EDUCATIONAL RESEARCH: A GUIDE TO THE PROCESS

EDUCATIONAL RESEARCH: A GUIDE TO THE PROCESS

Norman E. Wallen
San Francisco State University

Jack R. Fraenkel
San Francisco State University

McGraw-Hill, Inc.
New York St. Louis San Francisco Auckland Bogotá Caracas Hamburg
Lisbon London Madrid Mexico Milan Montreal New Delhi
Paris San Juan São Paulo Singapore Sydney Toyko Toronto

To Lina and Marge

This book was developed by Lane Akers, Inc.

Educational Research: A Guide to the Process

2 3 4 5 6 7 8 9 0 SEM SEM 9 5 4 3 2 1

ISBN 0-07-067945-2

This book was set in Bookman Light by Better Graphics, Inc.
The editors were Lane Akers and Holly Gordon;
the designer was Wanda Siedlecka;
the production supervisor was Janelle S. Travers.
Semline, Inc., was printer and binder.

Library of Congress Cataloging-in-Publication Data

Wallen, Norman E.
    Educational research: a guide to the process / Norman E. Wallen,
    Jack R. Fraenkel.
        p.   cm.
    Includes bibliographical references and index.
    ISBN 0-07-067945-2
    1. Education—Research.   I. Fraenkel, Jack R., (date).
II. Title.
LB1028.W275   1991
370'.7'8—dc20   90-39865

About the Authors

NORMAN E. WALLEN is currently Professor of Interdisciplinary Studies in Education at San Francisco State University, where he has taught since 1966. He received his Ph.D. from Syracuse University. An experienced researcher, he has taught courses in statistics and research design to master's and doctoral students for many years. His current work focuses on strategies for recruitment and retention of at-risk students.

JACK R. FRAENKEL is also Professor of Interdisciplinary Studies in Education and Director of the Research and Development Center, College of Education, San Francisco State University. He received his Ph.D. from Stanford University, and has taught courses in research methodology for more than 20 years. His current work centers around advising and assisting faculty and students in the generation and development of research endeavors.

Contents

APPENDIXES 333

INDEX 355

Preface

This text was motivated by our belief that many of the more traditional research texts currently available are either too difficult or too detailed (or sometimes both) for use in an introductory course. It is our view that those of us who teach the introductory course should strive to attain three fundamental objectives: (1) to introduce and make understandable certain concepts that are basic to the conduct of educational research, (2) to assist students in making sense out of the research literature they come across, and (3) to give students some sense of what it is like to actually do research of immediate interest to them.

Although we are advocates of basic research aimed at developing a widely applicable knowledge base, we are increasingly skeptical that such an approach to knowledge generation is sufficient. Educational practice at the local level might well be improved dramatically if teachers, principals, counselors, and case workers (to name a few examples) were to carry out studies, individually or collectively, on questions of immediate importance to them. We think it quite realistic to expect these professionals to acquire the necessary expertise to initiate such studies themselves. Indeed, some of our own students have done so!

As a result, we have written a different kind of research text. It consists of a series of realistic exercises that allow the student to experience what the research process is actually like. Thus, among other things, the student will learn to identify researchable issues, formulate and analyze research questions and hypotheses, prepare operational definitions, conduct library searches, locate or develop data collection instruments, analyze the adequacy of samples and the validity of conclusions drawn from such samples, examine research designs for alternative explanations for the outcomes of a study, and practice techniques for clarifying data. The emphasis throughout the book is on having students actively engage in the operations that researchers regularly perform rather than passively reading about such operations. As a result, we think that they will gain a much greater appreciation of what the process of doing research actually involves.

In attempting to produce a text that is interesting and involving as well as informative, we have built the following features into this book. Throughout we have:

- Used a conversational writing style rather than the more detached, formal style that characterizes most texts in the field.
- Prioritized and selected those topics of greatest importance to a basic understanding of good research practice.
- Attempted to keep the expository part of the book as simple and clear as possible without oversimplifying important concepts.
- Used real examples from our own research endeavors.

- Used illustrative examples that show how some of our students have handled recurring problems of research design.
- Provided numerous exercises that require the application of basic concepts and, thereby, help solidify understandings and skills.
- Provided Authors' Comments sections in which we analyze and evaluate the numerous examples presented in the text.
- Provided step-by-step directions for developing a research problem of personal interest to each student.
- Analyzed an actual research proposal prepared by a student in terms of both its strengths and its weaknesses.
- Analyzed a research report published by one of the authors.

Among these features, we feel that none is more important than the Authors' Comments sections, which are interspersed throughout each of the chapters. Students can, of course, skip those portions of the text where they are asked to respond to a question or complete an exercise, but in so doing they will be deprived of a particularly meaningful learning experience. Not only will they miss the opportunity of applying their understanding; they will also miss the opportunity to compare their thinking and ideas with ours and to discover that in some instances their thoughts are likely to be quite different from ours (and sometimes even better). Many of our students in past classes have reported this to be one of the most valuable features of the text. Furthermore, we sometimes provide new information in these Authors' Comments sections. We have done so deliberately as a way of extending learning on important concepts.

Special mention should also be made about the place of statistics in this text. It is our view that the role of statistics in an introductory course should be twofold: (1) to help students interpret information they have collected and (2) to provide an understanding of some of the basic ideas used in statistical reasoning. Therefore, detailed computation and mastery of complex statistical ideas have not been included in the chapters on descriptive and inferential statistics. Rather, emphasis is placed on understanding the underlying concepts and being able to interpret the use of statistics in published reports and articles. Statistics are tools that researchers use to make sense out of an otherwise large and unwieldy mass of data, and that is the way they are treated in this book.

In actuality, research does not consist of going through a series of defined steps. Rather, it is a continuing, dynamic process in which one aspect of planning a study often interacts with others, causing researchers to change their thinking about how they wish to proceed. For example, thinking through the matter of what subjects to include in a study may cause a researcher to change the overall direction of an investigation, and sometimes even to pursue a different question entirely. Books, however, are linear entities that must treat topics in some order. The particular organization of topics in this text, therefore, is by no means the only way they could have been organized. It may be helpful to keep this necessary artificiality in mind.

We believe that everyone involved in education should have at least some understanding of the basic concepts of research. As mentioned, we do not believe that educational research should remain the exclusive province of a relatively small group of "experts." Even those who say they see no value in research are increasingly affected by its results. School personnel are frequently asked to participate in research and to accept certain policies on the ground that "research has shown that. . . ." Surely, we ought, at the very least, to know what questions to ask about the findings of such research. There is no better way to become informed than to get involved in the research process itself. This book is designed to help do just that.

McGraw-Hill and the authors would like to thank the following reviewers for their many helpful comments and suggestions: David Andrews, Indiana State University; Robert Armstrong, Arizona State University; Paul Dixon, University of South Carolina; Bruce Gansneder, University of Virginia; David Hemphill, San Francisco State University; Jack Nelson, Rutgers University; Dianne Robertshaw, Virginia Technological University; and William Ware, University of North Carolina.

Norman E. Wallen
Jack R. Fraenkel

EDUCATIONAL RESEARCH: A GUIDE TO THE PROCESS

Chapter One

INTRODUCTION TO EDUCATIONAL RESEARCH

Education is a field about which everyone has opinions—often strong ones. Since virtually all of us have attended school, we know a lot about education through our own experiences. There are other fields in which we also have direct experience—medicine, for example. We have all received medical treatment of some kind, and most of us have been exposed to various home remedies to which we retain some attachment. Our opinions about health and medicine, however, are usually of a general nature: When we really need help or information, we are likely to rely on experts. This is much less the case in education, where we tend to think of ourselves as experts. We may complain about medical costs and may object to a specific treatment, but we do not try to tell physicians or hospitals what to do—as we frequently tell teachers and schools what they should be doing.

There are other reasons everyone is an expert on education. Schooling has a long-term and broad-gauged impact on people. During the 12 or more years when children are most susceptible to influence, schools affect not only their skills and specific knowledge but also their ideas, values, and social behavior. It is largely because schools are so important that people hold such strong views on what should take place in them.

None of this, we suppose, is news to you. We mention it here by way of making the case for the importance of research in education. A major purpose of educational research is to provide evidence to help people decide which opinions are correct—or at least more correct. Decisions affecting the greatest resource that human beings have, their children, should be informed by knowledge, not by the loudest voices that can be heard.

A second purpose of educational research is to help us develop better ways to think about the field of education. Just as other forms of scientific research have changed our conceptions of both the physical world and our own psychological worlds, educational research can be expected to lead to more fruitful ways to think about schooling.

As an initial exercise, we ask you to think about the issues in Table 1.1 and how much is known about them. We are focusing not on your opinion of the issue itself, but rather on the extent to which you think knowledge exists to support or refute the statement.

Please indicate, on a scale of 1–5, the extent to which you think research has demonstrated the truth of each statement (5 = the statement has been shown to be clearly supported by research; 1 = the statement has been shown to be clearly refuted by research; 3 = research on the topic does not support either conclusion). Circle your choice.

TABLE 1.1 Educational Research

Clearly refuted by research	Somewhat refuted by research	Inconclusive	Somewhat supported by research	Clearly supported by research	
1	2	3	4	5	1. The more time beginning readers spend on phonics, the better readers they become.
1	2	3	4	5	2. Bilingual education for nonnative speakers impairs their academic proficiency.
1	2	3	4	5	3. Increased contact with handicapped people results in a more positive attitude toward them.
1	2	3	4	5	4. Boys are better in math; girls are better in languages.
1	2	3	4	5	5. Requiring students who do not like one another to work together on a project results in an increase in their liking for each other.
1	2	3	4	5	6. Students who take moral education courses behave more ethically than students who do not take such courses.
1	2	3	4	5	7. The use of manipulatives in the elementary grades results in improved achievement in mathematics.
1	2	3	4	5	8. Behavior modification is an effective way of teaching skills to very slow learners.
1	2	3	4	5	9. Classroom discussion of real-life sexual issues and problems results in increased promiscuity among teenagers.
1	2	3	4	5	10. Among children who become deaf before language has developed, those with hearing parents become better readers than those with deaf parents.
1	2	3	4	5	11. The more teachers know about a specific subject matter, the better they teach it.

AUTHORS' COMMENTS

At present, there are relatively few issues in education that have been clearly resolved by research. However, each of the 11 statements in Table 1.1 has been addressed to some extent in the research literature. Although not every educator would agree with our assessment, we have rated the statements as follows:

1. Statement 1 is rated at 3. Despite a great deal of research on the topic, this statement can be neither clearly supported nor refuted. It is clear that phonics instruction is an important ingredient; what is not clear is how much time should be devoted to it.[1]
2. Statement 2 is rated at 2. Evidence is unclear as to whether or not bilingual methods are superior to English-only instruction, but several studies indicate no impairment of academic skills.[2]
3. Statement 3 is rated at 2. Evidence indicates that a more positive attitude results only if the nature of the contact is structured beforehand.[3]
4. Statement 4 is rated at 5. There is a considerable amount of evidence that these gender differences exist, though the reasons are not clear.[4]
5. Statement 5 is rated at 3. The evidence here is quite clear that the outcome *depends* on whether the students involved see one another as necessary to achieving success.[5]
6. Statement 6 is rated at 3, because there is relatively little research on ethical *behavior*.[6]
7. Statement 7 is rated at 4. The evidence is quite supportive of this method of teaching mathematics.[7]
8. Statement 8 is rated at 5, since there is a great deal of evidence to support the statement.[8]
9. Statement 9 is rated at 3, since not much evidence exists and the evidence that does exist is inconclusive.[9]
10. Statement 10 is rated at 1, since the findings of many studies refute the statement.[10]
11. Statement 11 is rated at 3, because the evidence is inconclusive despite the seemingly obvious fact that the teacher must know more than the students.[11]

The point of this exercise is not to review the state of current knowledge (some of our ratings might well be challenged), but rather to show that research can provide answers to some questions. The exercise also emphasizes the need for research on some of these (and other) issues about which little or no information exists or the information that does exist is inconclusive.

Notes
1. R. Calfee & P. Drum. 1986. Research on teaching reading. In M. C. Wittrock (Ed.). *Handbook of research on teaching* (3rd Ed.). New York: Macmillan, pp. 804–849.
2. D. Gunderson. 1982. Bilingual education. In H. E. Mitzel (Ed.). *Encyclopedia of educational research* (5th Ed.). New York: Macmillan, pp. 202–211.
3. S. L. Guskin. 1982. Attitudes toward the handicapped. In H. E. Mitzel (Ed.). *Encyclopedia of educational research* (5th Ed.). New York: Macmillan, pp. 189–193.
4. A. C. Peterson, L. Crockett, & M. H. Tobiu-Richards. 1982. Sex differences. In H. E. Mitzel (Ed.). *Encyclopedia of educational research* (5th Ed.). New York: Macmillan, pp. 1696–1712.
5. S. Oden. 1982. Social development. In H. E. Mitzel (Ed.). *Encyclopedia of educational research* (5th Ed.). New York: Macmillan, pp. 1715–1723.
6. F. V. Oser. 1986. Moral education and values education: The discourse perspective. In M. C. Wittrock (Ed.). *Handbook of research on teaching* (3rd Ed.). New York: Macmillan, pp. 917–941.
7. M. N. Suydam. 1986, February. Research report: Manipulative materials and achievement. *Arithmetic Teacher*, 10: 32.
8. S. L. Deno. 1982. Behavioral treatment methods. In H. E. Mitzel (Ed.). *Encyclopedia of educational research* (5th Ed.). New York: Macmillan, pp. 199–202.
9. P. A. Moseley. 1982. Sex education. In H. E. Mitzel (Ed.). *Encyclopedia of educational research* (5th Ed.). New York: Macmillan, pp. 1712–1715.
10. C. M. Kampfe & A. G. Turecheck. 1987, March. Reading achievement of prelingually deaf students and its relationship to parental method of communication: A review of the literature. *American Annals of the Deaf*, 10:11–15.
11. L. Shulman. 1986. Paradigms and research programs in the study of teaching. In M. C. Wittrock (Ed.). *Handbook of research on teaching* (3rd Ed.). New York: Macmillan, pp. 3–36.

Educational research can take many forms, including surveys, experiments, case studies, and ethnographies. Later in the book we will return to these types of research, along with several others. At this point, we want to distinguish between empirical and nonempirical research, and basic and applied research.

■ Empirical vs. Nonempirical Research

Empirical research is research that involves the collection of firsthand information. Nonempirical research does not involve the collection of information at firsthand. Thus, research that consists of locating and comparing references on a particular topic—the customary term paper—is not an example of empirical research. If a researcher is interested, for example, in finding out if girls read better than boys, he or she could locate and compare studies conducted during the past ten years as well as the opinions of authorities in reading. Although valuable and necessary, such research is not empirical. In order to do empirical research on this issue, a researcher would have to obtain firsthand information on the reading skills of an identified group and compare the performance (probably as indicated by scores on a reading test) of boys with girls. In this book, we are concerned primarily with empirical research; literature research will be discussed as a necessary background for conducting empirical research.

Here is an opportunity to check your understanding of the distinction between empirical and nonempirical research. In the list of research topics that follows, identify which are examples of empirical research and which are examples of nonempirical research.

1. A study of the effectiveness of a social learning program on the employability of severely disabled adults.
2. The relationship between television watching and school achievement—a review of the literature.
3. A reanalysis of the evidence on school effectiveness.
4. The relationship between self-esteem and age at school entrance of fourth-grade students in the San Francisco Unified School District.
5. Logical inconsistencies in the writings of Sigmund Freud.
6. A comparison of the effectiveness of behavior therapy as compared with client-centered therapy in homes for adolescent runaways.

AUTHORS' COMMENTS

Topics 1, 4, and 6 are examples of empirical research in that they clearly indicate that information will be obtained directly on the subjects in the study (severely disabled adults, fourth-grade students, and adolescent runaways). Topics 2, 3, and 5, on the other hand, are examples of non-empirical research. Topic 2 deals with a review of previous research that does not involve the direct collection of data. Topic 5 is a logical analysis of written material, but does not involve any raw data. Topic 3 implies that previously collected data are to be reexamined in a new way.

■ *Basic vs. Applied Research*

The distinction between basic and applied research is as follows:

Basic	*Applied*
Results apply to a great many people and situations.	Results are applicable only to a specific group of people in a particular situation.
Results are related to general theory or to a general field of knowledge.	Results are not necessarily related to a broader field of knowledge.
Results need not have immediate or even clear implications for practice.	Results must have immediate and clear implications for practice.

An example of basic research is an investigation of the relative effects of heredity and environment on academic performance. An example of applied research is a study that seeks the opinions of a school faculty toward merit pay. Many studies, of course, do not fit neatly into either of these categories, but fall on a continuum between the two extremes. Thus, a study of relaxation techniques as a method of increasing attention to task on the part of learning-handicapped students in a particular classroom has clear implications for that group of students. The results may also be consistent with studies on other groups of similar students and thus have wider application. Similarly, the results may be related to a particular theory.[1] If both of these criteria are met, the study can be considered basic research.[2] As stated in the Preface, we believe a text in research methods should pay more attention than is customary to the requirements for good applied research, and we have attempted to do so.

Use the following examples to check your understanding of the basic vs. applied research distinction. Which of the following topics represent examples of basic research and which represent examples of applied research?

1. A comparison of the attitudes of different student ethnic groups toward the general education requirements at Stanford University.
2. The effectiveness of counselors who are "recovering alcoholics" as compared with other counselors at the Rosewood Recovery Center.
3. A comparison of the effects of bilingual vs. English-only teaching on the achievement of Latino children in a particular subject, as based on the Cummins theory.
4. Employer perceptions of changes in essential secretarial skills between 1982 and 1992.
5. The relationship between adolescent self-esteem and alcoholism in parents.
6. The effectiveness of using manipulative materials in teaching first-grade mathematics.

---

[1] By theory, we mean a set of specific statements which, taken together, have wide-ranging explanatory power.

[2] Note that all of the issues evaluated on pages 2–3 fall under the category of basic research.

AUTHORS' COMMENTS

Topics 3, 5, and 6 are examples of basic research. They are clearly intended to have wide applicability. Topic 3 also has clear theoretical implications, whereas topics 5 and 6 have implied theoretical implications. Topics 1, 2, and 4, on the other hand, are examples of applied research. All focus on specific local groups, and topics 1 and 4 appear to have no theoretical basis.

The idea throughout this book is for you to cumulatively develop a plan for a research study that you could (and perhaps will) actually carry out. Accordingly, we will discuss a number of basic concepts having to do with research and ask you to think through a series of steps that will be presented in a particular sequence. Why do we follow this sequence? Because a book must be linear; it must, of necessity, treat topics in some order. There is no particular magic to this sequence, however—indeed, researchers seldom follow these steps in the exact order that we present them.

■ Summary

In this chapter, we attempted to place educational research in the context of our society and to illustrate the kinds of questions it can address. We also made distinctions among different types of educational research.

■ Key Concepts Discussed in This Chapter

empirical research   basic research
nonempirical research   applied research

■ How Far Along Should I Be at This Point?

By now, you should have some idea of what research involves and be able to distinguish between basic and applied research, as well as between empirical and nonempirical research.

Evaluate your progress, therefore, by checking each of the following. At this point, you should:

• Understand the differences between basic and applied research.
• Understand the differences between empirical and nonempirical research.

■ What's Next?

With this by way of introduction, let us now begin to involve you in the actual process of doing some research. We hope you find the process to be not only informative but also interesting and perhaps even exciting. May you have an enjoyable journey!

For Further Reading

Gross, R. 1982. *The independent scholar's handbook*. Reading, MA: Addison-Wesley.

Hunt, M. 1985. *Profiles of social research: The scientific study of human interactions*. New York: Basic Books.

Kerlinger, R. N. 1969. Research in education. In R. Ebel, V. Noll, & R. Bauer (Eds.), *Encyclopedia of educational research* (4th Ed.). New York: Macmillan.

Shulman, L. S. 1988. Disciplines of inquiry in education: An overview. In R. M. Jaeger (Ed.), *Complementary methods for research in education*. Washington, DC: American Educational Research Association.

Stouffer, S. 1962. *Social research to test ideas*. New York: Free Press.

Suppes, P. (Ed.). 1979. *The impact on research on education: Some case studies*. Washington, DC: National Academy on Education.

Chapter Two

THE RESEARCH QUESTION

In this chapter, we begin our discussion of the research process by introducing you to some of the basic concepts of research and its design. In particular, we discuss the idea of a researchable question and why some questions are researchable while others are not.

At the same time, we ask you to begin to apply the ideas you shall be learning about throughout this book to a research problem of your own choosing. In doing so, we believe you will acquire a deeper understanding and appreciation of what research is all about.

By the end of this chapter, you will have thought through a research question to the point where it is clear as to intent and meaning, and be able to defend the educational significance of the question.

Getting Started

As mentioned in Chapter One, the guiding idea throughout this book is for you to develop a plan for a study that you could (and perhaps will) actually carry out. Your first task in this regard is to decide on some aspect of a research problem that you would like to investigate. A research problem is exactly that—a problem of some sort that you would like to research. Research problems are usually stated as questions. The question format serves as the focus of the researcher's investigation. Here are some examples:

- Does client-centered therapy produce more satisfaction in clients than behavior modification therapy?
- Are the descriptions of people in social studies textbooks biased in any way?
- What goes on in an elementary school classroom during an average week?
- Do teachers behave differently toward students of different gender?
- How do mathematics teachers explain math concepts?

• How can we predict which sorts of students might have trouble learning certain kinds of subject matter?

Notice that what all of these questions have in common is that you can collect information of some sort to answer them (at least in part). That's what makes them researchable. On the other hand, here are two examples of questions about which you cannot collect data. They cannot (as stated) be researched:

1. Should elementary school teachers use the inquiry method to teach math concepts?
2. Is strategic family therapy the best method for counselors to use with alienated youngsters?

What is there about these two questions that prevents you from collecting data to answer them?

1. _____

_____

2. _____

_____

AUTHORS' COMMENTS

The difficulty with question 1 is that it requires a value judgment. This type of question (whether or not something should be done) can certainly be argued over, but it cannot be researched. The word "should" is a value term (implying notions of good and bad) and, as such, does not have empirical referents. Think about the question for a moment. How could you possibly determine if teachers *should* engage in a particular course of action (in this case, whether they should use the inquiry method to teach math)? There is no way to collect data that would enable you to answer the question. Note, however, that if the question were changed to "Do people think elementary school teachers should use the inquiry method to teach math concepts?" or "Does the use of inquiry methods to teach math concepts result in greater understanding?" it would be researchable. Why? Because you could collect information to help you answer the question.

The difficulty with question 2 is that it is unanswerable. It would be impossible to identify *all* the possible ways to counsel someone. Think about this for a moment. How could you ever be sure that all the possible methods had been identified? There is no way to go about answering it. You could, however, find out if strategic family therapy is the best of several specified methods.

Here are three more questions. Two are researchable and one is not. Circle the number in front of the two that are researchable.

3. Are children happier when they are taught by a teacher of the same gender?
4. Does high school achievement influence the academic achievement of university students?
5. What is the least effective way to teach grammar?

AUTHORS' COMMENTS

Questions 3 and 4 are researchable. Question 5, as stated, cannot be researched. Question 5 asks for the "least effective" way to do something (teach grammar). Think about this one for a moment. Is there any way we can determine the worst way to do anything? To be able to determine this, we must examine every possible alternative, and a moment's reflection brings us to the realization that this can never be accomplished. How would we ever be sure that all possible alternatives had been examined? We could, however, ask people what method they think is the least effective way to teach grammar—but that would be a different question.

◼ *Stating Your Question*

Try, now, to state a research question of your own. Many questions are being asked today about education. Think about a question you would like to investigate. Choose one that interests you and is related to your field of interest. As you do so, keep in mind that it is important that your question be within your own educational area of expertise or training and be one for which you would be able to collect firsthand information. Educational research need not always involve raw data, but you will learn more about the total research process if you think it through in its entirety.

As you think about your question, you should try to determine if it is a *feasible* question—that is, one that would allow you to collect enough information to provide at least a partial answer to it. Furthermore, try to formulate a question that will involve you in the process of collecting data, rather than simply compiling data from existing records. For example, a question that requires only the examination of school attendance records would not give you any experience in locating, evaluating, or developing techniques for collecting data, an essential element in most studies.

The emphasis we are placing on feasibility does not mean that you should select for study only that which is easy or obvious. The focus of this book is on helping you to learn and understand the process of research; hence, we want to minimize the frustration which goes with pursuing too many dead ends.

Listed below are five questions intended to help you think about the issue of feasibility. Think of a way that you could collect information (from friends, colleagues, students, and others) that would help you to answer (at least in part) each question. Check yes (or no) if you think you could (or could not) collect data to answer the question. If your answer is yes, briefly state how you would go about collecting information; if you answer no, briefly explain why you think you could not. You will probably notice that some of the questions contain ambiguous terms and are stated rather poorly. Don't let this disturb you. This is how most research questions are initially stated. Our intention at this point is to start you thinking about a research question of your own. You will refine it later.

Question 1: "Does the open classroom work?"

Could you collect data? Yes _____ No _____

How (or why not)? _____

_____

_____

Question 2: "How do teachers feel about special classes for the educationally handicapped?"

Could you collect data? Yes _____ No _____

How (or why not)? _____

_____

_____

Question 3: "Do second graders like school?"

Could you collect data? Yes _____ No _____

How (or why not)? _____

_____

_____

Question 4: "Are parents of autistic children detached in their relations with each other?"

Could you collect data? Yes _____ No _____

How (or why not)? _____

_____

_____

Question 5: "Should philosophy be required of all students in graduate school?"

Could you collect data? Yes _____ No _____

How (or why not)? _____

_____

_____

AUTHORS' COMMENTS

Question 1: "Does the open classroom work?" This question was formulated and later investigated by students in one of our graduate research seminars.[1] (We will refer to this investigation at various times throughout the text to provide examples of different aspects of the research process.) The investigation which resulted from this question is a good example of a beginning effort by students to engage in research. As such, and as you will see as we proceed, it has several flaws. Nevertheless, we think you will learn more from it than from a more sophisticated, and technically excellent, example.

To collect information on this question, you would need access to people who have had experience with an open classroom. If examples of such classrooms exist in your community, you might be able to observe in one of them, talk to students and/or teachers who are in them, or administer a questionnaire or test of some sort. Perhaps you have access to such a classroom outside of your community. If so, you may be able to think of a way to get the opinions of some of the people who are working in or with these classrooms. Without some form of access, however, it is difficult to see how you could investigate this question. (Remember that neither this nor any of the other questions we are considering at this point is as clear as it might be. We shall attempt clarification later. For the moment, we must address the question of feasibility.)

Question 2: "How do teachers feel about special classes for the educationally handicapped?" To investigate this question, you would need access to individuals (preferably teachers) who have had some experience with such classes.

Question 3: "Do second graders like school?" To investigate this question, you would need ac-cess to some second graders or to either the teachers or parents of second graders. There might be some difficulty in obtaining such access (some parents or teachers might not want their children or students to be interviewed, for example), but most likely there would be no objection to conducting the study. Consequently, the answer to the question of feasibility would probably be yes.

Question 4: "Are parents of autistic children detached in their relations with each other?" This question raises serious doubts as to feasibility. There are relatively few autistic children in most communities—even in highly populated areas—and getting permission to collect data on parent relations is likely to be difficult.

Question 5: "Should philosophy be required of all students in graduate school?" You should have checked no to this question, because there is no way to research it. This is another example of a question which asks for a value judgment. There is no way to determine if a particular course should be required. As we mentioned earlier, we can argue over this sort of question, or give our opinions concerning it, but there is no way to collect data to answer it. (Note again that if the question were changed to "Do graduate students think philosophy should be required . . . ," then data could be collected. To investigate this changed question, you would need access to some graduate students.)

Note

1. Although the term "open classroom" is currently not as fashionable as it was in the 1970s, the essential ideas have ancient historical roots and the approach is still being used and debated in many schools. The use of this study permits us to incorporate our experience with it as a teaching aid in our courses in educational research.

Now is the time to try writing the research question that you would like to investigate (you can reformulate it later, but at least write down the question you currently have in mind):

_____

_____

_____

_____

Could you collect data on this question? Yes _____ No _____

How (or why not)? _____

_____

_____

■ Refining the Question

Once we have determined that a question is feasible, we want to turn it into as good a question as we can. In addition to feasibility, a good research question possesses the following characteristics:

• The question is clear (i.e., most people would agree as to what the key terms in the question mean).
• The question is significant (i.e., it is worth investigating because it will contribute important knowledge about the human condition).
• The question is ethical (i.e., it will not involve physical or psychological harm or damage to human beings, or to the natural or social environment of which they are a part).
• The question indicates a relationship of some sort (i.e., two or more qualities are suggested as being connected or related to each other in some way).

We will discuss each of these characteristics in more detail shortly. To get started thinking about them, evaluate the following question in terms of each characteristic.

Question 1: "Is the phonics method more effective in teaching students how to read than the look-say method?"

Give your opinion of the quality of this question by circling the appropriate word or rating (1 = high, 5 = low) following each characteristic.

Feasibility:	Yes		No		Uncertain
Clarity:	Clear		Unclear		Needs work
Significance:	1	2	3	4	5
Ethicality:	1	2	3	4	5
Relationship:	Suggested		Not suggested		

AUTHORS' COMMENTS

We would judge this question to be a feasible one, though it is somewhat unclear. (What does "more effective" mean? What is meant by "phonics," "look-say," and "read"? What types of students are being talked about?) The question is also highly significant (we rated it a 1). We perceive no ethical problems in investigating the question. (Of course, we cannot be sure until we see how the investigator actually plans to research the question. More about ethics later on.) We also perceive a suggested relationship—between the method of teaching reading (phonics vs. look-say) and learning to read by students. We also shall discuss the idea of a relationship in more detail later.

Now, go back and consider your own question again. Write your question here (as originally stated, or as you may have changed it). _____

_____

_____

Evaluate your question in terms of the five characteristics previously mentioned.

Feasibility:	Yes		No	Uncertain
Clarity:	Clear		Unclear	Needs work
Significance:	1 2 3	4 5		
Ethicality:	1 2 3	4 5		
Relationship:	Suggested		Not suggested	

All of the above characteristics are important attributes of good research questions. As such, they deserve a bit more discussion.

FEASIBILITY

We discussed the notion of feasibility earlier, but it is important to stress again that the restraints imposed by reality must be considered early in the planning process. A feasible question is one that can be investigated without a goodly amount of money, time, or space, or other resources being required. There are times, of course, when questions that do require a lot of money, time, space, or energy are pursued (questions involving future space exploration, for example, or the study of the effects of special programs like Head Start, which take place over a long period of time). The beginning research student, however, should plan to investigate studies that are feasible—that focus on a question requiring subjects from whom data can be collected with a relatively modest expenditure of time, money, and energy.

CLARITY

The nature of a research investigation needs to be as clear as possible to all concerned. Since the research question is the focus of the investigation, it is only logical that it, too, should be clear. What exactly is being investigated? The research question that you have written may be perfectly clear to you and to others. Often, however, this is not the case. Look again at the questions presented on pages 10–12. In the first example, the term "open classroom" may seem quite straightforward to you. Nevertheless, many people may not be sure exactly what the term means. If we ask, "What are the essential characteristics of an open (compared, let us say, with a closed or traditional) classroom?" we begin to discover that it is difficult to specify them. Descriptions of open classrooms usually suggest that students have a wide choice of activities and that the teacher is a resource person of sorts rather than a director (in the traditional sense) of activities. Such descriptions go on to point out, however, that a great amount of variation exists from classroom to classroom (and school to school) in the sorts of activities in which students engage and in the strategies employed by the teacher. The way in which the classroom is physically arranged also varies. Thus, what initially may appear to be an easily understood and commonly agreed-on term becomes much more complex on closer examination.

This is true of many current educational concepts and methodologies. Consider such terms as "core curriculum," "client-centered counseling," "inquiry learning," and "humanistic teaching." What do such expressions mean? If you were to ask a sample of students or teachers that you know, you would probably get several different definitions. Although such ambiguity is valuable in some circumstances and for certain purposes, it presents a problem to the investigator of a research question. In examining a particular teaching method, a researcher needs to know precisely what is to be studied. The researcher has no choice but to try to be more specific about the terms used in the question. In making this effort, the researcher can gain a much clearer picture of how to proceed with an investigation. The very nature of the investigation, in fact, may change. Notice that it is the important or key terms which must be clarified. Sometimes these are individual words, but more commonly they are combinations of words, as in the term "open classroom." Defining the words "open" and "classroom" separately would be unlikely to convey the special meaning intended.

There are essentially three ways to clarify an important term in a research question. The first is to define the term *constitutively*—that is, to use what is often referred to as the dictionary approach. As researchers, we simply explain in other words what we mean by the term. Thus, open classroom might be further defined as we did above: "any classroom in which students have a wide number of choices with regard to activities and the teacher acts as a resource person to help them engage in the activities they choose." Notice, however, that this really doesn't provide too much clarity, since the synonyms used for "open" are themselves ambiguous. What, exactly, is meant by "choices"? What constitutes a "wide number" of choices? What does a teacher do in the role of "resource person"?

A constitutive definition is never perfect; some ambiguity is inevitable in the use of language. Our task, as researchers, is to be as clear as possible. There is no easy solution to the problem of ambiguity—we can only continue to revise our definitions while getting as much feedback as possible from our colleagues. You will find that your efforts at clarity at this stage will prevent many problems later on. When possible, of course, you should use a definition that is current in the literature, but only if it is relatively unambiguous and if it conveys your intended meaning.

A second way to clarify an important term is by *example*. You might mention some examples of open classrooms with which you are familiar, and then try to describe as fully as possible the essential characteristics of these classrooms. It is a good idea for people to observe such classrooms so they can see for themselves how they are different from other classrooms. This approach also has its problems, since descriptions may still not be as clear to others as we would like.

The third method of clarification is to define an important term *operationally*. Operational definitions require that a researcher specify the actions or operations required to *measure* or *identify* the term. Let us try to make this a bit clearer with some examples. Here are three possible operational definitions of open classroom:

1. Any classroom identified by a teacher or principal as using open classroom methods.
2. Any classroom identified as an open classroom by recognized experts.
3. Any classroom judged (by an observer spending at least 1 day per week in the classroom for 4 to 5 weeks) to possess the following attributes:

a. No more than three children work with the same materials at the same time.
b. The teacher never spends more than 20 minutes per day addressing the class as a group.
c. At least half of every class period is open for students to work on projects of their own choosing at their own pace.
d. Several (more than three) sets of different kinds of educational materials are available for every student in the class to use.
e. One-third of all objects in the classroom have been made by the students in the class.
f. The classroom uses nontraditional seating—students sit in circles, in small groupings, or even on the floor to work on their projects.

Notice in each of the three examples above that the activities or operations necessary to identify an open classroom (or to measure the "openness" of a classroom) have been specified. In the first example, we simply ask the principal or a teacher to identify a classroom in which the teacher uses open classroom methods. In the second example, we select a classroom recognized by acknowledged experts as being an open classroom. In the third example, we rely on a particular observational method.

Armed with any one of these definitions (and the necessary facilities), you could decide quickly whether or not a particular classroom matched the definition and, hence, qualified as an example of an open classroom that you could include in a research investigation.

Notice further that definitions 1 and 2 are not very satisfactory—even though they are operational. They do not help us understand the meaning intended by the researcher. This is often true of operational definitions, and is one reason they should always be accompanied by constitutive definitions. One strength of operational definitions is that their focus on specifying the identification or measurement process can help in developing constitutive definitions. They also help others who may wish to repeat the study.

Notice that there is another ambiguity in the question "Does the open classroom work?" Specifically, what is meant by "work"? Does the term mean "results in increased academic proficiency"? Does it mean "results in happier children" or "makes life easier for teachers" or "costs less money"? Maybe researchers mean all of these things and more. Once again, we have a term whose meaning is not clear. When students in one of our research classes decided to investigate this question, they eventually defined the term to mean "results in higher student motivation." Higher motivation was then itself defined. Here is how two students defined the term:

"A productive type of activity. A curiosity to learn more about or to study an observable person or object."

"Something that incites the organism to action or that sustains and gives direction to action once the organism has been aroused."

Which definition do you think is clearer? Why? _____

_____

_____

_____

_____

AUTHORS' COMMENTS

Although both definitions are somewhat lacking in clarity, we would judge the second definition to be less ambiguous. The phrases "incites . . . to action" and "sustains and gives direction to action," we think, are less ambiguous than "productive," "curiosity," and "study." If you try to apply each definition to another person's behavior, we think you will agree. Nevertheless, further clarification is needed and might be

gained from an operational definition such as this: "A class is highly motivated when the energy output of the class as a whole is judged high (as compared with that of other classes) by two independent observers for eight 30-minute periods, and the amount of tangible work produced during these sample periods is judged high by two different, independent judges."

Operational definitions, then, are useful tools. They can help us make clear to others what we mean when we use certain words. Here are some proposed definitions of the phrase "motivation to learn in history class." Circle the number in front of those definitions which are operational.

When a student is motivated in history, he or she:

1. Smiles a lot in class.
2. Is observed to ask questions about past and present reading assignments.
3. Is "turned on" to history.
4. States he likes the history teacher.
5. Is described by the teacher as a student who turns in all homework assignments on time.
6. Voluntarily checks out books on history from the school library.
7. Is listed on the membership roster of the school's history club.
8. Loves history courses.
9. Is observed carrying two or more history books around the halls.
10. Scores at least 90 percent on every history exam.

AUTHORS' COMMENTS

Definitions 2, 4, 5, 7, 9, and 10 are operational. Definitions 1, 3, 6, and 8 are not operational. The reason that 1 is nonoperational is not because the term "a lot" is ambiguous, but because the activities or operations necessary to measure the behavior have not been identified. In 3, "turned on" is not made operational, nor are "voluntarily checks out" in 6 or "loves" in 8. Remember that the key aspect of an operational definition is that

the *operations* or *activities* necessary to measure or identify the term have been specified. Adding "as shown by library records," for example, would make 6 operational. The key question to ask is either one of identification ("How do we know when we have an example of the term?") or one of measurement ("How do we know how much of the term we have?").

Now is the time for you to try your hand at defining terms clearly. See if you can identify and clarify any ambiguous terms that exist in two of the research questions we presented earlier. They are repeated here for your convenience.

Question 2: "How do teachers feel about special classes for the educationally handicapped?"

Define any terms that are not clear.

_____

_____

_____

_____

Question 3: "Do second graders like school?"

Define any terms that are not clear.

_____

_____

_____

_____

AUTHORS' COMMENTS

Question 2: "How do teachers feel about special classes for the educationally handicapped?" The phrase "feel about" is very ambiguous. Does it mean opinions or emotional reactions? Does it suggest actions? It should be noted that the term "feelings," although widely used in education today, is extremely difficult to define. We think this research question is most likely directed toward ascertaining teacher opinions about various aspects of special programs for educationally handicapped students. What do you think?

The terms "special classes" and "educationally handicapped" also need to be clarified further. One definition of an educationally handicapped student is "a minor who, by reason of marked learning or behavioral disorders, is unable to adapt to a normal classroom situation. The disorder must be associated with a neurological handicap or an emotional disturbance and must not be due to mental retardation, cultural deprivation, or foreign language problems." Note that this definition itself contains some ambiguous expressions (such as "marked learning disorders") which lend themselves to a wide variety of interpretations. (This is equally true of the term "cultural deprivation," which is not only ambiguous, but often offensive to members of ethnic groups to whom the term is frequently applied.)

The term "teachers" should also be defined, although, as in any study, the subjects or participants will be described in detail at a later time.

Question 3: "Do second graders like school?" The ambiguous term here is the word "like." Possible operational definitions of the term might be:

a. When questioned verbally, students state that they enjoy school.
b. When observed in school, students show a higher frequency of smiling and laughing behavior than of frowning and crying behavior.
c. When offered the option of attending school or staying at home, students choose to attend school.
d. When looking at a series of pictures depicting both pleasurable and unpleasurable reactions of children in school and asked, "Which one of these pictures is you?" students choose more pleasurable than unpleasurable pictures.

At this point, return to your initial attempt to state your research question on page 12. See which terms need clarification. In the space below, list both the terms and the ways that you propose to clarify them. Include operational definitions if at all possible.

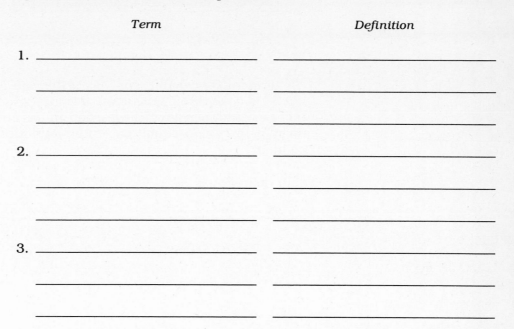

Term   *Definition*

1.

2.

3.

You now need to see how successful you have been in eliminating ambiguity in your research question. Identify two or three individuals who know something about the field of education (one of your professors, perhaps, or a student whose opinion you respect). Present your question to these individuals exactly as you have written it on page 12 (or as you may have amended it on page 14). Explain that you are thinking of doing a research study to investigate this question. Now ask each individual (independently) if he or she understands what you wish to investigate and if there is any part of the question that he or she finds confusing. Write their responses in the spaces provided below. If there are any questions which your respondents ask you in an attempt to clarify what you are after, write these down too. Now remove your question from view and ask each of your respondents to rephrase it so as to make it clearer. Record their efforts.

Respondent 1

Your question: _____

_____

_____

Respondent's reaction: _____

_____

_____

_____

Respondent's restatement of the question: _____

_____

_____

_____

Present your definitions. Ask if they are clear. Then ask if what you intend to do is clear. Write down any questions the respondent asks about the question. Then ask if the respondent has any suggestions as to how you might gather information concerning your question. Write down his or her opinions.

Your definitions: _____

_____

_____

_____

_____

Respondent's comments: _____

_____

_____

_____

_____

Respondent's suggestions for gathering information (i.e., the kinds of information that would be relevant for you to look for):

_____

_____

_____

_____

_____

Respondent 2

Your question: _____

_____

_____

Respondent's reaction: _____

_____

_____

_____

Respondent's restatement of the question: _____

_____

_____

_____

Your definitions: _____

_____

_____

_____

_____

Respondent's comments: _____

_____

_____

_____

_____

Respondent's suggestions for gathering information (i.e., the kinds of information that would be relevant for you to look for):

_____

_____

_____

_____

_____

Summarize the responses you obtained. Do the responses demonstrate a clear understanding of your question? It is our guess that your respondents will indicate a need for further clarification of some of the terms in your question. Perhaps you have discovered that your question means something quite different to your respondents than what it means to you. Consequently, you may wish to further revise your question and definitions and repeat the above exercise again with different respondents.

Summary of responses: _____

_____

_____

_____

_____

_____

Using the information you have gained from your respondents, rewrite your question in the clearest manner you can. Include any revisions necessary in definitions of key terms.

Your rewritten question: _____

_____

_____

_____

New or revised definitions of key terms: _____

_____

_____

_____

_____

SIGNIFICANCE

At this point, you need to consider whether your question, as it now stands, is worth investigating. In essence, we want to consider whether the question is worth expending time and energy (and often money) to try to answer. What, we might ask, is the value of investigating this question? In what ways will it contribute to our knowledge about education? to our knowledge of human beings? Is such knowledge important in some way? If so, how?

These questions ask you to think about why your question is a worthwhile (an important or a significant) one to investigate.

It probably goes without saying that your question is of interest to you, since you were asked initially to choose a question that was related to your field of interest. But is interest alone sufficient justification for an investigation? For some people, the answer is a clear yes! Any question that they sincerely want an answer to is worth investigating. Others, however, say that personal interest, in and of itself, is insufficient as a reason for investigating a question. Too often, they point out, personal interest can result in the pursuit of trivial or insignificant questions. Since most research efforts require some (and often considerable) expenditure of time, energy, materials, money, and/or other resources, it is easy to appreciate the point of view that some useful outcome or payoff should be forthcoming as a result of the research. The investment of self and others in a research enterprise should contribute some knowledge of value to the field of education.

Generally speaking, most researchers do not believe that research efforts based primarily on personal interest warrant investigation. There are too many important questions about education to be investigated which transcend personal curiosity. Furthermore, there is some reason to question a "purely curious" motive on psychological grounds. Most questions probably have some degree of hidden motivation behind them, and for the sake of credibility, these reasons should be made explicit.

One of the most important tasks for any researcher, therefore, is to think through the value of his or her intended research before too much preliminary work is done. There are three important questions to ask about any research question. Given the many questions about education that could be investigated:

- How might answers to this question advance knowledge in my field?
- How might answers to this question improve educational practice?
- How might answers to this question be of some help to human beings?

Return now to your question. Try to write a defense of it. Why would it be important to try to answer (at least in part) this question, other than that you are personally interested in doing so? Does the question have implications for the improvement of practice? administrative decision making? program planning? Is there an important issue that can be illuminated to some degree by a study of your question? Is it related to a current theory in your field?

It may be helpful to pretend for the moment that you are in a position of wanting to solicit funds to help you investigate the question. Any funding agency is almost certain to ask you to explain why your question is a worthwhile one to investigate. What arguments can you present? Write out a justification of your question in the space below and on the next page.

_____

_____

_____

_____

_____

_____

_____

_____

_____

_____

_____

Here are some sample defenses of the question about open classrooms.

Statement 1

The general purpose of this research is to add knowledge to the field of education at a time when classroom freedom is viewed by many as a key to the improvement of instruction in elementary school classrooms. Many authorities have argued that a strictly structured, teacher-directed classroom may not only detract from but even impede the learning process. It is this controversial thesis, coupled with a steadily growing onslaught of programmed learning materials, that has provoked many teachers and administrators to modify their classroom structures in the hope of achieving a greater amount of educational gain for their students. Although many teachers and others interested in education state that students will be more highly motivated to learn in a less structured environment, there are very little data in the literature to support this contention. Thus, the study is one attempt to provide data in this regard. If educators are to endorse an open classroom approach, they need something more than whim or personal inclination as a basis for doing so. This study is one attempt to look for "something more."

Statement 2

The education of children in elementary schools has always been a controversial issue among parents and teachers. Various ideas have been proposed concerning the type of setting that would produce the most constructive learning environment for young children. One such setting which some believe is especially motivating is the open classroom. This study is an attempt to determine if this is so.

Statement 3

The purpose of this study is to research open classrooms and structured classrooms and to discover in which setting the most student motivation occurs.

Compare these justifications and list as many differences as you can (other than length) which you think exist among them.

_____

_____

_____

_____

_____

_____

_____

      If you were in a position to approve (or fund) a study of open class-rooms, which of the three justifications would, in your opinion, provide the strongest basis for approval? Why?

_____

_____

_____

_____

_____

_____

_____

_____

AUTHORS' COMMENTS

Our reactions to the three justifications are as follows. Statement 3 is merely a description of what needs to be done. It contains no justification beyond the implication that discovery is a sufficient purpose in and of itself. Statement 2 gives some perspective on the study, but remains very general and fails to indicate how the results might be used. Statement 1 is, in our judgment, the best of the three (although not because it is the longest). It places the study in a context of both theoretical and practical work, indicates the importance of researching the question, and implies how the results might be used. This last point, however, could be spelled out in even more detail.

Look over the justification you have written. Is there any position or point of view expressed in our comments that you could use as additional justification in what you have written? If so, add to your justification in the space provided here and on the next page.

_____

_____

_____

_____

_____

_____

_____

_____

_____

▦ Summary

In this chapter, we introduced the idea of a research question—the focus of any research investigation. Not all questions, however, are researchable, and so we distinguished between those that are and those that are not. We emphasized that good research questions must be feasible—that is, they must be questions that permit a researcher to collect enough information to provide at least a partial answer to them.

Good research questions possess four additional characteristics: They should be clear, they should be significant, they should suggest a relationship of some sort, and they should be ethical. Clarity and significance were discussed in some detail in this chapter; ethics and relationships are discussed in Chapter Three.

▦ Key Concepts Discussed in This Chapter

research problem	operational definition
research question	constitutive definition
clarity	feasibility
significance	

▦ How Far Along Should I Be at This Point?

By now, you should have your research question pretty well in mind, and an adequate defense for it prepared. Thus, your question is presumably clear, has been justified as being worthy of investigation, and is a feasible one for you to investigate.

Evaluate your progress, therefore, by checking each of the following. At this point, you should have:

- Accomplished each of the tasks listed at the end of Chapter One.
- Written a research question that is feasible and that can be studied empirically.
- Defined the essential terms in your research question clearly.
- Justified the educational significance of your research question.

What's Next?

In the next chapter, we discuss the last two characteristics of good research questions: that they investigate a relationship and that they not violate certain ethical principles. We will introduce you to two very important concepts—the concept of variable and the concept of hypothesis—and discuss these in some detail. You will have an opportunity to identify different types of variables and to formulate a hypothesis. Finally, we will discuss the concept of ethics as it applies to research.

For Further Reading

Bart, P., & Frankel, L. 1976. *The student sociologist's handbook*. Morristown, NJ: General Learning Press.

Bunker, B. B., Pearlson, H. B., & Schulz, J. W. 1975. *A student's guide to conducting social science research*. New York: Human Sciences Press.

Burgess, R. G. (Ed.) 1986. *Key variables in social investigation*. London: Routledge & Kegan Paul.

Campbell, J. P., Daft, R. L., & Hulin, C. L. 1982. *What to study: Generating and developing research questions*. Beverly Hills, CA: Sage.

Ennis, R. H. 1964. Operational definitions. *American Educational Research Journal*, 1:183–201.

Hopkins, D. 1985. *A teacher's guide to classroom research*. Philadelphia: Open University Press.

Chapter Three

VARIABLES, HYPOTHESES, AND ETHICS

So far, we have identified a number of characteristics that good research questions possess. Three of these characteristics—feasibility, clarity, and significance—were discussed in detail in Chapter Two. The remaining two principles—that good research questions pose no ethical problems and that they usually suggest a relationship of some sort to be investigated—are discussed in this chapter. We will introduce three very important concepts in research: variables, hypotheses, and ethics. As you learn about these characteristics and concepts, we will in turn ask you to apply them to the research study that you are planning.

By the end of this chapter, therefore, you should be able to explain what is meant by the term "relationship" as it applies to a research question, and to discuss briefly some ethical principles that researchers should take care not to violate when conducting their research. You should be able to identify several different types of variables in a given study, including measured and categorical variables, independent and dependent variables, and outcome and extraneous variables. You should be able to explain what is meant by a hypothesis, and distinguish between directional and non-directional hypotheses. You should also be able to restate your own research question in the form of a hypothesis.

■ Relationships

What do we mean by a relationship as it applies to a research question? We mean that something "goes with" or is "associated with" something else. Figure 3.1 presents an example. Drawing (a) presents a group of 12 men and women, divided between those who wear glasses and those who do not. It illustrates that there is no relationship between gender and the wearing of

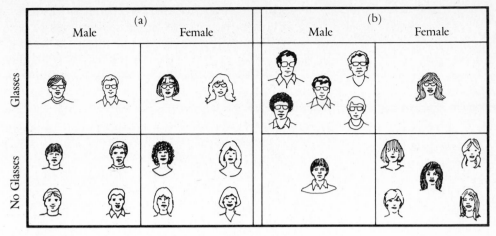

FIGURE 3.1
Illustration of a Relationship

glasses, since equal numbers of males and females wear glasses (both men and women, in other words, are equally likely to wear glasses). Drawing (b) also presents a group of 12 men and women. Contrary to drawing (a), however, it illustrates that there is a relationship between gender and the wearing of glasses, since more males than females wear glasses—that is, males are five times as likely to wear glasses as are females.

Not all research questions suggest relationships. Sometimes a researcher is interested only in obtaining descriptive information. The researcher wants to find out how people think or feel, or describe how they behave in a particular situation. At other times the intent is to describe a particular program or activity. This is referred to as *descriptive research*. As a result, the researcher may ask questions like the following:

• How do the parents of high school sophomores feel about the counseling program?
• What changes would the staff like to see instituted in the curriculum?
• Has the number of students enrolling in college preparatory as compared with noncollege preparatory courses changed over the last four years?
• How does the new reading program differ from the one used in this district in the past?
• What does an inquiry-oriented social studies teacher do?

Notice that no relationship is suggested in these questions. The researcher simply wants to identify characteristics, behaviors, feelings, or thoughts. Such information is often necessary to pave the way for designing other research or to make educational decisions of some sort.

Nevertheless, the problem with purely descriptive research questions is that answers to them do not help us understand why people feel or think or behave a certain way, why programs possess certain characteristics, why a particular strategy is to be used at a certain time, and so forth. We may learn what happened, or where or when (and even how) something happened, but not why it happened. As a result, our understanding of a situation, group, or phenomenon is limited. It is for this reason that research questions which suggest relationships to be investigated are considered so important: The answers to them help us to explain the nature of the world in which we live. We learn to understand the world by learning to explain how parts of it are related. We detect patterns. And we can make predictions. If drawing (b) in Figure 3.1 were true, we could predict that a male is more likely than a female to wear glasses.

At this point, check your understanding of what a relationship is. Here are four research questions. Which ones involve relationships?

1. To what extent are manipulatives used to teach mathematics in the primary grades in the Colma Elementary School District?
2. Do the principals in our district favor mainstreaming gifted students?
3. Are people with eating disorders more likely to have a history of sexual abuse in early childhood?
4. Do students who are taught Spanish in a language laboratory become more fluent in the language than students who are taught Spanish in a traditional classroom setting?

AUTHORS' COMMENTS

Questions 1 and 2 do not suggest a relationship. Question 1 asks for no more than a description regarding the current usage of manipulative materials in a particular school district. Similarly, question 2 asks only for a survey of administrative opinions. Investigations of such questions may be extremely useful in their own right, but they do not extend our knowledge as to why such conditions exist.

Questions 3 and 4, on the other hand, do indicate relationships. Question 3 seeks to investigate a possible relationship between eating disorders and sexual abuse. If a history of sexual abuse is related to eating disorders, this suggests (although it does not prove) that such abuse may be a cause of such disorders. It also suggests that counseling which addresses patient history may be helpful. Question 4 seeks to investigate a possible relationship between the type of language instruction and fluency in the language taught. If the language laboratory method is shown to be more effective than classroom instruction by individual teachers, this has clear implications for improving language learning.

Recall that in the question about phonics and look-say reading methods presented in Chapter Two, the suggested relationship was between the method of teaching reading and learning to read by students. To repeat, a relationship means that two qualities or characteristics are tied together (related) in some way. Does your research question suggest a relationship? If not, try to reformulate it so that it does.

Yes _____ The relationship suggested in my question is between

_____ and _____

No _____ I do not perceive a relationship in my question. My revised

question that does indicate a relationship is _____

_____

■ *Variables*

A relationship is a statement about variables. What is a variable? A *variable* is any characteristic that is not always the same—that is, any characteristic that varies. Examples of variables include gender, eye color, achievement, motivation, and running speed. In our earlier example, "gender" and the "wearing of glasses" were the variables. Even "spunk," "style," and "lust for life" are possible variables. The reason we describe such characteristics as "possible" variables is that they may not vary in a particular study. Although gender did vary in our example, it would not vary in a study relating the wearing of glasses to the occupations of males (only). In such a study, gender would be a constant, since it would be the same for all of the individuals involved (only males, no females). Thus a given characteristic can be a variable in some studies, but a constant in others.

As we mentioned above, much research involves a search for relationships among variables. Are motivation and learning related? If so, how? What about age and attractiveness? speed and weight? height and strength? counselor style and client anxiety? teacher personality and student interest in a subject? administrative policies and faculty morale?

There are many variables "out there" in the real world that can be investigated. Obviously, we can't investigate them all. So we must choose. We choose certain variables to investigate because we have a suspicion that they are somehow related, and that if we can discover the nature of this relationship, we will be able to make more sense out of the world in which we live.

Check your understanding of what we have discussed so far. Here is a potential research question:

"Are younger students more anxious in mathematics courses than older students?"

What are the variables in the question?

_____

_____

AUTHORS' COMMENTS

The variables are age and level of anxiety in mathematics courses.

MEASURED AND CATEGORICAL VARIABLES

Variables can be classified in several ways. One way is to distinguish between variables which are measured and those which are categorical. *Measured* (sometimes called quantitative) *variables* exist in some degree rather than all or none. They are measured along a continuum from "less" to "more," and we can assign numbers to different individuals or objects which indicate how much of the variable they possess. An example would be height. (John is 6 feet tall and Sally is 5 feet 4 inches.) Another would be weight. (Bill Adams weighs 150 pounds and Jane Adams weighs 140 pounds, but their son tips the scales at an even 200 pounds!) We can also assign numbers to various individuals to indicate how much "interest" they have in a subject, with a 5 indicating very much interest, a 4 indicating much interest, and so on down to a 1, indicating very little interest in the subject. If we can assign numbers in this way, we have the measured variable "interest."

By way of contrast, *categorical* (sometimes called qualitative) *variables* do not vary in degree, amount, or quantity, but are qualitatively different. Examples include eye color, gender, religious preference, occupation, position on a baseball team, and most kinds of "treatments" or "methods." For example, if a researcher wished to compare computerized and noncomputerized classrooms, the variable involved would be the presence or absence of computers. This is a categorical variable—a classroom is either one or the other, either computerized or noncomputerized, not somewhere on a continuum between being computerized and not being computerized. All members of the category are considered to be the same so far as the variable is concerned (see Figure 3.2).

Notice, for example, that gender, a categorical variable, consists of only two categories, male and female. When a study includes this variable, all males are considered to be the same, as are all females. The variable is not degree of maleness or femaleness, but whether an individual is male *or* female. Similarly, if the categorical variable were eye color, we would be interested not in the degree of blueness (or brownness or grayness) a person's eyes possess, but in which category of eye color a person, because of his or her eyes, would be placed.

Can "teaching method" be considered a variable? Yes, it can. Suppose a researcher is interested in studying teachers who use different methods in teaching. The researcher locates one teacher who lectures exclusively, another who buttresses her lectures with slides and filmstrips, and a third who uses the case study method and never lectures. Does not the teaching method "vary"? It does. You may need to practice thinking of differences in methods, or in groups of people (e.g., teachers compared with administrators) as variables, but mastering this idea is extremely useful in learning about research.

Sometimes a researcher has a choice of how to conceptualize variables. In the open classroom study, for example, the concept of openness was considered to be a measured variable, and each classroom was observed and given a score in terms of how "open" observers considered it to be. Other researchers might have preferred to treat the concept of openness as a categorical variable, involving only two categories—open and closed. In such a case, classrooms identified as "open" would be compared with others identified as "closed." This option, however, is seldom advisable, since it ignores distinctions within each category.

Here are several variables. Which ones are measured variables and which ones are categorical variables?

1. Type of automobile owned
2. Learning ability
3. Ethnicity
4. Family cohesiveness
5. Heartbeats per minute
6. Administrative style

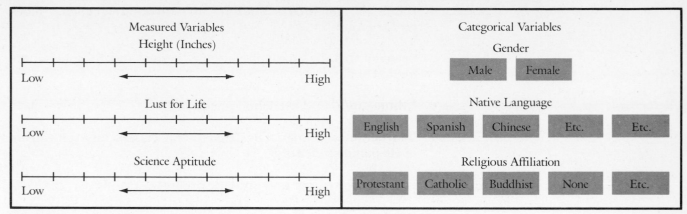

FIGURE 3.2
Measured vs. Categorical Variables

AUTHORS' COMMENTS

Items 1, 3, and 6 represent categorical variables: 2, 4, and 5 represent measured variables.

Relationships can take one of three forms. They can be between two measured variables, between one categorical and one measured variable, or between two categorical variables. Examples of each are given below.

- Two measured variables:
    age and amount of interest in school
    reading achievement and mathematics achievement
    classroom openness and student motivation
    amount of time watching television and aggressiveness of behavior
- One categorical and one measured variable:
    method used to teach reading and reading achievement
    counseling approach and level of anxiety
    nationality and liking for school
    student gender and amount of praise given by teachers
- Two categorical variables:
    ethnicity and father's occupation
    gender of teacher and subject taught
    administrative style and college major
    religious affiliation and political party membership

Listed below are a number of relationships. In front of the number in each example, write "MM" if the relationship involves two measured variables, or "CC" if two categorical variables are involved. If the relationship involves both a measured and a categorical variable, write "MC" and circle the categorical variable.

_____ 1. Gender of language-delayed children and gender of their friends.

_____ 2. Off-task behavior and reading achievement in emotionally disturbed adolescents.

_____ 3. Age and motor skill among children in grades 1–3.

_____ 4. Blind vs. sighted children on three-dimensional block construction.

_____ 5. Behavior therapy vs. client-centered therapy and dropping out of high school.

_____ 6. Ethnic group and academic major.

_____ 7. Instruction in bilingual or English-only classes and self-esteem of Hispanic students.

_____ 8. Parent involvement and student progress.

_____ 9. Gender and aggressive behavior among sixth graders.

AUTHORS' COMMENTS

The relationships in 2, 3, and 8 are between two measured variables. Each of these variables exists in some degree.

The relationships in 1, 5, and 6 are between two categorical variables. All of these variables do *not* exist in some degree—they exist as categories, and individuals are either a member of the category or not.

The relationships in 4, 7, and 9 involve both a measured variable and a categorical variable. In 4, the measured variable is block construction ability, whereas the categorical variable is degree of sightedness (some vs. none). In 7, the measured variable is amount of self-esteem among Hispanic students, whereas the categorical variable is type of language instruction (bilingual vs. English-only). In 9, the measured variable is amount of aggressive behavior among sixth graders, whereas the categorical variable is gender.

Note that all of the measured variables *could* be treated as categorical variables by defining specific categories such as "high" and "low" achievement. As stated earlier, however, doing so would ignore differences *within* each category and therefore should, in general, be avoided.

Generally speaking, most educational studies that include one measured variable and one categorical variable are comparisons of different methods or treatments. In such studies, the different methods or treatments represent the categorical variable. Often the other variable, the measured one, is referred to as an *outcome variable*. Can you see why?

The reason is rather clear-cut. The investigator, after all, is interested in the effect of the differences in method on one or more outcomes (e.g., the achievement of students, their motivation, their interest, and so forth). An outcome is a result of some sort, an observed behavior, product, or condition of an organism that has been stimulated in some way. Since these outcomes *vary* for different people in different situations, and under different conditions, they are a particular kind of variable called an outcome variable. All of the following are examples of outcome variables:

• The amount of uneasiness which job applicants express in an interview
• How anxious students are before an examination
• Neatness
• The "openness" of a classroom
• How disruptive students are in a history class

- The ability of people to express themselves in writing
- Fluency in a foreign language
- Teacher–student rapport

Notice two things about all of the above examples. First, each represents a possible result or outcome of some sort that can be produced by something else. Rarely are we certain what it is, exactly, that produces these outcomes, however. Thus, the level of anxiety which students feel before an examination may be caused by their previous performance on similar exams, the amount of studying they have done in preparation for the exam, how important a good grade on the exam is to them, or any one of several other factors. The "disruptiveness" of students in a history class may be due to their disrespect for the teacher, the teacher's failure to discipline them for past disruptions, their inability to do as the teacher requests, bad feelings among several students, and so forth.

This is why research is necessary. Many outcomes like the above are not very well understood by educators. Researchers have designed studies not only to broaden understanding of the nature of these (and other) outcomes, but also to gain insight into what causes them.

The second thing to notice about the examples above is that the amount or degree of each outcome can vary in different situations or under different conditions. Not all people have the same degree of fluency in Spanish, for example. The amount of rapport that exists between teachers and students varies for different teachers with different students, and vice versa. Neatness, expressiveness, anxiety—such qualities are possessed in varying amounts by different people. That is why they can be considered variables.

Let's check your understanding once more. Suppose a researcher plans to investigate the following question:

"Will students who are taught by a team of three teachers learn more than students taught by one individual teacher?"

What is the outcome variable in this question?

_____

_____

AUTHORS' COMMENTS

The outcome variable is amount of learning.

INDEPENDENT AND DEPENDENT VARIABLES

Two other types of variables that are frequently mentioned in the literature are independent and dependent variables. *Independent variables* are those the investigator chooses to study (and often manipulate) in order to assess their possible effect(s) on one or more other variables. An independent variable is presumed to have an effect on, to influence somehow, another variable. The variable that the independent variable is presumed to affect is called the *dependent variable*. In commonsense terms, the nature of the dependent variable "depends on" what the independent variable does to it, how it affects it. You also should realize that all outcome variables are dependent variables.

The relationship between independent and dependent variables can be portrayed graphically as follows:

Independent variable(s)   →   Dependent variable(s)
(presumed or possible cause)   (presumed results)

Consider the previous research question:

> "Will students who are taught by a team of three teachers learn more than students taught by one individual teacher?"

What are the independent and the dependent variables in the question?

The independent variable is _____

_____

The dependent variable is _____

_____

AUTHORS' COMMENTS

Do you see that the independent variable is the number of teachers, and the dependent variable is the amount of learning? Notice that there are two conditions (sometimes called levels) of the in- dependent variable—three teachers and one teacher. Also notice that the dependent variable is not "learning," but "amount of learning." Can you see why?

EXTRANEOUS VARIABLES AND CONSTANTS

A basic problem in research is that there are many possible independent variables that could have an effect on the dependent variable. Once a researcher has decided which variables to study, he or she must be concerned about the influence or effect of other variables which exist. Such variables are usually called *extraneous variables*. The task of the researcher is to control these extraneous variables somehow so as to eliminate or minimize their effect. Extraneous variables are independent variables that have not been controlled.

One way to control extraneous variables is to hold them constant. For example, if a researcher were to include only men as the subjects of a study, he or she would be controlling the variable of gender. We might say that in this study the gender of the subjects does not vary. Researchers refer to those potential variables that are not allowed to change as *constants*.

Look again at the research question about team teaching presented above. Now ask yourself, "What other variables might have an effect on the learning of students in a classroom situation?" List a few extraneous variables in the space provided below.

_____

_____

_____

_____

_____

AUTHORS' COMMENTS

There are many possible extraneous variables that you might have listed. The personality of the teachers involved is one possibility. The academic proficiency of the students is another. Time of day the classes are taught, nature of the subject taught, textbooks used, type of learning activities employed by the teachers, teaching methods used—all are possible variables that could affect learning. As such, they would be extraneous variables in this study.

A researcher must think about how he or she might control the possible effect(s) of extraneous variables. We will discuss how to do this in some detail in a later chapter. For now, you need to make sure that you understand the difference between independent and dependent variables, and to be aware of possible extraneous variables. Try your hand at the following question. What are the variables?

"Will students who are taught history by a teacher of the same gender like the subject more than students taught by a teacher of a different gender?"

The independent variable is _____

_____

The dependent variable is _____

_____

Possible extraneous variables are _____

_____

AUTHORS' COMMENTS

The dependent variable is a liking for history; the independent variable is gender correspondence. Possible extraneous variables include the personality of the teacher(s) involved, the ability level of the students, the materials (e.g., textbooks) used, the style of teaching, and ethnicity and/or age of the teacher and students. The researcher would want to control as many of these variables as possible.

Go back to your own research question. Check to make sure that it poses a possible relationship between variables. What are the variables in your question? Write them in the space below.

The variables to be investigated in my question are _____

_____ and _____

The independent variable is _____

_____

The dependent variable is _____

_____

Possible extraneous variables I would have to think about controlling

are _____

_____

◼ Ethics and Research

In addition to feasibility, clarity, and significance, researchers need to consider the ethics of their research. The basic question to ask in this regard is, "Will any physical or psychological harm come to anyone as a result of my research?" Naturally, no researcher wants to harm any of the subjects in a research study. Since this is such an important (and often overlooked) issue, we need to discuss it in more detail.

In a somewhat larger sense, ethics also refers to questions of right and wrong. When a person is behaving ethically, he or she is doing what is right. But what does it mean to be "right" so far as research is concerned?

One dictionary defines ethical (behavior) as "conforming to the standards of conduct of a given profession or group." What researchers consider to be ethical, therefore, is largely a matter of agreement among them. The American Psychological Association has published a list of ethical principles for the conduct of research with human subjects.[1] We have substituted the

[1] Committee on Scientific and Professional Ethics and Conduct. 1981. Ethical principles of psychologists. *American Psychologist*, 36:633–638.

word "educator" for the word "psychologist" in the association's general statement, and have summarized the major points.

> The decision to undertake research rests upon a considered judgment by the individual educator about how best to contribute to science and human welfare. Having made the decision to conduct research, the educator considers alternative directions in which research energies and resources might be invested. On the basis of this consideration, the educator carries out the investigation with respect and concern for the dignity and welfare of the people who participate and with cognizance of federal and state regulations and professional standards governing the conduct of research with human participants.

There are three very important issues that every researcher should address—the protection of participants from harm, the ensuring of confidentiality of research data, and the knowing deception of research subjects. Let us discuss each in more detail.

PROTECTING PARTICIPANTS FROM HARM

Participant protection is perhaps the most important ethical consideration of all. It is a fundamental responsibility of every researcher to do all in his or her power to ensure that participants in a research study are protected from any physical or psychological harm or danger that may arise from research procedures. Any study that is likely to cause lasting and/or serious harm or discomfort to any participant should not be conducted, unless the research has the potential to provide information of great benefit to human beings. Even when this is the case, participants should be fully informed of the dangers involved, and in no way required to participate.

A further question with regard to protecting participants involves obtaining the consent of individuals who may be exposed to any risk. Fortunately, almost all educational research involves activities which are within the customary procedures of schools or other agencies and, as such, involve little or no risk. Federal legislation recognizes this by specifically exempting most categories of educational research from extensive review processes. Nevertheless, the researcher should carefully consider whether there is any likelihood of risk involved and, if so, provide full disclosure as well as obtaining the formal consent of participants (or their guardians, if they are under 18 years of age). Three important ethical questions to ask about any study are:

- Could people be harmed?
- Can the study be conducted in another way and still find out what the researcher wants to know?
- Is the information that may be obtained from the study so important that it warrants possible harm to the participants?

These are difficult questions, and they deserve discussion and consideration by all researchers.[2]

---

[2] Universities and other agencies receiving federal funds are required to have a Human Subjects Review Board that reviews all research proposals (including master's and doctoral degree studies) for possible harm to subjects.

ENSURING CONFIDENTIALITY OF RESEARCH DATA

Graduate students and beginning researchers often have the impression that confidential information—in school or agency files, for example—is unavailable to them. This is not necessarily so; such data are regularly made available to people who can demonstrate (1) a legitimate research purpose and (2) professional integrity.[3] In many cases, supervision by a university faculty member or the equivalent is sufficient.

Once the data in a study have been collected, the researcher should make sure that no one else (other than a few key research assistants) has access to the data. Whenever possible, the names of the subjects should be removed from all data collection forms. To preserve confidentiality, a numeral or letter can be assigned to each form or subjects can be asked to furnish information anonymously. Ideally, not even the researcher will be able to link the data to a particular subject. Sometimes, however, it is important for the researcher to be able to identify individual subjects. When this is the case, the linkage system should be carefully guarded. It should go without saying (we hope) that all subjects should be assured that any data collected from or about them will be held in confidence. The names of individual subjects should never be used in any publications that describe the research. All participants in a study should always have the right to withdraw from the study, or to request that data about them not be used.

SHOULD SUBJECTS BE DECEIVED?

The issue of deception is a particularly troublesome one as far as ethics is concerned. Some studies cannot be carried out unless some deception of subjects takes place. It is often very difficult to find naturalistic situations in which certain behaviors occur frequently. A researcher may have to wait for a long time, for example, for a teacher to reinforce students in a certain way. It may be much easier for the researcher to observe the effects of such reinforcement by employing the teacher as a confederate.

Sometimes it is better to deceive subjects than to submit them to any pain or trauma that a particular research question might otherwise require. The famous Milgram study of obedience is a good example.[4] In this study, subjects were ordered to give increasingly severe electric shocks to another subject who was hidden behind a screen. What they did not know was that the individual to whom they thought they were administering the shocks was a confederate of the experimenter, and no shocks were actually being administered. The dependent variable was the level of shock that the subjects administered before they refused to continue. Out of a total of 40 subjects who participated in the study, 26 followed the "orders" of the experimenter and (so they thought) administered the maximum possible shock of 450 volts! Regardless of the fact that no shocks were actually administered, the publication of the results of the study produced widespread controversy. Many people felt the study was unethical. Others ar-

[3] The information contained in an individual education program (IEP) of a student receiving special education services is an exception. Recent court decisions require parental permission prior to such information being made available.

[4] S. Milgram. 1963. Behavioral study of obedience. *Journal of Abnormal and Social Psychology*, 67:371–378.

gued that the importance of the study and its results justified the deception. Notice that the study raises questions not only about deception but also about risk, since some participants could have suffered emotionally from later consideration of their actions.

Current professional guidelines[5] are as follows:

- Whenever possible, a researcher should conduct the study using methods that do not require deception.
- If alternative methods cannot be devised, the researcher must determine whether the use of deception is justified by the prospective study's scientific, educational, or applied value.
- If the participants are deceived, the researcher must ensure that the participants are provided with sufficient explanation as soon as possible.

Perhaps the most serious problem involving deception is what it may ultimately do to the reputation of the scientific community. If people in general begin to think of scientists and researchers as liars, or as individuals who misrepresent what they are about, the overall image of science may suffer. Fewer and fewer people will be willing to participate in research investigations. As a result, the search for reliable knowledge about our world may be impeded.

Here are brief descriptions of three research studies in which one of the authors participated. Evaluate each in terms of (1) presenting possible harm to the participants, (2) ensuring the confidentiality of the research data, and (3) knowingly practicing deception. If you detect a problem in any of these areas, suggest what the researcher might do to solve or minimize the problem.

Study 1

The researcher plans to observe (unobtrusively) students in each of 40 classrooms—eight visits each of 40 minutes' duration. The purpose of these observations is to look for relationships between the behavior of students and certain teacher behavior patterns.

Possible harm to participants: _____

_____

Ensuring confidentiality of the research data: _____

_____

Deception: _____

_____

Study 2

The researcher wishes to study the value of a workshop on suicide prevention for high school students. The workshop is to consist of three 2-hour meetings in which danger signals, causes of suicide, and community resources that provide counseling will be discussed. Students will volunteer,

[5] Ethical principles of psychologists, *op. cit.*

and half will be assigned to a comparison group that will not participate in the workshop. Outcomes will be assessed by comparing the information learned and attitudes of those attending with those who do not attend.

Possible harm to participants: _____

_____

Ensuring confidentiality of the research data: _____

_____

Deception: _____

_____

Study 3
The researcher wishes to study the effects of "failure" vs. "success" by teaching junior high students a motor skill during a series of six 10-minute instructional periods. After each training period, the students will be given feedback on their performance as compared with that of other students. In order to control extraneous variables (such as coordination), the researcher plans to randomly divide the students into two groups—half will be told their performance was "relatively poor" and the other half will be told that they are "doing well." Their actual performance will be ignored.

Possible harm to participants: _____

_____

Ensuring confidentiality of the research data: _____

_____

Deception: _____

_____

AUTHORS' COMMENTS

STUDY 1

Possible Harm to the Participants. This study would fall within the exempt category regarding the possibility of harm to the participants. Neither teachers nor students are placed under any risk, and observation is an accepted part of school practice.

Confidentiality of the Research Data. The only issue that is likely to arise in this regard is the possible but unlikely observation of a teacher behaving in an illegal or unethical way (e.g., physically or verbally abusing a student). In the former case, the researcher is legally required to report the incident. In the latter case, the researcher must weigh the ethical dilemma involved in not reporting the incident against that of violating assurances of confidentiality.

Deception. Although no outright deception is involved, the researcher is going to have to give the teachers a rationale for observing them. If the specific teacher characteristic being observed (e.g., need to control) is given, the behavior in question is likely to be affected. To avoid this, the researcher might explain that the purpose of the study is to investigate different teaching styles—without divulging the specifics. To us, this does not seem to be unethical. An alternative is to tell the teachers that specific details cannot be divulged until after data have been collected for fear of changing their behavior. If this alternative is pursued, some teachers might refuse to participate.

STUDY 2

Possibility of Harm to the Participants. Whether this study fits the exempt category with regard to any possibility of risk for the participants depends on the extent to which it is atypical for the school in question. We think that in most schools, this study would probably be considered atypical. In addition, it is conceivable that the material presented could place a student at risk by stirring up emotional reactions. In any case, the researcher should inform parents as to the nature of the study and the possible risks involved, and obtain their consent for their children to participate.

Confidentiality of the Research Data. No problems are foreseen in this regard, although confidentiality as to what will occur during the workshop cannot, of course, be guaranteed.

Deception. No problems are foreseen.

STUDY 3

Possibility of Harm to the Participants. This study presents several problems. Some students in the "failure" group may well suffer emotional distress. Although students are normally given similar feedback on their performance in most schools, feedback in this study (being arbitrary) may conflict dramatically with their prior experience. The researcher cannot properly inform students, or their parents, about the deceptive nature of the study, since to do so would in effect destroy the study.

Confidentiality of the Research Data. Confidentiality does not appear to be an issue in this study.

Deception. Deceiving participants is clearly an issue. One alternative is to base feedback on actual performance. The difficulty here is that each student's extensive prior history will affect both individual performance and interpretation of feedback, thus confounding the results. Some, but not all, of these extraneous variables can be controlled (perhaps by examining school records for data on past history or by pretesting students). Another alternative is to weaken the experimental treatment by trying to lessen the possibility of emotional distress (e.g., by saying to participants in the failure group: "You did not do quite as well as most") and confining the training to one time period. Both of these alternatives, however, would lessen the chances of the hypothesized relationship emerging.

At this point, explain how you would deal with each of these concerns in *your* research. If you feel the issue is not applicable to your study, explain why.

I would deal with the ethical issues of risk (possible harm to participants), confidentiality, and deception as follows:

I would protect participants from possible harm by _____

_____

_____

or   (*continues on next page*)

This issue is not a potential problem in my study because _____

_____

_____

_____

I would ensure confidentiality of the research data by _____

_____

_____

or

This issue is not a potential problem in my study because _____

_____

_____

_____

I plan to deal with the question of deception by _____

_____

_____

_____

or

This issue is not a potential problem in my study because _____

_____

_____

_____

■ *Hypotheses*

A research question often is restated as a hypothesis. A hypothesis is, simply put, a prediction of some sort regarding the possible outcomes of a study. For example, here is a research question followed by its restatement into a hypothesis:

Question: "Do individuals who see themselves as socially attractive want their romantic partners also to be socially attractive?

Hypothesis: "Individuals who see themselves as socially attractive will want their romantic partners also to be (as judged by others) socially attractive."

Let us restate the examples of research questions we presented in Chapter Two as possible hypotheses:

Question 1: "Does the open classroom work?"
Possible hypothesis: "The open classroom does work."
Question 2: "How do teachers feel about special classes for the educationally handicapped?"
Possible hypothesis: "Teachers feel that special classes for the educationally handicapped constitute a social stigma."
Alternative hypothesis: "Teachers feel that special classes for the educationally handicapped will help such students improve their academic skills."
Question 3: "Do second graders like school?"
Possible hypothesis: "Second graders like school."

Here are three additional examples of research questions. See if you can restate them as hypotheses:

1. Do teachers behave differently toward students of a different gender?
2. Does client-centered therapy produce more client satisfaction than behavior modification therapy?
3. Do students taught Spanish in a language laboratory become more fluent than students who are taught Spanish in a traditional classroom setting?

AUTHORS' COMMENTS

1. Teachers behave differently toward students of a gender different from their own than they behave toward students of their own gender.
2. Client-centered therapy results in more (or in less) satisfaction in clients than behavior modification therapy.
3. Students taught Spanish in a language laboratory become more (or less, or equally) fluent compared with students taught Spanish in a traditional classroom setting.

ADVANTAGES AND DISADVANTAGES OF STATING QUESTIONS AS HYPOTHESES

Stating questions as hypotheses has both advantages and disadvantages. What are some of the advantages? First, a hypothesis forces us to think more deeply about the possible outcomes of a study. Restating a question as a hypothesis can lead to a more sophisticated understanding of what the question implies and of the specific variables that are involved. Often, when more than one hypothesis seems to suggest itself, we are forced to think more carefully about what we really want to investigate.

Consider again the question of the open classroom. When a student in one of our research classes originally wrote this example, it read: "Does the open classroom work?" After considerable discussion, the student subsequently revised it to read, "Does the open classroom result in higher student motivation?" Let us now state this revised question as a hypothesis: "Open classrooms lead to higher student motivation."

Stating this hypothesis helps us to think further about the research question and what we really want to find out. It suggests that we need to consider many aspects of the open classroom, its advantages and disadvantages, and how it differs from more traditionally organized classrooms. Further, stating the hypothesis stimulates us to begin thinking of ways to test the prediction we have made. For example, it seems obvious (perhaps) that the testing of this hypothesis will require that we compare some open classrooms with less-open classrooms. Otherwise, there is no way for us to determine if higher motivation (should this be the case) is due to the "openness" of the classroom rather than to something else.

A second advantage of restating questions as hypotheses involves a philosophy of science. The rationale underlying this philosophy is as follows: If a researcher is attempting to build a body of knowledge in addition to answering a specific question, then stating hypotheses is a good strategy because it enables the investigator to make specific predictions on the basis of prior evidence or theoretical argument. If these predictions are borne out by subsequent research, the entire procedure gains in both persuasiveness and efficiency. A classic example is Albert Einstein's theory of relativity. Many hypotheses formulated as a result of Einstein's theory were later verified through research. As more and more of these predictions were shown to be fact, they not only became useful in their own right, but also provided increasing support for the ideas in Einstein's theory which generated the hypotheses in the first place.

There is no clear-cut theory about open classrooms to which we can refer at this time. There are, however, some general theories of behavior which are pertinent. Many of these theories suggest that people are more highly motivated when they are free to follow their own desires and satisfy their own needs than when they are directed or controlled by others. To the extent that open classrooms foster this sort of behavior (as opposed, say, to more traditional teacher-directed classrooms), verification of our hypothesis (that the open classroom leads to higher motivation) would tend to provide some support for such theories.

What are the disadvantages of stating research questions as hypotheses? Essentially they are twofold. First, stating a hypothesis may lead to either a conscious or unconscious bias on the part of the researcher. Once the investigator states a hypothesis, he or she may be tempted to arrange the procedures or manipulate the data in such a way as to bring about a desired outcome. This is probably more the exception than the rule. Researchers are assumed to be intellectually honest—although there are some famous exceptions. Furthermore, it is often argued that any particular study can be replicated in order to verify the findings. All studies should be subject to review; in the past, a review of suspect research has, on occasion, revealed such inadequacies of method that the reported results were cast into doubt. Unfortunately, educational research studies are seldom repeated, so this "protection" is somewhat of an illusion. Dishonest investigators stand a fair chance of getting away with falsifying results if they choose to do so. Why would investigators deliberately distort their findings? Because professional recognition and financial reward accrue to those who publish important results.

Even for the great majority of researchers who are honest, commitment to a hypothesis may lead to distortions that are unintentional and unconscious. Since it is probably unlikely that any researcher in the field of education is ever totally disinterested in the outcomes of a study, his or her attitudes and/or knowledge may favor a particular result. For this reason, it is probably desirable for a researcher to make his or her predelictions known in a hypothesis so that they are clear to others interested in the research. Furthermore, the investigator can then take steps to ensure (as much as possible) an unbiased study.

The second disadvantage of stating hypotheses is that focusing attention on a hypothesis may prevent the researcher from noticing other phenomena that might be important to study. For example, deciding to study the effect of the open classroom on student motivation might lead a researcher to overlook its effect on such characteristics as sex typing or decision making; these relationships might be quite noticeable to another researcher who was not focusing solely on motivation. Such "tunnel vision" seems to be a good argument for ensuring that not all research be directed toward hypothesis testing.

At this point, restate your research question as a hypothesis. That is, make a prediction of some sort about a possible answer (or answers) to your question. In stating your hypothesis, be careful to avoid terms like "can," "should," and "ought," since such words lead to statements that cannot be verified. As stated in Chapter Two, research cannot determine what should be, or what is ultimately possible.

My hypothesis is _____

_____

_____

Restating a research question as a hypothesis helps us see if we are investigating a relationship or not and, if we are not, to formulate one if possible. For example, in the open classroom hypothesis stated earlier, a relationship is only implied. A slight alteration of the hypothesis makes this implied relationship explicit:

Previous hypothesis: "Open classrooms lead to higher student motivation."
Revised hypothesis: "The greater the openness of a classroom, the higher the motivation of students."

The relationship to be investigated in this hypothesis is between _____

_____ and _____

The independent variable is _____

_____

The dependent variable is _____

_____

Extraneous variables the researcher might need to think about control-

ling include _____

_____

_____

AUTHORS' COMMENTS

The relationship in this hypothesis is between level of student motivation and degree of openness of a classroom. The independent variable is the degree of openness; the dependent variable is the level of student motivation. Extraneous variables that the researcher quite possibly would want to control include grade level of the students, type of subject taught, materials used, style of the teacher, and ability level of the students.

Consider the second example of a research question presented in Chapter Two: "How do teachers feel about special classes for the educationally handicapped?" We offered two (of many possible) hypotheses which might flow out of this question: (1) "Teachers feel that special classes for the educationally handicapped constitute a social stigma," and (2) "Teachers feel that special classes for the educationally handicapped will help such students improve their academic skills." Both of these hypotheses implicitly suggest a comparison between special classes for the educationally handicapped and some other kind of arrangement. Thus, the relationship to be investigated is between teacher feelings and type of class. Notice that it is important to compare how teachers feel about special classes with how they feel about other kinds of arrangements. If we were to look only at how teachers feel about special classes without also identifying how they feel about other kinds of arrangements, we would not know if their feelings were in any way unique or different. A comparison of some sort must be made to determine if a relationship exists.

Now consider the third example of a research question presented in Chapter Two: "Do second graders like school?" As we begin to think about this question, and how to restate it as a hypothesis, we can ask ourselves what we really want to know. We may think most second graders would say that they like school. But are we interested simply in how second graders feel about school? Aren't we interested, more broadly, in how second graders feel about school compared with other activities? For instance, how does their liking for school compare with their liking for television? What about staying home? If they were asked to choose, would they prefer to go to school rather than stay home? Perhaps we might compare the feelings of second graders about school with the feelings of students in other grades. Do second graders express more of a liking for school, for example, than first graders? As we begin to think about possible hypotheses suggested by the original question, we begin to see that some of them are more powerful than others. What do we mean by powerful? Simply that some may lead to more useful knowledge. Compare, for example, the following pairs of hypotheses. Which hypothesis in each pair would you say is the more powerful?

Pair 1
a. "Second graders like school less than they like watching television."
b. "Second graders like school less than first graders but more than third graders."

Pair 2
a. "Most students with academic disabilities prefer being in regular classes than in special classes."
b. "Students with academic disabilities will have more negative attitudes about themselves if they are placed in special classes than if they are placed in regular classes."

Pair 3
a. "Counselors who use client-centered therapy procedures get different reactions from students than do counselors who use traditional therapy procedures."
b. "Students who receive client-centered therapy express more satisfaction with the counseling process than do students who receive traditional therapy."

AUTHORS' COMMENTS

We judge the second hypothesis in each pair to be the more powerful, since in each case (in our judgment) the relationship to be investigated is clearer and more specific. Furthermore, investigation of the hypothesis seems more likely to lead to greater knowledge about the relationship. It also seems to us that the information to be obtained will be of more use to people interested in the general topic.

What relationship between variables is suggested by hypothesis (b) in each pair?

In hypothesis 1(b), _____ is related to

_____

In hypothesis 2(b), _____ is related to

_____

In hypothesis 3(b), _____ is related to

_____

AUTHORS' COMMENTS

In hypothesis 1(b), liking for school is related to grade level. In hypothesis 2(b), type of class is related to number of negative attitudes. In hypothesis 3(b), type of therapy is related to degree of satisfaction with the counseling process.

DIRECTIONAL VS. NONDIRECTIONAL HYPOTHESES

We now want to make a distinction between directional and nondirectional hypotheses. A *directional hypothesis* is one that indicates the specific direction (e.g., higher, lower, more, less) that a researcher expects to emerge in a relationship. The particular direction that is expected is based on what the researcher has found in the literature, in personal experience, or in the experience of others. Thus, the second hypothesis in each of the three pairs above is a directional hypothesis. By way of contrast, a *nondirectional hypothesis* does not make a specific prediction about what direction the outcome of a study will take. The above three hypotheses, in nondirectional form, would be stated as follows:

Nondirectional hypothesis 1: "First, second, and third graders will feel differently toward school."

Nondirectional hypothesis 2: "There will be a difference in scores on an attitude measure between students with academic disabilities who are placed in special classes and such students who are placed in regular classes."

Nondirectional hypothesis 3: "There will be a difference in expression of satisfaction with the counseling process between students who receive client-centered therapy and students who receive traditional therapy."

Think about the question concerning the open classroom. It seems reasonable to say that the findings of a study investigating this question will turn out in one of three ways. Specifically, the open classroom may show (1) higher motivation, (2) lower motivation, or (3) no difference with regard to motivation. Before the study is conducted and data are collected, we have no way of knowing which of these three outcomes will be the case. If we restate the question in terms of the first or second option, we have chosen a directional hypothesis—that is, we have stated the direction of the relationship we expect to emerge.

Sometimes it is difficult to make such specific predictions. If a researcher suspects that a relationship exists, but has no basis for predicting the direction of the relationship, he or she cannot make a directional hypothesis. In the example above, we might suspect that the level of student motivation in a classroom is somehow related to the degree of openness present in the classroom, but we may be uncertain as to how it relates. Still, we may feel that the relationship is important to investigate. In this case, we would state a nondirectional hypothesis: "The level of motivation of the students in a classroom is related to the degree of openness present in that classroom."

Which of the following statements are directional hypotheses and which are nondirectional hypotheses?

1. There is a relationship between reading improvement and off-task behavior in emotionally disturbed adolescents.
2. Males who are 60 years of age or older are more satisfied with their lives than females who are 60 years of age or older.
3. Counselors who are recovered alcoholics will experience less burnout after ten years in the counseling profession than counselors who are not recovered alcoholics.
4. Couples who receive marriage counseling will differ in marital satisfaction more than couples who do not receive marriage counseling.
5. Teachers with more positive attitudes toward their students will demonstrate better class management skills.

AUTHORS' COMMENTS

Statement 1 is nondirectional. It does not indicate whether high achievement goes with high off-task or low off-task behavior.

Statement 2 is directional. It states not only that gender is related to satisfaction but also that males are more satisfied with their lives than women in this same age group.

Statement 3 is directional. It states which group of counselors will experience less burnout, not just that there will be a difference in burnout.

Statement 4 is nondirectional. It does not state whether the counseled group will be more (or less) satisfied.

Statement 5 is directional. It indicates not only that a relationship exists between attitude and skills but also that a positive attitude goes with greater skill.

At this point, restate your research hypothesis in the space provided below.

_____

_____

_____

Check whether your hypothesis is _____ directional or _____ nondirectional.

■ *Summary*

In this chapter, we discussed the remaining two characteristics that good research questions should possess: They should suggest a relationship of some sort, and they should be ethical. You will recall that the other three characteristics—feasibility, clarity, and significance—were examined in Chapter Two.

We presented and discussed three basic ethical principles that researchers should take care not to violate. We discussed the concept of relationship in some detail and pointed out that a relationship is a statement about variables. Accordingly, we introduced and defined the concept of variable, and described and gave examples of several different kinds of variables. We presented examples of research questions that suggested a relationship between variables, and compared these with other examples that did not suggest a relationship.

We introduced the important concept of a research hypothesis. We restated a number of research questions as hypotheses, and discussed the advantages and disadvantages of stating questions as hypotheses. Finally, we described and illustrated the difference between directional and nondirectional hypotheses.

■ *Key Concepts Discussed in This Chapter*

relationship	dependent variable
variable	extraneous variable
measured variable	constant
categorical variable	hypothesis
independent variable	directional hypothesis
nondirectional hypothesis	ethics

■ *How Far Along Should I Be at This Point?*

By now, you should have restated your research question as a research hypothesis and indicated whether it is a directional or a nondirectional hypothesis. You should be able to recognize variables and hypotheses when you come across them in the literature. You should also have ensured that your research is ethical.

Thus, your question by now is clear not only to you but also to others. You have written a rationale as to why it is worth investigating, and have ensured that it possesses the five characteristics of a good research question—it is feasible, clear, and significant, it suggests a relationship, and it is ethical.

Evaluate your progress, therefore, by checking each of the following. At this point, you should have:

• Accomplished each of the tasks listed at the end of the preceding chapters. (If not, review and accomplish them before going any further.)
• Written a research question that suggests a relationship.
• Identified the independent, dependent, and extraneous variables in your study.
• Identified which of these variables are measured and which are categorical.
• Restated your research question as a hypothesis.
• Determined if your hypothesis is directional or nondirectional.
• Reviewed your study for any ethical problems regarding:
    possible harm to the participants
    confidentiality of the research data
    deception

■ *What's Next?*

In the next chapter, we describe how to conduct a literature review. We will introduce you to a number of different kinds of sources that you can review in order to find more information about the topic of your research. We also will take you through the steps involved in doing a computer search of the literature.

■ *For Further Reading*

American Psychological Association. 1982. *Ethical principles in the conduct of research with human participants.* Arlington, VA: American Psychological Association.

Committee on Scientific and Professional Ethics and Conduct. 1981. Ethical principles of psychologists. *American Psychologist*, 36:633–638.

Kimmel, A. J. 1988. *Ethics and values in applied social research.* Beverly Hills, CA: Sage.

Milgram, S. 1967. Behavioral study of obedience. *Journal of Abnormal and Social Psychology*, 67:371–378.

Tuckman, B. W. 1988. Identifying and labeling variables. In *Conducting educational research* (3rd Ed.). San Diego: Harcourt Brace Jovanovich.

Chapter Four

REVIEWING THE LITERATURE

Before planning the details of a study, researchers usually dig into the literature to find out what has already been written about the topic they are interested in investigating. Both the opinions of experts in the field and other research studies are of interest. Such reading is referred to as a *review of the literature*. A literature review is helpful in two ways. First, it helps researchers gain some knowledge of the ideas of others interested in a particular research question. Second, it lets researchers see the results of other (similar, or related) studies of the question. A detailed literature review is usually required of master's and/or doctoral students when they complete a thesis.

Types of References

There are no surefire rules to follow in trying to locate research studies on a particular topic. There are a number of sources, however, that are themselves reference works—that is, they suggest places for you to look. Although you will not be asked to do a detailed literature review in this chapter, you should become familiar with how to locate appropriate reference works in the library. We shall describe several of the more commonly used references and present sample pages for you to familiarize yourself with.

By the end of this chapter, you will know how to conduct both a manual and a computer search of the literature. You will be familiar with a number of different sources that you can use to locate more information on a topic of interest.

GENERAL REFERENCES

General references are the sources a researcher refers to first. They tell, in effect, where you can look in order to locate other sources, such as articles, monographs, and books that deal directly with your research question.

Most general references are either *indexes*, which list the author, title, and place of publication of articles and other materials on education, or *abstracts*, which give a brief summary of various publications along with the author, title, and place of publication. An index frequently used by researchers in education is *Current Index to Journals in Education*. A commonly used abstract is *Psychological Abstracts*.

SECONDARY SOURCES

Secondary sources refer to publications in which authors describe the work of others. The most common secondary sources in education are textbooks. A textbook in educational psychology, for example, may describe several different studies that have been done in psychology as a way of illustrating various ideas and concepts. Other commonly used secondary sources are educational encyclopedias, research reviews, and yearbooks.

PRIMARY SOURCES

Primary sources are those publications in which investigators report the results of their studies. The researcher communicates his or her findings directly to the reader. Most primary sources in education are journals, such as the *Journal of Educational Research* and the *Journal of Research in Science Teaching*. These journals are usually published monthly or quarterly, and the articles in them typically report on a particular research study.

If you are seeking information on a given topic, therefore, you should refer first to one or more general references in order to locate primary and secondary sources of value. For a quick overview of the problem at hand, secondary sources are probably your best bet. For detailed information about the research that others have done, consult primary sources.

Steps Involved in a Literature Review

1. Define the research problem as precisely as possible. General questions like "What sorts of teaching methods work well in the classroom?" and "How can a principal be a more effective leader?" are too fuzzy to be of much help when you start to look through a general reference. Narrow your question of interest down to a single area of concern. More specific questions in this instance might be "Is discussion more effective than slide-tape presentations in motivating students to learn social studies concepts?" and "What sorts of strategies do principals judged effective by their staffs use to improve faculty and staff morale?"

At this point, therefore, state the current version of your research question in the space provided below. Be sure that it is now as specific as possible.

_____

_____

_____

2. *Skim through some relevant secondary sources.* Once you have stated your research question in specific terms, it is a good idea to look through one or two secondary sources to get an overview of the previous work that has been done on your problem. Here are some of the most commonly used secondary sources in education.

Encyclopedia of Educational Research (current edition). This resource contains brief summaries of over 300 topics in education. It is an excellent source for getting a brief overview of your problem.

Handbook of Research on Teaching (current edition). This handbook contains longer articles on various aspects of teaching. Most are written by educational researchers who specialize in the topic on which they are writing. Includes extensive bibliographies.

National Society for the Study of Education (NSSE) Yearbooks. Published every year, these yearbooks deal with recent research on various topics. Each book usually contains from 10 to 12 chapters dealing with various aspects of the topic. The society also publishes a number of volumes on contemporary educational issues which deal in part with research on various topics. A list of these volumes can be found in the back of the most recent yearbook.

Review of Educational Research. Published four times a year, this journal contains reviews of research on various topics in education. Includes extensive bibliographies.

Review of Research in Education. Published yearly, each volume contains surveys of research on important topics written by leading educational researchers.

Each of the above sources contains reviews of research on various topics of importance in education. There are many topics, however, that have not been the subject of a recent review, in which case, the best chance of locating information discussing relevant research lies in recent books or monographs on the subject. The best source for identifying such books or monographs is the current edition of *Subject Guide to Books in Print*. Other places to look for new books on your topic are the card catalog[1] (see Figure 4.1) and the curriculum department (for textbooks) in the library. *Education Index* and *Psychological Abstracts* also list newly published professional books in the fields of education and psychology.

Indicate two general references you intend to consult on your research topic:

1. _____

2. _____

---

[1] Card catalogs may soon be a thing of the past. Most universities are converting the information in their card catalogs into a computer database. In the near future, rather than scanning through a number of cards, you will simply ask the computer to call up on screen the bibliographical data of the particular sources in which you are interested.

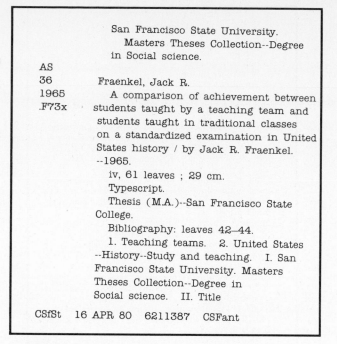

San Francisco State University.
Masters Theses Collection--Degree
in Social science.

AS
36
1965
.F73x

Fraenkel, Jack R.
A comparison of achievement between
students taught by a teaching team and
students taught in traditional classes
on a standardized examination in United
States history / by Jack R. Fraenkel.
--1965.
iv, 61 leaves ; 29 cm.
Typescript.
Thesis (M.A.)--San Francisco State
College.
Bibliography: leaves 42--44.
1. Teaching teams. 2. United States
--History--Study and teaching. I. San
Francisco State University. Masters
Theses Collection--Degree in
Social science. II. Title

CSfSt   16 APR 80   6211387   CSFant

FIGURE 4.1
Sample Card from University Card Catalog

3. *Peruse one or two appropriate general reference works.* There are many general references a researcher can consult. Here is a listing of the ones most commonly used in education.

Education Index. Published monthly, this source indexes articles from over 300 educational publications. Figure 4.2 illustrates part of a page listing under the topic of counseling. Note that the index gives only bibliographical data (author, title, and place of publication). For this reason, most researchers doing a literature search on a topic in education prefer the *Current Index to Journals in Education*, or *CIJE* (see below).

Psychological Abstracts. Published monthly by the American Psychological Association, this source covers over 900 journals, reports, monographs, and other documents (including books and other secondary sources). Abstracts (brief summaries of articles) are presented in addition to bibliographical data. Although there is considerable overlap with *CIJE*, *Psych Abstracts* (as it is often called) usually gives a more thorough coverage of psychological (as compared with educational) topics. It should definitely be consulted for any topic dealing with some aspect of psychology.

Resources in Education (RIE). Published monthly by the Educational Resources Information Center (ERIC), these volumes review speeches given at professional meetings, documents published by state departments of education, final reports of federally funded research projects, reports from school districts, commissioned papers written for government agencies, and other published and unpublished documents. Bibliographical

Group work

See also

Parents—Counseling services
Self help groups
Sensitivity training
Social group work

Adjustment to divorce: three components to assist children. R. G. Cantrell. bibl *Elem Sch Guid Couns* 20:163-73 F '86

Child, adult-interactional, and socioeconomic setting events as predictors of parent training outcome. J. E. Dumas. bibl *Educ Treat Child* 7:351-63 Fall '84

Circle of friends. G. J. Krysiak. *Sch Couns* 33:47-9 S '85

Coping with family change: a model for therapeutic group counselling with children and adolescents. R. Freeman and B. Couchman. bibl *Sch Guid Work* 40:44-50 My '85

Counseling children of divorce. R. K. Goldman and M. J. King. bibl *Sch Psychol Rev* 14 no3:280-90 '85

A curative factor framework for conceptualizing group counseling. M. Waldo. bibl *J Couns Dev* 64:52-8 S '85

Dual-career families: terminology, typologies, and work and family issues. C. C. Cherpas. bibl *J Couns Dev* 63:616-20 Je '85

The effect of small-group counseling on underachievers. M. Bland and P. Melang. *Elem Sch Guid Couns* 20:303-5 Ap '86

The effects of classroom meetings on self-concept and behavior. S. N. Sorsdahl and R. P. Sanchc. bibl *Elem Sch Guid Couns* 20:49-56 O '85

The effects of group and individual vocational counseling on career indecision and personal indecisiveness. S. E. Cooper. bibl *J Coll Stud Pers* 27:39-42 Ja '86

Engaging non-attending family members in marital and family counseling: ethical issues. S. A. Wilcoxon. bibl *J Couns Dev* 64:323-4 Ja '86

Group applications of hypnosis for college students. P. A. Payne and G. H. Friedman. bibl *J Coll Stud Pers* 27:154-60 Mr '86

Group counseling—it works! M. M. Omizo and S. A. Omizo. *Acad Ther* 21:367-9 Ja '86

A group for teaching job interview skills to international students. F. B. Wortham. *J Coll Stud Pers* 27:179-81 Mr '86

FIGURE 4.2
Part of a Page from *Education Index*
(*Education Index*, July 1985–June 1986, p. 321. Reprinted by permission of H. W. Wilson Co., Bronx, NY)

data are provided on all documents and an abstract is usually included. Because *RIE* reviews many reports that would otherwise never be published, it is an especially valuable resource. *RIE* should always be consulted, regardless of the nature of a research topic (see Figure 4.3).

Current Index to Journals in Education (CIJE). Also published monthly by ERIC, this index covers what *RIE* does not—journal articles. Abstracts of articles from almost 800 publications, including many from foreign countries, are provided (see Figure 4.4). Since the coverage is so thorough, a search of *RIE* and *CIJE* should be sufficient to locate the relevant references for most research problems in education.

Sociological Abstracts. Published five times a year, this source is similar in format to *Psych Abstracts*. It provides bibliographical data, plus

```
ED 276 643                    SO 017 565
Shoemaker, Rebecca S.
The Constitution and Citizenship Education.
Spons Agency—Indiana Committee for the Humani-
   ties, Indianapolis; Social Studies Development Cen-
   ter, Bloomington, Ind.
Pub Date—86
Note—16p.; Paper presented at a Rountable Meeting
   on the Constitution in the Education of Citizens
   (Evansville, IN, September 25, 1986).
Pub Type—Opinion Papers (120)—Speeches/Meeting
   Papers (150)
EDRS Price - MF01/PC01 Plus Postage.
Descriptors—Citizen Participation, *Citizenship Edu-
   cation, Community Education, Critical Thinking.
   Elementary Secondary Education, Governmental
   Structure, Political Influences, *Political Issues, *So-
   cial Studies, *Values Education
Identifiers—Power, *United States Constitution
   The paper takes the position that the study and
understanding of the United States Constitution should
be a critical part of citizenship education, especially as
its Bicentennial approaches. Several factors suggest that
the Constitution has become the most durable document
of its kind in history, and that its teaching should be
centered in both the school and the community. It is
proposed that the teaching of citizenship education
could be addressed through three topics: (1) principles,
including federalism, separation of powers, checks and
balances, the concept of limited government, and the
distinction between a democracy and a republic; (2)
issues, including judicial review, the power struggle
between states and the national government, civil
liberties, changing the document, and other contro-
versial subjects; and (3) values, such as representative
government, respect for rights, divided responsibilities,
and tradition. (TRS)
```

FIGURE 4.3
Excerpt from *RIE*

abstracts. It is worth consulting if your topic involves some aspect of sociology or social psychology.

Exceptional Child Education Resources (ECER). Published quarterly by the Council for Exceptional Children, *ECER* provides information on exceptional children from over 200 journals. Using a format similar to *CIJE*, it provides author, subject, and title indexes. It is worth consulting if your research topic deals with exceptional children, since it covers several journals not included in *CIJE*.

Doctoral Dissertations and Master's Theses. Most doctoral dissertations and many master's theses in education report on original research, and hence are valuable sources for literature reviews. The major reference for dissertations, *Dissertation Abstracts International (DAI)*, is published monthly. *DAI* contains the abstracts of doctoral dissertations submitted by almost 500 universities in the United States and Canada. There are two sections: Section A contains dissertations in the humanities and the social sciences, and includes education (see Figure 4.5). Section B contains dissertations in the physical sciences and engineering, and includes psychology.

With each monthly issue of *DAI* comes a Keyword Title Index. It is just what its title implies—an alphabetical listing of key words contained in the titles of the dissertations included in that issue. In looking for dissertations

EJ 343 588   CS 733 294
The Best Teaching: Intuition Isn't Enough. Abshire,
Gary M. *Clearing House*; v60 n2 p59-61 Oct 1986
(Reprint: UMI)
Descriptors: *Teacher Effectiveness; *Teacher Qualifi-
cations; *Teaching Methods; *Teacher Role; *Teacher
Education; Teacher Student Relationship; Material
Development; Elementary Secondary Education

Discusses factors, beyond intuition, that produce optimal teaching: written objectives; organization of exhaustive research;
selective rearrangement of subject matter; well-timed distribution of course syllabus and other handouts; planning of lesson
presentation, conclusion, classroom activities and outside assignments; sensitivity to level, time factor, environment, student participation, and an open mind. (JK)

EJ 343 589   CS 733 295
Improving Learning through Student Questioning.
Perez, Samuel A. *Clearing House*; v60 n2 p63-65 Oct
1986 (Reprint: UMI)
Descriptors: Elementary Secondary Education; *Cogni-
tive Processes; *Reading Comprehension; *Ques-
tioning Techniques; *Learning Strategies; Teaching
Methods
Identifiers: *Socratic Method

Uses the Socratic method as a point of departure and suggests
steps that teachers can take to teach students how to formulate
their own questions for better comprehension ability. (JK)

FIGURE 4.4
Sample Entries from *Current Index to Journals in Education (CIJE)*
(Reprinted from *Current Index to Journals in Education*, January–June 1987, p. 165. Copyright © 1987 by The Oryx Press, 2214 N. Central Ave., Phoenix, AZ 85004. Reprinted by permission.)

dealing with a specific topic, a researcher would identify key terms (see below) in his or her research question, and then see if any relevant abstracts are listed under these terms in the Keyword Title Index (see Figure 4.6).

Many universities now have *Dissertation Abstracts Ondisc*, a computer database with search software which allows an individual to do a computer search (by keyword, subject, author, even school!) of the dissertation database. It includes information on over 900,000 doctoral dissertations and master's theses in hundreds of subject areas, with some 30,000 new titles being added each year. We shall describe how to do a computer search of the literature later in the chapter.

Indicate two general references you intend to consult:

1. _____

2. _____

4. *Formulate search terms (key words or phrases) that are pertinent to your research question.* Once you have selected a general reference work to look through, formulate some search terms—descriptor words that will help you locate your primary sources. To do this, identify the most important words in your problem statement. For example, suppose that your question is the following: "Do students taught by a teaching team learn more than students taught by an individual teacher?" The key term in this question is "teaching team." This term, plus other terms that are similar to it, or synonyms for it, should be listed. Possibilities include "team teaching," "joint teaching," and "cooperative teaching." The general reference work would then be consulted to see what articles are listed under these terms, and those articles which seem to bear on the topic would be selected.

TOWARD A GROUNDED THEORY OF BURNOUT AMONG
SUBURBAN, ELEMENTARY SCHOOLTEACHERS
Order No. DA8702636

SIMKINS, MICHAEL BRIAN, ED.D. *University of California, Los Angeles,*
1986. 255pp. Chair: Charlotte Crabtree

Burnout has gained currency as a serious problem in many
professions, teaching among them. The purpose of the study was to
seek a theoretical perspective on teacher burnout which might guide
efforts to control or ameliorate it. In particular, the study sought to
answer three questions: (1) How do teachers themselves define
burnout? (2) Are there different varieties of teacher burnout? (3) What
specific factors account for burnout among teachers?

Because of its suitability for identifying meaningful categories from
qualitative data, the grounded theory approach of Glaser and Strauss
(1967) was selected as the method for the study. The core of this
approach is the constant comparative analysis of data, from which
theory is ''discovered'' and provisionally tested. The primary source of
data were ethnographic interviews held over a period of eighteen
months with twenty-five elementary schoolteachers. These teachers
spoke candidly and at length about their careers in general and about
burnout in particular. Excerpts from their comments were used
extensively in the exposition of the findings.

The study yielded a grounded, substantive theory of teacher
burnout, the key features of which include: (1) a conceptualization of
burnout as a generalized malfunctioning of the reward structure of
teaching; (2) a taxonomy of four varieties of burnout—the Dismayed,
the Nonchalant, the Valiant, and the Miserable—which are contrasted
in terms of teachers' attitudes toward continuing in teaching, the ways
in which they feel shortchanged, how they experience burnout, and
how they cope or contend with the problem; (3) a catalog and
detailed description of twenty factors which appear to contribute to
burnout; and (4) a set of propositions which describe ways in which
the factors influence the development and experience of burnout.
Implications for school leadership personnel and questions for further
research are included.

FIGURE 4.5

Excerpt from *Dissertation Abstracts International*

(From *Dissertation Abstracts International—A: Humanities and Social
Sciences,* 47, nos. 11–12, May–June 1987, p. 4032. Reprinted by
permission of University Microfilms International.)

COUNSELING
A DEVELOPMENTAL COUNSELING APPROACH TO ALTER
SELF-CONCEPT AND RACIAL PREJUDICE IN
ELEMENTARY CHILDREN—GUYTON, JANE MCCLARY
(ED.D 1987 UNIVERSITY OF ARKANSAS) 105p 48/05A,
p. 1116 DET87-18814
EFFECTS OF DIFFERENT LEVELS OF ACCULTURATION,
COUNSELOR ETHNICITY, AND COUNSELING STRATEGY
ON CLIENT'S PERCEPTIONS OF COUNSELOR
CREDIBILITY AND INFLUENCE (MEXICAN-AMERICAN)—
PONCE, FRANCISCO QUINTANILLA (PH.D. 1987
UNIVERSITY OF CALIFORNIA, SANTA BARBARA) 144p.
48/06A, p. 1399 DET87-19633
THE EFFECTIVENESS OF A CAREER COUNSELING
INTERVENTION, THE HARRINGTON-O'SHEA CAREER
DECISION-MAKING SYSTEM, AS AN AID TO HISPANICS
TO MAKE AND IMPLEMENT APPROPRIATE CAREER
DECISIONS (MCIP)—THOMPSON, DALE WILSON (PH.D.
1987 THE CATHOLIC UNIVERSITY OF AMERICA) 194p.
48/03A, p. 567 DET87-13912
A COMPARATIVE STUDY: THE EFFECT OF TRAINING ON
STUDENTS PERFORMANCE IN CAMPUS
INTERVIEWING (EMPLOYMENT, CAREER
DEVELOPMENT, COUNSELING)—BRANT, MARY BALL
(ED.D. 1987 INDIANA UNIVERSITY) 164p. 48/01A,
p. 56 DET87-08831
THE EFFECT OF RETIREMENT-LEISURE COUNSELING ON
LEISURE AND RETIREMENT ATTITUDE—LANGLIEB,
KENNETH ROGER (PH.D. 1987 KANSAS STATE
UNIVERSITY) 176p. 48/04A, p. 836 DET87-15221

FIGURE 4.6

**Excerpt from Keyword Title
Index of *DAI***

(*Comprehensive Dissertation Index 1987.*
Social Sciences and Humanities Supplement, Part I. Reprinted by permission
of University Microfilms International.)

List four search terms you intend to use for your research question.

1. _____

2. _____

3. _____

4. _____

5. *Search the general references for relevant primary sources.* Although there is no magic formula for searching a general reference, the following procedure is used by many educational researchers. Let us use *Education Index* as an example.

a. Find the most recent issue and work backward. The monthly issues are combined every quarter, and the quarterly issues in turn are combined into a yearly volume. You should search through each of the monthly issues for the current quarter, then the quarterly issues for the current year, and then the yearly volumes for as far back as you wish to go.

b. Look to see if there are any articles listed under each of your search terms in the current issue.

c. As you find the names of articles that seem pertinent to your research topic, it is helpful to list them on 3″ × 5″ (or larger) note cards.[2] Figure 4.7 is an example. Usually, the author, title, pages, publication date, and publication source are listed. Use a separate card for each reference. The important thing is to take care to record the bibliographical data completely and accurately. Nothing is more annoying than to find that you have listed a reference incorrectly and thus are unable to locate it.

d. Continue looking through other issues. If you find no articles relevant to your research topic under a particular search term, drop the term from your list. When you feel that you have gathered enough articles to obtain an adequate idea of what else has been written about your topic, stop the search. How many articles is enough? Again, there is no magic number. It depends on the purpose of your search. If you wish to obtain a fairly complete listing of what has been written on a topic, you should extend the search to issues covering several years. If you wish simply to obtain a few articles to get a "feeling" for the kinds of articles that have been written on a topic, you probably need to search only a few issues.

Psychological Abstracts. If you decide to search through *Psych Abstracts*, you should turn first to the index volume for a particular year to check for search terms. Only the subjects of the articles are listed there, followed by a number. The following is from Volume 73, Subject Index II, January–December 1986, p. 1151, under motivation:

> motivation and goal setting, skill & confidence in sports performance, athletes, 23150.

---

[2] Some researchers prefer a 4″ × 6″ (or 5″ × 8″) card so they can later make notes on the card pertaining to the contents of the reference.

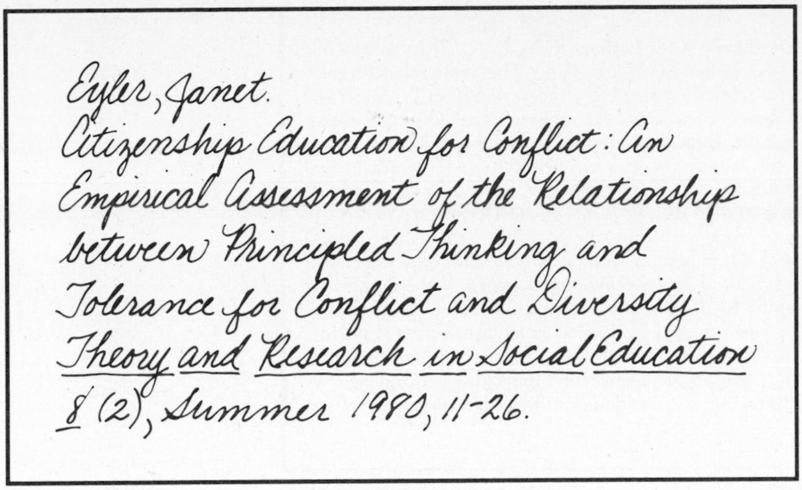

Eyler, Janet.
Citizenship Education for Conflict: An
Empirical Assessment of the Relationship
between Principled Thinking and
Tolerance for Conflict and Diversity
Theory and Research in Social Education
_8_ (2), Summer 1980, 11–26.

FIGURE 4.7
Sample Bibliographical Card

The number refers to the number of the abstract, which you can look up in the appropriate volume of abstracts. Figure 4.8 illustrates the abstract that would be found for the above subject listing.

As you can see, the abstracts provided in *Psychological Abstracts* are more informative than just the bibliographical data provided in *Education Index*. Thus it is perhaps somewhat easier to determine if an article is pertinent to a particular topic.

If your topic pertains strictly to education, little is to be gained by searching through *Psychological Abstracts*. If a topic involves some aspect of psychology, however (such as educational psychology), it often is useful to check *Psych Abstracts* as well as *Education Index*, *RIE*, and *CIJE*.

RIE and CIJE.   Searching through *RIE* and *CIJE* is similar to a search in *Psychological Abstracts*. You go first to the *Thesaurus of ERIC Descriptors* (a separate volume) and locate your search terms (called descriptors by ERIC). A sample of a thesaurus entry, with terms listed alphabetically, is shown in Figure 4.9. A key is provided to show you how ERIC uses the various terms in the descriptor display.

As you can see, other terms are suggested that might be considered for use as descriptors. You would look under the relevant descriptors in the Subject Index of monthly and cumulative issues of *RIE* and *CIJE* to find titles relevant to your topic. Again, the information should be listed on note cards, as suggested above. If you wish to obtain a document that is abstracted in *RIE* or *CIJE*, it can be ordered from ERIC. The latest issue of *RIE* tells how to obtain an ERIC document. In addition, most university libraries maintain a collection of ERIC documents on microfiche (small sheets of microfilm) which can be read in a special microfiche viewer.

In sum, the abstracts in *RIE* and *Psychological Abstracts* are presented in more detail than those in *CIJE*. In turn, *CIJE* is more comprehensive than *Education Index*, which gives only bibliographical information, not abstracts. *CIJE* also covers more journals.

23150, **Locke, Edwin A.** & **Latham, Gary P.** (U. Maryland, Coll of Business & Management, College Park) **The application of goal setting to sports.** *Journal of Sport Psychology,* 1985(Sep), Vol 7(3), 205–222.—Reviews clinical and field studies of goal setting. Results indicate that specific, difficult goals lead to better performance than vague or easy goals; short-term goals can help achieve long-term goals; goals affect performance by affecting effort, persistence, and attention and by motivating strategy development; progress feedback is necessary for goal setting to work; goals must be accepted if they are to affect performance; goal attainment is facilitated by a plan of action; and competition is a form of goal setting. Implications of these findings for athletics are discussed. In addition, suggestions are made regarding setting goals for both practice and game situations; setting goals for different elements of athletic skill as well as for strength and stamina; using goals to increase self-confidence; and improving performance by increasing task difficulty independently of goal difficulty. (52 ref)—*Journal abstract.*

FIGURE 4.8
Excerpt from *Psychological Abstracts*
(*Psychological Abstracts*, 73, pt. 3, p. 2499, July–September 1986. Reprinted by permission of American Psychological Association.)

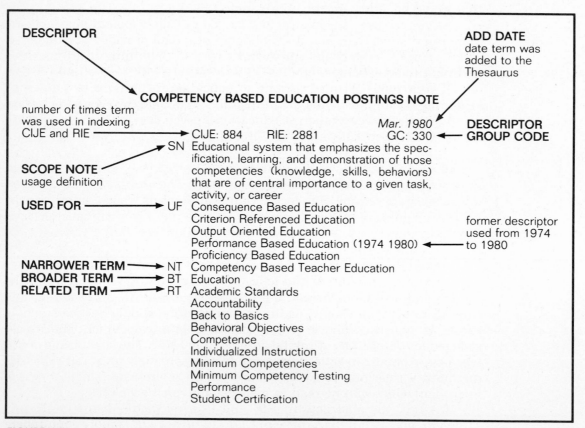

FIGURE 4.9
Sample *Thesaurus* Entry, Alphabetical Descriptor Display
(Reprinted from *Thesaurus of ERIC Descriptors*, 11th ed. Copyright © 1986 by The Oryx Press, 2214 Central Ave., Phoenix, AZ 85004. Reprinted by permission.)

The best strategy for a thorough search is as follows:

• Before 1965—search *Education Index*.
• From 1966 to 1968—search *RIE* and *Education Index*.
• From 1969 to the present—search *RIE* and *CIJE*.

6. *Read the relevant primary sources.* Once you have searched the general references, you should have a pile of bibliographical note cards. The next step is to locate each of the sources that you have listed, and then read and take notes on those that are relevant to your research problem. There are two major types of primary sources for you to be familiar with: journals and reports. Although space prevents a complete listing, what follows will give you a pretty good idea of what exists.

Professional Journals. There are many journals in education which publish reports of research. Some publish articles on a wide range of educational topics; others limit what they print to an area of specialization, such as social studies education. You should become familiar with the journals in your field of interest, and look them over from time to time. Here is a representative sampling of journals in education:

American Educational Research Journal. Washington, DC: American Educational Research Association.

Anthropology and Education Quarterly. Washington, DC: Council on Anthropology and Education.

British Journal of Educational Studies. London: Faber & Faber.

Canadian Education and Research Digest. Toronto: Canadian Education Association.

Child Development. Chicago, IL: Society for Research in Child Development, University of Chicago Press.

Educational Administration Quarterly. Columbus, OH.: University Council for Educational Administration.

Educational and Psychological Measurement. Durham, NC: Educational and Psychological Measurement.

International Journal of Aging and Human Development. Farmingdale, NY: Baywood Publishing Co.

International Journal of Behavioral Development. London: Lawrence Erlbaum Associates, Ltd.

International Journal of Rehabilitation Research. Heidelberg, Federal Republic of Germany: University of Education (Padagogische Hochschule).

International Journal of Social Education. Muncie, IN: Department of History, Ball State University.

International Review of Education. Federal Republic of West Germany: UNESCO Institute for Education.

Journal of Counseling and Development. Alexandria, VA: American Association for Counseling and Development.

Journal of Educational Measurement. Washington, DC: National Council on Measurement in Education.

Journal of Educational Psychology. Washington, DC: American Psychological Association.

Journal of Educational Research. Washington, DC: HELDREF Publications.

Journal of Educational Sociology. New York: Payne Educational Sociology Foundation, New York University.

Journal of Experimental Education. Washington, DC: HELDREF Publications.

Journal of Psychology. Provincetown, MA: Journal Press.

Journal of Research and Development in Education. Athens, GA: University of Georgia.

Journal of Research in Mathematics Education. Reston, VA: National Council of Teachers of Mathematics.

Journal of Research in Music Education. Vienna, VA: Music Educators National Conference.

Journal of Research in Science Teaching. New York: National Association for Research in Science Teaching and Association for the Education of Teachers in Science, John Wiley & Sons.

Journal of School Psychology. New York: Behavioral Publications.

Journal of Social Psychology. Provincetown, MA: Journal Press.

Psychological Bulletin. Washington, DC: American Psychological Association.

Psychological Review. Washington, DC: American Psychological Association.

Psychology in the Schools. Brandon, VT: Clinical Psychology Publishing Co.

Reading Research Quarterly. Newark, DE: International Reading Association.

Research in the Teaching of English. Urbana, IL: National Council of Teachers of English.

Research Quarterly for Exercise and Sport. Washington, DC: American Alliance for Health, Physical Education, and Recreation.

School Science and Mathematics. Tempe, AZ: School Science and Mathematics Association.

Sociology and Social Research. Los Angeles: University of Southern California.

Sociology of Education. Albany, NY: American Sociological Association.

Theory and Research in Social Education. Washington, DC: National Council for the Social Studies.

List three of the primary sources described above that you intend to peruse.

1. _____

2. _____

3. _____

Reports. Many important research findings are first published as reports. Almost all funded research projects produce a final report of their activities and findings when the research is completed. In addition, each year many reports on research activities are published by the U.S. government, by state departments of education, by private organizations and agencies, by local school districts, and by professional associations. Furthermore, many individual researchers give reports on their recent work at professional meetings and conferences.

These reports are a valuable source about current research efforts. Most of them are abstracted in the Documents Résumé section of *RIE*, and ERIC distributes microfiche copies of them to most college and university libraries. Many papers, such as the reports of presidential task forces, national conferences, and specially called professional meetings, are published only as reports. They are usually far more detailed than journal articles, and are much more up to date. Also, they are not copyrighted. Reports are a very valuable source of up-to-date information that you could not obtain anywhere else.

Locating Primary Sources. Most primary source material is located in journal articles and reports, since that is where most of the research findings in education are published. Although the layout of libraries varies, you may be able to go directly to the stacks where journals are shelved alphabetically. In some libraries, however, the stacks are closed and you must ask the librarian for the journals. When this is the case, it is a good idea to prepare call slips for about ten references at a time.

As is almost always the case, some of the references you desire will be missing, at the bindery, or checked out by someone else. If an article is particularly important for your research, you may be able to obtain a reprint directly from the author. Addresses of authors are listed in *Psychological Abstracts* and *RIE*, but not in *Education Index* or *CIJE*. Sometimes an author's address can be found in the directory of a professional association, such as the *American Educational Research Association Biographical Membership Directory*, or in *Who's Who in American Education*. If a reprint is not available directly from the author, you may be able to obtain the article from another library in the area or from an interlibrary loan, a service that nearly all libraries provide.

7. *Take notes and summarize the key points in the sources.* When you have the journal articles you intend to search gathered together, you can begin your review. It is a good idea to begin with the most recent articles and work backward. Recent articles often rely on earlier articles as a foundation and thus can give you a quicker understanding of previous work.

How should you read an article? Here are some ideas.

First, read the abstract or the summary. This will tell you whether the article is worth reading in its entirety. If it is, record the bibliographical data at the top of a note card.

As you take notes, concentrate on the following points.[3] Almost all research articles follow the same format. They usually include: (a) an abstract; (b) an introductory section which introduces the research problem or question and reviews other related studies; (c) the objectives of the study or the hypotheses to be tested; (d) a description of the research procedures, including the subjects studied, the research design, and the measuring instruments used; (e) the results or findings of the study; (f) a summary (if there is no abstract); and (g) the researcher's conclusions.

---

[3] Instead of taking notes, some researchers prefer to photocopy the abstract or summary.

Be as brief as possible in taking notes, but do not exclude anything that might be important to describe later in the full review. Before they begin, some researchers ditto off on note cards the essential steps mentioned above (problem, hypotheses, procedures, findings, conclusions), leaving space to take notes after each step. For each of these steps, you should note the following:

- Problem. List it verbatim.
- Hypotheses or objectives. List them exactly as stated in the article.
- Procedures. Describe the research methodology used (experiment, case study, and so on), the number of subjects and how they were selected, and the kinds of instruments (questionnaire, tally sheet, and the like) used. Make a note of any unusual techniques employed.
- Findings. List the major findings. Indicate whether the objectives of the study were obtained, or the hypotheses were supported. Often, the findings will be summarized in a table, which you can photocopy and paste to the back of a note card.
- Conclusions. Describe the author's conclusions. Note any disagreement you have with the author, and your reasons for such disagreement. Note any strengths or weaknesses of the study that make the results particularly applicable or limited with regard to your research question. See Figure 4.10 for an example of a completed note card based on the bibliographical data shown in Figure 4.7.

List the names of four of the journals you perused.

1. _____

2. _____

3. _____

4. _____

If they are different from the ones you originally intended to peruse, explain the reason for the difference.

_____

_____

Give the titles of the five studies you read.

1. _____

2. _____

3. _____

4. _____

5. _____

Problem: Is there a relationship btwn. principled polit. thinking & tendency to be polit. tolerant?

Hypotheses: Principl. thinkers more likely to: (1) apply principl. of democ. to specific cases than non-principl. thinkers; (2) accept polit. conflict as desirable & legitimate; (3) endorse an active citizenship role; (4) show more polit. involvement than citizens who reason predom. at conventional level.

Procedures: Sample = 135 college fr. & soph. median age 18/19. 2/3 fem. Sampled by classes in requir. gen'l ed. curricul. of small pvt. tchr's. college. Questionnaire study. Rest's Defining Issues Test (DIT) used to identify principled and non-principled thinkers of the 135, 15 Questionnaires discarded due to incomplete. 25 S_s indentif. as P thinkers; 34 as low in such thinking. sex ratio each group was same. Subjects asked respond various items on Q.

Findings: All hypotheses except #4 supported.

Conclusions: Civic tolerance & cognitive moral dvlpmnt. are associated. This intellectual growth is crucial for dvlpmnt. of citizen competence & must be fostered in schools. Tchrs should focus & promote discussions of kinds of conflict which generate controversy in the community. S_s also should be involved in polit. participation experiences in school involving decisions they make, and also in their community outside of school.

FIGURE 4.10
Sample Note Card

▣ A Computer Search of the Literature

Manual searches, unfortunately, take time. You can shorten this time considerably by conducting a computer search of the literature. Computer search facilities are available in almost all university libraries and most public libraries, in many state departments of education, and in some county offices of education and some large school systems. On-line computer terminals are linked to one or more information retrieval systems (such as the Lockheed DIALOG system) that retrieve information from a number of databases. The database most commonly used by educational researchers is ERIC, which can be searched by computer back to 1966. Examples of other databases are Psychological Abstracts, Exceptional Child Education Resources, and the Comprehensive Dissertation Index. All are available in the Lockheed retrieval system. Over 200 databases can be computer searched. Information about them can be obtained from most librarians. There are also a number of commercial information retrieval services which will conduct computer searches for a fee.

Conducting a computer rather than a manual search has a number of advantages. First, it is much faster than a manual search. Second, it is fairly inexpensive. Although the cost of an on-line search will vary with the length and complexity of the task, a typical search of the ERIC database, which includes all references located in *RIE* and *CIJE*, can be done for around $25, and take less than an hour.[4] Third, a printout of the search, including abstracts of sources, can be obtained. Fourth, and perhaps most important, more than one descriptor can be searched at the same time. We'll show you an example of this in a moment.

The steps involved in a computer search are similar to those involved in a manual search, except that much of the work is done by the computer. To illustrate the steps involved, we shall describe a search we conducted using the ERIC database.

Define the Problem as Precisely as Possible. As with a manual search, the research problem should be stated as specifically as possible so that relevant descriptors can be identified. A statement such as "How effective are questioning techniques?" is much too general. It is liable to produce an extremely large number of references, many of which probably will be irrelevant to the researcher's question of interest. For the purposes of our search, therefore, we posed the following research question:

"What sorts of questioning techniques help students understand historical concepts most effectively?"

Decide on the Extent of the Search. For a review for a journal article, a researcher might decide to include only 20 to 25 fairly recent references. For a more detailed review, such as a master's thesis, perhaps 30 or 40 references might be reviewed. For a very exhaustive review, as for a doctoral dissertation, 100 or more references might be searched.

Decide on the Database. As mentioned earlier, many databases are available, but the one most commonly used by educational researchers is ERIC. Descriptors must fit a particular database; some descriptors may not be applicable to different databases, although many do overlap. We used the ERIC database in our search.

Select Descriptors. Recall that descriptors are the words the researcher uses to tell the computer what to search for. The selection of descriptors is somewhat of an art. If the descriptor is too general, too many references may be located, and many of them are likely to be irrelevant. If the descriptor is too narrow, too few references will be located, and many references which might be applicable to the research question may be missed.

Since we used the ERIC database, we selected our descriptors from the *Thesaurus of ERIC Descriptors*. Descriptors can be used singularly or in various combinations to locate references. Certain key words, called *Boolean operators*, enable the retrieval of terms in various combinations. The most commonly used Boolean operators are "and" and "or." For example, by asking a computer to search for a single descriptor such as "inquiry," a researcher can gain access to all references which contain this term. By connecting two descriptors with the word "and," however, the researcher can narrow his or her search, since only those references which contain *both* of the descriptors will be located. Thus, asking the computer to search for "questioning techniques" *and* "history instruction" would narrow the

[4] To conduct the search described in this section, we were on-line for some 30 minutes at a cost of $11.93.

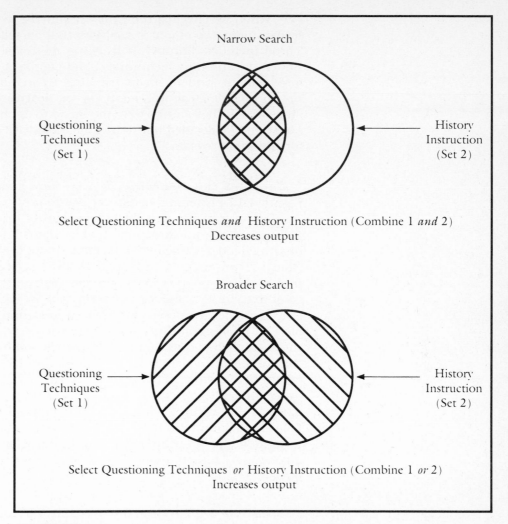

Narrow Search

Questioning Techniques (Set 1) → ← History Instruction (Set 2)

Select Questioning Techniques *and* History Instruction (Combine 1 *and* 2)
Decreases output

Broader Search

Questioning Techniques (Set 1) → ← History Instruction (Set 2)

Select Questioning Techniques *or* History Instruction (Combine 1 *or* 2)
Increases output

FIGURE 4.11
Venn Diagrams Showing the Boolean Operators "and" and "or"

search, because only references containing both descriptors would be located. On the other hand, by using the word "or," the investigator can broaden a search, since any references which contain *either* one of the descriptors will be located. Thus, asking the computer to search for "questioning techniques" *or* "history instruction" would yield a range of references containing either one of these terms. Figure 4.11 illustrates the results of using these Boolean operators.

All sorts of combinations are possible. For example, we might have asked the computer to search for questioning techniques *or* inquiry *and* history instruction *or* civics instruction. For a reference to be selected, it would have to contain *either* the descriptor term "questioning techniques" *or* the descriptor term "inquiry," *as well as either* the descriptor term "history instruction" *or* the descriptor term "civics instruction."

For our search, we chose the following descriptors:

• Questioning techniques
• Concept teaching
• History instruction

When we checked the ERIC thesaurus, we found a number of related terms under two of our descriptors that we felt should also be considered. These included "inquiry," "teaching methods," and "learning processes" under questioning techniques, and "concept formation" and "cognitive development" under concept teaching. Upon reflection, however, we decided not to include "teaching methods" or "learning processes" in our search, since we felt these terms were too broad to apply specifically to our research question. We decided not to include "cognitive development" in our search for the same reason.

Conduct the Search. We were now ready to conduct our search. Figure 4.12 presents a computer printout of our efforts.

As you can see, we asked the computer first to search for "questioning techniques" (S1), followed by "history instruction" (S2), followed by a combination (S3) of these two descriptors (note the use of the Boolean operator "and"). This resulted in a total of 2572 references for questioning techniques, 2157 references for history instruction, and 33 references for a combination of these two descriptors. We then asked the computer to search just for the descriptor "concept teaching" (S4). This produced a total of 1885 references. Since we were particularly interested in concept teaching as applied to questioning techniques and history instruction, we asked the computer to search for a combination (S5) of these three descriptors (again note the use of the operator "and"). This produced only 2 references. Since this was much too limited a harvest, we decided to broaden our approach by asking the computer to look for references which included the following combination (S9) of descriptors: "concept teaching" *or* "concept formation" *or* "inquiry" *and* "questioning techniques" *and* "history instruction." This produced a total of 19 references. At this point, we ended our search.

Broaden or Narrow the Search. If the initial effort at a search produces too few references, the search can be broadened by using more general descriptors. Thus, we might have used the term "social studies instruction" rather than "history instruction" had we not obtained enough references in our search. Similarly, a search can be narrowed by using more specific descriptors. As an example, we might have used the more specific descriptor "North American history" than the more inclusive term "history."

Obtain a Printout of the Desired References. Three printout options are available. To begin with, a researcher may obtain just the title of the reference and its accession number in ERIC (or whatever database is being searched). In ERIC, this is either the EJ or ED number (the number used to locate the reference). Here is an example:

EJ364977   HE523417
The Evaluation of a Course in Interviewing for First-Year Medical Students

This option is the least useful of the three, in that titles in and of themselves are often misleading or not very informative. Hence, most researchers choose one of the next two options.

The researcher can also obtain complete bibliographical data, the accession number, and a list of descriptors that apply to the particular reference. Here is an example:

```
File     1:ERIC--66-88/AUG


      Set   Items   Description

? ss questioning techniques and history instruction
      S1    2572    QUESTIONING TECHNIQUES   (METHODS USED FOR CONSTRUCTING
                    AND PRESENTI
      S2    2157    HISTORY INSTRUCTION
      S3      33    QUESTIONING TECHNIQUES AND HISTORY INSTRUCTION


  ss s3 and concept teaching
            33      S3
      S4    1885    CONCEPT TEACHING
      S5       2    S3 AND CONCEPT TEACHING


? ss (concept formation or concept teaching or inquiry) and s3
      S6    5846    CONCEPT FORMATION
      S7    1885    CONCEPT TEACHING
      S8    5318    INQUIRY (METHOD OR PROCESS OF SEEKING KNOWLEDGE,
                    UNDE . . .)
            33      S3
      S9      19    (CONCEPT FORMATION OR CONCEPT TEACHING OR INQUIRY) AND S3
```

FIGURE 4.12
Printout of Computer Search

EJ319126   SO514073
A New Challenge for Clio's Ancient Mask: Oral Sources for a History of Educational Institutions.
Christensen, Lawrence O; Ridley, Jack B.
Social Studies, v76 n2 p65–68 Mar–Apr 1985
Available from UMI
Language: English
Document Type: JOURNAL ARTICLE (080)

PROJECT DESCRIPTION (141)
Journal Announcement: CIJSEP85
Target Audience: Teachers; Practitioners
Descriptors: *Educational History; History Instruction
Interviews: *Oral History; Questioning Techniques; Research Methodology

As you can see, this type of printout provides the researcher with a better basis for judging the relevance of an article. The third option, however, is the most informative. It includes all of the information contained in the second option, plus an abstract of the article if one has been prepared. Here is an example, taken from the printout of our search:

EJ354834   SO516549
Focus Questions: The Engines of Lessons.
Killoran, James
Social Science Record, v24 n1 p38–41 Spr 1987
Available from UMI
Language: English
Document Type: JOURNAL ARTICLE (080)

INSTRUCTIONAL MATERIAL (051); TEACHING GUIDE (052)
Journal Announcement: CIJSEP87
Argues that teachers can easily structure social studies lessons to enhance

students' thinking skills by using carefully structured focus questions. States that such questions—often beginning with such words as "is," "could," "should," "does," and "can"—go beyond asking for simple recall of facts or shallow explanation, to requesting the solution to problems. Included are two model secondary-level government lessons. (JDH)

Descriptors: Critical Thinking; Curriculum Development; *History Instruction; *Instructional Improvement; Lesson Plans; *Logical Thinking; *Questioning Techniques; Secondary Education; *Social Studies; United States Government (Course)

■ Writing Your Summaries

Your task now is to conduct a "mini" literature review—to investigate the literature in order to learn something about what has been written pertinent to your topic. Try to locate at least five recent primary sources that are pertinent to your question. At least three of these should be *research reports* that present data of some kind (scores on a test, responses to a questionnaire, and so on). The other two may be the viewpoint or ideas of someone as expressed in an *article* (that is, merely an opinion piece that does not present data).

Limit your summary to approximately one-half page (200 words). A summary that is much shorter is unlikely to contain enough information; one that is much longer probably has too much information to be sufficiently focused on the important points contained in the reference you are summarizing.

Be sure to describe what the author did and what the author's conclusions were.

If the reference you are summarizing pertains to a research study, you should briefly describe the method the researcher used. Be sure that you also note how the author arrived at his or her conclusions. Was the author's work or opinion based on previous studies? on some sort of theory? on personal experience or argument? This should be made clear. A summary that describes the author's approach, but fails to summarize the end results, is just as frustrating as a summary that describes an author's conclusions, but gives no indication as to how they were derived.

Here is an example of a summary that you can use as a model:

Walberg, H. J., and Thomas, S. C. 1972. Open education: An operational definition and validation in Great Britain and the United States. *American educational research journal*, 9:197–216.

The purpose of this article is to describe the development of an observation scale and a teacher questionnaire for assessing the degree of "openness" of a given elementary school classroom. Items were written within each of eight "themes" obtained from available literature and reviewed by a panel of authorities.

The resulting instruments were used in approximately 20 classrooms for each of three types: British open, American open, and American traditional. The classrooms were identified by reputation and personal knowledge. Approximately equal numbers of lower and middle socioeconomic-level classrooms were included.

Results showed that overall assessments obtained with the two different instruments (observation scale and questionnaire) agreed quite highly. Differences between the open and traditional classrooms were much greater than those between socioeconomic levels or between countries.

Evaluate the above summary using the criteria described immediately preceding it.

_____

_____

_____

_____

AUTHORS' COMMENTS

The above summary is a good one. It describes what the authors did (how they developed and field-tested two instruments), and it describes the results obtained and the authors' conclusions. However, in our judgment, it could have been im-proved if the writers had included a little more detail on (1) the format of each instrument, (2) the numbers of observation periods and their length, and (3) the magnitude of relationships (rather than just the phrase "quite highly").

In the space provided below, summarize three of the five studies or articles you read as a part of your review of the literature on your topic.

Summary of reference 1:

_____

_____

_____

_____

_____

_____

_____

_____

_____

_____

_____

Summary of reference 2:

_____

_____

_____

_____

_____

_____

_____

_____

_____

_____

Summary of reference 3:

_____

_____

_____

_____

_____

_____

_____

_____

_____

_____

Has your review of the literature related to your topic affected your thinking in such a way that you now wish to change your original question and/or your definitions? If so, state your revisions below.

_____

_____

_____

_____

_____

_____

■ Summary

In this chapter, we presented several examples of different types of references that researchers consult to obtain information on a topic of interest. These include such general references as indexes and abstracts; such secondary sources as encyclopedias, research reviews, and yearbooks; and such primary sources as journals and reports. We also described the steps involved in both a manual and a computer search of the literature. These include defining the research problem as precisely as possible, skimming relevant secondary sources, perusing appropriate general references, formulating search terms, searching the general references for appropriate primary sources, reading these primary sources, and taking notes and summarizing the key points in the sources. We also presented an example of an actual computer search that we performed.

■ Key Concepts Discussed in This Chapter

review of the literature   search term
general reference work   descriptor
secondary source   bibliographical note card
primary source   Boolean operators

■ How Far Along Should I Be at This Point?

By now, you should be quite firm about your research question. It should be clear to all concerned, defensible, feasible, and ethical. It should suggest a relationship. You should have restated it as a hypothesis, and you should be able to identify the variables in the hypothesis.

You also should have conducted a mini literature review, consulting various sources (as necessary) to obtain more information about your topic. Accordingly, you should have read five reports (at least three of which were research reports) and summarized three of them dealing with your topic.

Evaluate your progress, therefore, by checking each of the following. At this point, you should have:

- Accomplished each of the tasks listed at the end of the preceding chapters. (If not, you should review and accomplish them before going any further.)
- Familiarized yourself with at least one general reference in the library.
- Familiarized yourself with at least one secondary source in the library.
- Familiarized yourself with at least two primary sources in the library.
- Learned where to locate each of the following sources:
  Education Index
  RIE
  CIJE
  Dissertation Abstracts
  At least one professional journal in your field
- Learned how to conduct a computer search of the literature.
- Read at least five references (three or more of which were research reports) related to your topic.

What's Next?

In the next chapter, we will introduce you to the concept of instrumentation—the process of selecting or developing instruments that can be used to collect data related to a research question, together with a specification of the conditions under which these instruments are to be used. We will illustrate how the members of one research class developed two instruments that they in turn used in an actual study. We also shall introduce you to two very important concepts—reliability and validity—that researchers apply in judging the value of an instrument for use in a particular study. These concepts will be discussed in some detail.

For Further Reading

Berry, D. M. 1980. *A bibliographic guide to educational research* (2nd Ed.). Metuchen, NJ: Scarecrow Press.

Gover, H. R. 1981. *Keys to library research on the graduate level: A guide to guides.* Lanham, MD: University Press of America.

Yarborough, J. 1975, September. *How to prepare a computer search of ERIC: A nontechnical approach.* Stanford, CA: ERIC Clearinghouse on Information Resources (ED 110 096).

Chapter Five

INSTRUMENTATION

W hat instruments can be used to obtain information to test a hypothesis? For many students, instrumentation is one of the most interesting parts of planning a study. It is, at the same time, one of the most important and sometimes difficult aspects of research. There are many tools that may be used to obtain information. In the following pages, we will look at some examples of the most widely used types of instruments. We will also discuss, in some detail, two very important concepts that are related to the process of instrumentation: reliability and validity. Finally, we will describe some ways to assess the reliability and validity of the scores obtained when different kinds of instruments are used.

By the end of this chapter, you should be able to analyze some specific instruments in terms of their value for a specific purpose.

Instrument Development

Whenever possible, a researcher makes use of previously developed instruments. There are times, however, when appropriate instruments are not available, as in the following example.

A research class investigated the hypothesis "The more open the classroom, the higher the student motivation." That process resulted in the development of two instruments: a *rating scale* and an *observation record*. As these instruments are described, the meaning of these terms will become clear. It is important to keep in mind that these instruments are the products of a particular group of people who worked on the problem. There are undoubtedly other ways to tackle the problem, although they are likely to contain the same basic features.

At the outset, it was clear that the class needed some way or ways to assess both the degree of openness and the level of student motivation within a particular classroom. Only by having a measurement of each of these variables could the members of the class determine if a relationship existed between them. Two commonly used measuring techniques were

TABLE 5.1 Indicators of Classroom Openness

Physical environment: Are the desks placed in rows? Are the desks in study centers? Are there specific learning centers for subjects? Are classes sometimes held outdoors? Are they ever held in the outside community? Is there a general meeting area for students in the classroom? Are any other types of furniture besides desks (sofas, rocking chairs, tables) used? Are students free to move outside without an adult present? How many adults (teachers, paraprofessionals, volunteers) are there in the classroom? Are students grouped by age, or are different ages present?

Curriculum: What amount of time does the teacher spend on planning? on evaluating students? What type of planning (written lesson plans, behavioral objectives, and so forth) does the teacher use? Does the teacher have a list of overall objectives? How much time is spent on the academic curriculum? on arts and crafts? on discussions or problem solving? Do the students direct their own planning or curriculum? Is there a contract system in effect? Are affective objectives included in the curriculum? Are students taught to express their feelings? Are grades given?

Teacher–student relationships: How often does the teacher give directions? help students? How often do students initiate activities? Can students leave the classroom on their own, or must they request permission? Does the teacher work with students individually? work in small groups? teach the entire class? Do students and teachers evaluate together? Are class meetings teacher- or student-directed? Can students make their own schedule? Can students choose their own free time?

Materials: Are students assigned specific materials to use? What kinds of materials exist for students to use? How much time is spent on workbook assignments? Are there manipulative materials? Are students free to choose these materials? Are the materials easily accessible, or do students have to request them? Is the use of materials directed by teacher or students? Do students use available books freely? Are there art materials available?

Social environment: Are students encouraged to help one another? to tutor? Are students free to talk to one another? How often? Do students work alone, or can they choose to work together? Do students group themselves, or are groups arranged by the teacher? Do students share in room cleanup? How many times does the teacher have to ask for quiet? Does physical aggression ever occur between students? How often? Is aggression handled by teacher or students?

Parent participation: Are parents allowed in classrooms? observers? others? Are parents free to enter the classroom when they wish, or is there a formal procedure for them to go through? Is there a volunteer parent-aide program? If so, how many volunteers are there? What kinds of tasks do parents perform?

selected to assess openness. The first was direct observation in the classroom and the second was the questioning of both students and teachers.

As is the case with the development of most instruments, the class's first task was to become more familiar with previous work. Each student expanded on his or her knowledge of the open classroom by reading pertinent literature, talking with other students, or visiting classrooms that had been described as open classrooms. Further input was obtained from two documents brought to the class by students. One was a statement of intent on the part of a nearby school district to move in the direction of openness; it indicated some specific changes that the district intended to make. The other document, although not concerned with the particular problem being investigated, listed examples of the kinds of things an observer could look for in a classroom.

The next step the class undertook involved the production of items related to openness. Typically, this took the form of an open-ended "brainstorming" session in which the goal was the production of as large a number of items as possible. Each student in the class was asked to make a list of specific things that could be taken as indicators of openness. These suggestions were subsequently pulled together to form the basis for developing a usable instrument. The procedure involved committee work, followed by review and discussion by the class as a whole. This step required both the critical review of prospective items and their organization into useful groupings.

The committee procedure was as follows: The class was divided into four committees. Each committee was asked to consolidate the lists that individual class members had developed. As part of the consolidation, some progress was made in defining key terms, an ongoing process of clarification. The resulting four lists were then duplicated for each member of the class. At a subsequent meeting, it was decided that the four committees would each focus on certain groupings that seemed to emerge from the list of indicators. For example, a number of indicators seemed to concern the physical arrangement of the classroom, so this constituted one group. Table 5.1 shows the list of suggested indicators within each category. (We realize that this list is fairly extensive, but it is unavoidable—and desirable—at this stage. Why? Because a large pool of items are needed for later refinement.)

Each committee then attempted to refine and clarify the indicators within its particular category or categories. The question then arose as to how the presence or absence of the various indicators would be measured. The instructor suggested that one appropriate instrument would be a *rating scale*, consisting of a number of items about which an observer would make a judgment. The observer would assess the degree to which the indicator, as represented by the item, was present in the classroom. (Other indicators would be better assessed by an observation record, discussed later in the chapter.) Once the decision to use a rating scale was made, it became clear to the class that for optimal use at least the ends of the scale had to be defined.

▪ The Rating Scale

The class then began to convert the statements listed in Table 5.1 into items for the rating scale. The members of each committee prepared a list of items; then the students came together as a class to review what had been prepared. The final items, as agreed to by the total class, are shown in Table 5.2.

TABLE 5.2 Rating Scale for Classroom Openness

Left statement	1	2	3	4	5	Right statement
1. Students do not move without teacher permission.	1	2	3	4	5	1. Students may move in or out of class without permission.
2. All students work at the same task at the same time.	1	2	3	4	5	2. A great variety of tasks are performed at the same time.
3. The teacher is the only resource in the classroom.	1	2	3	4	5	3. Several human resources other than the teacher are in the classroom.
4. Human resources are only clerical or housekeeper aides to the teacher.	1	2	3	4	5	4. Human resources interact with students and/or with small groups.
5. Furniture is permanently arranged.	1	2	3	4	5	5. Furniture is spontaneously arranged.
6. Everyone works at own desk.	1	2	3	4	5	6. There are many floating study centers.
7. Desks, tables, and chairs have a traditional arrangement.	1	2	3	4	5	7. There is a complete variety of furniture—couches, rocking chairs, pillows—in a variety of arrangements.
8. Students cannot interact without direct permission from the teacher.	1	2	3	4	5	8. Students are free to interact with others in any way they desire.
9. The teacher initiates all activities.	1	2	3	4	5	9. Students also initiate activities.
10. The teacher teaches class as a group.	1	2	3	4	5	10. The teacher works with small groups or individual students.
11. The teacher is formally addressed (Mrs. X, Mr. B; hand raised).	1	2	3	4	5	11. The teacher is addressed informally (first name or nickname, no name).
12. Reprimands are punitive.	1	2	3	4	5	12. No reprimands or only friendly reminders are given.
13. No feeling is verbally expressed.	1	2	3	4	5	13. Much feeling is verbally expressed.
14. The text is followed closely.	1	2	3	4	5	14. No formally prepared materials are used in class.

Record any differences that you notice between the original set of indicators (Table 5.1) and the final rating scale (Table 5.2).

_____

_____

_____

_____

_____

_____

_____

The idea of developing questions to be asked of students and/or teachers was abandoned at this time because it lacked feasibility. The class did not have sufficient time to both observe and interview. It is not uncommon

AUTHORS' COMMENTS

Only a few of the indicators in Table 5.1 were converted directly into rating scale items (Table 5.2). All items except 2 and 11 relate quite directly to one or more indicators. For example, item 1 encompasses two indicators: "Are students free to move outside without an adult present?" and "Can students leave the classroom on their own, or must they request permission?" In most cases the wording has been changed in the transition. Items 2 and 11 do not relate to specific indicators; rather, they emerged from the conversion process. The focus on items that can be directly observed eliminated many indicators, particularly under the headings of curriculum and parent participation. Rating scales can be substantially improved by giving explicit descriptions of each point of the scale, as in the following example for item 1:

	1	2	3	4	5
1. Students are observed to move around without teacher permission.	(never)	(less than 11 instances)	(11–30 instances)	(31–50 instances)	(more than 50 instances)

to have to omit desirable features of a study because of a lack of feasibility. A more extensive study, of course, does not encounter the same difficulties as a class project.

Look back over the list of suggested indicators of openness in Table 5.1 and determine which ones could be better assessed through the use of interviews. Write down the specific indicator and whether you would assess it with interviews of students, teachers, or both. Also state why you think that the interview approach would be superior to classroom observation for that particular indicator.

Indicator	Who is to be interviewed?	Why is the interview superior to observation?
_____	_____	_____
_____	_____	_____
_____	_____	_____
_____	_____	_____
_____	_____	_____
_____	_____	_____
_____	_____	_____

AUTHORS' COMMENTS

Items better assessed through interview include those that are difficult to observe directly, those that lie within the province of knowledge of the respondent, and those that are likely to elicit straightforward replies. Here are some examples:

"Are classes ever held outdoors?"

"Do students choose free time?"

"Are children free to choose (manipulative) materials and are they easily accessible or do children have to ask for them?"

"Are children free to talk to one another?"

"Do children share in room cleanup?"

Teachers would best be asked:

"Is multiage grouping or self-contained grouping according to age level better?"

"What amount of time does teacher spend in planning?"

"Do students and teacher evaluate together?"

"Are children assigned specific materials?"

"Are parents free to enter school as they wish?"

You may wonder why it was necessary for the class to develop a measure of classroom openness rather than use an already available instrument. So far as we could determine, no appropriate instrument existed.[1] Often, there is an instrument available that does suit a researcher's needs for a particular study. The problem is then one of becoming familiar with the instrument and evaluating it in the context of the specific study. When an existing instrument cannot be located, however, an appropriate instrument must be developed. There is no simple way of doing this. The development of a good instrument can be a very time-consuming process, in many cases requiring a good deal of specialized knowledge and a considerable degree of talent. It is for these reasons that researchers make use of instruments previously developed whenever they can.

No matter what kind of instrument is chosen, it is useful only when it provides the investigator with an index (measure) of the particular characteristic in question. In our example, the rating scale in the open classroom study had value only to the extent that it provided an index of the degree of openness in the particular classrooms that were observed.

Did the rating scale do this? Yes, it did. We could simply add together the ratings, on each of the 14 specific items, for a particular classroom to obtain an "openness" score for that classroom. Thus, a classroom rated at the bottom of the scale on each item (a score of 1) would receive a total of 14 points. A classroom rated at the top of the scale on each item (a score of 5) would receive a total of 70 points (the greatest degree of openness possible). This numerical rating for a particular classroom is referred to as the *measurement*, or score, for that classroom. It is very desirable, though not essential, to summarize information in research studies through the use of scores, which greatly simplifies subsequent analysis of the information.

It is helpful to make a distinction between instrument and instrumentation. An *instrument* is a device or procedure for systematically collecting information. Common types of instruments include tests, questionnaires, rating scales, checklists, and observation forms. *Instrumentation* refers not

---

[1] The report describing a similar approach to instrument development that is summarized in Chapter Three (see p. 41) had not yet been published.

only to the instrument itself but also to the conditions under which it is used, when it is to be used, and by whom it is to be used. All of these can affect the instrumentation process, especially if the procedure is done incorrectly, by someone disliked by the respondents, if testing conditions are noisy or inhospitable, or if respondents are exhausted. Keeping this in mind, researchers must decide upon the instruments to be used in a particular study. Later in this chapter we will review examples of commonly used instruments and ask you to evaluate them in relation to the information needed.

■ *Reliability and Validity*

Two concepts that are extremely useful in judging the value of an instrument are reliability and validity. *Reliability* refers to the consistency of the information obtained. If we used a yardstick to measure a desk three times and obtained different readings each time, we would conclude that the information was unreliable—either because the yardstick was defective (perhaps it was made of rubber), or because it was used improperly (perhaps the user had poor vision). In either case, we would have no way of knowing which measurement to use.

Validity refers to the extent to which an instrument gives us the information we want. If we were foolish enough to use a yardstick (even a reliable one) to assess the artistic merit of our desk, we would clearly obtain information of no validity. A less obvious example is the assessment of student knowledge (of economics, for example) by means of test items that require students to read and analyze written passages. For poor readers, such tests give misleading information about what they know.

How do the concepts of reliability and validity apply to the rating scale of classroom openness? We need to have total scores for each classroom that are consistent across observers and over time. If different observers do not get similar scores, a serious problem arises—and it is a problem of inconsistency. If we obtain different scores for the same classroom at different times, we again have a problem of inconsistency. Unless our "reading" of each classroom remains consistent across observers and over some period of time, there is no point in trying to study differences in classroom openness; either the variable is meaningless or we lack an adequate way to assess it.

In terms of validity, the question is whether our scale really measures openness as we have defined it. Perhaps observers are actually responding to the degree of affluence reflected in the classroom or to the friendliness of the teacher and students rather than to the intended variable.

■ *The Observation Record*

The next task of the class was to develop an instrument to measure the amount of "motivation" existing in a classroom. Given the limited time the class had available for instrument development, an observation record that had been used in prior research appeared appropriate.

The observation procedure was as follows: During each of six consecutive 5-minute intervals, the classroom observer recorded the number of students who were judged NOT to be attending to any learning activity for at least half the time (defined as 2.5 minutes). Attending to a learning activity was defined as having one's sensory apparatus directed toward some object(s) that contained academic content (broadly defined). Thus, nonattenders were primarily those who had books or other materials open but who were not looking at them, and/or those who were engaged in social conversation or some routine preparatory activity such as pencil sharpening. The number of nonattenders was divided by the total number of students to give the percentage of nonattenders. A motivation score was obtained by averaging across the six intervals.

Might use of this instrument have resulted in unreliable scores? Yes _____

No _____ If you checked yes, explain how.

_____

_____

_____

_____

What might a researcher who used this instrument be assessing other than motivation (as intended)?

_____

_____

_____

AUTHORS' COMMENT

As with the rating scale, the issue of reliability is one of consistency. Do different observers get similar results? Are scores for each classroom consistent over time? We might expect better agreement on the observation record than on the rating scale, since only one attribute is being observed. On the other hand, observers are required to watch many students and to arrive at a decision on each—a difficult task which may impair agreement.

The validity of scores obtained with this instrument depends on whether attention is considered the same as motivation. As always, we must compare the instrument and how it is used with the definition of the variable of interest.

We shall discuss the important concepts of reliability and validity in more detail later in the chapter. To further your understanding at this point, however, use the following procedure to draw some conclusions about reliability and validity with regard to the rating scale and the observation record described earlier. If possible, use both of them. Try to locate a classroom, preferably at the elementary level. Spend at least 10 minutes observing in the classroom, then rate it on each of the 14 items listed in the rating scale (see Table 5.2). As a further check, take a time block of at least 5 minutes and use the procedure for assessing motivation on the observation record.

Using an instrument is extremely helpful in judging reliability and validity. As a result of your experience in using these two instruments, you should be able to make some judgments concerning the probable reliability and validity of any information obtained using them. Please do so below, including the reasoning for your judgment.

Rating scale (openness)

Your judgment concerning reliability: _____

_____

_____

Your judgment concerning validity: _____

_____

_____

Observation record (motivation)

Your judgment concerning reliability: _____

_____

_____

Your judgment concerning validity: _____

_____

_____

More about Reliability and Validity

We now wish to introduce the notion of collecting *evidence* on the reliability and validity of instruments, and to discuss some ways to obtain such evidence. We shall also distinguish between different forms of reliability and validity.

VALIDITY

Validity is the most important idea to consider when preparing or selecting an instrument for use. More than anything else, a researcher wants the information obtained with an instrument to serve his or her purposes. Suppose, for example, that a researcher wants to know what teachers in a particular school district think about a recent policy passed by the school board. The investigator needs not only an instrument to find this out but also some sort of assurance that the information obtained with the instrument will lead to *correct conclusions* about the opinions elicited. The drawing of correct conclusions on the basis of data obtained through an instrument is what validity is all about.

It is essential that a researcher consider not only the instrument itself, but also how it is used and with whom. The same instrument may provide valid information about one group but not another. We shall illustrate this later.

In recent years, validity has been defined to include the appropriateness, meaningfulness, and usefulness of the specific *inferences* a researcher makes on the basis of the data he or she collects. The *validation* of an instrument refers to the process of collecting evidence to support such inferences. There are many ways to collect evidence, and we shall discuss some of them shortly. The important point here is that validity refers to the degree to which such evidence supports any inferences a researcher makes on the basis of data collected with a particular instrument. It is the inferences regarding the specific uses of an instrument that are validated, not the instrument itself. These inferences should be appropriate, meaningful, and useful.

An appropriate inference is one that is *relevant* (related) to the purposes of the study. If the purpose of a study is to determine what students know about African culture, for example, it makes little sense to draw inferences about this from their scores on a test about African physical geography.

A meaningful inference is one that says something about the *meaning* of the information (e.g., test scores) obtained through an instrument. What exactly does a high score on a particular instrument mean? What does such a score allow us to say about the individual who received it? In what way is an individual who receives a high score different from one who receives a low score? And so forth. It is one thing to collect information from people. We do this all the time—we gather names, addresses, birthdates, shoe sizes, car license numbers, and so on. But unless we can make inferences that mean something from the information we obtain, it is of little use. The purpose of research is not just to collect information but to use it to draw warranted conclusions about the people (and others like them) from whom the information was collected.

The degree to which an instrument is valid, therefore, depends on the amount and type of *evidence* available to support the interpretations that researchers wish to make on the basis of information they have collected. The crucial question is: Does the instrument provide useful information regarding the topic or variable as defined by the researcher?

What kinds of evidence might a researcher collect? Essentially, there are three main types.

Content-related evidence refers to the nature of the content included within the instrument, and the specifications the researcher used to formulate the content. How appropriate is the content? How comprehensive? Does it logically get at the intended variable? Such evidence most often relies on the judgments of people who are presumed to be knowledgeable about the variable being observed. It is sometimes referred to as "logical" or "face" validity.

Criterion-related evidence refers to the relationship between scores obtained using the instrument and scores obtained using one or more other instruments or measures (often called criteria). How strong is this relationship? How well do such scores estimate present or predict future performance of a certain type?

Construct-related evidence refers to the nature of the psychological construct or characteristic being measured by the instrument. How well does this construct explain differences in the behavior of individuals or their performance on certain tasks?

Listed below are three basic questions a researcher needs to ask and answer with regard to each of the types of evidence we have discussed. To which type of evidence does each question apply?

1. How accurately does individual performance as measured by the instrument *predict* future performance, or estimate *present* performance, on some other valued measure or criterion?
2. How adequately does the sample of items contained in the instrument represent the domain of content to be measured as judged by experts?
3. How well can individual performance as measured by the instrument be explained in terms of theoretical characteristics?

AUTHORS' COMMENTS

Question 1 refers to criterion-related evidence; 2 refers to content-related evidence; and 3 refers to construct-related evidence.

Let us discuss each of these types of evidence in more detail. Ideally, a researcher is armed with evidence from all three of these categories. The important thing to remember, however, is that the more evidence a researcher has concerning the validity of inferences he or she makes, the better.

CONTENT-RELATED EVIDENCE

Suppose a researcher is interested in the effects of a new math program on the mathematics ability of fifth graders. Upon completion of the program, the researcher expects students to be able to solve a number of different types of word problems. To assess their mathematics ability, the researcher plans to administer a math test containing about 15 such problems. The performance of the students on this test is important only to the degree that it provides evidence of their ability to solve these kinds of problems. Hence, the instrument in this case (the math test) would provide valid evidence of the mathematics ability of students only to the degree that it contained an adequate sample of the types of word problems learned about in the program. If only easy problems were included in the test, or only very difficult or lengthy ones, or only problems involving subtraction, the test would be unrepresentative, and hence not provide information from which valid inferences could be made.

One key element in content-related evidence, then, revolves around the adequacy of the *sampling.* Most instruments provide only a sample of the kinds of problems that might be solved, the questions that might be asked, and so forth. Content validation, therefore, is partly a matter of determining if the content that the instrument contains is an adequate sample of the domain of content it is supposed to represent.

Another key element of content validation is the format of the instrument. Format refers to the clarity of printing, size of type, adequacy of work space (if needed), appropriateness of language, clarity of directions, and so on. Regardless of the adequacy of the questions in an instrument, if they are presented in an inappropriate format (e.g., giving a test in English to children whose English is minimal), valid results cannot be obtained.

How can content-related evidence of validity be obtained? A common approach is to have someone look at the content and format of the instrument and judge whether they are appropriate. The "someone," of course, should not be just anyone, but rather an individual who logically can be expected to render an intelligent judgment concerning the adequacy of the instrument. In other words, the person should know enough about what is to be measured to be a competent judge. Finally, and of great importance, the preceding must be judged in the context of usage, that is, appropriateness for the intended respondents.

Typically, the researcher writes out a definition of what he or she wants to measure and then gives this description, along with the instrument and a description of the intended "subjects," to one or more judges. The judges look at the definition, read over the items or questions in the instrument, and then place a checkmark in front of each question or item which they feel does not measure one or more of the objectives. They also note any aspects of the definition that are not assessed by any of the items. The researcher then rewrites any item or question so checked and resubmits it to the judges; the researcher may also write new items for aspects that are not adequately covered. The process continues until the judges approve all of the items or questions in the instrument and indicate that they feel the total number of items is an adequate representation of the domain of content covered by the variable being measured and that the format is appropriate.

To illustrate how a researcher might go about trying to establish content-related validity, let us consider two examples.

Example 1

Suppose a researcher desires to measure the following: Students' ability to *use information that they are given or have previously acquired*. When asked what this phrase means, the researcher offers the following definitions:

As *evidence* that students can use previously acquired information, they should be able to:

- Draw a correct conclusion (verbally or in writing) that is based on information they are given.
- Identify one or more logical implications that follow from a given point of view.
- State (orally or in writing) whether two ideas are identical, similar, unrelated, or contradictory.

How might such evidence be obtained? The researcher decides to prepare a written instrument that will contain various questions for students to answer. Their answers will constitute the evidence being sought. Here are three examples of the kinds of questions the researcher has in mind, one designed to produce each of the three types of evidence listed above.

1. If A is greater than B, and B is greater than C, then:
   a. A must be greater than B.
   b. C must be smaller than A.

c. B must be smaller than A.

d. all of the above are true.

2. Those who believe that increasing consumer expenditures is the best way to stimulate the economy would advocate:

a. an increase in interest rates.

b. an increase in depletion allowances.

c. tax reductions in the lower income brackets.

d. a reduction in government expenditures.

3. Compare the amount of trade between the English colonies in North America and England from 1750 to 1783 with the amount of trade between the states and the U.S. government from 1789 to 1865.

Now, look at each of the questions and the corresponding objective it is supposed to measure. Do you think each question measures the objective it was designed for?

Yes _____ No _____ If no, why not? _____

_____

AUTHORS' COMMENTS

We would rate correct answers to questions 1 and 2 as valid evidence, although 1 could be considered questionable, since students may view it as somewhat tricky. We would not rate answers to question 3 as valid, since students are asked to contrast facts, not ideas.

Example 2

Here is what another researcher designed as an attempt to measure (at least in part) the ability of students to *explain why events occur.* By "explain," the researcher meant the ability to provide a logical cause-and-effect sequence.

Read the following directions and then answer the question.

Directions: Here are some facts.

Fact W	*Fact X*
A camper started a fire to cook dry food on a windy day in a forest.	A fire started in some grass near a campsite in a forest.

Here is another fact that happened later the same day in the same forest.

Fact Y
A house in the forest burned down.

Now imagine that you have been asked to explain what might have caused the house to burn down (Fact Y). Would Facts W and X be useful as parts of your explanation?

1. Yes, both W and X and the possible cause-and-effect relationship between them would be useful.
2. Yes, both W and X would be useful, even though neither was likely a cause of the other.
3. No, because only one of W and X was likely a cause of Y.
4. No, because neither W nor X was likely a cause of Y.[2]

Once again, look at the question and the objective it was designed to measure. Does it measure this objective?

Yes _____ No _____ If not, why not? _____

_____

AUTHORS' COMMENTS

We would rate a correct answer to this question as potentially valid evidence of students' ability to explain why events occur. Our main concern is that students are asked only to recognize logical cause-effect sequences; yet the verb "explain" usually implies the ability to originate such sequences. (The correct answer is 1.)

Attempts to obtain evidence of some sort (in the above instances, the support of independent judges that the items measure what they are supposed to measure) typify the process of content validation. As we mentioned earlier, however, the qualifications of the judges are always an important consideration. While such evidence is indispensable, it can also be in error since judgment is always fallible.

CRITERION-RELATED EVIDENCE

When a researcher tries to obtain criterion-related evidence of validity, he or she usually compares performance on one instrument (the one being validated) with performance on some other, independent measure. A *criterion* is a second instrument by which something can be measured. For example, if an instrument has been designed to measure academic motivation, student scores on the instrument might be compared with their grade point averages (the criterion). If the instrument does indeed measure academic motivation, then students who score high on the test would also be expected to have high grade point averages. Can you see why?

There are two forms of criterion-related validity: the predictive form and the concurrent form. In the *predictive* form, a time interval elapses between administering the instrument and obtaining the criterion-related data. For example, a researcher might administer a science aptitude test to a group of high school students, and later compare their scores on the test with their end-of-semester grades in science courses.

[2] Norman E. Wallen, Mary C. Durkin, Jack R. Fraenkel, Anthony J. McNaughton, & Enoch I. Sawin. 1969. *The Taba curriculum development project in social studies: Development of a comprehensive curriculum model for social studies for grades 1 through 8, inclusive of procedures for implementation and dissemination.* Menlo Park, CA: Addison-Wesley, p. 307.

In the *concurrent* form of criterion-related validity, the instrument data and the criterion data are gathered at nearly the same time, and the results are compared. For example, a researcher may administer a self-esteem inventory to a group of eighth graders and then compare their scores with teacher ratings of their self-esteem, obtained at about the same time.

Validity Coefficients. A key index in both forms of criterion-related validity is the validity coefficient, which indicates the degree of relationship that exists between the scores individuals obtain on two different instruments. A positive relationship is indicated when high scores on one of the instruments are accompanied by high scores on the other and when low scores on one are accompanied by low scores on the other. A negative relationship is indicated when high scores on one instrument are accompanied by low scores on the other, and vice versa. Validity coefficients fall somewhere between -1.00 and $+1.00$. An r of .00 indicates that no relationship exists.

Suppose that a validity coefficient of $+1.00$ is obtained between a set of scores on a mathematics aptitude test (the predictor) and another set of scores on a mathematics achievement test (the criterion) for the same individuals. Such a coefficient would indicate that each individual in the group had exactly the same relative standing on both measures. It would also allow the researcher to predict math achievement perfectly on the basis of aptitude test scores. Such a validity coefficient is highly unlikely, of course, but it does illustrate what validity coefficients mean. The closer to $+1.00$ a validity coefficient is, the more accurate a researcher's predictions are likely to be. A rule of thumb is that validity coefficients above $+.50$ provide evidence for validity.

It is important to realize that the nature of the criterion is the most important factor in the gathering of criterion-related evidence. High validity coefficients do not mean much if the criterion measure does not make logical sense. A high coefficient, for example, between scores on an instrument designed to measure aptitude for science and scores on a physical fitness instrument would not provide relevant criterion-related evidence for either instrument.

Further, some criteria are better than others. Grade point average (GPA) is often used as a criterion for a test of academic motivation. Though legitimate, it is a weak criterion because GPA clearly reflects other characteristics (such as ability) in addition to academic motivation. Thus, a criterion having greater content validity is to be preferred. In this example, teacher or peer ratings of academic motivation would provide a more direct and hence more useful measure.

At the same time, use of a criterion that is too similar to the first instrument is to be avoided. It is not unusual, for example, to read test manuals that report a relationship between "their" test and another instrument as evidence of (concurrent) validity. Examination of the two tests, however, may show that they are virtually identical in format, item type, and content. If this is the case, a high relationship between them is to be expected and is only weak evidence of validity. Any defects in content, format, or item type that limit the validity of one test will affect the other in the same way. An ideal criterion, then, is one which differs from the first instrument in format, content, and, if possible, source of information, but for which there exists evidence of content- related validity. Judgments made by knowledgeable people provide such evidence.

Students in our classes sometimes object to the use of such judgments on the ground that they are "subjective." It is true that scientific research attempts to transform subjective judgments, reactions, and so forth, into objective (communicable, public) forms by means of definition and training. Nevertheless, subjective judgments (incompletely specified and based on personal experience) can never be eliminated from the research process. A researcher must make many such judgments in the course of a study. In instrument validation particularly, use of experienced (although subjective) judgment should not be discouraged. The goal is instrumentation that is largely free of subjective judgment, but some judgment nonetheless is indispensable in reaching that goal. If instrument scores that represent students' academic motivation are in agreement with teacher ratings or rankings of that motivation, this is impressive evidence of validity, because the instruments differ both in format and in source of information: individual self-reports vs. teacher judgments that are based on accumulated prior experience with the students.

Sometimes the same instrument can serve as both predictor and criterion, provided that the *source* of information is different. Evidence of the validity of a self-esteem scale can be obtained, for example, by comparing self-rating scores with scores obtained by asking knowledgeable people to fill out the scale on the basis of their perceptions of the individuals. Even though the items are the same, the source of information is different.

Think back to the example presented earlier of the questions designed to measure ability to explain. What sort of criterion could be used to establish criterion-referenced validity for those items? _____

_____

_____

AUTHORS' COMMENTS

People who know the students who have taken the test could be asked to judge each of them on the ability to explain. Or these same students could be observed in class, and their spontaneous or requested explanations could be recorded. Alternatively, students could be asked to provide oral or written explanations for specified events.

CONSTRUCT-RELATED EVIDENCE

Construct-related evidence is the broadest of the three categories of evidence for validity that we are considering. There is no single piece of evidence that carries the day for construct-related validity. Rather, researchers attempt to collect a variety of *different* types of evidence—the more and varied the better—which will allow them to make warranted inferences. Such evidence enables researchers to assert, for example, that the scores obtained from administering a self-esteem inventory permit accurate inferences about the degree of self-esteem which people who receive those scores possess.

There are three steps involved in obtaining construct-related evidence of validity:

- The researcher formulates a clear definition of the variable being measured.
- Hypotheses, based on a theory underlying the variable, are formed about how people who possess a "lot" vs. a "little" of the variable will behave in a particular situation.
- The hypotheses are tested both logically and empirically—that is, by collecting additional information.

The sum total of all the available evidence is then used to judge whether the instrument does indeed measure the intended variable.

For example, a researcher might predict that individuals scoring high on a self-esteem inventory would also (1) score high on a projective test of self-esteem; (2) be described by their friends as high in self-esteem; (3) be rated as high in self-esteem by their teachers; and (4) show less deterioration in task performance when placed under stress. Confirmation of these predictions would support the contention that the inventory does, indeed, measure self-esteem.

■ *Reliability*

Reliability, you will recall, refers to the *consistency* of scores or answers— how consistent they are for each individual from one administration of an instrument to another, and from one set of items to another. Consider, for example, an instrument designed to measure typing ability. If the instrument provides reliable information, a student who receives a high score the first time he or she takes the instrument would be expected to receive a high score the next time he or she takes the instrument. The scores would probably not be identical, but they should be close.

Notice that the scores obtained from an instrument can be quite reliable, but not valid. Suppose a researcher gave a group of eighth graders two forms of a test designed to measure their knowledge of the Constitution of the United States, and found their scores to be very consistent. Those who scored high on Form A also scored high on Form B; those who scored low on A scored low on B; and so forth. The researcher would say that the instrument provides reliable information. But if these same test scores were then used to predict the success of students in their physical education classes, the researcher would probably be looked at in amazement. Any inferences about success in physical education that were based on scores on a test of the U.S. Constitution would have no validity.

What about the reverse? Can an instrument with poor evidence of

reliability yield valid score-based inferences? Yes _____ No _____

AUTHORS' COMMENTS

No! If scores are completely inconsistent for a person, they provide no useful information. We have no way of even knowing which score to use to infer an individual's ability, attitude, and so forth.

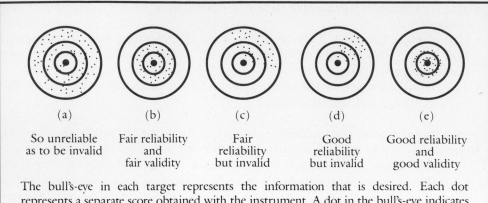

(a)	(b)	(c)	(d)	(e)
So unreliable as to be invalid	Fair reliability and fair validity	Fair reliability but invalid	Good reliability but invalid	Good reliability and good validity

The bull's-eye in each target represents the information that is desired. Each dot represents a separate score obtained with the instrument. A dot in the bull's-eye indicates that the information obtained (the score) is the information the researcher desires.

FIGURE 5.1
Reliability and Validity

The distinction between reliability and validity is shown in Figure 5.1. The bull's-eye in each target represents the information that is desired. Unless an instrument has some degree of reliability, it cannot lead to useful inferences, as target (a) reveals. As reliability improves, validity may improve, as target (b) reveals; or it may not, as shown in target (c). An instrument may also have high reliability, but low validity, as shown in target (d). What is desired, of course, is both high reliability and high validity, as shown in target (e). A point which must be stressed again is that reliability, like validity, depends on the characteristics of the group being studied. An instrument may well have high reliability at some grade levels, for example, but not at others.

ERRORS OF MEASUREMENT

Whenever people take the same instrument twice, they seldom perform exactly the same—that is, their scores or answers are not usually identical. This may be due to a variety of factors (changes in the characteristic itself or in motivation, anxiety, the testing situation, the wording of questions, and so forth), but it is inevitable. Such factors result in *errors of measurement*.

Since errors of measurement are always present to some degree, researchers expect some variation in instrument scores (answers, ratings, and so on) when an instrument is administered to the same group more than once or when two different forms of an instrument are used. Reliability estimates provide a researcher with an idea of how much variation to expect. Such estimates are usually expressed as *reliability coefficients*.

As mentioned earlier, a validity coefficient expresses the relationship which exists between scores of the same individuals on two *different* instruments. A reliability coefficient, by contrast, expresses a relationship between scores of the same individuals on the *same* instrument at two different times, or between two forms of the same instrument. Here is a description of the most commonly used methods.

THE TEST-RETEST METHOD

The test-retest method involves administering the same instrument twice to the *same* group after a certain time interval has elapsed. A reliability coefficient is then calculated to indicate the degree of stability of the scores obtained.

Retest coefficients are affected by the length of time that elapses between the two administrations of the instrument. The longer the time interval that passes, the lower the reliability coefficient is likely to be, since there is a greater likelihood of changes in the individuals taking the instrument. When test-retest reliability coefficients are used, therefore, the time interval between the two testings should always be reported. In checking this type of reliability, an appropriate time interval should be selected. The interval should be that during which individuals are assumed to retain their relative positions in a meaningful group. There is no point in studying, or even conceptualizing, a variable that has no permanence. When researchers assess a person as being academically talented, or as possessing skill in typing, or as having a poor self-concept, they assume that these characteristics will continue to differentiate the person from others for some period of time—otherwise, there is no utility to the assessment. Furthermore, there is no possibility of studying a variable which is continually changing.

Researchers do not, however, expect all variables to be equally stable. Prior experience and/or evidence suggests that some abilities, such as writing, are more subject to change than others, such as abstract reasoning. Some personal characteristics, such as self-esteem, are considered more stable than others, such as vocational interests among teenagers. Meaningful studies, in fact, have been carried out on "mood," a type of variable that is considered, by definition, to be stable only for short periods of time—a matter of hours or even minutes. Even here, unless the instrumentation is reliable over such a short time period, meaningful relationships with other (perhaps causal) variables will not be found. For most educational research, stability over a two- or three-month period is probably sufficient, but this rule of thumb may not always be appropriate.

THE EQUIVALENT FORMS METHOD

A second source of inconsistency is relatively unique to behavioral science. It occurs because any measurement of human behavior uses indicators; measurement virtually never encompasses all behavior included in the characteristic of interest. For example, an algebra test must sample from the possible problems that could be given; and observers must look for certain indicators of "openness" even though there are undoubtedly others that exist. A check can be made by comparing measurements with different indicators (or different test items).

When this method is used, two different, but equivalent (also called alternative or parallel) forms of an instrument are administered to the same group of individuals during the same time period. Although the questions are different, they sample the same content. A reliability coefficient is then calculated between the two sets of scores obtained. A high coefficient indicates that there is a high level of reliability, that is, the two forms are measuring the same thing. Such evidence tells us how consistent scores are across different content as contrasted to their stability over time.

It is also possible to combine the two methods mentioned above. Here, two different forms of the same instrument are given with a time interval between the two administrations. A high reliability coefficient indicates not only that the two forms are measuring the same sort of performance but also how stable individual performance is.

INTERNAL CONSISTENCY METHODS

The methods mentioned so far all require two administration or testing sessions. There are several *internal consistency* methods of estimating reliability, however, that require only a single administration of an instrument. They provide the same kind of information as the equivalent forms method; that is, consistency over differing content.

Split-Half Testing

The split-half method involves scoring two halves (usually odd items vs. even items) of a test separately for each person. This reliability coefficient indicates the degree to which the two halves of the test provide the same results, and hence describes the internal consistency of the test.

The reliability coefficient is calculated using what is known as the Spearman-Brown prophecy formula. A simplified version of this formula is as follows:

$$\text{Reliability of total test} = \frac{2 \times \text{reliability for 1/2 test}}{1 + \text{reliability for 1/2 test}}$$

Thus, if we obtained a coefficient of .56 for two halves of a test, the reliability for the total test would be:

$$\text{Reliability of total test} = \frac{2 \times .56}{1 + .56} = \frac{1.12}{1.56} = .72$$

This illustrates an important characteristic of reliability. The reliability of any instrument can generally be increased by increasing its length, if the items added are similar to the original ones.

The Kuder-Richardson Approaches

Perhaps the most frequently employed method for determining internal consistency is the Kuder-Richardson method, particularly their formulas KR20 and KR21. These formulas require only three pieces of information: the number of items in the test, the mean, and the standard deviation.[3] A form of Kuder-Richardson that is more generally applicable and that is obtained in a similar way is called the alpha coefficient.

As with validity coefficients, there are two benchmarks we can use to evaluate reliability coefficients. First, we can compare a given coefficient with the extremes that are possible. As with validity, a coefficient of .00

---

[3] See Chapter Twelve for an explanation of standard deviation.

indicates a complete absence of a relationship—hence, no reliability at all. Perfect reliability is indicated by +1.00.

Second, we can compare a given reliability coefficient with the sorts of coefficients that are usually obtained for measures of the same type. The reported reliability coefficients for many commercially available achievement tests, for example, are typically .90 or higher when Kuder-Richardson formulas are used. Many classroom tests report reliability coefficients of .70 and higher. For research purposes, a rule of thumb is that reliability should be at least .70 and preferably higher.

Below is a descriptive summary of the four methods of estimating the reliability of an instrument. Which method does each summary describe?

1. Scores (answers, ratings, and so on) are consistent over two different forms of an instrument.
2. Scores are consistent over two different forms and a time interval.
3. Scores are stable over time.
4. Scores are consistent over different parts of an instrument.

AUTHORS' COMMENTS

Summary 1 describes equivalent forms; 2, equivalent forms plus test-retest; 3, test-retest; and 4, internal consistency.

OBSERVER AGREEMENT

Most tests and many other instruments are administered with specific directions and are scored objectively—that is, with a key that requires no judgment on the part of the scorer. Although differences in the resulting scores with different administrators or scorers are still possible, it is generally considered highly unlikely that they would occur. This is not the case with instruments that are susceptible to differences in administration, scoring, or both. In particular, instruments that use direct observation are highly vulnerable to observer differences. Researchers who use such instruments are obliged to investigate and report the degree of observer agreement. Such agreement is enhanced by training the observers and by increasing the number of observation periods.

Instruments differ in the amount of training required for their use. In general, observation techniques require considerable training for optimum use. Such training usually consists of explanation and discussion of the procedures involved, followed by use of the instruments by trainees as they observe videotaped or live classrooms. All trainees observe the same behaviors and then discuss any differences in scoring. This process, or some variation thereon, is repeated until an acceptable level of agreement by independent observers is reached. Usually, even after such training, 8 to 12 observation periods are required to get adequate evidence of reliability. What is desired is a correlation of at least .90 among observers or agreement of at least 80 percent.

Checking Reliability and Validity

A major aspect of research design is the obtaining of reliable and valid information. Since both reliability and validity depend on the way that instruments are used and on the inferences researchers wish to make from these instruments, we can never simply assume that a particular instrument will provide satisfactory information. We can have more confidence in instruments for which there is previous evidence of reliability and validity, provided we use the instruments in the same way—that is, under the same conditions as existed previously. Even then, we cannot be sure; even if all else remains the same, the mere passage of time may have impaired the instrumentation we wish to use. What this means is that there is no substitute for checking reliability and validity as part of the research procedure. There is seldom any excuse for failing to check internal consistency, since the necessary information is at hand—no additional data collection is required. In most cases, reliability over time does require an additional administration of instruments, but this can often be done. It should be noted that not all members of the sample need to be retested, although it is desirable. It is better to retest a randomly selected subsample, or even a convenience subsample, than to have no evidence of reliability whatsoever. Another option is to use a different, although very similar, sample to obtain retest evidence.

Obtaining evidence of validity is more difficult, but seldom prohibitive. At a minimum, a second instrument should be administered. Locating or developing an additional means of instrumentation is sometimes difficult and occasionally impossible (e.g., there is probably no way to validate a self-report questionnaire on sexual behavior), but the effort is well worth the time and energy expended. As with retest reliability, a subsample or different sample can be used (by obtaining data on them with both instruments). Table 5.3 summarizes these approaches to checking validity and reliability.

At this point, return to the instruments used in the open classroom study (see pages 82 and 85–86). Indicate below how you could obtain evidence of reliability and validity for each instrument.

The rating scale (classroom openness)

To check observer agreement, I would _____

_____

_____

To check retest reliability (stability over time), I would _____

_____

_____

To check internal consistency, I would _____

_____

_____

TABLE 5.3 Methods of Checking Validity and Reliability

Validity ("truthfulness")	
Type	*Procedure*
Content-related evidence	Expert judgment
Criterion-related evidence	Relate to another measure of the same variable
Construct-related evidence	Assess evidence on predictions made from theory

Reliability ("consistency")			
Type	*Content*	*Time Interval*	*Procedure*
Test-retest	Identical	Varies	Give identical instrument twice
Equivalent forms	Different	None	Give two forms of instrument
Internal consistency	Different	None	Divide instrument into halves and score each or use K–R
Observer agreement	Identical	None	Compare scores obtained by two (or more) observers

To obtain content-related evidence of validity, I would _____

_____

_____

To obtain criterion-related evidence of validity, I would _____

_____

_____

The observation record (class motivation)

To check observer agreement, I would _____

_____

_____

To check retest reliability (stability over time), I would _____

_____

_____

To check internal consistency, I would _____

_____

_____

To obtain content-related evidence of validity, I would _____

_____

_____

To obtain criterion-related evidence of validity, I would _____

_____

_____

AUTHORS' COMMENTS

The Rating Scale. The rating scale was used by several pairs of student observers working independently in the same classroom at the same time. In spite of only limited training in use of the scale, most of the pairs of students agreed quite well in their ratings. Subsequent discussion suggested that certain items were difficult to rate, particularly those dealing with how the teacher is addressed (11), the use of resource people (4), and the arrangement of furniture (5). Consequently, the reliability of these items was questionable.

Reliability over time could be checked by observing the same classroom on several occasions and deriving two scores—each one a total (or average) based on half the observation periods (e.g., periods 1 and 2 vs. periods 3 and 4). A comparison of these scores would provide evidence of stability over the time period during which data were collected. Internal consistency could be checked by obtaining separate scores (across all observation periods) for odd-numbered items (1, 3, 5, etc.), summing these scores, and then comparing the total with the score obtained by summing the scores for all the even-numbered items (2, 4, 6, etc.).

Validity could be checked by asking students and/or teachers to answer questions on the same or additional indicators—as was originally intended. A score based on these questions could then be compared with the rating score for each classroom. A high (or low) score on both would be evidence of validity. Content-related evidence could be obtained by asking knowledgeable people to evaluate the instrument and by making a thoughtful analysis after it is used (as you did earlier in the chapter).

The Observation Record. In spite of the obvious difficulties in observing whether another person is paying attention, the observation record does provide reliable evidence of classroom attention when it is used by observers who have received prior training and when several visits are made to each classroom and the average of these visits is used as the measurement. Evidence on stability can be obtained in the same way as for the rating scale—that is, by combining scores for the first half of the observation periods and comparing this total with the score obtained for the second half. Internal consistency cannot be assessed because there is no way to compare one set of indicators with another; the way the instrument was designed implies that all possible behaviors indicating "attentiveness" are included, but they are not measured separately.

Evidence of validity rests on the assumption that a group that appears to be attending closely is in fact attending closely. However, this instrument provides an index of only a limited aspect of what is encompassed by most definitions of motivation, including the one used in this study.

Consequently, evidence of validity of the scale ultimately must be judged to be questionable for the purpose of the open classroom study. At this point, had our purpose been sophisticated research rather than instruction, the class would have had either to locate or to develop additional instruments for assessing motivation or to revise the hypotheses so that "attention" rather than "motivation" became the focus of the study.

An instrument for checking validity could consist of questions asked of students by means of interviews or, possibly, questionnaires. Since it is the classroom for which motivation is assessed, questioning teachers (who may find it hard to be objective) seems less defensible.

■ Summary

In this chapter, we introduced the concepts of instrument and instrumentation. An instrument is a device or procedure for systematically collecting information of some sort. Instrumentation refers not only to the instrument itself but also to the conditions under which the instrument is used in a research study. We also introduced the concepts of reliability and validity, and discussed them in some detail.

■ Key Concepts Discussed in This Chapter

instrumentation
instrument
rating scale
reliability
validity
observation record
criteria
validity coefficient
observer agreement
content-related evidence of validity
criterion-related evidence of validity

construct-related evidence of validity
predictive form of criterion-related validity
concurrent form of criterion-related validity
test-retest method
equivalent forms method
internal consistency
split-half method
errors of measurement
Kuder-Richardson approaches

■ How Far Along Should I Be at This Point?

By now, you should have completed all of the tasks listed at the end of the preceding chapters. (If not, review and accomplish these before going any further.) You should understand what is meant by the terms "instrument" and "instrumentation." You also should understand what is meant by the terms "reliability" and "validity" as they apply to a research instrument.

Evaluate your progress, therefore, by checking each of the following. At this point, you should be able to explain:

• The meaning of the terms "reliability" and "validity."
• What is meant by the terms "content-related evidence," "criterion-related evidence," and "construct-related evidence" of validity.
• What is meant by the terms "validity coefficient" and "reliability coefficient."
• How to use the test-retest, equivalent forms, and split-half methods for checking reliability.
• What a rating scale is, and when it is appropriate to use.
• What an observation record is, and when it is appropriate to use.

■ What's Next?

In the next chapter, we present a number of additional examples of instruments that are frequently used in educational research and assist you in the process of selecting or developing an instrument for use in your own study.

■ For Further Reading

Brinberg, S., & McGrath, J. E. 1985. *Validity and the research process.* Beverly Hills, CA: Sage.

Feldt, L. S., & Brennan, R. L. 1989. Reliability. In R. L. Linn (Ed.), *Educational measurement* (3rd Ed.). New York: Macmillan.

Kirk, J., & Miller, M. L. 1986. *Reliability and validity in qualitative research.* Beverly Hills, CA: Sage

Messick, S. 1989. Validity. In R. L. Linn (Ed.), *Educational measurement* (3rd Ed.). New York: Macmillan.

Yalow, E. S., & Popham, W. J. 1983, October. Content validity at the crossroads. *Educational Research*, 12(8):10–21.

Wainer, H. 1986, Summer. Can a test be too reliable? *Journal of Educational Measurement*, 23(2):171–173.

(See also the suggestions listed at the end of Chapter Six.)

Chapter Six

MORE ON INSTRUMENTATION

$\mathbf{I}$n the preceding chapter, you have seen examples of two common forms of instrumentation: the rating scale and the observation record. In this chapter, we present some further examples of commonly used instruments, and discuss evidence of their reliability and validity. We also discuss how to locate and/or develop an instrument you can use in your own study.

By the end of this chapter, you should be able to identify a variety of types of instruments and describe when they would be appropriate to use. You will also have begun the process of either selecting or locating the instrument for use in your proposed study.

■ The Structured Interview

The *structured interview* is an instrument in which individuals are asked to respond to a series of specific questions. For example, another research class led by one of the authors expressed interest in the open classroom study. This class wanted to assess student opinion on a variety of issues that were of theoretical interest as well as of interest to the teachers in a particular school. The class developed an instrument to interview a sample of children from each of ten classrooms in a new school that had from its beginning included several open classrooms.

The structured interview technique requires that the interviewers ask the questions exactly as they are worded. They may be allowed some latitude, however, in clarifying terms. It is important that the interviewer do nothing to bias or influence the answers that are given. It is equally important that the interviewer establish rapport with each respondent before beginning to ask any questions. The questions shown in Table 6.1 were intended for use with children in grades 4–6.

Use these questions to interview a fourth, fifth, or sixth grader in your area. If any of the questions are inappropriate, you may delete them. It is important, however, that you use as many of them as possible. Record

TABLE 6.1 Interview Schedule

Question/Student Response

1. How do you feel* about your teacher?_____

   Why?_____

   How do the other students in the class feel about the teacher?_____

2. Do most of the other students in the room like their classmates?_____

   How does it compare with last year?_____

   How do you feel about having different ages in the same class?_____

   Is there much fighting in class?_____

   How does it compare with last year?_____

   How do you settle problems?_____

3. Do most of the students in the class find school interesting?_____

   Why?_____

   If you could not come to school for some reason, would you be disappointed?_____

4. Are you doing more kinds of things this year than last?_____

   What things?_____

   Do you do a lot of things without being told to do them?_____

   More than last year?_____

   How do you feel about doing more things?_____

5. Is this classroom a happy place for you?_____

   How does it compare with last year?_____

6. How do you feel about the amount of noise in the room?_____

   How does it compare with last year?_____

7. Do you help your classmates with their work when they ask you?_____

   Do you ask other students for help with things you do not understand?_____

8. Are the things you are learning in school important to you?_____

   How does it compare with last year?_____

9. Do you talk with your parents about what you do in school?_____

   How much?_____

   What do they say?_____

   Do your parents say any bad things about school?_____

* As discussed in Chapter Two, terms such as "feel" are ambiguous and need to be clarified. This does not preclude their use in instruments for which their ambiguity may, in fact, be an asset when a researcher does not wish to limit responses too narrowly.

student responses. After completing the interview, record your reactions to the questions, paying particular attention to their validity.

Did the student understand all of the questions you asked?

Yes _____ No _____

Do you think the student told you what he or she really thought?

Yes _____ No _____

What variable do you think the instrument was designed to measure?

_____

Assuming you are correct as to the intended variable, how would you evaluate the content validity of the interview process as a whole?

_____

How might you obtain evidence of criterion-related validity?

_____

_____

_____

AUTHORS' COMMENTS

This instrument was intended to assess students' "liking for school." The structured interview was administered individually to a total of 60 students—6 selected from each of 10 classrooms. The students in each class were in grades 4–6, represented a variety of ethnic groups, and, for the most part, came from a lower socioeconomic background than the average student. Most of the questions were understandable to the students and appeared to function as had been intended. The exceptions were the questions that asked about talking with parents about school. These were unclear to some of the students.

There was considerable difference in replies to certain questions among the ten classrooms. For example, in one classroom all six of the students said the things they were learning in school were important to them; in another classroom, only two of six answered yes. In the first of these classrooms, however, only one of six students said that the importance of what they were learning was better than last year, whereas in the second all six said it was better. This inconsistency raised some questions about the validity of either or both parts of question 8. Further, since it was not feasible to take the time to train the interviewers in this situation, it is conceivable that differences in interviewing style or in the way in which the questions were asked may have influenced students' responses.

On logical grounds, the interview procedure itself may have been questionable, since the interviewer was not known to the students. Further, the interviews were conducted in a classroom setting, and one might expect a reluctance on the part of elementary school children to make negative statements about their teacher or their school, even if they had such feelings.

As a part of the same study, the research class also observed in these classrooms and rated them on the same characteristic as those sampled in the questions asked of the students. A considerable correspondence was found between the assessment of a particular classroom on the basis of what the students said and the impressions gained from observations. This is some evidence that both procedures were to some extent valid.

In summary, we think that this measure leaves a good deal to be desired. It would certainly need to be further refined before being recommended for widespread use. There is some evidence, however, primarily in terms of the agreement of the responses with the observations in the classroom, that even as presently constituted, the instrument can provide valid information.

Since interviewing is time-consuming, questions are often printed and distributed in the form of questionnaires. This procedure has a major drawback in that a substantial number of questionnaires will probably not be returned unless they are filled out in a group setting, which may itself influence responses.

The following suggestions should be helpful in preparing questions for inclusion in either interview schedules or questionnaires:

1. Keep the purpose of your study in mind as you prepare each question.
2. Phrase the questions so as to keep the respondent attentive.
3. Avoid complex and/or ambiguous words or phrasing.
4. Keep in mind the probable frame of reference of the respondent.
5. Avoid unrealistic assumptions about the amount of background information respondents possess.
6. Avoid leading questions—that is, ones which suggest an expected or "correct" answer.
7. Place the questions in a sequence that is sensible from the respondent's point of view.
8. Ask general questions before specific ones.
9. Place any questions that may be offensive to a respondent toward the end.
10. Do not let one question (or its response) influence answers to subsequent questions.

■ Ability Tests

If you have lived in our society for any appreciable length of time, you are undoubtedly quite familiar with ability tests. The most common of such tests are the so-called achievement tests that range from kindergarten (e.g., the Metropolitan Reading Readiness Test) to graduate school (e.g., the Graduate Record Examination). Another type of ability instrument is the so-called intelligence test, which assesses intellectual abilities that are less directly related to what is taught in school. The vast literature on this type of instrument (and on some particular tests) demonstrates that many of these tests display a considerable amount of evidence of reliability and validity when they are used with certain kinds of people and for certain purposes (e.g., predicting the college grades of middle-class Caucasian students). At the same time, such tests have come increasingly under attack when used with other groups and/or for other purposes (e.g., identifying Hispanic students for placement in special classes). Further, there is increasing recognition that these tests do not currently measure many important abilities (e.g., the ability to see unusual relationships). Consequently, researchers must carefully evaluate any such tests before using them and

TABLE 6.2   The Q–E Intelligence Test

Directions: Read each of the following questions and write your answer on a separate sheet of paper. Suggested time for the test is 10 minutes.

_____ 1. I went to bed at eight o'clock in the evening and set the alarm to get up at nine o'clock in the morning. How many hours of sleep would this allow me?

_____ 2. Who is buried in Grant's tomb?

_____ 3. Some months have 30 days, some have 31. How many have 28 days?

_____ 4. If you had only one match and entered a dark room in which there was an oil lamp, an oil heater, and some kindling wood, what would you light first?

_____ 5. If a physician gave you three pills and told you to take one every half hour, how long would they last?

_____ 6. A person builds a house with four sides to it—a rectangular structure, with each side having a southern exposure. A big bear comes wandering by. What color is the bear?

_____ 7. A farmer had 17 sheep. All but 9 died. How many did he have left?

_____ 8. Divide 30 by $\frac{1}{2}$. Add 10. What is the correct answer?

_____ 9. Take two apples from three apples. What do you have?

_____10. How many animals of each species did Moses take aboard the ark?

judge whether they are appropriate to the purpose of their study. It is important to look for empirical evidence (in test manuals, research reports, or instrument reviews) of reliability and validity for these tests.[1]

Table 6.2 presents a nontypical "intelligence" test.[2] Please take it. Answer each question in the space provided.

Now look at the key in the footnote at the bottom of this page[3] and score yourself. Give yourself 1 point for each correct answer. Presumably the score on this test gives a measure of intelligence. If so, each of the ten items should be an indicator of intelligence. We could, therefore, use only five items instead of ten. Suppose the test were composed of only items 1, 3, 5, 7, and 9. What would your score be? We could just as well use only the even-numbered items (2, 4, 6, 8, 10). What would your score be on these five items? Compare the two scores. If either half of the test provides an equally good measurement of "intelligence," your scores should agree fairly closely. If they don't agree, then the separate five-item tests do not provide consistent results. If this is true, then the total test of ten items probably does not provide consistent results either, in which case the reliability of the test would be suspect.

[1] Anne Anastasi. 1988. *Psychological testing* (6th Ed.). New York: Macmillan.
[2] Author unknown.
[3] *Scoring key:* (1) 1 hour, (2) Ulysses S. Grant, (3) all of them, (4) the match, (5) 1 hour, (6) white, (7) 9 sheep, (8) 70, (9) 2 apples, (10) none (it wasn't Moses, but Noah who took the animals on the ark).

Ask some other people to take the test. List in the spaces below the score of each individual on each of the separate five-item tests.

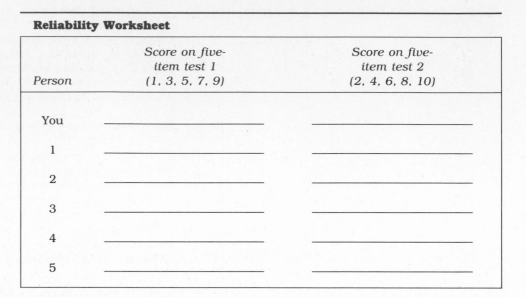

Reliability Worksheet

Person	Score on five-item test 1 (1, 3, 5, 7, 9)	Score on five-item test 2 (2, 4, 6, 8, 10)
You	_____	_____
1	_____	_____
2	_____	_____
3	_____	_____
4	_____	_____
5	_____	_____

Examine the scores you have obtained. What would you conclude (from this small amount of evidence) about the reliability of scores obtained with this instrument? Which method of assessing reliability does this exercise illustrate?

AUTHORS' COMMENTS

If the two scores for each individual are identical, this is very strong evidence for the reliability of the instrument. If, on the other hand, many people have discrepancies of 3, 4, or 5 points, this indicates poor reliability. Results obtained by the students in our research classes provided evidence of fair reliability, but not sufficient for drawing conclusions about individuals. The scores of most students differed by only 1 or 2 points, but there were quite a few that differed by 3 or more points. This procedure illustrates the split-half method of assessing reliability.

We have examined only one aspect of reliability for this instrument. We still do not know how much a person's score might change over time—that is, whether his or her scores would change if the test were taken again at a different time. We could get a better idea of this if we gave one of the five-item tests at one time and the other five-item test at another. If feasible, administer the test to a new group of people, making a reliability worksheet such as the one above. For a true measure of reliability, at least 100 people should be tested. Also, it has been found that tests with many more than ten items produce more consistent results, presumably because they provide a larger sampling of a person's behavior.

What is your analysis of the validity of the inferences made from the instrument presented in Table 6.2? Do you think the instrument measures intelligence? Why or why not?

AUTHORS' COMMENTS

The instrument appears to primarily measure a person's lack of gullibility or ability to see through attempts to mislead. Whether or not this is intelligence depends on the definition or view of intelligence. It would seem that most current psychological definitions incorporate the lack of gullibility as one, but only one, of many aspects of intelligence. The instrument also appears to measure knowledge to some extent. Almost anyone in our society over the age of 10 would be expected to understand the concept of time as it is presented in item 1. In contrast, at least a passing acquaintance with the Judeo-Christian tradition is needed in order for item 10 to function as an indicator of gullibility. Also, item 8 clearly requires knowledge of how to divide by fractions.

Notice also that item 1 illustrates how an item can be invalidated by the passage of time. The answer of 13 hours was incorrect prior to the advent of digital clocks, but is now equally correct as 1 hour—depending on the type of clock the respondent has in mind.

The entire instrument assumes sufficient ability to read English to comprehend the statements; some recent immigrants to the United States would receive a low score on this basis alone. Adequate evidence for validity would depend on research that explores the relationship of this instrument to other measures. The instrument is an adaptation of a teaching device that is widely used in tests and measurement courses, but the original author is unknown.

Existing tests are frequently criticized because they do not adequately measure "thinking skills," such as the ability to make legitimate inferences, to recognize assumptions, to make logically defensible deductions, and/or to apply ideas in new contexts. The Watson-Glaser Critical Thinking Appraisal is a published instrument that attempts to measure some of these characteristics in students of high school age or older.

Another instrument, the Application of Generalizations Test, was developed by the authors as part of a major social studies curriculum project.[4] This instrument assesses the ability to apply previously learned ideas in a new context. One of the objectives of the Taba Curriculum, of which this instrument is a part, is to have students learn, through inductive processes, important generalizations (ideas) in social studies and subsequently to apply these generalizations in new situations. The Application of Generalizations Test, designed specifically for sixth graders, consists of seven passages, each followed by a series of statements. There are a total of 65 statements. Both the passages and the statements are read to students so as not to penalize poor readers. Students are asked to respond to each statement as either probably true or probably false, having been told in the directions that a clearly true or clearly false answer is, in most cases, not defensible. The example shown in Table 6.3 includes one passage and the statements to which students are asked to respond. Also shown are the generalizations that are intended to be applied to each item. (These do not appear in the test; nor are students expected to express them as we have.) The student follows along as the passage and the statements are read. After the examiner reads each statement, students mark their answer. The statements cannot be answered from the text alone; students must use other ideas (or guess) to arrive at an answer. Students who have learned the ideas intended by the curriculum will supposedly be able to be apply them to the

[4] N. E. Wallen, M. Durkin, J. R. Fraenkel, A. H. McNaughton, & E. I. Sawin. 1969. *The Taba Curriculum development project in social studies.* Menlo Park, CA: Addison-Wesley.

TABLE 6.3 **An Example from the Application of Generalizations Test**

Hunteros and Farmanos

This is about two groups of people, the Hunteros and the Farmanos, who live in the same valley surrounded by mountains. The Hunteros hunt and fish to get food. They often have to move because the herds of animals travel from place to place. Most of the Farmanos are farmers, although some of them make simple tools.

Remember: Hunteros are hunters.
                 Farmanos are farmers.

Statement	*Generalization**
1. The Farmanos have more schools for their children than the Hunteros, (pt)†	1. Geographic stability and increased technology lead to more formalized educational institutions, permanent buildings, and other facilities.
2. The Hunteros' way of life shows that their ability to learn is less than that of the Farmanos. (pf)	2. "Way of life" is not a good index of learning ability; it is a product of many factors.
3. The Farmanos should be worried if the Hunteros have a poor hunting season. (pt)	3. Interdependence of groups in the same geographic area is likely. The suffering of one group has repercussions on others.
4. The Farmanos will develop modern conveniences before the Hunteros. (pf)	4. Technology breeds technology.
5. The Hunteros have practically no contacts with the Farmanos. (pf)	5. Groups living in the same geographic area almost certainly interact.
6. The Farmanos are suspicious of the Hunteros. (pt)	6. Strangeness in, or differences among, groups usually leads to suspicion.
7. The Hunteros will be more concerned that their leaders be daring than will the Farmanos. (pt)	7. Expectations for leaders depend largely on group needs.
8. The Hunteros do not have musical or artistic activities. (pf)	8. Almost all cultures or societies have some form of art.
9. The Farmanos will increase in population (number) faster than the Hunteros. (pt)	9. Geographic stability and a less hazardous life lead to population growth.
10. If both groups had their lodgings destroyed, the Farmanos would be harmed more than the Hunteros. (pt)	10. Geographic stability leads to greater investment, economically and psychologically, in permanent structures.

*The generalizations are not included in the test as administered.

†Correct responses (pt = probably true; pf = probably false) are included parenthetically.

situation and respond to the statements. For example, students who have grasped the generalization listed next to statement 1 should answer "probably true."

In the space on p. 113, indicate your overall impression of the validity of the statements in Table 6.3 for measuring students' ability to apply generalizations. List also any statements that seem to have questionable validity and your reasons for thinking so.

My overall evaluation of the responses to the statements in Table 6.3 as providing content-related evidence of validity for the Application of Generalizations Test is:

_____

_____

_____

_____

The following statements seem to be questionable to me.

Statement	My reasons for thinking so

AUTHORS' COMMENTS

The main evidence for the validity of the responses to this instrument was obtained by giving the instrument in an interview format to a sample of 31 sixth-grade students. Both the passage and questions were read to the students as they followed along with their own copies. Students were asked to answer "probably true" or "probably false" to each question and to explain their answer. The task of the interviewer was to pursue the point until a student's reasoning was clear. These interviews were recorded verbatim and subsequently typescripted so they could be reviewed independently by two analysts. Each response to a statement by a student was classified into one of 15 different categories that covered all possible responses. Only the five major categories are presented in Table 6.4. Each of the categories is illustrated using an early version of statement 2: "The Hunteros live the way they

do because they are less able to learn than the Farmanos." Responses which suggested that some students interpreted the question as referring to school learning led to the revised wording that appears in the final form.

Responses in categories 1, 2, and 4 indicate that the statement is functioning as intended. That is, the students who get it right are using an appropriate generalization and logical reasoning. The students who get the wrong answer do so because they used an erroneous idea or reasoned illogically. Categories 3 and 5, however, indicate that the question is not functioning properly. In category 3, for example, students gave the right answer, as keyed, but based it on an erroneous idea; in category 5, students gave the wrong answer, although their ideas and thought processes were appropriate and logical.

This analysis was carried out for all 65 state-

TABLE 6.4   Examples of Responses in the Interview Study of the Application of Generalizations Test

Category 1: Answered correctly using intended generalization (regardless of particular wording).
 Example: "Not necessarily, because instead of learning to . . . , that's their way of life. They learned how to hunt, and the others learned how to farm, so it is probably false."

Category 2: Answered correctly using different but defensible generalization or reasoning.
 Example: "Well, I think that's false because they move around a lot, and, well, they can learn things."

Category 3: Answered correctly, based on erroneous generalization or reasoning.
 Example: "Well, I think that's probably false because neither of them has schools."

Category 4: Answered incorrectly, using erroneous generalization or reasoning.
 Example: "True, because they have the tools to do all of their fishing and hunting and cooking and stuff."

Category 5: Answered incorrectly, using a defensible generalization or reason.
 Example: "I think it's true because the Farmanos can build schools. They can go to them and learn all the knowledge. The Hunteros keep on moving around and they don't have a school to learn."

---

ments in the instrument. It was done independently by two analysts who agreed quite well in their categorizations of student responses. A score was derived on the basis of a student's reasoning as revealed during the interview. An answer in categories 1, 2, or 5 was considered correct. This score agreed quite well with the score obtained from the student's initial answer of "probably true" or "probably false," showing that, in general, the instrument was functioning as intended. There were certain statements, however, that were identified as poor. These were either altered or deleted.

Another way to assess the validity of interpretations using this instrument is to use other instruments (such as teacher ratings) to see if those students who score high on this instrument also are identified as high in ability to apply specified ideas.

How might an instrument of this type be used in the open classroom study? Would it be valuable? Why or why not?

_____

_____

_____

_____

_____

AUTHORS' COMMENTS

An ability test is sometimes used as a measure of motivation. The task must be such that a student's score reflects, not ability, but persistence or motivation. Whether such a test could be designed to fit the definition of motivation used is problematical. It is difficult to see how an ability test could be used to measure openness.

■ *Projective Tests*

Projective tests have a unique feature: They permit individuals to project themselves into the test. This type of instrument has no clear-cut "right" answers, and the format of the instrument permits individuals to express something of their own personality, with room for a wide variety of possible responses. The best-known examples of this type of instrument are the Rorschach Inkblot Test, which asks individuals to tell what each of a series of inkblots looks like, and the Thematic Apperception Test (TAT), which presents pictures of events and asks the individual to make up a story about them.

Another common format is the cartoon approach. The best-known example is the Rosensweig Picture Frustration Study. An application of this approach to the classroom setting is the Picture Situation Inventory, which consists of a series of cartoonlike drawings, each portraying a classroom situation in which a student is saying something to a teacher.[5] The individuals taking the test are asked to write in the response of the teacher (thereby presumably indicating what they would be likely to say in such a situation). Two pictures from this test are shown in Figure 6.1. Write in your own reactions (put yourself in the position of the teacher) in the balloons in the figure.

With instruments of this kind, or with any open-ended procedure that permits a wide variety of responses, some procedure must be developed for arriving at a score. One technique, a variation of *content analysis*, is to define categories on the basis of a sample of responses. Once developed, new responses can be categorized by comparing them with examples of each category. This procedure was illustrated in Table 6.5 in connection with the Application of Generalizations Test. For the Picture Situation Inventory, scoring systems have been developed to assess two characteristics of teachers. These are need for control, defined as the extent to which teachers are motivated to control the moment-to-moment activities of their students; and communication, defined as the extent to which teachers attempt to keep channels of communication open. The scoring system permits the assignment of 1–5 points on each picture for each characteristic. Each point category is described and several examples are given. Abbreviated examples of the scoring categories for the two pictures in Figure 6.1 are given in Table 6.5. Two examples of each point category are presented.

[5] N. T. Rowan. 1967. The relationship of teacher interaction in classroom situations to teacher personality variables. Salt Lake City: University of Utah. Unpublished doctoral dissertation.

FIGURE 6.1
Sample Items from the Picture Situation Inventory

(N. T. Rowan. 1967. The relationship of teacher interaction in classroom situations to teacher personality variables. Unpublished doctoral dissertation. Salt Lake City: University of Utah, p. 68.)

Score your own responses using the categories in Table 6.5. First, compare your response to picture 1 to the examples listed under Control-Need Score, picture 1. Find the example that is closest to your own. Then compare your response to those listed under Communication Score, picture 1 in the same way. Enter your response. Repeat the procedure for picture 2.

	Control	*Communication*
Picture 1	_____	_____
Picture 2	_____	_____
Total	_____	_____

How well do the two scores for each characteristic agree? Now add the two scores for control together and do the same for communication. How well do these scores correspond to your view of your actual or probable behavior in the classroom? Do they agree with your perception of your need to control, or with the extent to which you keep communication open with students? Using this analysis, write an evaluation of the evidence you have for the validity of each of the two scores in the space below.

TABLE 6.5 Scoring Categories for the Picture Situation Inventory

Control-Need Score: Rationale—the more controlling or directive the response, the higher the score.

Picture 1:
1 point	"I thought you would enjoy something special."
	"Is this a job you should do?"
2 points	"I'd like to see how well you can do it."
	"Would you like me to help?"
3 points	"Some children don't do as well or as much as others."
	"You and Tom are two different children."
4 points	"Yes, I would appreciate it if you would finish it."
	"Yes, sometimes children do different things."
5 points	"This is your assignment, not Tom's."
	"Do it quickly, please."

Picture 2:
1 point	"Do you think you would like a harder book?"
	"Do you want to?"
2 points	"All right, why don't you try this one."
	"Why don't I discuss it with your mother?"
3 points	"Let's hear you read and then I'll decide where you should be reading."
	"If you'll read two easier ones while I help you with the harder ones, maybe we can keep everybody happy."
4 points	"For now, let's read where we are comfortable. Before long we can read harder books."
	"I will call your mother and talk to her so she'll understand why you are in that book."
5 points	"When we are able, we'll read in a hard book."
	"Tell your mother we have a regular method of progressing from one book to another. When this one is completed, we'll go to another.

Communication Score: Rationale—the more the response keeps communication open, the higher the score.

Picture 1:
1 point	"Yes, please do as you were told."
	"This is your assignment, not Tom's."
2 points	"I have reasons for wanting you to do it."
	"Yes, Tom doesn't need the practice."
3 points	"You do things for your own benefit."
	"You and Tom are two different children."
4 points	"I thought you would enjoy something special."
	"I'd like to see how well you can do it."
5 points	"Would you like me to help?"
	"Why don't you want to do it?"

Picture 2:
1 point	"Tell your mother we have a regular system for progressing."
	"Why doesn't your mother talk to me about such things?"
2 points	"I'll call your mother and explain why you're in this book."
	"I don't think you're ready yet."
3 points	"You can when you are able to."
	"Let's hear you read and then I'll decide where you should be reading."
4 points	"Do you think you can?"
	"Why don't I discuss it with your mother?"
5 points	"Do you want to?"
	"Let's see if we can find one you'll like."

Need for Control

_____

_____

_____

_____

Communication

_____

_____

_____

_____

AUTHORS' COMMENTS

In addition to the appeal to logical or apparent validity, there is some evidence in support of the validity of these two measures (control and communication) when they are based on all 20 pictures in the test. The evidence is summarized below.

Rowan[1] studied relationships between the two Picture Situation Inventory (PSI) scores and several other measures with a group of elementary school teachers. She found that teachers scoring high on control need were more likely to (1) be seen by classroom observers as imposing themselves on situations and having a higher content emphasis; (2) be judged by interviewers as having more rigid attitudes of right and wrong; and (3) score higher on a test of authoritarian tendencies. Teachers scoring high on communication were more likely to (1) be observed as doing less imposing; (2) be judged by interviewers as having less rigid attitudes of right and wrong, more acceptance of themselves, and higher feelings of self-worth; and (3) be judged better teachers by administrators.

In a study of ability to predict success in a program preparing teachers for inner-city classrooms, one of the authors found evidence that the PSI control score had predictive value. Although the study had serious limitations, there were relationships between the control score obtained on entrance to the program and a variety of measures subsequently obtained through classroom observation in the student teaching and subsequent first-year teaching assignments. The most clear-cut finding was that those scoring higher in control need had classrooms observed as less noisy. This finding adds somewhat to the validity of the measurement, since a teacher with higher control need would be expected to have a quieter room.

The reliability of both measures was found to be high when assessed by the split-half procedure. When assessed by follow-up over a period of 8 years, the consistency over time was considerably lower, as would be expected.

Note
1. N. T. Rowan. 1967. The relationship of teacher interaction in classroom situations to teacher personality variables. Salt Lake City: University of Utah. Unpublished doctoral dissertation.

Might a projective test be used in the open classroom study?

Yes _____ No _____ If so, how? _____

_____

_____

_____

_____

AUTHORS' COMMENTS

A projective test might portray classroom situations of various kinds, such as students engaged in a variety of activities or students in conflict. Students and/or teachers would write in responses of individuals, as in the PSI. A measure of openness might be obtainable from the responses. With respect to motivation, a considerable literature exists on the use of such instruments for assessing certain motivations (e.g., achievement, affiliation, power) in adults. Adaptations might be appropriate for this study.

You have now seen examples of the most commonly used forms of instrumentation. They constitute only an introduction to the topic. There are a number of references that expand upon this topic in detail.[6]

The next task is for you to determine the instrumentation for the study that you are planning. You have essentially two choices: Either locate one or more existing instruments that could be used in your study or develop your own instrument. For purposes of an introductory course, it is probably appropriate to attempt to develop your own instrument, provided it is in the form of a rating scale, a structured interview, a questionnaire, or an observation record. It is unlikely that you will have sufficient time to develop the other forms of instrumentation that have been discussed here.

■ *Locating a Suitable Instrument*

There is no surefire way to gain access to available instruments which might serve your purpose. It may be that a literature search will turn up some instruments. Advisers or colleagues may be able to suggest possibilities. University libraries often have test files, as do some psychology and education departments. The references listed below provide the most systematic means of surveying existing instruments, but they are not all-encompassing. After identifying possible instruments, you will need to

---

[6] See, for example, Jack R. Fraenkel & Norman E. Wallen. 1990. *How to design and evaluate research in education.* New York: McGraw-Hill.

review them, which in most cases means getting a copy of the instrument itself and, hopefully, an accompanying technical manual containing evidence on reliability and validity. Often, manuals include only descriptions of the instrument and directions for administration. Although these descriptions are necessary, such manuals fail to provide the essential data on reliability and validity. In addition, you should attempt to locate reviews of the instrument—a task made much easier if the instrument is reviewed in one of the issues of the *Mental Measurements Yearbook*. If an instrument is not reviewed in the latest volumes, be sure to check the previous ones. Publishers will, in most cases, provide specimen sets of tests and manuals, though some publishers may require the purchaser to provide credentials. In this case, your adviser may agree to get these materials for you. An illustrative review from the *Mental Measurements Yearbook* follows the list of references below.

Mitchell, J. V., Jr. 1989. *Mental Measurements Yearbook* (10th Ed.). Lincoln: University of Nebraska.

Buros, O. 1987. *Tests in Print*. Highland Park, NJ: Gryphon Press.

Robinson, P., & Shaver, P. R. 1976. *Measures of Social/Psychological Attitudes*. Ann Arbor: Institute for Social Research, University of Michigan.

Sweetland, R. C., & Keyser, D. J. 1986. *Tests* (2nd Ed.). Kansas City: Test Corp. of America.

Coopersmith Self-Esteem Inventories.[7] Ages 8–15, 16 and above; 1981; SEI; norms consist of means and standard deviations, no norms for adults; 2 levels labeled forms; manual ('81, 22 pages); 1984 price data: $5.50 per manual; $6 per specimen set (both forms, no scoring keys); (10–15) minutes; Stanley Coopersmith; Consulting Psychologists Press, Inc.

a. SCHOOL FORM. Ages 8–15; 6 scores: general self-subscale score, social self-peers subscale score, home-parents subscale score, school-academic subscale, total self score, lie scale score; separate answer sheets may be used; $5 per 25 tests; $9.50 per 50 machine-scoreable answer sheets; $2 per scoring key; scoring service available from the Center for Self-Esteem Development, 669 Channing Ave., Palo Alto, CA 94301.

b. ADULT FORM. Ages 16 and above; 1 form (2 pages); $3.25 per 25 tests; $1.25 per scoring key.

Review of Coopersmith Self-Esteem Inventories by CHRISTOPHER PETERSON, Associate Professor of Psychology, and JAMES T. AUSTIN, Graduate Assistant, Department of Psychology, Virginia Polytechnic Institute and State University, Blacksburg, VA:

The Coopersmith Self-Esteem Inventories (SEI) are three self-report questionnaires intended to measure "the evaluation a person makes and customarily maintains with regard to him- or herself." Each questionnaire presents respondents with generally favorable or generally unfavorable statements about the self, which they indicate as "like me" or "unlike me." The School Form is a 50-item inventory to be used for 8- to 16-year-old children. It may be broken into four subscales pertaining to different self-esteem domains: peers, parents, school, and personal interests. The School Form is accompanied by an 8-item Lie Scale to assess defensiveness. The School Short Form contains the 25 items from the School Form with the highest item-total correlations. The Adult Form is an adaptation of the School Short Form for individuals over 15 years of age.

[7] Christopher P. Peterson & James T. Austin. 1985. "Review of Coopersmith Self-Esteem Inventories." In James V. Mitchell (Ed.). *Ninth Mental Measurements Yearbook*, Vol. 1. Lincoln: University of Nebraska, pp. 396–397.

The Coopersmith Inventories have much to recommend them as measures of self-esteem. They are among the best-known and most widely used of the various self-esteem measures (Johnson, Redfield, Miller, & Simpson, 1983). They are brief and easily scored. They are reliable and stable, and there exists an impressive amount of information bearing on their construct validity. Finally these measures are straightforwardly based on a general theory of self-esteem and its relationship to academic performance. One of the interesting aspects of the SEI manual is a brief discussion of how to boost the self-esteem of students.

These measures do have some drawbacks, however, some of them endemic to all measures of self-esteem and self-concept (Crandall, 1973; Wylie, 1974). Most basically, researchers have been unable to agree on the precise meaning of self-esteem. In the SEI measures, this disagreement is reflected in several ways. "Self-esteem" is defined unidimensionally (see above), but the School Form is composed of subscales. Personal standards of evaluation are assumed, but some of the items seem to reflect assessment by others (e.g., "People usually follow my ideas").

Relatedly, there is not enough evidence that different self-esteem measures tap the same underlying construct. Some recent research has shown that the Coopersmith questionnaires indeed converge with other self-report measures of self-esteem (e.g., Johnson et al., 1983), but there is less indication that they diverge from measures of conceptually distinct constructs (e.g., Cowan, Altmann, & Pysh, 1978). . . .

Finally, measures of self-esteem may be confounded by social desirability biases, tendencies to answer questions in terms of social appropriateness rather than "true" self-esteem (Wells & Maxwell, 1976). Crandall (1973) reported substantial correlations of .44 and .75 between the SEI and the social desirability scales of Marlowe-Crowne and Edwards, respectively. At this time, social desirability is not itself well understood. Nonetheless, that it may confound measures of self-esteem should not be ignored.

There are several more specific problems with the SEI, and these involve possible clinical uses of the measures. First, the provided norms could be based on better-defined samples. We suspect that teachers may use these measures to make decisions about individual students and we doubt that the norms are sufficient for such clinical use. Similarly, the user of the SEI is cautioned to supplement scores with additional observations and information, but no clear guidelines are provided about how to do this. In light of a recent study showing that teacher-completed scales of behaviors indicating self-esteem have little relationship to students' self-reports of self-esteem (Benner, Frey, & Gilberts, 1983), this recommendation must be better explained.

Second, detailed instructions are not provided about how to use the Lie Scale that accompanies the School Form. The user is told that high scores may indicate defensiveness, but we were left wondering just what is a "high" score and what is the evidence linking such a score to defensiveness or to lying, behaviors with different denotations and connotations. . . .

In sum, we find the Coopersmith self-esteem measures to possess enough reliability and validity to recommend their use in research. These questionnaires share some problems in common with most measures of self-esteem and self-concept. Additionally, there is reason to be careful about the clinical use of these questionnaires. Differential validity of the subscales needs to be established, guidelines for the use of the Lie Scale need to be provided, and the cutoff values contained in the manual need to be justified.

Reviewer's References

Crandall, R. 1973. The measurement of self-esteem and related concepts. In J. P. Robinson & P. R. Shaver (Eds.), *Measures of social psychological attitudes* (2nd Ed.). Ann Arbor, MI: Institute for Social Research. pp. 46–167.

Shavelson, R. J., Hubner J. J., & Stanton, G. C. 1976. Self-concept: Validation of construct interpretations. *Review of Educational Research*, 46:407–441.

Wells, L. E., & Maxwell, G. 1976. *Self-esteem: Its conceptualization and measurement*. Beverly Hills, CA: Sage.

Cowan, R., Altmann, H., & Pysh, F. 1978. A validity study of selected self-concept instruments. *Measurement and Evaluation in Guidance*, 10:211–221.

Johnson, B. W., Redfield, D. L., Miller, R. L., & Simpson, R. E. 1983. The Coopersmith Self-Esteem Inventory: A construct validation study. *Educational and Psychological Measurement*, 43:907–913.

Fleming, J. S., & Courtney, B. E. 1984. The dimensionality of self-esteem: II. Hierarchical facet model for revised measurement scales. *Journal of Personality and Special Psychology*, 46:404–421.

■ *Developing Your Own Instrument*

The following steps are those used by most researchers in instrument development; they may require adaptation to special circumstances.

1. Be sure you are clear as to what variable or variables are to be assessed. Much time and effort can be wasted by definitions that are too ambiguous. If more than one variable is involved, be sure to keep both their meanings and specific items distinct. In general, a particular item or question should be used for only one variable.

2. Review existing instruments that are similar in intent in order to decide on item format and to obtain ideas on specific items.

3. Decide on format. Although it is sometimes appropriate to mix multiple-choice, true-false, matching, rating, and open-ended items, doing so complicates scoring and is usually undesirable.

4. Begin compiling and/or writing items. Be sure that, in your judgment, each has logical validity—that is, that the item is consistent with the definition of the variable. Try to ensure that vocabulary is appropriate for the intended respondents.

5. Have colleagues review the items for content validity. Supply colleagues with a copy of your definition and a description of the intended respondents. Be sure they evaluate format as well as content.

6. Revise items on the basis of colleague feedback. At this point, try to have about twice as many items as you intend to use in the final form (generally at least 20 to 30). Remember that more items generally means higher reliability.

7. Locate a group of people with experience appropriate to your study. Have them review your items for logical validity. Make any revisions needed and compile your items. You should have half again as many as intended in the final form.

8. Try out your instrument with a group of respondents who are as similar as possible to your study respondents. Have them complete the instrument and then discuss it with them—to the extent that this is feasible given their age, sophistication, and so forth.

9. If feasible, conduct a statistical item analysis. Such analyses are technically beyond the scope of this book, but are not difficult to carry out—especially if you have access to a computer. The information provided on each item indicates how effective it is and, sometimes, even suggests how to improve it.

10. Select and/or revise items until you have the number you want.

State below the proposed means of instrumentation for your study. If you plan to use instruments that you have located, identify them by name and description. If appropriate, include sample items, and then write an analysis of the appropriateness of this instrument for your purpose, based on whatever information you have located. If you plan to develop your own instrument, describe the procedure that you will follow and include at least some sample items or some examples from the instrument itself.

It may not be appropriate for you to spend a great deal of time developing your own instrument. If, however, you plan to carry out your study, it is necessary that you use some form of instrumentation during the information-gathering aspect of your study. You will probably want to return to this section and add to it as time goes on. At this point, record as much as possible regarding the instrument you are planning to use or develop. As soon as you have your instrumentation firmed up, ask several other people, preferably ones knowledgeable about research, to assess the validity of the content of your instrument(s). Ask whether they think the instrument(s) will measure what you are after. Record their responses. To the extent possible, try out your instrument. There is no substitute for tryout and concomitant evaluation.

Description of instrumentation for your study: _____

_____

_____

_____

_____

_____

_____

_____

_____

_____

_____

_____

Evaluation of content-related evidence of validity by others: _____

_____

_____

_____

How could you assess the reliability of the scores obtained by using your instrument(s)? Check one or more:

By using the equivalent forms method _____

By using the test-retest method _____

By checking internal consistency _____

How could you obtain criterion-related evidence on the validity of your instrument(s) for your purpose?

_____

_____

_____

■ Summary

You have become acquainted with some of the major types of instruments and have examined a few in some detail. You have begun to select or develop instruments for your own study. You will probably need to continue the process of instrumentation as you move ahead to other topics in this book.

■ Key Concepts Discussed in This Chapter

structured interview
interviewing
interview schedule

ability test
intelligence test
projective test

■ How Far Along Should I Be at This Point?

By now, you should have a better idea of the many different kinds of instruments that can be used to collect data. You should have begun the process of selecting or developing an instrument for use in your own proposed study.

Evaluate your progress, therefore, by checking each of the following. At this point, you should have accomplished each of the tasks listed at the end of the preceding chapters. (If not, review and accomplish them before going any further.) Furthermore, you should be able to:

• Explain what a structured interview involves, and when it is appropriate to use this type of instrument.

- Explain the purpose of an ability test, and when it is appropriate to use this type of instrument.
- Explain the purpose of a projective test, and when it is appropriate to use this type of instrument.
- Suggest what would count as evidence of the validity of scores obtained on your instrument(s).
- Suggest what would count as evidence of the reliability of scores obtained on your instrument(s).

■ *What's Next?*

In the next chapter, we begin to talk about sampling—the process of selecting the subjects of a study. We will discuss the difference between a sample and a population, and distinguish between a target population and an accessible population. We will also discuss a number of different ways to obtain a sample and say a few words about sample size.

■ *For Further Reading*

Anastasi, A. (1988). *Psychological testing* (5th Ed.). New York: Macmillan.

Bernard, H. R. 1988. Collecting data. In *Research methods in cultural anthropology*. Beverly Hills, CA: Sage.

Carey, L. 1988. *Measuring and evaluating school learning.* Boston: Allyn & Bacon.

Gronlund, N. E. 1988. *How to construct achievement tests* (4th Ed.). Englewood Cliffs, NJ: Prentice-Hall.

Sawin, N. I. 1969. *Evaluation and the work of the teacher.* Belmont, CA: Wadsworth.

Webb, E. T., Campbell, D. T., Schwartz, R. D., Sechrest, L., & Grover, J. B. 1981. *Nonreactive measures in the social sciences* (2nd Ed.). Boston: Houghton Mifflin.

(See also the suggestions listed at the end of Chapter Five.)

Chapter Seven

SAMPLES AND POPULATIONS

One of the most important steps in the research process is to select the sample of individuals who will participate (e.g., be observed or questioned) in the study. Who is to be observed, questioned, or tested? *Sampling* refers to the process of selecting these individuals.

After completing this chapter, you should be able to recognize examples of poor sampling and inappropriate generalizing of results. You will have identified both an ideal and a feasible procedure for selecting subjects for your proposed study.

■ Selecting a Sample

Let us continue to use the open classroom study as an illustration. After the research class decided to test the hypothesis "The more open the classroom, the higher the motivation of the students," they decided to try to identify classrooms that differed in terms of their "openness," and then find out how they compared with regard to student motivation. Only the elementary level was chosen to be studied, for two reasons: The membership of the class consisted primarily of elementary-level personnel, and the class wanted to limit the extent of the study in order to keep it manageable. There were a number of elementary schools in the local area that had a reputation for having open classrooms. Members of the class contacted the administrators of these schools and received permission to visit them.

Discussion now centered around the question of how many classrooms to study. The sample that was selected consisted of 27 classrooms in five schools. This number—27—evolved from considerations of desirability and feasibility. Students felt that for this study, a sample of 27 classrooms was adequate, although not as large as they desired. For reasons that we will discuss later, it is almost always desirable to have as large a sample as is feasible.

There are no clear-cut rules for deciding on sample size. If a good deal is known about the measuring instruments to be used and about the subjects, it is possible to employ a somewhat technical procedure to estimate the sample size necessary to provide a fair test of the hypothesis. Unfortunately, in many studies this degree of detailed information does not exist. A rule of thumb that you might consider is the following: The size of the sample should consist of at least 30 subjects, but a larger sample is all to the good and should be obtained whenever possible. Note that sample size refers to the units that are to be measured. In many studies, the units are individual people. In the open classroom study, however, the hypothesis dealt with classrooms. The classroom, therefore, not the individual student, was the unit of sampling and measurement in that study.

After the five schools to be observed had been identified and the school administrators had given permission to collect the kind of information desired, 40 classrooms in grades 4–6 were made available to the members of the research class. These grades were chosen because many students felt it might be difficult to use the instruments they had developed with primary-grade students. (You may recall that the class originally desired to interview students.) After some discussion, it was decided that 18 members of the class would be involved in the data collection process. The class wished to have two observers collecting data at the same time in each classroom so that measurements could be compared. This meant that there would be 9 teams of 2 people each. Although only one afternoon was available to the class for data collection, it still seemed feasible for each team to visit three classrooms. Thus, a total of 27 classrooms would be visited. The actual sample from which data were obtained turned out to be only 26, however, since one of the teams of observers was able to visit only two rather than three classrooms.

When researchers plan a study, they do not expect to encounter such severe and artificial restrictions as inevitably accompany a class project. Nevertheless, the type of planning presented above must be done in any study. In some cases, feasibility restrictions may be so severe as to result in a judgment that the likelihood of an adequate test of the hypothesis is too slight to undertake data collection.

All those who undertake educational research—particularly in schools—must come to grips with such practical questions as the following:

• Can permission be obtained to visit classrooms?
• Will the school staff be cooperative?
• How much data can be collected given the human and financial resources available?

These are important questions that researchers must be prepared to answer in any study.

It is important to describe the sample and how it was obtained in as much detail as possible. In this study, the team of observers assigned to each school asked the principal to identify classrooms that represented an open classroom style. They then made an effort to observe in at least one or two of these classrooms, as well as in one or two classrooms not so identified (if such classrooms existed in the school). Aside from this, the observers simply chose classrooms to visit with no particular system in mind. In one of the five schools, however, it became necessary to observe some second- and third-grade classrooms, because there were not enough fourth-through sixth-grade classrooms available. Thus, the final sample was drawn predominantly from the intermediate grades but also included several primary classrooms.

Let us examine two student descriptions of the kinds of classrooms that were observed in the sample.

Student 1

The sample consisted of classes that were available for observation in schools that would allow us entry. Our sample was approximately 27 elementary classrooms from five schools, most of which were on an open classroom basis.

Student 2

The sample of 26 classrooms was obtained from five schools in the San Francisco Bay area that were reputed to have open classrooms. Three of the schools were in urban settings and two were in suburban situations. The schools had at least some classrooms identified by the administration as open. Of the actual classrooms observed, approximately three-fourths were identified as open. Some of the classrooms were multiage; others were not. Grades 2–6 were included; approximately three-fourths of the rooms included grade 4 and above. Class sizes ranged from 25 to 30. The schools differed in the socioeconomic backgrounds of the students. One school was upper middle class; two others were generally middle class; the other two contained many students of low to low-middle socioeconomic classification.

What differences (other than length) do you notice in these descriptions?

_____

_____

_____

_____

_____

AUTHORS' COMMENTS

The description made by student 2 is much more informative. It provides information on geographic location, urban and suburban variations, grade levels, socioeconomic levels, and degree of anticipated openness. As a rule, it is a good idea to provide as much information as possible about the characteristics of the sample.

Most people, we think, base their conclusions about a group of people (students, Republicans, football players, actors) on the experiences they have with a fairly small number, or *sample*, of individual members. Sometimes such conclusions are an accurate representation of how the larger group of people acts, or what that group believes, but often they are not. It all depends on how *representative* (similar) the sample is of the larger group.

Samples vs. Populations

A *sample*, then, refers to any group on which information is obtained. Often, it is selected from a larger group. The larger group is called a *population*. All of the 700 students at San Francisco State University who are majoring in mathematics, for example, would constitute a population of students. Fifty of those students would represent a sample. Those students who own automobiles would be another population, as would all of those who live in the campus dormitories. Notice that a group may be both a sample and a population at the same time. All of the San Francisco State University students who own automobiles would constitute the population of automobile owners at San Francisco State, yet also represent a sample of all the automobile owners at state universities in the United States.

Whenever possible, a researcher tries to study the entire population in which she or he is interested. Often, however, this is very difficult to do. Many populations of interest are very large, diverse, and scattered over a large geographic area. Finding, let alone contacting, all of the members can be very difficult, time-consuming, and/or expensive. For that reason, researchers must, of necessity, often select a sample to study. That is what happened in the open classroom study.

DEFINING THE POPULATION

The first task in the selection of a sample is to define the population of interest. In what group, exactly, is the researcher interested? To whom does he or she want the results of the study to apply? The population, in other words, is the group of interest to the researcher, the group to which the researcher would like to generalize the results of the study. Here are some examples of populations:

- All of the high school principals in the United States
- All of the elementary school counselors in the state of California
- All of the students attending Central High School in Omaha, Nebraska, during the academic year 1987–1988
- All of the students in Mrs. Brown's third-grade class at Wharton Elementary School

The above examples reveal that a population can be any size, and that it will have at least one characteristic (and sometimes several) which sets it off from any other population. Notice that a population is always *all* of the individuals who possess a certain characteristic (or set of characteristics).

Here are brief descriptions of three groups on which information is to be collected. Do they represent samples or populations?

Group 1
A researcher is interested in studying the effects of diet on the attention span of third-grade students in a large city. There are 1500 third graders attending the elementary schools in the city. The researcher selects 150 of these third graders, 30 each in five different schools, to study.

Group 2

An administrator in a large urban high school is interested in determining the opinions of his faculty about a new counseling program that has recently been instituted in the district. He plans to mail a questionnaire to each faculty member asking his or her opinion of the program.

Group 3

The principal of an elementary school district wants to investigate the effectiveness of a new U.S. history textbook being used by some of the teachers in her district. Out of a total of 22 teachers who are using the text, she selects 6, comparing the achievement of students in the classes of these 6 teachers with those of another 6 teachers who are not using the text.

AUTHORS' COMMENTS

Groups 1 and 3 are examples of samples. Group 2 is an example of a population (notice that all of the members of the faculty are sent the questionnaire).

TARGET VS. ACCESSIBLE POPULATIONS

Unfortunately, the actual population (called the *target population*) to which a researcher would like to generalize is often not available. The population to which a researcher is *entitled* to generalize, therefore, is the *accessible population*. The former is an ideal choice; the latter, a realistic choice. Consider this example.

Research problem to be investigated: The effects of computer-assisted instruction on the reading achievement of first and second graders in California.

Target population: All of the first- and second-grade children in California.

Accessible population: All of the first- and second-grade children in the Laguna Salada Elementary School District of Pacifica, California.

Sample: 10 percent of the first- and second-grade children in the Laguna Salada District in Pacifica, California.

Check your understanding. Here is another example. What is the accessible population?

Research question to be investigated: The attitudes of fifth-year teachers-in-training toward their student teaching experience.

Target population: All the fifth-year students enrolled in teacher training programs in the United States.

Sample: 200 fifth-year students selected from those enrolled in the teacher training programs in the State University of New York.

AUTHORS' COMMENTS

The accessible population is all the fifth-year students enrolled in teacher training programs in the State University of New York.

The more narrowly researchers define their population, the more they save on time, effort, and (probably) money—but the more they limit generalizability. It is also possible, of course, to restrict the population so severely that it becomes of little interest to most people. How many people, for example, are interested in the population composed of all left-handed, blue-eyed, bald men who wear glasses?

One of the essential things for any researcher to do is describe the population and the sample in sufficient detail so that interested others can determine the applicability of the researcher's findings to their situations. Failure to define in detail the population of interest, and the sample studied, is one of the most common weaknesses to be found in published research reports.

■ *Random vs. Nonrandom Sampling*

There are two main types of sampling: random sampling and nonrandom sampling. Here is an example of each.

Example 1 (random sampling)
The dean of a school of education in a large Midwestern university wishes to find out how her faculty members feel about the sabbatical leave requirements currently in operation at the university. She places all 150 names of the school faculty in a hat, mixes them thoroughly, and then draws out the names of 25 individuals to interview.[1]

Example 2 (nonrandom sampling)
The president of the same university wants to know how his junior faculty members feel about a new promotion policy which he has recently (with the advice of a faculty committee) introduced. He decides to interview the officers of the campus faculty union, the officers of the academic senate, and several department chairs whose judgment and awareness of faculty concerns he has learned to respect.

In example 1, a sample of 25 names was selected from a hat after all of the names had been mixed thoroughly. This procedure is called *random sampling* because every member of the population (the 150 faculty members in the school) presumably had an equal chance of being selected. There are better ways of drawing a random sample, but they all have the same intent—to select a *representative* sample from the population. The basic idea is that the individuals selected are just like the ones who are not

---

[1] A better way to draw a random sample will be discussed shortly, but this gives you the idea.

selected. A researcher can never be sure of this, of course; but if the sample is selected randomly, and is sufficiently large, the researcher should get an accurate view of the larger group. The best way to ensure randomness is to make sure that no *bias* enters into the selection process—that the researcher (or something else) cannot consciously, or unconsciously, influence who gets chosen to be in the sample. We'll talk more about sample size and bias a bit later in the chapter.

In example 2, the president wants to make sure that he talks to those most likely to give him the information he wants; perhaps a random sample of junior faculty members would not feel free to respond honestly. Each member of the population (the entire junior faculty of the university) does *not* have an equal chance of being selected. Most, in fact, have *no* chance of being selected. Hence, the selection process involves nonrandom sampling, or what is sometimes called purposive sampling.

Consider another example.

Example 3
A third-grade teacher compares the number of words spelled correctly by two groups of her students after she has taught each group by a different spelling method.

Does example 3 illustrate random or nonrandom sampling? Explain.

_____

_____

_____

AUTHORS' COMMENT

Example 3 is a nonrandom sample. Notice that the teacher studied her own class—subjects who conveniently were available to her. She has no basis for generalizing to any other population.

Ideally, of course, a researcher wants *not* to sample, but to study the entire population. As mentioned earlier, however, a population study is usually not feasible; so a sample must be selected. When a researcher has made a decision to sample, therefore, he or she should try as hard as possible to obtain a sample that is representative of the population of interest. There are many different ways of obtaining this type of sample, but the three most common are simple random sampling, stratified random sampling, and cluster sampling.

SIMPLE RANDOM SAMPLING

A simple random sample is one in which each and every member of the population has an equal chance of being selected. It is the best way yet devised by human beings for obtaining a sample that is representative of the population from which it has been selected. Define a population as all the eighth-grade students in School District Y. Imagine that there are 500 such students. Select one student at random from this population. His or her chance of being selected is 1 in 500, if the sampling procedure is indeed random.

The larger a random sample is in size, the more likely it is to be representative of the population. There is no guarantee, of course, that the sample will be a representative one, but the likelihood of it being so is much greater with this method than with any other. Any differences that exist between the sample and the population should be small and unsystematic. Any differences that do occur should be the result of chance rather than bias on the part of the researcher.

Here are two more examples of samples. One is a random sample and one a nonrandom sample. Which is which?

Example 4
A researcher wishes to conduct a survey of all of the social studies teachers in a Midwestern state to determine their attitudes toward the new state guidelines for teaching history in the secondary schools. There are a total of 700 social studies teachers in the state. The names of these teachers are obtained and listed alphabetically. The researcher then selects 100 teachers for the sample by selecting every seventh name on the list.

Example 5
The manager of the campus bookstore at a local university wants to find out how students feel about the services the bookstore provides. Every day for two weeks during his lunch hour, he asks every person who enters the bookstore to fill out a short questionnaire he has prepared, and drop it in a box near the entrance before leaving the store. At the end of the two-week period, the manager has a total of 235 completed questionnaires.

AUTHORS' COMMENTS

Example 4 is a random sample; example 5 is a nonrandom sample.

As mentioned earlier, the key to obtaining a random sample is to ensure that each and every member of the population has an equal and independent chance of being selected. This can be done by using what is known as a table of random numbers—an extremely large list of numbers that have no order or pattern to them. Such lists can be found in the back of most statistics books. Table 7.1 illustrates what part of such a table might look like.

For example, if a researcher desired to obtain a sample of 200 from a population of 2000 individuals, he or she would open the book to any page, select a column of numbers, start anywhere in the column, and begin reading four-digit numbers. (Why four digits? Because the population numbers 0001 through 2000 consist of four digits, and the same number of digits must always be used for each person. Person 1 would be identified as 0001; person 2 as 0002; person 635 as 0635; and so forth.) The researcher would then proceed to write down the first 100 numbers in the column that have a value of 2000 or less.

TABLE 7.1   Part of a Table of Random Numbers

011723	223456	222167	032762	062281	565451
912334	379156	233989	109238	934128	987678
086401	016265	411148	251287	602345	659080
059397	022334	080675	454555	011563	237873
666278	106590	879809	899030	909876	198905
051965	004571	036900	037700	500098	046660
063045	786326	098000	510379	024358	145678
560132	345678	356789	033460	050521	342021
727009	344870	889567	324588	400567	989657
000037	121191	258700	088909	015460	223350
667899	234345	076567	090076	345121	121348
042397	045645	030032	657112	675897	079326
987650	568799	070070	143188	198789	097451
091126	021557	102322	209312	909036	342045

Let us take the first column of four numbers in Table 7.1 as an example. Look at the first four digits of the first number in the column: 0117. This indicates that number 117 in the list of individuals in the population would be selected for the sample. Look at the second number. It is 9123. There is no 9123 in the population (Why? Because there are only 2000 individuals in the entire population!) So the researcher goes on to the third number. It is 0864. Hence number 864 in the list of individuals in the population would be chosen. The fourth number in the table of random numbers is 0593. And so number 593 gets selected. The fifth number is 6662. There is no number 6662 in the population, so the researcher goes on to the next number. The process continues until the researcher has selected a total of 100 numbers, each representing an individual in the population who will be selected for the sample. If the table is exhausted before all 100 numbers are identified, the researcher can simply substitute a new system of reading numbers (e.g., the last four digits or the middle four digits).

The advantage of random sampling is that it is very likely to produce a representative sample. Its biggest disadvantage is that it is not easy to do. Each and every member of the population must be identified. In most cases, the researcher must be able to contact the individuals selected. He or she must know *who* number 117 (for example) is. Furthermore, when the researcher wishes to *ensure* that certain subgroups are present in the sample in the same proportion as they are in the population, simple random sampling will not suffice. In this case, the researcher must engage in stratified sampling, as discussed below.

Try another example to check your understanding. Suppose a researcher wishes to obtain a sample of 10 subjects from a population of 100. If the researcher refers to the table of random numbers in Table 7.1 and uses the *leftmost* three numbers in the *second* column to select a sample, what would the number of the first individual be?

AUTHORS' COMMENT

The first individual would be number 16 (016 is part of the third number in the second column, 016265). Notice that the first two numbers in the column cannot be used, since no student would be numbered either 223 or 379 (there are only 100 individuals in the population).

STRATIFIED RANDOM SAMPLING

Stratified sampling is a process whereby certain subgroups, or *strata*, are selected for the sample in the same proportion as they exist in the population. Suppose that the director of research for a large school district wants to find out student opinions about a new ninth-grade general science textbook that the district is considering adopting. She wants to ensure that both male and female students are included in the sample in the same proportion as they exist in the population of students taking ninth-grade general science—a total of 365 students. The steps in the sampling process would be as follows:

1. The director identifies the target population: all 365 ninth-grade students enrolled in general science courses in the district.
2. She finds out that there are 219 females (60 percent) and 146 males (40 percent) in the population.
3. Since she has reason to believe that gender is an important variable which may affect the outcome of her study, she decides to ensure that the proportion of males and females in the study is the same as in the population. She decides to have a sample made up of 30 percent of the target population. Using a table of random numbers, she then randomly selects 30 percent of each gender from the population, which results in 66 female (30 percent of 219) and 44 male (30 percent of 146) students being selected from these subgroups. The proportion of males and females is the same in both the population and the sample—40 percent and 60 percent (see Figure 7.1).

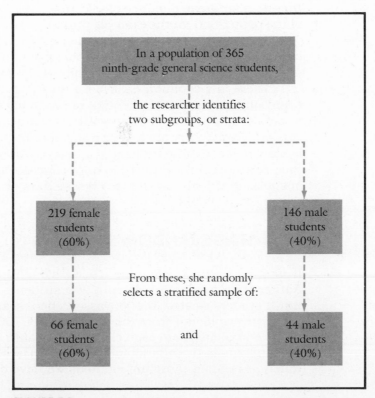

FIGURE 7.1
Selecting a Stratified Sample

The advantage of stratified random sampling is that it increases the likelihood of representativeness, especially if the sample is not very large. With stratified sampling, key characteristics of individuals in the population are included in the same proportion in the sample. The disadvantage is that it requires still more effort on the part of the researcher.

RANDOM CLUSTER SAMPLING

There are times when it is not possible to select a sample of individuals from a population. Sometimes, for example, a list of all members of the population of interest is not available. Obviously, then, simple random or stratified sampling cannot be used. A researcher may not be able to select a random sample of individuals because of administrative or other restrictions. This is especially true in schools. For example, if a researcher's target population is all the eleventh-grade students enrolled in U.S. history courses in a district, it is unlikely that the principals of the various high schools in the district would allow the researcher to select a certain number of individual students randomly from each of the eleventh-grade U.S. history classes for testing. About the best the researcher could hope for would be to study a number of intact classes—that is, classes that are already in existence. The selection of groups, or clusters, of subjects rather than individuals is known as *cluster sampling*. Just as simple random sampling is more effective with larger numbers of individuals, so cluster random sampling is more effective with larger numbers of clusters.

Cluster sampling, then, is similar to simple random sampling except that groups rather than individuals are randomly selected. The advantages of cluster sampling are that it can be used when random sampling of individuals is difficult or impossible, it is often far easier to implement in schools, and it is frequently less time-consuming. The disadvantage is that there is a far greater chance of selecting a sample that is not representative of the population. In the example presented above, the students to be tested would all come from a portion of the classes in the district. It might be the case that these classes differ in some ways from the other classes in the district (thereby distorting the results of the study).

There is a common error with regard to cluster sampling that many beginning researchers make; that of randomly selecting only *one* cluster as a sample, and then observing or interviewing all the individuals within that cluster. Even if there are a large number of individuals within the cluster, it is the cluster, not the individuals, that has been randomly selected; hence, the researcher is not entitled to draw conclusions about a target population of such individuals. Sometimes researchers do draw such conclusions. We repeat, they should not.

TWO-STAGE RANDOM SAMPLING

It is often useful to combine cluster sampling with individual sampling. Rather than randomly selecting 200 students from a population of 3000 ninth graders located in 100 classes, the researcher might decide to select 25 classes randomly from the population of 100 classes and then randomly select 8 students from each class. (Why would this be better than using all the students in three randomly selected classes?[2]) Figure 7.2 illustrates the different random sampling methods we have been discussing.

---

[2] Because three classes are too few to ensure representativeness, even though they are selected randomly.

Populations

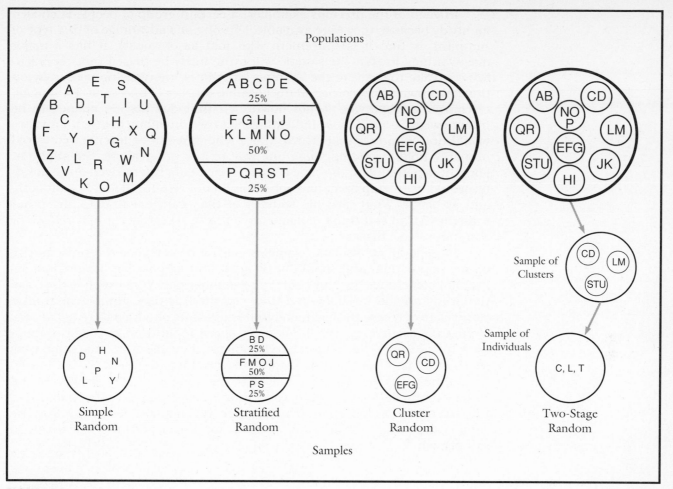

Samples

FIGURE 7.2
Random Sampling Methods

CONVENIENCE SAMPLING

Often, it is extremely difficult (sometimes even impossible) to select a random sample. At such times, a researcher will select a convenience sample. A convenience sample is a group of individuals who (conveniently) are available for study. Thus, a researcher might decide to study two third-grade classes at a nearby elementary school because the principal asked the researcher to help teachers compare the effectiveness of a new spelling text. Here are some examples of convenience samples.

- The manager of the student union at an East Coast university wants to find out how students feel about the food service in the union. He places himself outside the main door of the cafeteria on a Monday morning, and interviews the first 50 students who walk out of the cafeteria.
- A high school counselor interviews all of the students who come to her for counseling about their career plans.
- A news reporter for a local television station asks passersby on a downtown street corner their opinions concerning plans to build a new baseball stadium in a nearby suburb.
- A university professor compares student reactions to two different textbooks she tries out in her statistics classes.

In each of the previous examples, a certain group of people is chosen for study because they were available. The obvious advantage of this type of sampling is that it is convenient. But just as obviously, it has a major disadvantage in that the sample will quite likely be biased (not representative). Take the case of the TV reporter who is interviewing passersby on the downtown street corner. Many possible sources of bias exist. First of all, of course, anyone who is not downtown that day has no chance to be interviewed. Second, those individuals who are unwilling to give their views would not be interviewed. Third, those who agree to be interviewed would probably hold strong opinions one way or the other about the stadium. Fourth, depending on the time of day, those being interviewed quite possibly would be unemployed, have jobs that do not require them to be indoors, and so forth. What possible sources of bias can you find in the other examples? Can you think of some ways that a researcher might reduce or eliminate these biases?

In general, convenience samples cannot be considered representative of any population, and should be avoided if at all possible. Unfortunately, they are sometimes the only choice a researcher has. When such is the case, the study should be *replicated* (i.e., repeated) with a number of similar samples to decrease the likelihood that the results obtained were not simply a one-time occurrence. (We'll talk more about replication in the next chapter.) In addition, the researcher is obligated to describe the sample as thoroughly as possible with respect to variables pertinent to the study. Sometimes it is possible to show that the sample is very similar to the intended population in certain ways. In this case, the researcher can *argue* that the sample is representative. However, it is impossible to show that the sample and population are similar with respect to all pertinent variables. Do you see why?

AUTHORS' COMMENTS

Think about this for a moment. How would a researcher even know what *all* the pertinent variables were?

PURPOSIVE SAMPLING

On occasion, using previous knowledge of a population and the specific purpose of his or her research, an investigator uses personal judgment to select a sample. The researcher assumes that personal knowledge of the population can be used to judge whether a particular sample will be representative. Here are some examples.

• For the past 5 years, the leaders of the teachers' association in a Midwestern school district have represented the views of three-fourths of the teachers in the district on most major issues. This year, therefore, the district administration decides just to interview the leaders of the association rather than to select a sample from all the district's teachers.

- An eighth-grade social studies teacher chooses six students in his class—the two students with the highest grade point average, the two whose grade point average falls in the middle, and the two with the lowest grade point average—in order to get an idea of how the class feels about including a discussion of current events as a regular part of classroom activity. In the past, the teacher has found that the opinions of similar samples have represented the viewpoint of the total class quite accurately.

- A graduate student wants to know how retired people age 65 and over feel about their "golden years." She has been told by one of her professors, an expert on aging and the aged population, that the local association of retired workers is a representative cross-section of retired people age 65 and over. She decides to interview a sample of 50 people who are members of the association to get their views.

Purposive sampling is different from convenience sampling in that the researcher does not simply study whoever is available, but uses his or her judgment to select the sample for a specific purpose. The major disadvantage of purposive sampling is that the researcher's judgment may be in error. He or she may not be correct in estimating the representativeness of a sample. In the first example above, this year's leaders of the teachers' association may hold markedly different views from those of their members. Figure 7.3 illustrates the methods of convenience and purposive sampling.

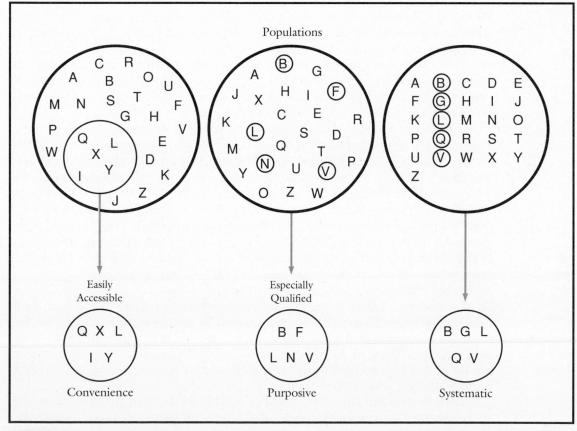

FIGURE 7.3
Nonrandom Sampling Methods

Here are two examples of samples. Which one is a convenience sample and which is a purposive sample?

Example 1
A university professor interviews two leaders of the Progressive Students Association, a campus group noted for its radical position on every issue affecting the campus community.

Example 2
A high school teacher of physical education interviews several people sitting near him at a major-league baseball game about the comparative merits of professional baseball players vis-à-vis professional football players.

AUTHORS' COMMENT

Example 1 is a purposive sample; example 2 is a convenience sample.

■ *Sample Size*

Drawing conclusions about a population after studying a sample is never totally satisfactory, since a researcher can never be sure that the sample is perfectly representative of a population. There are bound to be some differences between the sample and the population; however, if the sample is randomly selected and of sufficient size, these differences are likely to be relatively insignificant. The question remains, therefore, as to what constitutes an adequate, or sufficient, sample size.

Unfortunately, there is no clear-cut answer to this question. Suppose a researcher's target population consists of 1000 eighth graders in a given school district. Some sample sizes, of course, would obviously be too small. Samples with only 1 or 2 or 3 individuals, for example, could not possibly be representative. Probably any sample with fewer than 20–30 individuals would be too small, since it represents only 2 or 3 percent of the district's eighth-grade population. On the other hand, a sample can be too large, given the amount of time and effort the researcher must put into obtaining it. In the current example, a sample of 250 or more—or a quarter of the population—would probably be needlessly large. But what about samples of 50 or 100? Would these be sufficiently large? Would a sample of 200 be too large? At what point, exactly, does a sample stop being too small and become sufficiently large? The best answer is that a sample should be "as large as the researcher can obtain with a reasonable expenditure of time and energy." This, of course, is not as useful a guideline as researchers would like, but it suggests that researchers should try to obtain as large a sample as they reasonably can.

Students often question whether a table of random numbers actually gives everyone in a population an equal chance of being selected. Intuitively, it seems that a person with a sequence of identical numbers (e.g., 666) has less of a chance of being selected than a person whose number is 682. This

TABLE 7.2 **Illustration of Equal Probability of Numbers in a Population**

	1	2	3	4	5	6	7	8	9
0	01 = Albert	02 = Sue	03 = Bill						
1	11 = Ramon								
2									
3									
4									
5	51 = Bud								
6						66 = Juan		68 = Lee	
7									
8									
9									

is not the case, however, as is illustrated in Table 7.2. Assume that a population consists of 99 people, each of whom is assigned a number from 01 to 99. The researcher wishes to draw a random sample of 20 people. With a random process, each of the individuals listed in Table 7.2 has the same chance of being selected—that is, the person numbered 66 is no less (or more) likely to be selected than the person numbered 68, or 51, or 2.

■ *A Final Word*

Our discussion so far has addressed various ways of obtaining or selecting a sample. It is crucial to remember, however, that the actual sample in a study does *not* consist of those selected or originally identified, but those on whom information is obtained. Many times the final sample is different from the sample originally selected because some subjects refuse to participate, move away, become ill, and so forth. When generalizations are made to any population, it is the final sample that counts.

■ *Summary*

In this chapter, we introduced the concept of sampling—the process of selecting the subjects of a study. We discussed the difference between a sample and a population, and distinguished between a target population and an accessible population. We discussed the difference between random and nonrandom sampling. We then presented several types of sampling, including stratified random sampling, cluster random sampling, two-stage sampling, convenience sampling, and purposive sampling. Finally, we offered a few comments about sample size.

Key Concepts Discussed in This Chapter

sample
sampling
population
target population
accessible population
random sample
table of random numbers
nonrandom sample

simple random sampling
stratified random sampling
two-stage random sampling
cluster sampling
convenience sampling
purposive sampling
sample size

How Far Along Should I Be at This Point?

At this point, you should understand what is meant by the terms "sampling" and "sample." You should be able to explain what a random sample is—and be able to use a table of random numbers to obtain one—but also understand why such a sample is often difficult to obtain. You should be able to explain the difference between an accessible population and a target population.

Evaluate your progress, therefore, by checking each of the following. At this point, you should have accomplished each of the tasks listed at the end of the preceding chapters. (If not, review and accomplish them before going any further.) Furthermore, you should be able to:

• Explain the difference between a sample and a population.
• Explain the difference between a target and an accessible population.
• Explain what is meant by the term "random sample."
• Identify examples of random as opposed to purposive and/or convenience samples.
• Use a table of random numbers to select a random sample.

What's Next?

In the next chapter, we begin to talk about generalizing from a sample to a population, and introduce the concept that represents this process—external validity. We will distinguish between population generalization and ecological generalization, and explain when generalization is, and when it is not, appropriate. We will also suggest a procedure to follow when generalizing is not warranted.

For Further Reading

Jaeger, R. M. 1984. *Sampling in education and the social sciences.* New York: Longman.
Kish, L. 1965. *Survey sampling.* New York: John Wiley & Sons.
Rosenthal, R., & Rosnow, R. L. 1975. *The volunteer subject.* New York: John Wiley & Sons.
Sudman, S. 1976. *Applied sampling.* New York: Academic Press.
Williams, B. 1978. *A sampler on sampling.* New York: John Wiley & Sons.

Chapter Eight

GENERALIZING FROM SAMPLES TO POPULATIONS

I n this chapter, we talk about generalizing from a sample to a population, and introduce the concept that represents this process—*external validity*. We will distinguish between population and ecological generalization, and explain when both types of generalization are, and when they are not, appropriate. We will also suggest a procedure to follow when generalizing is not warranted.

You will be asked to look at several examples of research (in which one of the authors has participated) for which random sampling was not feasible. You will be asked to evaluate both the adequacy of the description of the sample involved and the legitimacy of generalizing to the intended population.

After completing this chapter, you will have identified both a target and an accessible population for your proposed study, and stated not only an ideal but also a feasible sampling procedure to follow.

■ *Generalizing*

As indicated in Chapter Seven, we generalize when we apply the findings of a particular study to people or settings that go beyond the particular people or settings used in the study. The former is referred to as *population generalizability*; the latter (with respect to settings), as *ecological generalizability*. Scientific knowledge is built on the idea of generalizing. Every science seeks to find basic principles or laws that can be applied to a great variety of situations and, in the case of the social sciences, to a great many people. Most researchers wish to generalize their findings to appropriate populations. But when is generalizing warranted? When can a researcher say with confidence that what he or she has learned about a sample is also true of the population? Both the nature of the sample and the environmental conditions—the setting—within which a study takes place must be considered in thinking about generalizability. The extent to which the results of a study can be generalized determines the *external validity* of the study.

■ *Population Generalizability*

Population generalizability refers to the degree to which a sample represents the population of interest. If the results of a study apply only to the group being studied, and if that group is a fairly small or narrowly defined one, the usefulness of any findings is very seriously limited. This is why trying to obtain a representative sample is so important. Since the conduct of a study takes a considerable amount of time, energy, and (frequently) money, researchers usually want the results of an investigation to be as widely applicable as possible.

When we speak of representativeness, however, we are referring only to the essential, or *relevant*, characteristics of a population. What do we mean by relevant? Only that the characteristics referred to might possibly be a contributing factor to any results that are attained. For example, if a researcher wished to select a sample of first and second graders to study the effect of color on the teaching of reading, such characteristics as height, eye color, and jumping ability would be judged to be irrelevant—that is, we would not expect any variation in them to have an effect on how easily a child learns to read, and hence we would not be overly concerned if those characteristics were not adequately represented in the sample. On the other hand, characteristics such as age, gender, and visual acuity might (logically) have an effect, and hence should be appropriately represented in the sample. Whenever purposive or convenience samples are used, generalization is made more plausible if data are presented to show that the sample is representative of the intended population on at least some relevant variables. This procedure, however, can never guarantee representativeness on *all* relevant variables.

A misconception that is common among beginning researchers is illustrated by the following statement: "Although I obtained a random sample only from schools in San Francisco, I am entitled to generalize my findings to the entire state of California because the San Francisco schools (and hence my sample) reflect a wide variety of socioeconomic levels, ethnic groups, and teaching styles." This statement is incorrect. Can you explain why?

AUTHORS' COMMENTS

The statement is incorrect because variety is not the same thing as representativeness. In order for the San Francisco schools to be representative of all the schools in California, they must be very similar (ideally, identical) with respect to characteristics like the ones mentioned. Ask yourself: "Are the San Francisco schools representative of the entire state with regard to the ethnic composition of students?" The answer, of course, is that they are not.

One aspect of population generalizability which is often overlooked in methods studies pertains to the teachers, counselors, administrators, or others who administer the various methods or other forms of treatment. We must remember that such studies involve not only a sample of students, clients, or other recipients of the method, but also a sample of those who implement the various methods. Thus a researcher who randomly selects students but not teachers is entitled to generalize the outcomes only to the population of students—and only then if the students are taught by the *same* teachers. In order to generalize to other teachers, the sample of teachers must also be selected randomly—and must be sufficiently large.

Does a researcher always want to generalize? The only time a researcher is not interested in generalizing beyond the confines of a particular study is when the results of an investigation are of interest only as applied to a particular group of people at a particular time—and when all the members of the group are included in the study. An example is a study of the opinions of an elementary school faculty on the issue of implementing a new math program. The results might be of value for decision making or program planning to that faculty, but not to anyone else.

When Random Sampling Is Not Feasible

As we have shown, sometimes it is not possible to obtain or retain a random sample. When this is the case, the researcher should describe the sample as thoroughly as possible (age, gender, ethnicity, socioeconomic status, and the like) so that interested others can judge for themselves the degree to which any findings apply, and to whom and where. This is clearly an inferior procedure compared with random sampling, but sometimes it is the only alternative a researcher has available.

In the vast majority of studies that have been done in education, random samples have not been used. There seem to be two reasons for this. First, educational researchers may not be sufficiently aware of the hazards involved in generalizing from a study that is not based on a random sample. Second, in many studies it simply is not feasible for a researcher to invest the time, money, or other resources necessary to obtain a random sample. As a result, for the findings of a particular study to be applicable to a larger group, the researcher must argue convincingly that the sample employed, even though not chosen randomly, is in fact representative of the target population. This is difficult, however, and always subject to contrary arguments.

Another alternative when random sampling is impossible is *replication*. The researcher (or others) repeats the study using different groups of subjects and different situations. If a study is repeated several times, with different groups of subjects, especially if the groups differ in geographic location, socioeconomic level, ability, and so forth, and the results obtained are essentially the same in each case, the researcher may have additional confidence about generalizing his or her findings.

■ *Ecological Generalizability*

A researcher must also make clear the nature of the environmental conditions—the setting—under which a study takes place. These conditions must be the same in all important respects in any new situation in which the researcher wishes to assert that his or her findings apply. For example, if a researcher studies the effects of a new reading program on third graders in a large urban school system, generalizing the results of the study to the teaching of mathematics is probably not warranted. Furthermore, research results which apply to urban school environments may not apply to suburban or rural school environments. Results obtained with transparencies may not apply to textbooks. What holds true for one subject, or with certain materials, or under certain conditions, or at certain times may not generalize to other subjects, materials, conditions, or times.

An example of inappropriate ecological generalizing occurred in a study which found that a particular method of instruction in map reading resulted in substantially greater transfer to general map interpretation on the part of fifth graders in several schools. The researcher accordingly recommended that the method be used in other content areas, overlooking the unusually varied geography materials that were available and used in his study. Improper ecological generalizing such as this remains the bane of much educational research.

Unfortunately, application of the powerful technique of random sampling is virtually never possible with ecological generalizing. Although it is conceivable that a researcher could identify populations of organization patterns, materials, classroom conditions, and the like, and then randomly select a sizable number of combinations from all possible combinations, the logistics of doing so quickly boggle the mind. Therefore, researchers must be very cautious about generalizing the results from any one study. Only when outcomes have been shown to be similar through replication across specific environmental conditions can researchers generalize across those conditions.

Return now to the earlier description of the sample used in the open classroom study (see pages 126–127 in Chapter Seven).

To what population could the results of this study legitimately be generalized? _____

_____

What additional information would it be helpful to have about this sample?

_____

Suppose that the investigators conducting this study wished to generalize to all elementary classrooms in the San Francisco Bay area. Would they be justified in doing so? Yes _____ No _____

Explain your choice. _____

_____

_____

If you were planning this study and wished to generalize to all elementary classrooms in the San Francisco bay area, describe in detail how you would go about selecting your sample.

_____

_____

_____

_____

AUTHORS' COMMENTS

We cannot generalize with confidence to any population because random sampling was not used. It might be _argued_ that findings could be generalized to open classrooms at the elementary level that are located in schools in heavily populated areas with much variation in socioeconomic level and ethnic background. In so doing, we might wish more information on such dimensions as teacher age, teacher philosophy, parent attitudes, resources available to the schools, administrator attitudes, and extent of school experience with openness.

It would be extremely questionable to generalize to all elementary classrooms in the San Francisco Bay area because (1) only schools reputed to be "open" were included, and (2) two-thirds of the classrooms were identified as being open, a much higher proportion than is true for this population. Thus, we can be fairly certain that these 26 classrooms were _not_ representative of all the elementary classrooms in the Bay area.

There are two ways to select an appropriate sample for such a study. The first is to identify all the classrooms within the grade range desired in the defined geographic area. Each classroom would be given an identifying number, and the classrooms comprising the sample would be randomly selected by use of a table of random numbers. In this particular study, this procedure would pose a problem if the sample size could not be increased to more than 30 classrooms. Not enough classrooms are likely to be found that exhibit a substantial degree of openness. If a sample of 60 or 70 classrooms could be obtained, more open classrooms would likely be found. In order to relate the degree of openness to motivation, it is essential to have classrooms that differ in their degree of openness. (Remember that variability is essential to the study of relationships.)

The second approach is not only to identify the classrooms in a particular grade range, but also to identify them initially as to degree of openness or perhaps simply as open or traditional. We could then sample randomly within each of these classifications to obtain a sample of, say, 15 open and 15 traditional classrooms and then compare these as to degree of student motivation. The difficulty here is that we would need much more information at the outset about the degree of openness of any given classroom and, further, that we must be careful when generalizing not to extrapolate any obtained relationship to include classrooms not falling under one of these two designations. Nevertheless, either of these approaches would be a great improvement upon the sampling procedure that was actually used by the research class.

■ _Another Example of Sampling_

In this section, another example of research in which one of the authors has participated is provided. Again, in this instance, random sampling was not feasible. Following the example, you will be asked to evaluate both the adequacy of the description of the sample and the legitimacy of generalizing to the intended population.

In this study, the researchers investigated relationships between characteristics of teacher behavior in the classroom, as assessed through rating scales and observation records, and certain personality characteristics of teachers, as assessed through questionnaires and projective tests.

The target population for the study was all female elementary school (K–6) teachers in the United States. Since the study was viewed as basic research, the intent was to look for relationships between teacher personality and classroom behavior that would have wide applicability and would constitute general laws of teacher behavior. It was assumed that relationships between teacher personality and classroom behavior would be essentially the same throughout the elementary grades (an assumption that was later shown to be a questionable one). It was decided not to include male teachers because the proportion of male teachers in the elementary grades was low at the time the study was conducted.

The nature of the study virtually precluded the use of a random sample. It was considered essential to maintain a good deal of personal contact with the teachers, because research of this kind can be threatening. In addition, the research procedure necessitated frequent observations in each classroom over a period of time. These considerations, along with the funds and staff time available for the project, precluded use of a sample much larger than 130 teachers. Finally, it was clearly impractical to travel throughout the country collecting data on individual teachers in 130 different locations, as would have been almost certain if a random sample had been obtained.

Instead, two separate samples of teachers in two somewhat different settings (although both in the same geographic area) were used. All the teachers were located in the vicinity of Salt Lake City, Utah. Sample 1 consisted of 83 teachers comprising almost all the faculties of four elementary schools in Salt Lake City itself. Sample 2 consisted of 41 teachers from a school district that included a number of small towns and suburban areas, all approximately 20 miles from Salt Lake City. This sample included almost the entire faculties of two elementary schools.

The procedure for locating these teachers was the same for both samples. The researcher contacted district officials and, after explaining the project and securing their cooperation, requested that schools be identified to meet two conditions. The first was that the principal would be supportive of the study and that no special problems existed in the school to make the collection of data difficult. The second condition was that the schools involved represented the various areas of the community and various backgrounds of the students. After the schools were so identified, meetings were held with the principals; subsequent to their agreement, the researchers met with the entire faculties. The project was described, questions were answered, and the cooperation of the teachers was solicited.

All but four teachers in the city and one teacher in the suburban setting cooperated in the study. In both samples virtually the entire range of age and teaching experience was found. The city sample comprised four schools representing different neighborhoods and different socioeconomic levels. These schools varied from a very modern structure with the latest facilities to an old building with much poorer facilities. In the second sample, both schools served middle-class communities in suburban residential areas. Most of the parents worked in the nearby city. The two samples of teachers differed in some respects: The relationships among certain of the attributes studied were different in the two samples, and the rate of turnover was much higher in the urban setting. On most of the measures obtained, however, the two samples of teachers were quite similar.

Evaluate the adequacy of the sample for generalizing to the intended population. _____

_____

_____

_____

_____

_____

What additional information about these samples would you like to have to determine where the findings of this study might apply? Be specific.

_____

_____

_____

_____

_____

_____

_____

AUTHORS' COMMENTS

Clearly the lack of random sampling makes generalization to the intended population tentative. The information provided about the sample does suggest that it *may* be representative of teachers in many schools throughout the United States. Further, some support for generalizing the findings is to be found in the fact that two separate samples that differed in certain respects were used and that the major findings of the study were essentially the same for both samples. (This, of course, could not be known before the study was completed.) A major finding of the study was that the extent to which teachers exhibited controlling behavior in the classroom was predicted by their score on a questionnaire measure of control need. The fact that a wide variety of age levels, teaching experience, and socioeconomic backgrounds of students was included in the two samples is a positive feature. On the negative side, it seems likely that the sample of teachers would be different from the total population of elementary school teachers in that very few members of ethnic minorities were included in the sample, and no teachers in inner-city areas were included. It could also be argued that teachers in this location might differ from teachers elsewhere with regard to certain attitudes, expectations, and the like. If the study were to be repeated in a large metropolitan area containing a large representation of ethnic minorities in a different geographic locale using more recent data and the results were much the same, one would have much more confidence in generalizing these results.

Your next task is to identify two examples of questionable generalizing from a sample. Take them from your own experience. The media provide a good source of examples. On a television talk show, for example, one psychiatrist discussed his study of airplane hijackers. He described a number of hijackers at some length and pointed out that their outstanding characteristic (which he had discovered by extensive psychiatric interviewing) was a consistent history of failure. His sample consisted of approximately 20 hijackers who were interviewed while they were in jail. Although not explicitly stated, it seemed obvious that the population to whom he intended to generalize was "all hijackers." Would it be appropriate to generalize to

this population? Yes _____ No _____ If not, why not? _____

_____

AUTHORS' COMMENTS

Because there have been many more than 20 hijackings of airliners (many of them successful), those hijackers who were caught are clearly not a representative sample to study. Perhaps the outstanding characteristic of successful hijackers is their consistent history of success.

As you collect your two examples, keep in mind that what you want are examples of generalizations that are questionable because of lack of representativeness of the sample. This process can be seen when people, as they often do, generalize about how individuals will behave in a given situation on the basis of a small and often unrepresentative past sampling of their behavior.

Describe your examples of inappropriate generalizing below.

Example 1

Purpose and/or findings of the study: _____

_____

_____

_____

_____

Description of the sample: _____

_____

_____

_____

_____

Population (stated or implied) to whom a generalization is made: _____

_____

_____

_____

_____

Reason generalizing is questionable: _____

_____

_____

_____

_____

Example 2

Purpose and/or findings of the study: _____

_____

_____

_____

_____

Description of the sample: _____

_____

_____

_____

_____

Populaton (stated or implied) to whom a generalization is made: _____

_____

_____

_____

_____

Reason generalizing is questionable: _____

_____

_____

_____

_____

Assume that you wish to study the following hypothesis:

"Introducing a program of relaxation will improve word recognition for learning-handicapped students in the upper elementary grades."

To what target population would you want to generalize? _____

_____

_____

What population would be sufficiently accessible? _____

_____

_____

How might you get a random sample from the accessible population? _____

_____

_____

_____

If you had to use a convenience sample—in just one or two schools, for example—what descriptive information would you want to try to obtain?

_____

_____

_____

_____

AUTHORS' COMMENTS

The ideal population is probably all the learning-handicapped students in the upper elementary grades in the United States. An accessible population might be all the learning-handicapped students in a metropolitan area—such as the seven counties in the San Francisco Bay area. Random sampling of individuals would require identification of all learning-handicapped students in schools in this area—a difficult, but possible, task. Further, since some students must receive the relaxation program, it is probably necessary to select classes rather than individuals—that is, cluster sampling would be needed. All learning-handicapped classes could be identified without excessive effort. It might be possible to pick 20 classes at random, with 10 to receive relaxation and the other 10 to serve as controls. Although 20 classrooms is not enough to guarantee representativeness, it is a reasonable compromise with feasibility. If fewer than 20 classes must be used, replication is probably a better model to follow.

If you had to use a convenience sample—say, 10 classrooms to which access could be easily arranged—a detailed description of the classrooms and the students becomes important. Variables to be described should include the specific type of learning handicap, gender, age, length of time in special education, and socioeconomic level as a minimum. You would then have a choice as to whether to (1) compare the 5 relaxation classes with the 5 control classes in toto, that is, to ignore particular class membership, or (2) treat the data as 5 replications—that is, to compare pairs of classes, one exposed to each method. We favor the latter approach when so few classes are involved. Such a study might even be done with only one class, divided into two subgroups, one relaxation, one control. In this case, generalization would be extremely hazardous, however, and even more descriptive information about the sample would be needed.

Try another example. Assume you wish to study the hypothesis that among career women age 30–50 career satisfaction is related to the adequacy of their relationship with their father during adolescence.

To what target population would you want to generalize?

_____

_____

What population would be sufficiently accessible?

_____

_____

How might you get a random sample from the accessible population?

_____

_____

_____

_____

If you had to use a convenience sample—in just one or two locations, for example—what descriptive information should you try to obtain?

_____

_____

_____

AUTHORS' COMMENTS

The initial target population is probably all the career women between the ages of 30 and 50 in the United States (or even the world). Although it might be possible to identify (through census or IRS information) all such women, the difficulties involved would probably be prohibitive. Some restriction of the population to be generalized to seems necessary. Limiting the population geographically, for example, to Illinois or even to Chicago is not much help—though these would be meaningful populations. One possibility is to limit the number of careers to be studied (by limiting the population to, say, "self-employed professionals") or perhaps more feasibly to limit the study to a particular career (teaching, nursing, acting). The latter option opens up the likelihood of locating a roster of all population members (even nationwide) through certification agencies or professional organizations. Of course, getting the necessary permission to use their membership lists might be difficult.

Once such lists are obtained, randomly selecting 200 (or 300) individuals would be a simple matter. Since data collection presumably would require responding to questionnaires, collecting the data would be feasible once the respondents were identified—although, as with all survey studies, cooperation might be a problem. Perhaps you can think of a better way to locate a representative sample.

If a convenience sample were to be selected (e.g., members enrolled in certain classes at a local university), it should be described on at least the following variables: number in each career, years employed in career, income and/or status in career, ethnicity, and amount of training received.

At this point, specify both a target population and a procedure for obtaining the sample for the study that you are designing. In defining the population, specify the individuals or groups to be included so that you could proceed to identify all such individuals or groups. You should then describe how you would go about selecting the sample for your study, including how large the sample is to be. It may be that either the nature of your question or practical considerations will prevent you from actually carrying through on the sampling procedure that you would prefer to use. Nevertheless, for this exercise, design the sampling procedure in the best way you can. If you foresee that this ideal procedure will not be feasible, specify how you could in fact obtain a sample in order to collect data for your study. Then state to what population you feel you would be entitled to generalize and why.

Desired (target) population: _____

_____

_____

What would an ideal sampling procedure be for you? Be as specific as possible.

_____

_____

_____

_____

What would your actual sampling procedure be? (If it is the same, write "same.") _____

_____

_____

_____

_____

To what population would you be justified in generalizing?

_____

_____

You now should be sensitized to the dangers of generalizing the findings of a particular study to an inappropriate population or setting. You have also learned an extremely powerful technique for obtaining a sample that does permit generalizing to other individuals, classrooms, and schools, and to other settings—the technique of random sampling. Unfortunately, very few educational researchers obtain random samples for use in their investigations. This is partly because of the difficulties involved, although we believe many more researchers could use randomization if its importance were sufficiently emphasized.

As mentioned earlier, there is an alternative that researchers can employ when a random sample is impossible to obtain. The alternative is replication—repeating a study.

We believe that the replication of studies should be actively promoted in the field of educational research. Too many topics and issues are investigated once and then not pursued. Rarely do we find the same study repeated using different subjects, under different conditions, and with different materials. Knowledge about issues in education could be improved, perhaps dramatically, if replication became more the rule than the exception.

Replication easily can be done at the local level. Several master's degree students at the same college or university, for example, might replicate a previous study as their thesis topics. Similarly, school districts and other local agencies could make it possible for interested teachers, counselors, principals, or others to cooperate in replicating studies locally. Such local replications would, of course, eventually need to be replicated more broadly in order to develop a general body of knowledge; but in the meantime much valuable information could be made available for local decision making. It may be that an enduring body of knowledge may not be possible in education and that ongoing research must and should be carried out on a local scale in order to address local problems. At present, few positions in schools and other agencies include a research function—nor do time demands and resources even permit it—but there is no reason why this need be so. The necessary research skills, we believe, are well within the grasp of many who are (or could become) interested in participating in research.

■ Summary

In this chapter, we introduced the concept of external validity—the process of generalizing appropriately from a sample to a population. We distinguished between population and ecological generalization, and explained when either or both types of generalization were and were not appropriate. We also suggested that the procedure of replication be followed when generalizing is not warranted.

■ Key Concepts Discussed in This Chapter

population generalizability   external validity
ecological generalizability   replication

■ How Far Along Should I Be at This Point?

By now, you should understand what is meant by the terms "population generalizability," "ecological generalizability," "external validity," and "replication." You should be able to explain when generalizing to a particular population is, and when it is not, warranted.

Evaluate your progress, therefore, by checking each of the following. At this point, you should have:

- Accomplished each of the tasks listed at the end of the preceding chapters. (If not, review and accomplish them before going any further.)
- Identified the target population for your proposed study.
- Described an ideal sampling procedure for your study.
- Described the actual sampling procedure you would use.
- Specified the population to which you would be justified in generalizing.

Furthermore, you should be able to:

- Explain the difference between population generalizing and ecological generalizing.
- Explain what is meant by the term "external validity."
- Explain what is meant by the term "replication."
- Identify examples of appropriate as opposed to inappropriate generalizing from a sample to a population.

■ *What's Next?*

In the next chapter, we will begin a discussion of one of the most interesting aspects of planning a study—how to avoid misleading interpretation of the results. Often the intended hypothesis does not really get tested because other factors may account for the results the researcher obtains. Planning ways to avoid this possibility has occupied much of the time and ingenuity of many a researcher.

■ *For Further Reading*

Bracht, G. H., & Glass, G. V. 1968. The external validity of experiments. *American Educational Research Journal*, 5:437–474.

Phillips, D. C. 1981. Toward an evaluation of the experiment in educational contexts. *Educational Researcher*, 10(6):13–20.

Rosenthal, R. 1976. *Experimenter effects in behavioral research: Enlarged edition.* New York: Irvington.

Rosenthal, R., & Jackson, L. 1968. *Pygmalion in the classroom.* New York: Holt, Rinehart & Winston.

Chapter Nine

INTERNAL VALIDITY

Now that you have begun to think about the kinds of instrumentation you will need to obtain the necessary information on your intended sample, the next step is to think through how you will actually get this information. At the same time, you must consider how you will use the information to test your hypothesis. This is often referred to as the "design" of a study.

Obtaining and using information are directly related to a major concern in planning any study—how to avoid misleading interpretations of results. Many times an intended hypothesis does not really get tested because other factors account for the results a researcher obtains. In the language of research, these alternatives are threats to the *internal validity* of a study. Later in the chapter, you will be asked to look at several alternative explanations for the results of a study, and evaluate the likelihood of their occurring.

After completing this chapter, you will have detailed the procedures to be followed in your study. You also will have practiced identifying some of the threats to internal validity that can occur in a study, and examined your proposed study for the existence of such threats.

■ The Procedures Section of a Research Proposal

The procedures section of a proposal describes the arrangements to be made for the collection of data. These include contacting people for permission, selecting subjects, planning how the data will be collected and by whom, scheduling a time for data collection, training data collectors, and so forth. In studies that compare methods or treatments, the procedures for locating or establishing the different methods must also be described. Although it is impossible to specify every detail in advance, a researcher should be as specific as possible. Here is an example, taken from the open classroom study:

> Eighteen observers will be divided into nine teams of two observers each. Each team will visit three classrooms in the same school, one of which is to be a traditional classroom if available. All visits will be made during the same week. Prior to the observation, the principal of each school will be called by one of the observers to arrange the time of the visit. Each classroom will be visited once for a period of 30 to 40 minutes.[1] During this time, the two observers will independently complete both the rating scale for openness and the observation record for attentiveness.[2]

In those instances where details about the selection of the sample and instrument usage have not previously been described, they should be included in this section of the research proposal.[3]

At this point, describe any of the details of your study that have not been discussed in previous sections of your proposal.

Obtaining permission and/or cooperation of subjects: _____

_____

_____

Selecting subjects: _____

_____

_____

Scheduling data collection: _____

_____

_____

Training data collectors: _____

_____

_____

Establishing treatments (if applicable): _____

_____

_____

---

[1] This is a weak part of the procedure because it is unlikely that reliable measurements can be obtained from only one observation period.
[2] Note that no information is given as to how (or whether) observers are to be trained.
[3] In the open classroom study, these details were provided earlier (see Chapters Five and Seven).

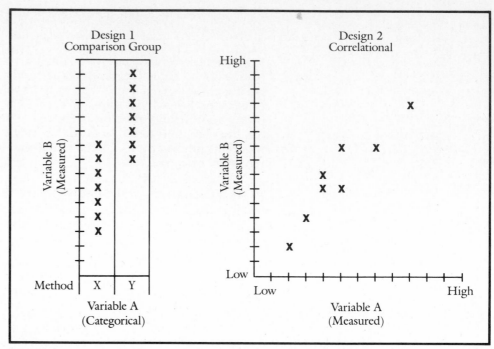

FIGURE 9.1
A Comparison of a Comparison-Group and a Correlational Design

■ The "Design" of a Study

In educational research, two basic designs are used to investigate relationships: the comparison-group design and the correlational design. The *comparison-group design* compares two or more groups or sets of scores in order to test the hypothesis. A common example occurs when a group receiving a particular intervention or treatment is compared with a group not receiving the treatment. When this design is used, one of the variables is a categorical variable; the other is (usually) a measured variable. In a *correlational design*, both variables are measured variables and a score on each is obtained for each unit (usually a person) studied.

These different designs require different planning for data collection and different methods for presenting data in order to test a hypothesis. In the comparison-group design, one set of scores (as a whole) is compared with one or more other sets of scores (as a whole). In the correlational design, pairs of scores are plotted and the resulting pattern is analyzed to determine results.

It is important at this stage of planning to be clear as to how the data, once collected, will be studied in relation to your hypothesis. Figure 9.1 illustrates the difference between the two designs. Each small **x** represents one score. The fictitious data presented for the comparison-group design illustrate that those subjects who were taught by Method Y obtained higher scores on Variable B. The fictitious data presented for the correlational design illustrate that those subjects who scored higher on Variable A also scored higher on Variable B (whereas those who scored lower on Variable A also scored lower on Variable B).[4]

---

[4] You may need to study these diagrams in order to see that this is the case.

Let us apply these designs to the open classroom study. You will recall in that study that the two variables, openness and motivation, were both measured variables, and hence a correlational design was the appropriate one to use. In the correlational design in Figure 9.1 (Design 2), imagine that A represents scores on the variable openness, and that B represents scores on the variable motivation. What can you say about the hypothesis stated earlier that higher openness will be accompanied by higher motivation?

_____

_____

_____

AUTHORS' COMMENTS

Figure 9.1 would support the hypothesis because classrooms with higher scores on openness also tend to have higher scores on motivation.

You may recall our earlier discussion[5] of how measured variables, such as openness, can be treated as categorical variables, as when classrooms identified as "high" in openness are compared with those identified as "low" in openness. If this were done (although we would not recommend doing so, since it would ignore differences within each category), the comparison-group design would then be the appropriate one to use. In the comparison-group design in Figure 9.1 (Design 1), Variable A would represent degree of openness ("high" vs. "low"), and Variable B would represent motivation. If a comparison-group design were used, the procedures section of the proposal would have to state how classrooms of each type would be identified. This could be done by measuring the amount of openness (as in the correlational design) in a sample of classrooms, and then selecting high-scoring and low-scoring classes (see Figure 9.2). It could also be done in other ways, such as by having the principals of the schools identify classrooms of each type or by

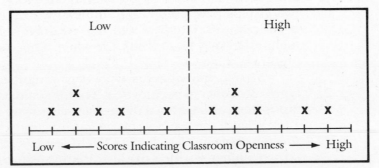

FIGURE 9.2
Changing a Measured Variable to a Categorical Variable

[5] See pages 31–34 in Chapter Three.

training teachers to establish these types of classrooms. In many studies of course, the comparison-group method *must* be used. Why?

_____

_____

_____

AUTHORS' COMMENTS

The comparison-group method must be used when the categorical variable cannot be measured—it does not exist as a matter of degree (e.g., a study comparing phonics with whole-word methods of teaching reading).

We will return to the topic of design in Chapter Ten, but for now it is important to be clear about which basic design you plan to use since it makes a difference when we consider the issue of internal validity. Therefore, in the space below, indicate which design you intend to use, and why.

_____

_____

_____

The Meaning of Internal Validity

Let us imagine that the results of a study show that high school students taught by the "inquiry method" score higher on a test of critical thinking, on the average, than do students taught by the "lecture method." Is this difference in scores due to the difference in methods—to the fact that the two groups have been taught differently? Certainly, the researcher who is conducting the study would like to draw such a conclusion. Your first inclination may be to think the same. This may not be a legitimate interpretation, however.

What if the students who were taught by the inquiry method were better students to begin with? What if some of the students in the inquiry group were also taking a related course during this time at a nearby university? What if the teachers of the inquiry group were simply better teachers? Any of these (or other) factors might serve to explain why the inquiry group scored higher on the critical thinking test. Should this be the case, the researcher may be mistaken if he or she concludes that there is a difference in effectiveness between the two methods, for the obtained difference in results may be due *not* to the difference in methods, but to something else.

The concept of internal validity can be illustrated by the old story "The Dog Who Barked the Sun Up." Each morning after waking, the dog noticed that its barking was followed shortly by the appearance of the sun. "How marvelous," thought the dog, "to be responsible for the appearance of the sun!" Why was the dog mistaken?

_____

_____

_____

AUTHORS' COMMENTS

The dog, of course, was mistaken as to what caused the sun to appear. In research terms, we would say that the dog was ignorant of the operation of other variables.

In any study that either describes or tests relationships, there is always the possibility that the relationship shown in the data is, in fact, due to or explained by something else. If so, then the relationship observed is not at all what it seems, and it may lose whatever meaning it appears to have. Many alternative hypotheses may exist, in other words, to explain the outcomes of a study. These alternative explanations are often referred to as threats to internal validity.

When a study has internal validity, any relationship observed between two or more variables is meaningful in its own right, rather than being due to "something else." The "something else" may, as we suggested above, be any one (or more) of a number of factors—the age or ability of the subjects, the conditions under which the study is conducted, the type of materials used, and the like. If these factors are not in some way controlled or accounted for by the researcher, he or she can never be sure that they are not the reason for any observed results.

Consider another example. Suppose a researcher finds a strong correlation between height and mathematics test scores for a group of elementary school students (grades 1–5). Such a result is quite misleading. Why? Because it is clearly a by-product of age. Fifth graders are taller and better in math than first graders simply because they are older and more mature. To explore this relationship further is pointless; to let it affect school practice would be absurd.

Or consider a study in which the researcher hypothesizes that, in classes for students with learning-handicaps, teacher expectation of failure is related to amount of disruptive behavior. Suppose the researcher finds a high correlation between these two variables. Should he or she conclude that this is a meaningful relationship? Perhaps. But the correlation might also be explained by another variable, such as the ability level of the class (classes low in ability might be expected to have more disruptive behavior _and_ higher teacher expectation of failure). Can you suggest any other variables that would explain a high correlation (should it be found) between a teacher's expectation of failure and the amount of disruptive behavior that occurs in his or her classes?

In our experience, a systematic consideration of possible threats to internal validity receives the least attention of all the aspects of planning a study. Often, the possibility of such threats is not discussed at all. Probably this is due to the fact that such consideration is not seen as an essential step in carrying out a study. Researchers cannot avoid deciding on what variables to study, or how the sample will be obtained, or how the data will be collected and analyzed. They can, however, ignore or simply not think about possible alternative explanations for the outcomes of a study until after the study is completed—at which point it is almost always too late to do anything about them. Identifying possible threats during the planning stage of a study, on the other hand, can often lead a researcher to design ways of eliminating or at least minimizing these threats.

In recent years many useful categories for considering possible threats to internal validity have been identified. Although most of these categories were originally designed for application to experimental studies (see Chapter Ten), some apply to other types of methodologies as well. The most important of these possible threats are discussed below.

Some General Threats to Internal Validity

SUBJECT CHARACTERISTICS[6]

The selection of people for a study may result in the individuals (or groups) differing from one another in unintended ways that are related to the variables to be studied. In comparison-group studies, subjects in the groups to be compared may differ in age, gender, ability, socioeconomic background, and other variables. If not controlled, these variables may "explain away" whatever differences between groups are found. The list of such characteristics is virtually unlimited. Here are some examples.

Age	Speed	Reading ability
Strength	Academic ability	Fluency
Maturity	Vocabulary	Manual dexterity
Gender	Attitude	Socioeconomic status
Ethnicity	Political beliefs	Religious beliefs
Coordination		

In a particular study, the researcher must decide, on the basis of previous research or experience, which variables are most likely to create problems, and do his or her best to prevent or minimize their effects. We shall discuss some ways to do this in Chapters Ten and Eleven.

LOSS OF SUBJECTS[7]

No matter how carefully the subjects of a study are selected, it is common to "lose" some as the study progresses. For one reason or another (illness, family relocation, the requirements of other activities, and so forth), some individuals may drop out of the study. This is especially true in intervention studies,[8] since they take place over time. Subjects may be absent during the

---

[6] Sometimes referred to as selection bias.
[7] Also referred to as mortality.
[8] Studies in which the outcomes of one or more treatments or methods are studied.

collection of data or fail to complete tests, questionnaires, or other instruments. Failure to complete instruments is especially a problem in questionnaire studies, in which 20 percent or more of the subjects commonly do not return their forms. Remember, the actual sample in a study is not the total of those selected, but only the total of those from whom data are obtained.

Loss of subjects, of course, limits generalizability, as we discussed in Chapter Eight. It can also introduce bias—*if* those subjects who are lost would have responded differently from those who completed the study. Many times this is quite likely, since those who do not respond or fail to appear probably do so for a reason. In the example we presented earlier in which the researcher was studying the possible relationship between amount of disruptive behavior by students in class and teacher expectations of failure, it is likely that those teachers who failed to describe their expectations to the researcher (and who would therefore be "lost" for the purposes of the study) would differ from those who did provide such information.

In comparison-group studies, loss of subjects probably would not be a problem if the loss were about the same in all groups. But if there are sizable differences between groups in the numbers who drop out, this is certainly a conceivable alternative explanation for whatever findings appear. In comparing students taught by different methods (such as lecture vs. discussion), for example, a researcher might expect the poorer students in each group to be more likely to drop out. If more of the poorer students drop out of either group, the other method may appear more effective than it actually is.

Here are two fictitious examples[9] in which a loss-of-subjects threat is possible. In each case, see if you can explain why it might be an alternative explanation for any results the teacher or the researcher obtains.

Example 1

A counselor wishes to compare changes in achievement motivation of males and females during high school. During his study he discovers that more males than females fail to complete high school.

Example 2

A researcher wishes to study the effects of a new diet on building endurance in long-distance runners. He receives a grant to study, over a 2- year period, a group of such runners who are on the track team at several nearby high schools in a large urban school district. The study is designed to compare runners who are given the new diet with similar runners in the district who are not given the diet. However, about 5 percent of the runners receiving the diet and about 20 percent of those not receiving the diet are seniors, and they graduate at the end of the first year of the study.

My explanation of how loss of subjects might be a threat in these two examples is as follows:

1. _____

_____

_____

[9] All such examples in this chapter are fictitious.

2. _____

_____

_____

_____

AUTHORS' COMMENTS

Example 1. If the students who dropped out had a greater decrease in achievement motivation than those who remained (as seems likely), their loss will affect the male group more than the female group. The remaining male group will appear to have less decline in motivation than is really the case for the whole group.

Example 2. Since seniors are probably stronger runners, this loss will cause the remaining "no diet" group to appear weaker than the "diet" group.

LOCATION

The particular locations in which data are collected, or in which an intervention is carried out, may create alternative explanations for results. For example, classrooms in which students are taught by the inquiry method may have more resources (texts and other supplies, equipment, parent support, and the like) than classrooms in which students are taught by the lecture method. The classrooms themselves may be larger, offer better lighting, or have more fully equipped work stations. Such variables may account for higher performance by students. In our "disruptive behavior vis-à-vis teacher expectations" example, the availability of support (resources, aides, parent assistance) might explain the correlation between the major variables of interest. Classes having fewer resources might be expected to have more disruptive behavior and higher teacher expectations of failure.

The location in which tests, interviews, or other instruments are administered may affect responses. Parent assessments of their children may be different if they are performed at home than if they are done at school. Student performance on tests may be lower if tests are given in noisy or poorly lighted rooms. Observations of student interaction may be affected by the physical arrangement in certain classrooms. Such differences might provide defensible alternative explanations for the results in a particular study.

Here are two examples in which a location threat is possible. In each case, see if you can explain why it might be an alternative explanation for any results the researchers obtain.

Example 1
A researcher designs a study to compare the effects of team teaching vs. individual teaching of U.S. history on student knowledge of history. The classrooms in which students are taught by a single teacher are markedly smaller than the ones in which students are taught by a team of three teachers.

Example 2
A researcher decides to interview counseling and special education students in order to compare their attitudes toward their respective master's degree programs. Over a 3-week period, she manages to interview all the students enrolled in the two programs. Although she is able to interview most of the students in one of the university classrooms, scheduling conflicts prevent this classroom from being available for her to interview the remainder. As a result, the researcher interviews 20 of the counseling students in the coffee shop of the student union.

My explanation of how location might be a threat in these two examples is as follows:

1. _____

   _____

   _____

2. _____

   _____

   _____

AUTHORS' COMMENTS

Example 1. The difference in size of the rooms in which the students are taught might have an effect. For example, since the room in which the students are taught by only one teacher is markedly smaller, this might produce adverse learning conditions. As a result, the students in that group may do less well on tests—even though, on the average, they may be no different from the team-taught students. The researcher might mistakenly conclude that the team-teaching arrangement was more conducive to learning than was really the case.

Example 2. The informal atmosphere of the coffee shop where 20 of the counseling students were interviewed might cause them to be more relaxed, be less attentive, or take the interview less seriously than the other students who were interviewed in one of the university classrooms. This difference in location could, in turn, affect their responses for better or for worse.

The way in which instruments are used may also constitute a threat to the internal validity of a study. As discussed in Chapter Five, the instrumentation used in a study can lack validity. Lack of instrument validity does not necessarily present a threat to *internal* validity—but it may.[10]

---

[10] In general, we expect lack of instrument validity to make it *less* likely that any relationships will be found. There are times, however, when "poor" instrumentation can *increase* the chances of "phony" or "spurious" relationships emerging.

INSTRUMENT DECAY

Instrumentation can create problems if the nature of the instrument (including the scoring procedure) is *changed* in some way. This is usually referred to as instrument decay. For example, if the instrument is of a type which permits differing interpretations of results (as in essay tests), or is especially long or difficult to score, the scorer may experience fatigue. When a researcher scores a number of tests one after the other, he or she often becomes tired and scores the tests differently at different times (more rigorously at first, more generously later).

Here are two examples in which instrument decay poses a threat. In each case, see if you can explain why it might offer an alternative explanation for any results the researchers obtain.

Example 1
A professor grades 100 essay-type final examinations in a 5-hour period without taking a break. Each essay encompasses between 10 and 12 pages. He grades the papers of each class in turn, and then compares the scores of the first 50 with those of the last 50.

Example 2
The administration of a large school district changes its method of reporting absences. Only students who are considered truant (absence is unexcused) are reported as absent; students who have a written excuse (from parents or school officials) are not reported. The district reports a 55 percent decrease in absences under the new reporting system.

My explanation of how instrument decay might be a threat in these two examples is as follows:

1. _____

   _____

   _____

2. _____

   _____

   _____

AUTHORS' COMMENTS

Example 1. The professor may be placing the students in the class whose papers are graded last at a disadvantage. He may unwittingly be giving them lower (or higher) scores, not because of any difference in performance, but simply because he is tired and is thus giving these papers less careful attention than the ones he graded earlier. Grading papers without letup for 5 hours is a pretty tiring business!

Example 2. The district has changed its scoring system. Since only students who are truant are now counted as absent, it may appear on paper that the number of absences has been reduced. In reality, the reduction is due only to the fact that students who have a written excuse for being absent are no longer counted.

DATA COLLECTOR CHARACTERISTICS

The characteristics of the data gatherers—an inevitable part of most instrumentation—also can affect results. Gender, age, ethnicity, language patterns, or other characteristics of the individuals who collect the data in a study may have an effect on the nature of the data they obtain. If these characteristics are related to the variables being investigated, they may offer an alternative explanation for whatever findings appear. Return to the example we presented earlier of a researcher wishing to study the relationship between disruptive classroom behavior and teacher expectations. Suppose that both male and female data gatherers were used in the study. It might be that the female data collectors (as compared with males) would elicit more confessions of an expectation of failure on the part of teachers, and more incidents of disruptive behavior on the part of students during classroom observations.[11] If so, any correlation between teacher expectations of failure and the amount of disruptive behavior by students might be explained (at least partly) as an artifact of who collected the data.

Here are two examples in which data collector characteristics may pose a threat. In each case, see if you can explain why they might be an alternative explanation for any results the researchers obtain.

Example 1

Two groups of students are compared with regard to their attitude toward a career in the military. Two different recruiting officers administer the same attitude scale to each group. The recruiter who administers the scale to the first group is in uniform; the second recruiter is in civilian clothes.

Example 2

All the teachers in a large elementary school district in California are interviewed by a researcher regarding their future goals and their views on faculty organizations. The researcher's hypothesis is that those who are planning for an administrative career will be more negative in their views on faculty organizations than those who plan to continue teaching. The interviews are conducted in each of the district's schools by the vice-principal of that school.

My explanation of how the characteristics of the data collector might be a threat in these two examples is as follows:

1. _____

_____

_____

2. _____

_____

_____

---

[11] The opposite, of course, could also occur—male data collectors may elicit more negative expectations and more disruptive behavior.

AUTHORS' COMMENTS

Example 1. Responses (pro or con) regarding a military career may well be influenced by the students' personal reactions to the way the recruiting officers are dressed.

Example 2. Responses are likely to be influenced by the teachers' perceptions of the vice-principals. A conclusion in support of the hypothesis may be a result of such perceptions (that administrators don't like faculty organizations) rather than a reflection of the teachers' true opinions.

DATA COLLECTOR BIAS

There is also the possibility that the data collector(s) and/or scorer(s) may unconsciously distort the data in such a way as to make certain outcomes (e.g., support for the hypothesis) more likely. Examples include (1) data collectors allowing some classes more time on tests than other classes; (2) interviewers asking "leading" questions of some interviewees; (3) observer knowledge of teacher expectations affecting quantity and type of observed behaviors in class; and (4) judges of student essays favoring (unconsciously) one instructional method over another.

Here are two examples in which data collector bias poses a threat. In each case, see if you can explain why it might be an alternative explanation for any results that are obtained.

Example 1
An interviewer unconsciously smiles at certain answers to certain questions during an interview.

Example 2
An observer with a preference for inquiry methods observes more "attending behavior" in inquiry-oriented classes compared with noninquiry-oriented classes.

My explanation of how data collector bias might be a threat in these two examples is as follows:

1. _____

_____

_____

_____

2. _____

_____

_____

_____

AUTHORS' COMMENTS

Example 1. The interviewer may cause the interviewees to give more answers of the same kind.

Example 2. Since the observer is biased toward inquiry methods, he or she may unconsciously be

biased to "see more" attending behavior on the part of students in inquiry-oriented classes.

TESTING

In intervention studies, in which data are collected over a period of time, it is common to test[12] subjects at the beginning of the intervention(s). If substantial improvement is found in posttest (compared with pretest) scores, the researcher may conclude that the improvement is due to the intervention. An alternative explanation, however, may be that the improvement is due to use of the pretest. Why is this so?

Suppose the intervention in a particular study involves the use of a new textbook. The researcher wants to see if students score higher on an achievement test if they are taught the subject using the new text as compared with students who have used the regular text in the past. The researcher pretests the students before the new textbook is introduced, and then posttests them at the end of a 6-week period. The students may be "alerted" to what is being studied by the questions in the pretest, however, and accordingly may make a greater effort to learn the material. This increased effort on the part of the students (rather than the new textbook) could account for the improvement from pretest to posttest. It may also be that "practice" on the pretest by itself is responsible for the improvement; students may discuss the test or they may look up the answers.

Consider another example. Suppose a counselor in a large high school is interested in finding out whether student attitudes toward mental health are affected by a special unit on the subject. He decides to administer an attitude questionnaire to the students prior to the introduction of the unit, and then administer it again after completion of the unit. Any change in attitude scores may be due to the students thinking about and discussing their opinions as a result of the pretest rather than as a result of the intervention.[13] In some studies, the possible effects of pretesting are considered so serious that such testing is eliminated.

A similar problem is created if the instrumentation process permits subjects to figure out the nature of the study. This is most likely to happen in correlational studies of attitudes, opinions, or other variables other than ability. Students might be asked their opinions, for example, about teachers and also about different subjects (in order to test the hypothesis that students' attitude toward teachers is related to students' attitude toward

---

[12] By testing, we mean any form of instrumentation, not just "tests."

[13] Notice that it is not always the administration of a pretest per se that creates a possible testing effect, but rather the "interaction" which occurs between the taking of the test and the intervention. A pretest sometimes can make students more alert or aware of what may be going to take place; as a result, they may be more sensitive to and responsive toward the treatment which subsequently occurs.

the subjects taught). The students may see a connection between the two sets of questions (especially if both sets are included on the same form) and answer accordingly.

Here are three examples in which a testing threat is possible. In each case, see if you can explain why it might be an alternative explanation for any results the researcher obtains.

Example 1
A researcher uses the exact same set of problems to measure change over time in students' ability to solve mathematics word problems. She first administers the test at the beginning of a unit of instruction and administers it again at the end of the unit of instruction, 3 weeks later.

Example 2
A researcher incorporates items designed to measure "self-esteem" and "achievement motivation" in the same questionnaire.

Example 3
A researcher uses pretests and posttests of "anxiety level" to compare students given relaxation training to students in a control group.

My explanation of how testing might be a threat in these three examples is as follows:

1. _____

_____

_____

_____

2. _____

_____

_____

3. _____

_____

_____

AUTHORS' COMMENTS

Example 1. If improvement in scores occurs, it may be due to sensitization to the problems produced by the first test and the practice effect rather than to any increase in problem-solving ability.

Example 2. The students may see a connection (or think they do) between the two types of items, and adjust their responses accordingly.

Example 3. Lower scores for the "relaxation" group on the posttest may be due to the training. But they also may be due to sensitivity (created by the pretest) to the training.

EXTRANEOUS EVENTS[14]

On occasion, one or more unanticipated, and unplanned for, events may occur during the course of a study which can affect the responses of subjects. In the study of students being taught by the inquiry vs. the lecture method, for example, a boring visitor who "dropped in" on, and spoke to, the lecture class just before an upcoming examination would be an extraneous event. Should the visitor's remarks in some way discourage or "turn off" students in the lecture class, they might do less well on the examination than if the visitor had not appeared.

In comparison-group studies, a researcher can never be certain that one group has not had experiences which differ from those of other groups. As a result, he or she should continually be alert to any such influences which may occur (in schools, for example) during the course of a study.

Here are two examples in which an extraneous event poses a threat. See if you can explain why it might be an alternative explanation for any results the researchers obtain.

Example 1

A researcher designs a study to investigate the effects of simulation games on ethnocentrism. She plans to select two high schools to participate in an experiment. Students in both schools will be given a pretest designed to measure their attitudes toward minority groups. School A will then be given the simulation games during social studies classes over a 3-day period while School B sees travel films. Both schools will then be given the same test to see if attitudes toward minority groups have changed. The researcher conducts the study as planned, but a special documentary on racial prejudice is shown in School A between the pretest and the posttest.

Example 2

The achievement scores of five elementary schools using team teaching are compared with the achievement scores of five schools in which the classes are self-contained. During the course of the study, the faculty of one self-contained school is engaged in a disruptive conflict with the principal.

My explanation of how extraneous events might be a threat in these studies is as follows:

1. _____

_____

_____

2. _____

_____

_____

---

[14] "History" is the term usually found in educational research texts. We prefer the phrase "extraneous events" because we think it describes the nature of the threat more accurately.

AUTHORS' COMMENTS

Example 1. The special documentary on racial prejudice shown between the pretest and the posttest in School A may affect the responses of the students. The documentary, in research terms, is the extraneous event.

Example 2. The scores of the school in which the disruption occurred may well suffer as a result, thereby making the self-contained schools as a whole score lower than those that use team teaching.

MATURATION

Often, change during an intervention may be due to factors associated with the passing of time rather than to the intervention itself. Over the course of a semester, for example, very young students in particular will change in many ways simply because of aging and experience. Suppose, for example, that a researcher is interested in studying the effect of special "grasping exercises" on the ability of 2-year-olds to manipulate various objects. She finds that a group of children using these exercises show a marked increase in manipulative ability over a 6-month period. Two-year-olds mature very rapidly, however, and the increase in their manipulative ability may be due simply to this fact rather than to the grasping exercises. Maturation is a serious threat in studies which use only pretest and posttest data for the intervention group, or in studies which span a number of years.

Here are two examples in which a maturation threat is possible. In each case, see if you can explain why it might be an alternative explanation for any results the researcher obtains.

Example 1
A researcher reports that students in liberal arts colleges become less accepting of authority between their freshman and senior years. He attributes this to the many "liberating" experiences students have undergone in college.

Example 2
A researcher tests a group of students enrolled in a special class for "students with artistic potential" every year for 6 years, beginning when they are 5. She finds that their drawing ability improves markedly over the years.

My explanation of how maturation might be a threat in these two examples is as follows:

1. _____

_____

_____

2. _____

_____

_____

AUTHORS' COMMENTS

Example 1. It may be that the "liberating experiences" are the reason for the decreasing acceptance of authority by students between their freshman and senior years, but decreased acceptance also may be due to the fact the students simply have grown older and more experienced.

Example 2. The alternative explanation for the results noticed by the researcher are the same as in example 1—the students simply have grown older, regardless of the instructional method.

ATTITUDE OF SUBJECTS

The way in which subjects view a study and their participation in it can create a threat to internal validity. This phenomenon was first documented at the Hawthorne plant of the Western Electric Company some years ago.[15] It was accidentally discovered that productivity increased not only when physical working conditions were improved (an increase in the number of coffee breaks, better lighting, and so forth) but also when such conditions were made *worse* (a reduction in the number of coffee breaks, dimmer lighting, and so forth). The usual explanation here is that the special attention and recognition received by the workers were responsible. This increased attention and recognition of subjects have subsequently been referred to as the *Hawthorne effect*.

An opposite effect can occur in intervention studies whenever the members of the control group receive no treatment at all. As a result, they may become demoralized or resentful, and hence perform more poorly than the treatment group. It may thus appear that the experimental group is performing better as a result of the treatment when this is not the case. It has also been suggested that recipients of an experimental treatment may perform better because of the novelty of the treatment rather than because of the specific nature of the treatment.

It might be expected, then, that subjects who know they are part of a study may show improvement as a result of feeling that they are receiving some sort of special treatment—no matter what this treatment may be. Although this possibility should not be overlooked, it does not seem to us to be prevalent in education. If it were, we should expect new, innovative interventions to show much more dramatic, and consistent, effects than has usually been the case. Perhaps, unlike the Hawthorne workers, students and teachers do not see interventions as attempts to improve their conditions.

The attitude of subjects is also important with respect to data collection. If respondents do not take a test (or any instrument) seriously, or if they deliberately distort their answers, a major threat to instrument validity arises. This does not necessarily create a threat to internal validity, however, if all treatment groups or individuals are equally subject to such distortion. On the other hand, if one treatment group tries harder on a test, this "extra effort" rather than the treatment itself may account for the group's superior performance. Thus, any reaction (positive or negative) to any part of the instrumentation process can create a threat if it is different in different treatment groups.

[15] F. J. Roethlisberger & W. J. Dickson. 1939. *Management and the worker*. Cambridge, MA: Harvard University Press.

Here are two examples in which an attitudinal threat is possible. In each case, see if you can explain why it might be an alternative explanation for any results the researcher obtains.

Example 1

A researcher decides to investigate the possibility of a reduction in test anxiety through the playing of classical music during examinations. She randomly selects ten freshman algebra classes from all such classes in the five high schools in a large urban school district. In five of these classes, she plays classical music softly in the background during the administration of examinations. In the other five (the control group), she plays no music. The students in the control group, however, learn that music is being played in the other classes, and express some resentment when their teachers tell them that the music cannot be played in their classes.

Example 2

A researcher hypothesizes that critical thinking skill is correlated with attention to detail. He administers a somewhat novel test that provides a separate score for each of these variables (critical thinking and attention to detail) to a sample of eighth graders.

My explanation of how the attitude of the subjects might be a threat in these two examples is as follows:

1. _____

_____

_____

2. _____

_____

_____

AUTHORS' COMMENTS

Example 1. The resentment of the students in the control group may actually cause them to be more anxious during exams, and hence (unconsciously) to inflate their anxiety scores.

Example 2. The novelty of the test may confuse some students; others may think it silly. In either case, the scores of those students may be lower on *both* variables because of the format of the test, not because of their abilities. It may therefore appear that the hypothesis is supported. For such students, neither score is a valid indicator of their ability, and the lack of instrument validity also creates a threat to internal validity.

REGRESSION

Regression may pose a threat whenever change is studied in a group which is extremely low or high in its preintervention performance. Studies in special education are particularly vulnerable to this threat, since the students in such studies are frequently selected on the basis of previous low performance. The regression phenomenon can be explained statistically, but for our purposes it simply describes the fact that a group selected because of unusually low (or high) test performance will, on the average, score closer to the mean on subsequent testing regardless of what transpires in the interim. Thus, a class of students of markedly low pretest ability may be expected to score higher on posttests regardless of the effect of any intervention to which they are exposed.

Here are two examples in which a regression threat is possible. In each case, see if you can explain why it might be an alternative explanation for any results that are obtained.

Example 1

An Olympic track coach selects the members of her team from those who have the fastest times during the final trials for various events. She finds that their average time decreases the next time they run, however—a change that she attributes to differences in track conditions.

Example 2

Those students who score in the lowest 20 percent on a math test are given special help. Two weeks later their average score on a test involving similar problems has improved.

My explanation of how regression might be a threat in these two examples is as follows:

1. _____

_____

_____

2. _____

_____

_____

AUTHORS' COMMENTS

Example 1. Since only the team members with the fastest times are selected, it is very likely that their average time will regress toward the mean, and hence be lower (it is unlikely that the time would be higher). The decrease in average time may be due to this regression effect rather than to a difference in track conditions, as the coach mistakenly assumes.

Example 2. Since all the students who took the second test were poor students to begin with (they scored in the lowest 20 percent on the first test), their higher average score on the test 2 weeks later may be due to the fact that their scores regressed upward toward the mean, rather than to the special help they received.

IMPLEMENTATION

The treatment or method in any intervention study must be administered by someone—the researcher, the teachers involved in the study, a counselor, and so forth. This fact raises the possibility that the intervention group may be treated in unintended ways that are not necessarily part of the method but that give the group an advantage of one sort or another. This is known as an *implementation effect* and it can happen in at least two ways.

The first way is when different individuals are assigned to implement different methods, and they differ in ways related to the outcome. Consider our earlier example in which two groups of students are taught by either the inquiry or the lecture method. The inquiry teachers may simply be better teachers than the lecture teachers.

The second way an implementation effect can occur is when some individuals have a personal bias for one method over the other. Their enthusiasm for the method, rather than the method itself, may account for the superior performance of students taught by this method. This is a good reason a researcher should, if at all possible, *not* be one of the individuals who implement a method in an intervention study. It is sometimes possible to keep individuals who are implementers ignorant of the nature of a study, but it is generally very difficult—in part because most teachers or others involved in a study will usually need to be given a rationale for their participation. Note that preference for a method as a *result* of using it is not a threat; it is one of the by-products of the method itself.

Here are two examples in which an implementation threat is possible. In each case, see if you can explain why it might be an alternative explanation for any results the researcher obtains.

Example 1

A teacher is interested in studying the effects of a new diet on the attentiveness of young children. She gets the parents of her first-grade class to agree to try the diet for 1 month and then compares the attentiveness of her class with that of the other first-grade class in her school.

Example 2

A group of stuttering clients is given a relatively new method of therapy called generalization training. Both client and therapist interact with people in the "real world" as a part of the therapy. After 6 months of receiving the therapy, the fluency of these clients is compared with that of a similar group of clients who are receiving traditional "in office" therapy.

My explanation of how implementation might be a threat in these two examples is as follows:

1. _____

_____

_____

2. _____

_____

_____

AUTHORS' COMMENTS

Example 1. The teacher is overlooking the fact that the children in her class may be affected more by her (probably unconscious) efforts to improve attentiveness than by the diet.

Example 2. Speech therapists who use new methods are likely to be more generally compe-

tent and dedicated than those treating the comparison group. If so, greater posttherapy fluency might have occurred with their clients regardless of whether they used the new method.

■ *Two Studies to Examine*

What follows are descriptions of two studies in which the authors participated. In each case, you should first identify the dependent variable, and then consider each of the threats to internal validity that we have discussed in this chapter. In each of these categories, see whether you can find any specific factors that might threaten the internal validity of the study.

STUDY 1: AN INNOVATIVE CURRICULUM

The purpose of this study was to assess the effects of an innovative social studies curriculum designed for use at the elementary school level. A comparison-group design was used. Ten sixth-grade classrooms that were using the curriculum were compared with ten other sixth-grade classrooms that were not using the curriculum. Since the innovative curriculum required a style of teaching that is somewhat unique, it was necessary to give special training to the teachers who were to use the curriculum. Eight of the curriculum teachers were located in the San Francisco Bay area: the other two were located in a residential suburb of Portland, Oregon. A wide range of pupil characteristics and school environments were represented in the curriculum classrooms. One classroom, located in an inner-city school, contained mostly black children; a second contained a sizable proportion of Mexican-American children who were predominantly of lower economic status. At the other extreme economically were several classrooms in schools located in affluent, exclusively white, residential settings. Altogether, there were nine different schools represented in the curriculum group. The comparison group of classrooms was selected entirely from one suburban school district; seven elementary schools were represented.

The instrumentation consisted of the Application of Generalizations Test[16] given early in the school year and again near the end of the school year in order to assess the ability of students to "apply generalizations," a major goal of the innovative curriculum.[17] The hypothesis of the study was that the students in the curriculum classrooms would show greater gain in being able to apply generalizations than the students in the comparison classrooms.

---

[16] See Chapter Six for examples of the kinds of questions asked in this test.
[17] Other tests were used to assess other objectives of the curriculum.

In the space which follows, list all the possible threats to the internal validity of this study that you can detect in each of the categories listed.

1. Subject characteristics: _____

_____

_____

_____

_____

2. Loss of subjects: _____

_____

_____

_____

_____

3. Location: _____

_____

_____

_____

_____

4. Instrumentation: _____

_____

_____

_____

_____

5. Data collector characteristics: _____

_____

_____

_____

6. Data collector bias: _____

_____

_____

_____

_____

7. Testing: _____

_____

_____

_____

_____

8. Extraneous events: _____

_____

_____

_____

_____

9. Maturation: _____

_____

_____

_____

_____

10. Attitude of subjects: _____

_____

_____

_____

_____

11. Regression: _____

_____

_____

_____

_____

12. Implementation: _____

_____

_____

_____

_____

AUTHORS' COMMENTS

1. *Subject characteristics.* The question must be raised as to whether students in the curriculum and noncurriculum classrooms were comparable with regard to such characteristics as socio-economic status, ethnic composition, and general academic skills that may be related to the attribute tested.

2. *Loss of subjects.* In this study, loss of subjects would presumably be due to absence on the testing date. At the sixth-grade level, it seems unlikely that absence would be related to anything systematically affecting the types of measurements that were made. The exception is that those students from the poorest economic stratum might have a higher probability of being absent. It is possible for a systematic bias to occur if these absences were higher in either the curriculum or comparison groups and if the absent students would score consistently lower or higher.

3. *Location.* A bias could be introduced if more classrooms in either the curriculum or comparison groups contained features that were conducive to the achievement of the objectives of the innovative curriculum, but were not part of the curriculum itself. An example is any schoolwide practice which favored independent thinking. The use of two classrooms in a different geographic location could introduce a bias if certain characteristics of the community tended to foster or retard development of the innovative curriculum objectives.

4. *Instrument decay.* Decay could be a problem if either the tests themselves or the test administrators were subject to some form of systematic deterioration as a result of repeated testing. An example is students writing their answers on the test booklets or defacing them in some way.

5. *Data collector characteristics.* A threat might be present if there is a systematic difference in data collectors for the two groups (e.g., if the testers of one group include more females, more whites, or more young people).

6. *Data collector bias.* The possibility does exist that the individuals doing the testing could differ in their test administration behavior so as to favor (unconsciously) one or the other of the two groups. There is also the possibility that the people scoring the tests might bias the results by knowing to which group a particular classroom belonged.

7. *Testing.* The initial testing might well have a bearing on how students would respond a second time because the exact same instrument was used in both the pretest and the posttest. Because this factor was constant for both groups, it would not in itself introduce any systematic bias. It is possible, however, that the curriculum was made more effective through student "awareness" from the pretest.

8. *Extraneous events.* A problem arises from the possibility of unknown factors occurring dur-

ing the course of the year that might have affected pupil gains (e.g., in-service programs that might have affected the teacher's behavior in the classroom, or unique events that might have affected the students' behavior, such as special television programming).

9. *Maturation.* Because the study was restricted to one grade level, and the period of time between testings was essentially the same for the two groups, it seems unlikely that there would be a maturation bias in this study.

10. *Attitude of subjects.* There are two possibilities here. The first has to do with the attitude of the students concerning test taking. The manner in which they approached the test certainly could affect their performance. It is possible that students in either group might systematically differ in their attitudes and thus create a bias. Second, a Hawthorne effect may exist.

11. *Regression.* No threat should be posed by regression because neither of the two groups was selected on the basis of extreme scores.

12. *Implementation.* The curriculum teachers had received special training in order to be able to implement the innovative curriculum. Since the training was *part* of the curriculum, however, it would not be, in and of itself, an extraneous variable—although generalization to "untrained teachers" clearly is not justified. Still, it is conceivable that the curriculum teachers differed from the comparison-group teachers in other ways such as general teaching competence or general teaching style. If so, that could create a bias.

STUDY 2: THE OPEN CLASSROOM

The second study for you to consider is the open classroom study that we have referred to previously. By now you should be fairly familiar with the details of this study. As you will recall, 27 classrooms in grades 2–6 were visited, each for 30–40 minutes. Each of nine teams of two observers visited three classrooms in the same school. The two members of each observer team independently completed the rating scale for classroom openness and also the observation record for classroom motivation.

Since this was a correlational study, remember that you are looking for other variables (factors) that might account for the finding that the variables of openness and motivation are related.

1. Subject characteristics: _____

_____

_____

_____

_____

2. Loss of subjects: _____

_____

_____

_____

_____

3. Location: _____

_____

_____

_____

_____

4. Instrumentation: _____

_____

_____

_____

_____

5. Data collector characteristics: _____

_____

_____

_____

_____

6. Data collector bias: _____

_____

_____

_____

_____

7. Testing: _____

_____

_____

_____

_____

8. Extraneous events: _____

_____

_____

_____

_____

9. Maturation: _____

_____

_____

_____

_____

10. Attitude of subjects: _____

_____

_____

_____

_____

11. Regression: _____

_____

_____

_____

_____

12. Implementation: _____

_____

_____

_____

_____

AUTHORS' COMMENTS

The dependent variable is class motivation (or, more accurately, attention).

1. *Subject characteristics*. In the open classroom study, the subjects are the classes of students. We must ask: "What student characteristics are likely to be related to motivation?" Two that come immediately to mind are ability and socioeconomic status. It seems reasonable to assume that academically able students are more motivated toward academic activities than those less able, and that students from higher socioeconomic levels are more motivated toward school than those from lower socioeconomic levels. It is also likely that more open classrooms will be found in schools where students are more able and where students are from higher socioeconomic levels.

The most troublesome variable is grade level. Since grades 2–6 were studied, it may be that any relationship between openness and motivation is due to grade level. Students in the lower grades may be more motivated (and their classrooms more open) than those in the upper grades. Perhaps you can think of other characteristics that might explain a relationship between openness and motivation.

2. *Loss of subjects*. There are two possibilities here. First, more of the less motivated students are likely to be absent on the days the data are being collected. The effect of their absence would be to raise the class motivation score. The second possibility is that data would be unavailable for an entire class. Whether this would create a threat would depend on the reason for the unavailability of the data. If, for example, some information was unavailable because teachers refused to supply it, the refusal might suggest a class that is low in motivation.

3. *Location*. It has been our experience that both the parents and the teachers in more affluent schools are more receptive to the open classroom idea than their counterparts in less affluent schools. If this is indeed the case, schools that have open classrooms are more likely to have a greater amount of other resources as well, such as a variety of learning materials and teaching aids—plus a greater amount of parental involvement and support than are found in schools with more traditional classrooms. Such resources would be expected to foster higher motivation in students.

4. *Instrument decay*. There is a potential problem here. If the observers became tired or bored during the later observations, they may have overlooked nonattenders and/or become less aware of indicators of openness.

5. *Data collector characteristics*. The age, ethnicity, and gender of the data collectors might affect the level of observed "motivation."

6. *Data collector bias*. Since each data collector made assessments on both variables for the same class, collector bias is a major problem. Initial impressions of openness might well color subsequent assessments of attention, particularly since the observers were well aware of the hypothesis. Further, at least some observers knew that certain classrooms had been identified by the school principals as either open or traditional.

7. *Testing*. There should be no testing threat because the subjects are not required to respond to any instruments.

8. *Extraneous events*. An extraneous event such as an assembly, a fight on the playground, or a breakdown in cafeteria service might well affect the level of attention of a class during any one observation period.

9. *Maturation*. There is no maturation threat because there is no time interval involved in this study.

10. *Attitude of subjects*. Since the subjects are not required to do anything in the study, the only way in which an attitudinal threat might exist is if students behave differently because of the presence of the two observers.

11. *Regression*. There is no regression threat because the study does not assess change on the part of a group that is extreme in any way.

12. *Implementation*. There may be an implementation threat if teachers of the more open classrooms are also better teachers (regardless of the method they use) because of their experience, training, or personal characteristics.

At this point you should examine *your* proposed study for specific threats in each of these 12 categories. State any problems that you foresee in the spaces provided below.

1. Subject characteristics: _____

_____

_____

_____

_____

2. Loss of subjects: _____

_____

_____

_____

_____

3. Location: _____

_____

_____

_____

_____

4. Instrumentation: _____

_____

_____

_____

_____

5. Data collector characteristics: _____

_____

_____

_____

_____

6. Data collector bias: _____

_____

_____

_____

_____

7. Testing: _____

_____

_____

_____

_____

8. Extraneous events: _____

_____

_____

_____

_____

9. Maturation: _____

_____

_____

_____

10. Attitude of subjects: _____

_____

_____

_____

_____

11. Regression: _____

_____

_____

_____

_____

12. Implementation: _____

_____

_____

_____

_____

◾ *Summary*

In this chapter, we introduced the concept of internal validity. When a study has internal validity, any relationship observed between two or more variables is meaningful in its own right, and cannot be attributed to some other factor(s). Such other factors are, in the language of educational research, threats to internal validity. They include the characteristics of the subjects, the conditions under which a study is conducted, the kinds of materials that are used in a study, and the like. We described and illustrated several such threats in this chapter.

◾ *Key Concepts Discussed in This Chapter*

internal validity	subject characteristics
loss of subjects (mortality)	location effect
instrument decay	data collector characteristics
data collector bias	testing effect
extraneous events (history)	maturation
attitudinal effect	Hawthorne effect
regression effect	implementation effect

■ *How Far Along Should I Be at This Point?*

By now, you should understand what is meant by the term "internal validity," and be able to explain briefly each of the threats to internal validity described in this chapter. You should have described, in some detail, the procedures to be used in your proposed study and have examined it for potential threats within each of the 12 categories discussed.

Evaluate your progress. At this point, you should have accomplished each of the tasks listed at the end of the preceding chapters. (If not, review and accomplish them before going any further.) Furthermore, you should be able to:

• Explain what is meant by the term "internal validity."
• Explain briefly how each of the following factors might be a threat to the internal validity of a study:
   subject characteristics
   mortality
   location
   instrument decay
   data collector characteristics
   data collector bias
   testing
   history
   maturation
   attitude of subjects
   Hawthorne effect
   regression
   implementation effect
• Identify the basic design of your proposed study.
• Review your proposed study for potential threats within each of these categories.

■ *What's Next?*

In the next chapter, we discuss further the comparison-group design and, in particular, a very powerful technique for controlling threats to internal validity—the experiment.

■ *For Further Reading*

Borg, W. R. 1984. Dealing with threats to internal validity that randomization does not rule out. *Educational Researcher*, 13(10):11–14.

Fraenkel, J. R., & Wallen, N. E. 1990. Internal validity. In *How to design and evaluate research in education*. New York: McGraw-Hill, pp. 212–238.

Kenny, D. A. 1979. *Correlation and causality*. New York: John Wiley & Sons.

Rosenthal, R., & Rosnow, R. L. (Eds.) 1969. *Artifact in behavioral research*. New York: Academic Press.

Chapter Ten

RESEARCH DESIGN

In Chapter Eleven we shall return to specific ways in which a study can be planned so as to avoid, or at least minimize, the various threats to internal validity described in Chapter Nine. Before we do so, however, we need to make a further distinction among studies which fit the comparison-group design. We will contrast *experimental* studies with *causal-comparative* studies. As you will see, the experiment is a very powerful way to handle many of the threats to internal validity.

After completing this chapter, you will understand how experimental studies differ from causal-comparative studies, but also how they are similar. You will also be able to describe several commonly used experimental designs and explain their strengths and weaknesses.

Experimental Research

The basic idea underlying all experimental research is really quite a simple one: Try something and systematically observe what results. Somewhat more formally, all experiments consist of two basic conditions. First, at least two (but often more) conditions or methods are *compared* to assess the effect(s) of a particular condition or treatment (the independent variable). Second, the independent variable is directly *manipulated* by the researcher. Change is planned for and deliberately manipulated in order to study its effect(s) on one or more outcomes (the dependent variable). Let us discuss each of these characteristics in a bit more detail.

THE CONTROL OR COMPARISON GROUP

An experiment usually involves at least two groups of subjects: an experimental group and a control or comparison group. (It is possible to conduct an experiment with only one group—by providing all treatments to the same subjects—or with three or more groups.) The experimental group receives a treatment of some sort (a new textbook, a different method of teaching, and so forth), while the control or comparison group receives no treatment, receives a different treatment, or is treated as usual. The control or comparison group is important in experimental research, for it serves the purpose of determining if the treatment has had an effect or if one treatment is more effective than another.

A pure control group is, historically, one which receives no treatment at all. Although this is often the case in medical or psychological research, it is rarely true in educational research. The control group almost always receives a different treatment of some sort. Some educational researchers, therefore, prefer to refer to comparison groups rather than control groups.

Consider an example. Suppose a researcher wished to study the effectiveness of a new method of teaching science. The students in the experimental group would be taught by the new method, but the students in the control group would continue to be taught by their teacher's usual method. The researcher would not administer the new method to the experimental group, and have the control group *do nothing*. Why?

_____

_____

AUTHORS' COMMENTS

Any method of instruction would likely be more effective than no method at all!

MANIPULATION OF THE INDEPENDENT VARIABLE

Another essential characteristic of all experiments is that the researcher actively manipulates the independent variable. What does this mean? Simply put, it means that the researcher deliberately and directly determines what forms the independent variable will take, and then which group will get which form. For example, if the independent variable in a study is the amount of enthusiasm an instructor displays, a researcher might train two teachers to display differing amounts of enthusiasm as they teach their classes.

After the treatment has been administered for an appropriate length of time, the researcher measures the two groups (by means of a posttest of some sort) to see if they differ. Another way of saying this is that the researcher wants to see if the treatment made a difference. If the average scores of the two groups on the posttest do differ, and the researcher cannot find any feasible alternative explanations for this difference, he or she can conclude that the treatment did have an effect and is, indeed, the cause of the difference.

Experimental research, therefore, enables researchers to go beyond identifying relationships to at least a partial determination of what causes them. Correlational studies may demonstrate a strong relationship between socioeconomic level and academic achievement, but they cannot demonstrate that improving socioeconomic level will necessarily improve achievement. Only experimental research has this capability.

RANDOMIZATION

An important aspect of experiments is the random assignment of subjects to groups. Although there are certain kinds of experiments in which random assignment is not feasible, it is a crucial ingredient in the best of experiments and is used whenever possible. Random assignment is similar, but not identical, to the concept of random selection. Random *assignment* means that every individual who is participating in the experiment has an equal chance of being assigned to any of the experimental or control conditions being compared. Random *selection*, on the other hand, means that every member of a population has an equal chance of being selected to be a member of the sample. Under random assignment, each member of the sample is given a number (arbitrarily), and a table of random numbers is then used to select the members of the experimental and control groups.[1]

Three things should be noted about the random assignment of subjects to groups. First, it takes place *prior* to the beginning of the experiment. Second, it is a *process* of assigning or distributing students to groups, not a result of such distribution. This means that you cannot look at two groups that have already been formed and be able to tell, just by looking, whether they were formed randomly or not. Third, random assignment allows the researcher to form groups that, right at the beginning of the study, are as *equivalent* as possible. This is the beauty—and the power—of random assignment. Its use is one of the fundamental strengths of experiments compared with other kinds of research.

The previous statement must be tempered, of course, by the realization that the groups formed through random assignment may still differ somewhat. But usually these differences will be slight, and will not seriously affect the outcome(s) of the study. Random assignment only ensures that groups are equivalent (or at least as equivalent as human beings can make them) at the beginning of an experiment.

Furthermore, random assignment is no guarantee of equivalent groups unless both groups are sufficiently large. No one would count on random assignment having much of an effect if only five subjects were assigned to each group, for example. There are no rules for determining how large groups must be, but most researchers are uncomfortable relying on random assignment if fewer than 40 subjects are in each group.

Here are four examples of randomization. Write RS if random selection is involved, RA if random assignment is involved, B if *both* random selection and random assignment are involved, or O if no randomization is involved.

Example 1 _____
Using all fifth-grade classes in the campus demonstration school, a researcher divides the students in each class into two groups by drawing their names from a hat.

Example 2 _____
All students with learning handicaps in a school district are identified and the names of 50 are pulled from a hat. The first 25 are given an experimental treatment, and the remainder are taught as usual.

Example 3 _____
All third-grade students in an elementary school district who are being taught to read by the literature method are identified, as are all students

---

[1] See Chapter Seven.

who are being taught with basal readers. The names of all students in each group are placed in a hat and then 50 students from each group are selected.

Example 4 _____
The third-period history class is compared with the sixth-period history class.

AUTHORS' COMMENTS

The correct choices are as follows: 1—RA, 2—B, 3—RS, 4—O. Notice that in example 2 random selection is used to obtain the total sample. The researcher subsequently could randomly divide the sample into two groups. However, placing the first 25 selected in the experimental group and the second 25 in the comparison group accomplishes the same end—that is, each student selected has an equal chance at the outset of being placed in either group.

■ *Causal-Comparative Research*

Causal-comparative research attempts to determine the cause or consequences of differences which *already exist* among groups of individuals. A researcher might observe, for example, that two groups of individuals differ on some variable (e.g., teaching style) and then attempt to determine the *reason* for, or the *results* of, this difference. Again, the difference between the groups has *already occurred*. This is in contrast to an experimental study, in which a researcher *creates* a difference between groups, and then compares their performance (on one or more dependent variables) to determine the effects of the created difference.

The difference among groups in a causal-comparative study is either a variable that cannot be manipulated (e.g., ethnicity) or one that might have been manipulated but for one reason or another has not been (e.g., teaching style). Sometimes, ethical constraints prevent a variable from being manipulated, thus precluding an experimental study. A researcher might be interested, for example, in the effects of a new diet on very young children. Ethical considerations, however, might prevent the researcher from deliberately varying the diet to which the children are exposed. Causal-comparative research, however, would allow the researcher to study the effects of the diet if he or she could find a group of children who have *already been exposed to* the diet. The researcher could then compare them with a similar group of children who had not been exposed to the diet. Much of the research on smoking and lung cancer is causal-comparative in nature.

Another example is the comparison of scientists and engineers in terms of their originality. As in correlational research, explanations or predictions can be made from either variable to the other. Originality could be predicted from group membership or group membership could be predicted from originality. However, most causal-comparative studies attempt to explore causation rather than foster prediction. Are "original" individuals

TABLE 10.1 Types of Causal-Comparative Research

Type 1. Exploration of *effects* (dependent variable) caused by membership in a given group.
  Question: "What differences in abilities are caused by gender?"
  Hypothesis: "Females have a greater amount of linguistic ability than males."
Type 2. Exploration of *causes* (independent variable) of group membership.
  Question: "What causes individuals to join a gang?"
  Hypothesis: "Individuals who join gangs have more aggressive personalities than individuals who don't join gangs."
Type 3. Exploration of the *consequences* of an intervention.
  Question: "How might students taught by the inquiry method react to propaganda?"
  Hypothesis: "Students taught by the inquiry method are more critical of propaganda than those taught by the lecture method."

more likely to become scientists? Do scientists become more original as they become immersed in their work? And so forth. Notice that if it were possible, a correlation study would be conducted, but that it is not appropriate when one of the variables (in this case, the nature of the groups) is a categorical variable. Table 10.1 gives some examples of different types of causal-comparative research.

Causal-comparative studies have been used frequently to study the differences between males and females. They have demonstrated the superiority of girls in language and of boys in math (at least at certain age levels). The attribution of these differences to gender—as cause—must be tentative. Gender could hardly be viewed as being caused by ability, but there are many other probable links in the causal chain—including societal expectations of males and females. Like correlational studies, causal-comparative investigations do not involve the manipulation of variables and therefore provide weaker evidence of causation. Causal-comparative investigations often identify relationships that later are studied experimentally.

Once again, the basic causal-comparative approach is to begin with a noted difference between two groups and to look for possible causes, or consequences, of this difference. A researcher might be interested, for example, in the reason(s) that some individuals become addicted to alcohol while others develop a dependence on "pills." How can this be explained? Descriptions of the two groups (alcoholics and pill poppers) might be compared to see if their characteristics differ in ways that might account for the differing choice of drug.

Sometimes, causal-comparative studies are conducted solely as an alternative to experiments. Suppose, for example, that the curriculum director in a large urban high school district is considering implementing a new English program, yet is hesitant because of the cost involved. The director might try the curriculum out experimentally in a few randomly selected classes throughout the district and then compare student performance in these classes with the performance of comparison groups who continue to experience the regular curriculum. Such an experiment might take a considerable amount of time, however, and be quite costly in terms of materials, teacher preparation workshops, and other resources. As an alternative, the director might undertake a causal-comparative study, and compare the achievement of students in school districts that are currently using the new curriculum with the achievement of students in similar districts that do not use the new curriculum. If the results show that students in districts (similar to the director's) using the new curriculum are achieving higher scores in English, the director would have a basis for going ahead and implementing the new curriculum in his district.

Despite their advantages, causal-comparative studies do have serious limitations. The most serious lie in the lack of control over threats to internal validity. Thus, considerable caution must be expressed in interpreting the outcomes of a causal-comparative study. Relationships can be identified, but causation cannot be established. The alleged cause may really be an effect, the effect may be a cause, or there may be a third variable which caused both the alleged cause and effect.

Here are a number of hypotheses conceptualized by our students. Which could be studied best as an experiment and which could be best carried out as a causal-comparative study?

> *Hypothesis 1:* "Deaf high school students in residential settings who receive instruction in English through a combination of signed English and American Sign Language will demonstrate higher levels of written English than those taught using only signed English."
>
> *Hypothesis 2:* "Adult homosexual males have had greater exposure to sexual abuse in childhood than adult heterosexual males."
>
> *Hypothesis 3:* "Male high school students who participate in a 4-week simulation of pregnancy will subsequently demonstrate more responsible attitudes toward parenthood than similar students not participating in the simulations."

AUTHORS' COMMENTS

Hypothesis 1. This hypothesis could be studied using *either* method. The experimental method would require that teachers be trained in each method and students randomly assigned to each method. The causal-comparative method would require the researcher to locate classes already being taught by teachers using the different methods.

Hypothesis 2. This hypothesis could be studied only by identifying groups of male homosexuals and heterosexuals and obtaining information on the sexual history of each. The experimental method, clearly, is not possible. A third method, a longitudinal study in which the researcher followed a sample of boys throughout their early years, would provide better information, but it would be extremely difficult to carry out.

Hypothesis 3. This hypothesis could be studied most appropriately by means of an experiment. Existing examples of the simulation-of-pregnancy technique, as required by the causal-comparative approach, are likely to be rare. Furthermore, the nature of the intervention is such as to make it likely that the more powerful experimental method could be used without great expense or inconvenience.

SIMILARITIES AND DIFFERENCES BETWEEN CAUSAL-COMPARATIVE AND EXPERIMENTAL RESEARCH

Similarities

Both causal-comparative and experimental studies require at least one categorical variable (group membership). Both compare group performances (average scores) to determine relationships. Both typically compare separate groups of subjects.

Differences

In experimental research, the independent variable is manipulated; in causal-comparative research, it has already occurred. Causal-comparative studies provide much weaker evidence for causation than do experimental studies. In experimental research, the researcher can sometimes assign subjects to treatment groups; in causal-comparative research, the groups are already formed—the researcher must locate them. In experimental studies, the researcher has much greater flexibility in formulating the structure of the design.

To check your understanding of the experimental and causal-comparative methods, state below how each might be used as an alternative to the correlational method in the open classroom study.

Experimental method: _____

_____

_____

_____

_____

_____

_____

Causal-comparative method: _____

_____

_____

_____

_____

_____

_____

AUTHORS' COMMENTS

EXPERIMENTAL METHOD

This method requires that at least two groups be formed by the researcher so as to differ in openness. One group of teachers must be willing to restructure their classrooms in order either to fit the definitions of the open classroom (see pages 14–16 in Chapter Two) or to be rated high on all, or most, items on the rating scale for openness (see page 82 in Chapter Five). Since most classrooms, presumably, are not this open, the researcher might use existing classrooms as the comparison group or obtain a second group of teachers willing to structure their classrooms so as to be "nonopen." Thus, the researcher would directly manipulate the independent variable by arranging the classrooms into two types: open and nonopen. If desired, a third group of classrooms might be structured to represent an intermediate level of openness.

The researcher next would attempt to assign students randomly to each classroom type. In order to do so, the researcher must have at least two teachers in each school, teaching the same grade, with each representing one of the two types of classroom. Further, the teachers and the principal must agree to having students assigned randomly—rather than assigning students to classrooms on the basis of prior history, student characteristics, parental preference, or any of the other factors that often affect student placement. As you can see, the conditions needed to carry out an experiment are often difficult to arrange.

CAUSAL-COMPARATIVE METHOD

This method requires that the researcher locate teachers in classrooms that exemplify different degrees of openness. This could be done by observing classrooms, perhaps using the "openness" rating scale, hopefully in randomly selected schools and classes until a number at each extreme (on overall rating) are identified. Note that it is not reasonable to expect, nor is it necessary, that all classrooms of each type be identical. What is essential is that the two types of classrooms be sufficiently different so that the difference can be expected to affect the dependent variable. Since this observation procedure is time-consuming and somewhat inefficient (some classrooms presumably will not fit either type), most researchers would probably shorten it through prior identification. The principal of each school could be asked to identify classrooms of each type—perhaps, again, using the rating scale. These nominations could be verified by observation.

Once classrooms of each type are identified, the researcher might arrange for random assignment of students to classrooms, although the difficulties here are the same as in an experimental study. More likely, the researcher will need to use students who have been, or will be, assigned to classrooms in a nonrandom fashion.

■ *Types of Experiments*

There are many variations of the experimental method; some texts are devoted entirely to them. Although such detail is beyond the scope of this text, we want to introduce you to a few of the most common ones.[2]

WEAK EXPERIMENTAL DESIGNS

Experimental designs are called "weak" when they are very vulnerable to the threats to internal validity discussed in Chapter Nine. Let us illustrate these weak designs with the *one-group pretest-posttest design* shown in Figure

[2] For greater detail, see Jack R. Fraenkel & Norman E. Wallen. 1990. *How to design and evaluate research in education.* New York: McGraw-Hill.

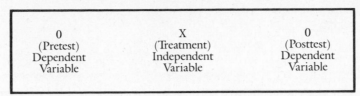

FIGURE 10.1
Example of a Weak Design: The One-Group Pretest-Posttest Design

10.1. The *X* indicates that a treatment of some sort is given; the *O* indicates that one or more measurements are made. Only one group is involved; it is pretested, exposed to the experimental treatment, and then tested again (usually called a posttest). Which of the threats to internal validity discussed in Chapter Nine are present in this design?

_____

_____

_____

_____

AUTHORS' COMMENTS

Possible threats include *maturation* (subjects may have improved regardless of the treatment), *instrument decay* (if the same tests are used), *data collector bias* (if collectors know the intent of the study), *testing* (since a pretest is given), *extraneous events* (during the treatment period), *attitude of subjects* (since subjects are likely to know they are receiving special treatment), *regression* (if subjects are selected on the basis of low pretest scores), and *implementation* (since improvement may well depend upon characteristics of the implementer).

There are times, however, when this deservedly chastised design may be effective. In order to use it, four conditions should be met. First, the outcome variable must be one that is highly unlikely to be affected by maturation, extraneous events, or pretesting. Second, instrumentation must be independent of data collector bias and instrument decay. Third, implementer characteristics must not affect the treatment, or must be an integral part of it. Fourth, the subjects must not be selected on the basis of the pretest. Examples which meet these conditions are rare. See if you can think of one and describe it here.

_____

_____

_____

AUTHORS' COMMENTS

Here are two possibilities.

1. The outcome variable is the performance of a highly specialized ability such as detecting errors in technical language; the instrumentation is mechanical (e.g., computer-recorded errors); the treatment is mechanical (e.g., interactive video); and the group is not preselected.

2. The outcome variable is the application of a particular theory of parenting that requires un-

common behavior such as "paraphrasing" and "ignoring criticism"; instrumentation is carried out by several observers who are different for pretesting and posttesting; training is given by several trained counselors who are appropriately considered an essential part of the treatment; and parents are not selected on the basis of preobservations.

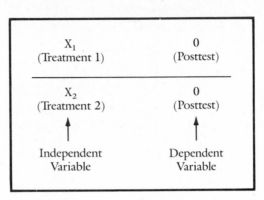

FIGURE 10.2
A Second Example of a Weak Design: The Static-Group Comparison Design

Another weak design, the *static-group comparison*, is diagrammed in Figure 10.2. Here X_1 indicates that an already existing group receives one treatment, and X_2 indicates that another already existing group receives a second treatment. Why is this a weak design?

_____

_____

AUTHORS' COMMENTS

There is no guarantee that the two groups are equivalent at the outset; hence, any difference in results between the two groups may well be due to differences in initial subject characteristics.

TRUE EXPERIMENTAL DESIGNS

True experimental designs are powerful because they provide good control over many of the threats to internal validity that we have discussed. They do so either by including a presumably equivalent comparison group as part of the study or by using the subjects as their own controls. An example is the *randomized posttest-only control group* design, as shown in Figure 10.3. R indicates that subjects are randomly assigned to groups. X_1 indicates that

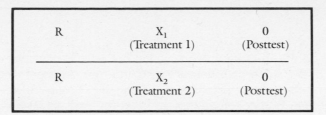

R	X_1 (Treatment 1)	0 (Posttest)
R	X_2 (Treatment 2)	0 (Posttest)

FIGURE 10.3
An Example of a True Experimental Design: The
Randomized Posttest-Only Control Group Design

one randomly formed group receives treatment 1, and X_2 indicates that another randomly formed group receives treatment 2.

The randomized posttest-only design involves two or more groups, each formed by random assignment of subjects. Each group receives a different treatment (or one group receives a treatment and the others do not). All groups are then assessed in some way on the dependent variable. The control of certain threats is excellent. The random assignment of subjects provides for control of subject characteristics, maturation, and regression threats—provided the groups are sufficiently large.[3] Also, since none of the subjects is measured twice, testing is not a threat.

Unfortunately, there are some threats that are not contolled by this design. The first is loss of subjects. Since the groups are presumably equivalent at the outset, we might expect an equal dropout rate for each group. However, exposure to the experimental treatment(s) may cause more individuals to drop out (or remain) than in the comparison group. This may result in the groups becoming dissimilar in their characteristics, which in turn may affect the results, In addition, implementer characteristics, data collector characteristics, data collector bias, and extraneous events are not controlled.

The randomized posttest-only design is often modified through the addition of a pretest. Doing so permits a check on the equivalence of groups at the outset and also if subjects are lost. The negative side of this modification, however, is that it adds the possibility that a testing threat may affect results.

Figure 10.4 presents a diagram of the *Solomon four-group design*.

How would you characterize it? Strong _____ Weak _____

R	0 (Pretest)	X_1 (Treatment 1)	0 (Posttest)
R	0 (Pretest)	X_2 (Treatment 2)	0 (Posttest)
R		X_1 (Treatment 1)	0 (Posttest)
R		X_2 (Treatment 2)	0 (Posttest)

FIGURE 10.4
The Solomon Four-Group Design

[3] At least 40 in each group.

AUTHORS' COMMENTS

This is another strong design. It offers the advantages of pretesting while at the same time assessing its effect. If there is no difference in results for groups 1 and 3, the researcher can conclude that the pretest did not have an effect. The necessity of having four different treatment groups, however, makes this design difficult to arrange.

QUASI-EXPERIMENTAL DESIGNS

Some experimental designs do not include random assignment of subjects to treatment groups. Researchers who use such designs rely instead on other techniques to control (or at least reduce) the subject characteristics threat. Let us discuss two of these designs: the pretest-posttest matched subjects design and the time-series design.

In the *pretest-posttest matched subjects design* (see Figure 10.5), two or more treatment groups are used, but instead of relying on random assignments to equate the groups, the researcher matches subjects on certain characteristics. Existing groups of subjects, such as classes, are used. In the most straightforward method, pairs (triplets, or larger groups) of subjects are matched on one or more characteristics, with one of each pair selected from each treatment group. The matching may be done on the pretest and/or on other variables, provided they have been measured—scores must be available to permit the matching. Two students, for example, whose pretest scores on the dependent variable of reading comprehension and on test scores of vocabulary and "liking for reading" are similar might be paired. M indicates that the subjects are matched.

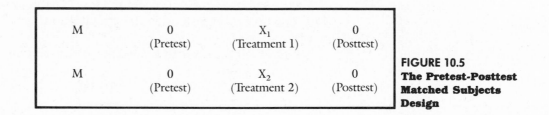

FIGURE 10.5 The Pretest-Posttest Matched Subjects Design

Unfortunately, two problems limit the usefulness of this type of (mechanical) matching. First, it is very difficult to match on more than two or three variables at the same time. People just do not pair up on more than a few characteristics, thus very large groups are needed to begin with. Second, it is almost inevitable that some subjects will be eliminated from the study because no "matchee" can be found for them. When this occurs, the sample is no longer random, although it may have been before matching occurred.

Another form of matching can be done statistically. Each subject receives a predicted posttest score based on the correlation between the posttest and the variable(s) to be controlled. The difference between the predicted and actual posttest scores for each individual is then used to compare treatment groups. This procedure (often referred to as the statistical equating of groups) has two advantages: No subjects are eliminated and any number of variables can be controlled.

Unfortunately, this technique also has its limitations. We will explain more about this procedure in Chapter Eleven, but for now you should simply be aware that it is available as a way to control the subject characteristics threat to internal validity. Remember, however, that both forms of matching are inferior to random assignment. Why?

AUTHORS' COMMENTS

Because it is impossible to match on every variable that might be important to control.

One final, and very important, point about matching (mechanical or statistical): In order to match, the variable to be controlled must be measured—matching is impossible without the necessary information. Many a researcher has overlooked this fact. Obtaining information usually requires planning to do so before or during the study.

The *time-series design* (see Figure 10.6) requires repeated measurements over a period of time, both before and after a treatment. An extensive amount of data is collected on one group through a series of pretests and posttests. If the pattern of scores changes substantially once the treatment is introduced, the researcher is justified in concluding that the treatment is responsible.

$$O_1 \quad O_2 \quad O_3 \quad O_4 \quad X \quad O_5 \quad O_6 \quad O_7 \quad O_8$$

(Treatment Introduced)

FIGURE 10.6
The Basic Time-Series Design

Figure 10.7 illustrates some possible outcomes. The vertical line indicates the point at which the experimental treatment is introduced. The change between time periods O_5 and O_6 gives the same information that would be obtained by a one-group pretest-posttest design. The collection of additional data before and after the introduction of the treatment shows how misleading information obtained through the one-group pretest-posttest design may be.

Check your understanding of the time-series design by interpreting each of the patterns shown in Figure 10.7.

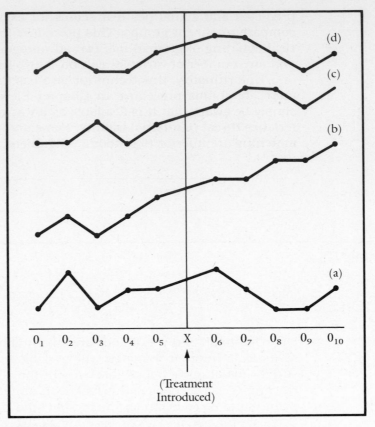

FIGURE 10.7
Possible Outcome Patterns in a Time-Series Design

Interpretation of the results shown in (a) in Figure 10.7:

_____

_____

Interpretation of the results shown in (b) in Figure 10.7:

_____

_____

Interpretation of the results shown in (c) in Figure 10.7:

_____

_____

Interpretation of the results shown in (d) in Figure 10.7:

_____

_____

AUTHORS' COMMENTS

In (a), the improvement is shown to be no more than what occurs from one data collection period to another—regardless of method. You will notice that performance does improve from time to time, but no trend or overall increase is apparent. In (b), the gain from period O_5 to O_6 appears to be part of a trend already started before the treatment was begun (quite possibly an example of maturation). Introduction of the treatment at X has no apparent effect, as the line following appears to be an extension of the line prior to X. In (d), the higher score in period O_6 is only temporary, as performance soon reverts to what it was before the treatment was introduced (suggesting an extraneous event of transient impact). Only in (c) is there evidence of a consistent effect of the treatment.

The time-series design is a strong one, although it is vulnerable to extraneous events (something external could occur between periods O_5 and O_6) and to testing and instrumentation threats (several test administrations are made at different points in time). The extensive amount of data collection required is a likely reason that this design is infrequently used in educational research. In many studies, especially in schools, it simply is not feasible to give the same instrument eight to ten times. Even when it is possible, serious questions of instrument validity are raised with so many administrations. An exception is the use of observational devices which can be used over many occasions with no subsequent threat to their validity (see pages 82 and 85 for examples of such instruments).

All the designs presented so far involve the study of *groups*. At times, however, group designs are not appropriate, particularly when the researcher cannot rely on the usual instruments and observation must be the method of data collection. Sometimes, also, there just are not enough subjects available to make a group design practical. In special education, in particular, an adaptation of the time-series design known as the *single-subject design* has received widespread use. Here data are collected and analyzed for only one subject at a time. For example, researchers who wish to study children suffering from multiple handicaps (such as blindness *and* deafness) may have only a very small number of such children available— say, ten or fewer. It would make little sense to form two groups of five each in such an instance. The use of a single-subject design is preferable.

The basic approach of a researcher using a single-subject design is to expose the same subject, operating as his or her own control, to two conditions or phases. The first condition or period is the pretreatment condition, typically called the *baseline* period, and is identified as A. During the baseline period, the subject is observed for several sessions until it appears that his or her typical behavior has been reliably determined. Then a treatment of some sort, typically identified as B, is introduced. During or following each administration of the treatment, the subject is again observed until the researcher can determine the effects of the treatment.

Typically, though not necessarily, a highly specific behavior is taught during the intervention condition, with the instructor also serving as the data collector—usually by recording the number of correct responses (e.g., object identifications) or behaviors (e.g., looking at the teacher) given by the subject during a fixed number of trials.

In the simplest, or AB design, the baseline measurements or observations are repeatedly made until the researcher feels that stability has been established. The treatment is then introduced, and a series of measurements or observations are made during or after each administration of the treatment. If the behavior of the subject improves during the treatment period, the effectiveness of the treatment is presumed. As an example of the AB design, consider a researcher who is interested in the effects of verbal praise on the attentiveness of a particularly inattentive junior high school music student during orchestra rehearsals. The researcher could observe the student's behavior for, say, 5 days during the orchestra's daily practice sessions, then praise the student verbally after each session and observe the student's behavior immediately following the praise. The problem with this design is that the researcher does not know if any behavior change occurred *because* of the treatment. It is possible that some other variable (other than praise) actually caused the change, or even that the change would have occurred naturally, without any treatment all.

The ABA design simply adds another baseline period. This improves the design considerably. If the behavior is different during the treatment period than during either baseline period, the researcher has stronger evidence for its effectiveness. In the previous example, after praising the student for 5 days, the researcher could eliminate the praise and observe the student's behavior for 5 days when no praise is forthcoming.[4]

The ABAB design features two baseline periods and two treatment periods. This further strengthens any conclusions about the role of treatment, because it permits the effectiveness of the treatment to be demonstrated *twice*. In fact, the second treatment period can be extended indefinitely if the researcher desires. If the behavior of the subject is essentially the same during both treatment phases, and different from both baseline periods, the likelihood of another variable being the cause of the change is decreased markedly.

To implement an ABAB design in the previous example, the researcher would reinstate the experimental treatment (B) for 5 days after the second baseline period and observe the subject's behavior. As with the ABA design, the researcher hopes to demonstrate that the dependent variable (attentiveness) changes whenever the independent variable (praise) is applied. If the subject's behavior changes from the first baseline to the first treatment period, from the first treatment period to the second baseline, and so on, the researcher has evidence that praise is indeed the cause of the change. Look, for example, at Figure 10.8, which illustrates the results of a hypothetical study involving a single subject.

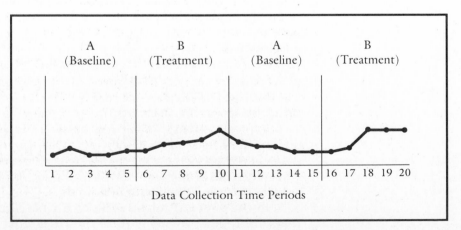

FIGURE 10.8
Hypothetical Illustration of Results of Study Involving an ABAB Design

[4] You will sometimes see ABA designs referred to in the literature as reversal designs.

How would you interpret the results shown in Figure 10.8? _____

_____

_____

_____

AUTHORS' COMMENTS

Notice that a clear baseline is established, followed by improvement during treatment, followed by a decline in performance when treatment is stopped, followed by improvement once treatment is instituted again. This provides fairly strong evidence that it is the treatment, rather than extraneous events, maturation, or something else, that is responsible for the improvement.

Normally, evidence such as that shown in Figure 10.8 would be considered a strong argument for causation. You should be aware, however, that the ABAB design suffers from two limitations: the likelihood of data collector bias (the individual who is giving the treatment also usually collects the data), and the possibility of an instrumentation effect (the need for an extensive number of data collection periods can lead to changes in the administration conditions). The design is also suspect on ethical grounds, in that the second baseline condition is introduced during an attempt to change behavior considered to be important. At least temporarily, the welfare of the subject is presumably sacrificed in the interest of clear research results.

An alternative to the ABAB design is the *multiple-baseline design*. Multiple-baseline designs are used when it is not possible or ethical to withdraw a treatment and return to baseline. When a multiple-baseline design is used, the researcher does more than collect data on one behavior for one subject in one setting. He or she collects data on several behaviors for one subject, obtaining a baseline for each during the *same* period of time. The researcher then systematically applies the treatment at *different* times for each behavior until all the behaviors are undergoing treatment. If behavior changes in each case only after the treatment has been applied, then it is judged to be the cause of the change.

It is important that the behaviors being treated, however, remain independent of one another. If behavior 2, for example, is affected by the introduction of the treatment to behavior 1, the effectiveness of the treatment on behavior 2 cannot be assessed.

For example, a researcher might investigate the effects of "wait time" (waiting quietly until an objectionable behavior ceases) on decreasing various undesirable classroom behaviors in a particular student. Suppose the behaviors are (1) talking out of turn, (2) chewing gum, and (3) making derogatory remarks toward another student. The researcher would begin by applying the treatment first to behavior 1, then to behavior 2, and then to behavior 3. At that point, the treatment will have been applied to all three behaviors. The more behaviors that are eliminated or reduced, the more effective the treatment can be judged to be. How many times the researcher must apply the treatment, of course, is a matter of judgment and depends on the subjects, the setting, and the behaviors involved.

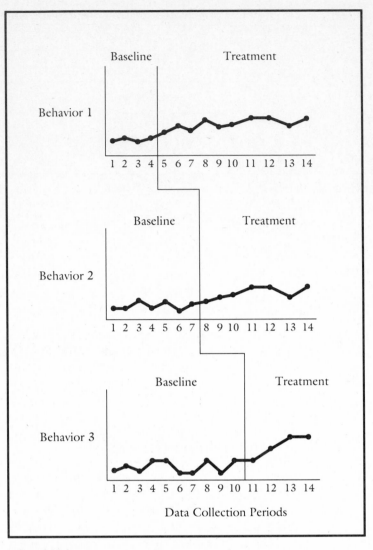

FIGURE 10.9
Hypothetical Illustration of Multiple-Baseline Design

An illustration of the effects of a treatment in a hypothetical study using a multiple-baseline design is shown in Figure 10.9. Notice that each of the behaviors involved changed only when the treatment was introduced.

In practice, results of studies like this hypothetical one rarely fit the ideal model in that the data points often show more fluctuation, making trends less clear-cut. This feature makes data collector bias even more of a problem, particularly when the behavior studied is relatively complex.

To check your understanding at this point, try to apply each of the designs discussed in this chapter to your own study. We recognize that application is easier with some studies than with others. If your study is a correlational one, you can change one of the measured variables to a categorical variable. (We suggest that you do so for purposes of this exercise only—it is generally not a good idea to make such a change.) For each experimental design, draw a diagram and indicate what the X's and O's represent.

Causal-comparative design:

One-group pretest-posttest design:

Static-group comparison design:

Randomized posttest-only control group design:

Solomon four-group design:

Pretest-posttest matched subjects design:

Basic time-series design:

ABAB design:

Multiple-baseline design:

■ *Summary*

In this chapter, we explained why the experiment is a powerful tool for controlling threats to internal validity, and we compared several types of experimental designs with another type of design commonly used in educational research—the causal-comparative design.

■ *Key Concepts Discussed in This Chapter*

experiment	pretest-posttest matched subjects design
experimental research	
experimental design	randomization
causal-comparative design	random assignment
one-group pretest-posttest design	control group
static-group comparison design	comparison group
ABAB design	Solomon four-group design
randomized posttest-only control group design	time-series design
	multiple-baseline design

■ *How Far Along Should I Be at This Point?*

By now, you should understand the differences between experimental and causal-comparative research and be able to describe briefly and draw a simple sketch of several types of experimental designs. You should have identified an experimental design that could conceivably be used in your proposed study.

Evaluate your progress. At this point, you should have accomplished each of the tasks listed at the end of the preceding chapters. (If not, review and accomplish them before going any further). Furthermore, you should be able to:

- Explain how an experiment is a powerful device for controlling threats to internal validity.
- Describe some of the differences and similarities between experimental and causal-comparative research.
- Describe how each of the experimental designs discussed in this chapter can be used.
- Explain the strengths and weaknesses of each of the designs discussed in this chapter.

■ *What's Next?*

In the next chapter, we discuss further some specific ways for planning a study in order to avoid the various threats to internal validity described in Chapter Nine.

■ *For Further Reading*

Borg, W. R., & Gall, M. D. 1989. Exploring relationships among variables: The causal-comparative method. In *Educational research: An introduction* (5th Ed.). New York: Longman.

Campbell, D. T., & Stanley, J. C. 1966. Experimental and quasi-experimental designs for research on teaching. In N. L. Gage (Ed.), *Handbook of research on teaching*. Chicago: Rand McNally.

Cook, T. D., & Campbell, D. T. 1979. *Quasi-experimentation: Design and analysis issues for field settings*. Chicago: Rand McNally.

Fisher, R. 1951. *The design of experiments* (6th Ed.). New York: Hafner.

Fraenkel, J. R., & Wallen, N. E. 1990. Experimental research. In *How to design and evaluate research in education*. New York: McGraw-Hill, pp. 230–273.

Gage, N. 1989. The paradigm wars and their aftermath: A historical sketch of research on teaching since 1989. *Educational Researcher*, 18(7):4–10.

Chapter Eleven

CONTROLLING THREATS TO INTERNAL VALIDITY

Let us now reconsider the various threats to internal validity. What can a researcher do about them? Later on we will ask you to consider ways in which the threats identified in the examples in Chapter Nine might be controlled. You can then compare your ideas with what was actually done.

After completing this chapter, you will have identified specific ways to avoid or minimize many of the threats to internal validity that you recognized in your own study.

◼ General Methods of Controlling Threats to Internal Validity

By now, you have probably recognized that the experimental method is so powerful precisely because it permits more confidence in the internal validity of a study. It does this by (1) ensuring that the treatment is given as intended, since the researcher arranges it, and (2) controlling at least some of the threats discussed in Chapter Nine.

Experimental designs, as you have seen, differ considerably as to how well they achieve these purposes. Also, unfortunately, there are some threats that cannot be controlled by any experimental design—notably data collector bias, implementation, and attitude of subjects. Fortunately researchers have several other general techniques available for controlling (or at least assessing) threats to internal validity. These include:

- Holding a troublesome variable constant (as in limiting the subjects of a study to those of only one gender) or standardizing conditions by holding them constant.
- Obtaining additional information on subjects, conditions, and the like, and then using this information to eliminate or reduce threats, perhaps by matching.
- Using planned ignorance (as in keeping data collectors or implementers from having the information they would need to bias the study).

Let us discuss these techniques as they apply to each of the threats to internal validity we have previously described.

SUBJECT CHARACTERISTICS

In comparison-group studies, random assignment is a powerful control mechanism when it can be used. When it cannot, or when the researcher wishes to have further assurance that certain characteristics are equated, additional information (if available) can be used to match groups mechanically or statistically.

In correlational studies, mechanical matching is impossible, but a statistical procedure similar to statistical matching can be used. We will discuss this procedure in Chapter Twelve.

LOSS OF SUBJECTS (MORTALITY)

Loss of subjects (also known as *mortality*) is perhaps the most difficult to control of all the threats to internal validity. A common misconception is that the threat is eliminated simply by replacing the lost subjects. No matter how this is done—even if lost subjects are replaced by new subjects selected randomly—a researcher can never be sure that the replacement subjects respond as those who are lost would have. In most cases, they are more likely to respond differently. Those who drop out voluntarily are likely to be different[1] from random replacements in ways that affect the dependent variable.

It is sometimes possible for a researcher to argue that the loss of subjects in a study is not a problem. The researcher explores the reasons for such a loss, and then offers an argument as to why these reasons are not relevant to the particular study at hand. In most cases, for example, absence from class on the day of testing probably would not favor a particular treatment group, since it would be incidental rather than intentional—unless the day and time of the testing were announced beforehand.

Another attempt to eliminate the problem of mortality is to provide evidence that the subjects lost were similar to those remaining on pertinent

---

[1] That is, they may possess some characteristics (e.g., lack of interest, no home support, outside jobs) that those who do not drop out do not possess.

characteristics such as demographics (e.g., age, gender, ethnicity), pretest scores, or other variables that presumably might be related to the study outcomes. While desirable, such evidence can never demonstrate conclusively that those subjects who were lost would *not* have responded differently from those who remained. When all is said and done, the best solution to the problem of mortality is to do one's best to prevent or minimize the loss of subjects, perhaps by paying them for their time.

LOCATION

The best way to handle location threats is to hold location constant—that is, to keep it the same for all participants (or as nearly so as possible). In comparison-group studies, for example, a location threat is more serious when experimental and comparison classrooms are in different schools than when there is one classroom of each method in every school in the study. An alternative is to assign locations (e.g., schools) randomly to treatments, but this requires a large number of locations and may be difficult to arrange. If none of these is possible, the researcher should try to obtain information on the different locations. As far as the researcher can determine, do locations differ with regard to resources or other characteristics that might affect outcomes? If this is the case, the researcher should try to equalize such characteristics as much as possible. In correlational studies, the location and conditions of data collection should be standardized (held constant) as much as possible.

INSTRUMENT DECAY

Instrument decay can be controlled in two ways: (1) by standardizing the instrumentation process (by examining test booklets to ensure that parts are not illegible, do not have answers written in them, and so forth) and/or (2) by scheduling data collection so as to avoid data collector (especially observer) fatigue or boredom.

DATA COLLECTOR CHARACTERISTICS

Data collector threats are best handled by using the same data collector(s) throughout. Another possibility is to balance data collectors across treatments or comparison groups, thereby ensuring that each data collector is used equally for all comparison groups. This presumably gives no advantage to any of the groups. It does not, however, handle the situation in which characteristics of a particular data collector might affect different groups differently. For example, the gender of the data collector might affect groups of males differently from groups of females.[2]

In correlational studies, the best solution is to have a different data collector obtain information on each variable, thereby ensuring that a given characteristic of the data collector cannot affect both variables.

---

[2] To control such a threat, male and female data collectors should be "balanced" across such subgroups.

DATA COLLECTOR BIAS

One method of handling data collector bias is to standardize conditions (perhaps by providing training to the collectors) so that data collectors cannot influence the data. Clearly, this approach is more effective when the data collected are less susceptible to personal influence—for example, in pencil-and-paper achievement testing as compared with on-site observation. No matter how hard a researcher tries, however, there is always the possibility that a data collector may unintentionally affect the data. Consequently, we have much more confidence in planned ignorance. There is seldom (if ever) any need for data collectors to know the purpose or hypothesis of a study. Without such information, they cannot consciously affect the data so as to favor the hypothesis.

Still, there are times when it is difficult to prevent data collectors from figuring out the hypothesis—as, for example, when the same observers are used in all treatments. The solution here is to use different collectors for different treatments. Another possibility is to obtain information directly about the data collection process by having an observer present or by making an audio or videotape of the process. This at least permits the researcher to determine whether bias was present.

In correlational studies, the best approach is the same as that suggested for data collector characteristics—use different collectors with each instrument.

TESTING

As you have seen, some experimental designs handle a testing threat by having a pretest administered to all groups. Unfortunately, this does not rule out the possibility that the pretest may make some treatments more (or less) effective. The Solomon four-group design does control for such a possibility, but it is often cumbersome and requires a large enough sample to allow for four groups. An alternative, favored by many researchers, is to eliminate the use of a pretest entirely and rely on random assignment to equate groups whenever possible. When random assignment is not possible, we favor risking a testing threat in order to ensure the equating of groups on at least some subject characteristics through matching.

In correlational studies, the testing threat takes the form of subjects "psyching out" the intent of the study. The best solution is to keep administration of the instruments as independent as possible so that the subjects are less likely to see a connection between them.

EXTRANEOUS EVENTS (HISTORY)

The threat of extraneous events applies only to intervention-type studies. It can ultimately be addressed only by collecting additional information. The researcher should give thought to the kinds of events that might affect the study and plan to keep track of such events whenever possible. This often means staying in sufficient contact with the various groups in the study so as to be aware of extraneous events (changes in the curriculum, community events, and so forth). Sometimes it is advisable to question participants sytematically regarding such occurrences to see if they might have affected results. The best way to control this threat is to have enough subgroups receiving each treatment so that any such events are unlikely to favor one treatment group over another.

MATURATION

The maturation threat also is of concern primarily in intervention-type studies. Maturation can usually be controlled either by random assignment or by matching—that is, by the design of the study. Either method should ensure that groups are equivalent at the outset. If the time interval is the same for all groups, maturation should not favor any particular treatment. In certain types of studies, however, different groups may be expected to mature at different rates. For example, a causal-comparative study might be designed to compare the effectiveness of a particular instructional method for boys vs. girls. Even though the groups were matched on a pretest, any differences in improvement might be attributable to differences in growth between genders, regardless of the instructional method. This possibility can be controlled by adding groups who are receiving no intervention at all (or who are receiving a different method) and then comparing the amounts of growth shown.

ATTITUDE OF SUBJECTS

One solution to an attitude threat is to treat all groups as though they were "special"—not only the experimental groups, but also the control or comparison groups. This might be done, for example, by providing the comparison groups with a special experience that has no direct relationship to the outcome(s) being studied. Another possibility is to inform *all* groups that they are part of the research—although doing so increases the chances that preexisting attitudes toward the treatment(s) may influence outcomes. Another approach is to make the intervention as unobtrusive and matter of fact as possible and thus keep the experimental subjects from knowing they are being treated in a special way (a form of planned ignorance). Finally, the researcher may be able to collect "attitude" information from participants and use it to match groups.

It is important to remember that an attitude threat exists only if the subjects have positive or negative reactions to participating in the study. If their reactions are *due to* the treatments used, then they *should* affect the outcome(s) and they do not constitute an alternative explanation for what occurs.

REGRESSION

The threat of regression is present only in intervention-type studies, and then only if an extreme group (e.g., gifted students or very low-scoring students) is involved. It can be controlled through the design of the study— by obtaining an equivalent comparison group through random assignment and/or matching.

IMPLEMENTATION

An implementation threat also is of concern only in intervention-type studies. There are a number of ways it can be controlled. The researcher can attempt to evaluate the individuals who implement each method on some pertinent characteristic (e.g., teaching ability) and then try to equate the treatment groups on this dimension (e.g., by assigning or using teachers of equivalent ability for each method). Clearly, this is a difficult and time-consuming task.

Another approach is to require that each method be taught by all teachers in the study. When feasible, this solution is preferable, although it also is vulnerable to the possibility that some teachers may have a differing ability in, or preference for, one method over another.

Finally, several different individuals can be used to implement each method, thereby reducing the chances that any one method will gain an advantage. In the event that none of these solutions is applicable, the researcher should attempt to describe the implementation of each treatment and make an assessment of the degree of possible threat.

■ *Two Studies Revisited*

We now return to the two studies analyzed in Chapter Nine for the purpose of identifying specific threats to internal validity. Your task at this point is to suggest ways to eliminate, or at least reduce, the possibility of such threats. We will then describe what was actually done by the researchers who conducted these studies.

STUDY 1: AN INNOVATIVE CURRICULUM

Please reread pages 182–183 in Chapter Nine to refresh your memory as to the threats that impinged on that study. Next, indicate below what, specifically, you would do (if you were planning this study) to minimize each of these threats.

1. Subject characteristics: _____

_____

_____

_____

_____

2. Loss of subjects: _____

_____

_____

_____

_____

3. Location: _____

_____

_____

_____

_____

4. Instrument decay: _____

_____

_____

_____

_____

5. Data collector characteristics: _____

_____

_____

_____

_____

6. Data collector bias: _____

_____

_____

_____

_____

7. Testing: _____

_____

_____

_____

_____

8. History: _____

_____

_____

_____

_____

9. Maturation: _____

_____

_____

_____

10. Attitude of subjects: _____

_____

_____

_____

_____

11. Regression: _____

_____

_____

_____

_____

12. Implementation: _____

_____

_____

_____

_____

AUTHORS' COMMENTS

Here is what the researchers who conducted the study did to try to control these threats. Note that some threats were not completely controlled.

1. *Subject characteristics.* In order to try to ensure comparability of students in the curriculum and noncurriculum groups, the researchers matched each of the noncurriculum classrooms with a curriculum classroom of similar socioeconomic status and ethnic composition. School district personnel provided the information on these variables using somewhat crude indices of socioeconomic level and ethnic composition. Nevertheless, the researchers were fairly confident that the match-up on these variables was quite good, except for one classroom in the curriculum group that was comprised of a large number of children of very low socioeconomic status. A matching classroom that included students with the same degree of economic deprivation in the comparison group could not be found. A subsequent finding that the curriculum and noncurriculum groups scored very nearly the same in the pretest on the various measures provided additional assurance that the treatment groups were comparable at the outset.

2. *Loss of subjects.* No special provision was made to control for loss of subjects. A follow-up of absentees would have been desirable, but this was deemed to require more effort and expense than was warranted. The researchers noted that the number of subjects lost in both curriculum and noncurriculum groups was quite similar, however.

3. *Location.* The only systematic attempt that was made to control location was to select noncurriculum classrooms that matched curriculum classrooms in the socioeconomic and ethnic characteristics of students. Since economic and ethnic characteristics are usually found to be related to such variables as adequacy of the physical plant and resources available to teachers and students, it was believed that some control of these variables was achieved. Further, observations in the classrooms suggested that the curriculum and comparison groups were comparable with regard to school atmosphere, philosophy, and the like— except for some curriculum schools that exhibited a philosophy more consistent with the curriculum. A location bias, therefore, remained a possibility in this study.

4. *Instrument decay.* The test booklets were examined and any with marks on them were thrown out. The tests were not used so extensively as to be subject to much deterioration, nor did the testers work so exhaustively as to make it likely that their performance was affected.

5. *Data collector characteristics.* The same group of three data collectors was used throughout, with each collector testing equal numbers of curriculum and noncurriculum classes.

6. *Data collector bias.* The three testers were hired specifically for that purpose and had no vested interest in how the study came out. Furthermore, in most cases, they were unaware as to which of the comparison groups they happened to be testing. In addition, the prescribed testing procedures were spelled out in detail to decrease the possibility of such a bias intruding.

None of the classroom teachers saw copies of any test until the posttest was completed. In only one class was the teacher present during the pretesting, and this was done to ensure attention to the task. Results showed that her class did not show an atypical amount of gain in test score. All tests were machine-scored to ensure comparability of scoring. If the interview format had been used (as in validating the test), or if students had been asked to provide written comments, it would have been necessary to code each classroom so that the scorer would not know which of the treatment groups was being scored.

7. *Testing.* A pretest was given to both treatment groups. Although it is possible that the pretest might have enhanced the effectiveness of the curriculum, this seems unlikely, since the pretest content was not specifically included in the curriculum itself.

8. *Extraneous events.* Since a number of different schools were involved, it seems unlikely that particular programs or outside events would have affected these different schools in such a way as to introduce a bias in favor of one treatment method. It was determined that there were no districtwide programs affecting any of the classrooms in the study. Some communitywide impact on the students did remain a possibility, however.

9. *Maturation.* Maturation was controlled for by the design of the study. The curriculum and

noncurriculum groups were compared, with the time lapse between pretesting and posttesting for both groups kept the same.

10. *Attitude of subjects.* To ensure student co-operation, all testing was done by people who had previous experience in testing children, and who were trained by the project staff. A statement was given to students in all classes, explaining in a general way the nature of the study and soliciting their cooperation. In addition, each of the testers filled out observation reports on the attitude of the students during testing. For the most part, these reports indicated that the attitude of the students during test taking was as intended. There were, however, a couple of exceptions, primarily in the low-income classrooms where the observer reported that some students were not taking the test appropriately. Such a bias would have worked *against* the research hypothesis, since the inappropriate test-taking behavior occurred more often in the curriculum than in the noncurriculum classrooms.

Unfortunately, the possibility of a Hawthorne effect cannot be ruled out, because both the teachers and the students in the curriculum group were aware that they were part of a study evaluating the curriculum.

11. *Regression.* The design of the study made regression unlikely. No extreme groups were selected.

12. *Implementation.* Teachers in the noncurriculum group were identified through a process comparable to that used in locating the curriculum teachers. Supervisory personnel in the district were asked to identify teachers who were interested in new developments, who had a high degree of professional identity, and who were sufficiently flexible to be able to adjust fairly easily to a new teaching style. Because these were the same criteria that were used to identify teachers for training in the curriculum, it was hoped that the comparability of the teacher groups on the variables mentioned earlier would be ensured. Subsequent encounters with teachers in the course of testing supported this judgment, with the exception of one or two individuals. It would appear that this threat was controlled to some extent, but not eliminated.

STUDY 2: THE OPEN CLASSROOM

Please reread page 186 in Chapter Nine to refresh your memory as to the threats that impinged on that study. Then see if you can suggest, in the spaces provided below, how each of these threats might be eliminated or reduced.

1. Subject characteristics: _____

_____

_____

_____

_____

2. Loss of subjects: _____

_____

_____

_____

3. Location: _____

_____

_____

_____

_____

4. Instrument decay: _____

_____

_____

_____

_____

5. Data collector characteristics: _____

_____

_____

_____

_____

6. Data collector bias: _____

_____

_____

_____

_____

7. Testing: _____

_____

_____

_____

_____

8. History: _____

_____

_____

_____

_____

9. Maturation: _____

_____

_____

_____

_____

10. Attitude of subjects: _____

_____

_____

_____

_____

11. Regression: _____

_____

_____

_____

12. Implementation: _____

_____

_____

_____

_____

AUTHORS' COMMENTS

1. *Subject characteristics.* In a correlational study, the only means of controlling a subject characteristics threat is through a statistical matching technique known as *partial correlation.* In Chapter Twelve, we shall describe the reasoning on which this technique is based. At this point, you need to know only that it provides a useful means of controlling variables such as grade level, academic ability, and socioeconomic status. The essential requirement is that information on the variable(s) to be controlled must be obtained. In this example, it would be necessary to have scores on these variables for each class, since the class is the unit of analysis. For the variables of academic ability and socioeconomic level, scores would likely be obtained by getting the information on each student and then determining the class average.

2. *Loss of subjects.* Subject loss is a problem only if more students are absent from some classes than from others. Why? Because it is the motivation score for each class that is being studied. If equal numbers of the less-motivated students are absent from *all* classes, the overall motivation score will presumably be equally reduced. On the other hand, if more of the less-motivated students are absent from the less "open" classes, this could account for a higher motivation score. Although the number absent would most likely be very similar for all classes, plans should have been made to check whether this was actually the case.

Loss of an entire class presents a serious problem in that there is no good way to determine whether the loss made it more or less likely that the hypothesis would be supported. All the researcher can do is attempt to find out the reason for the nonparticipation, and judge whether it is likely to affect the results. The level of "openness" and "motivation" of the missing class might also be determined through some other means (such as interviewing the principal). Neither of these controls the threat of subject loss, but they do make it possible to judge how serious the loss might be.

3. *Location.* Although it might have been possible to hold location constant in this study (by collecting all the data in the same school, for example), it is unlikely that an adequate number of classrooms could have been obtained. Most elementary schools usually have only 15 or fewer classes in grades 2–6, and differences in classroom "openness" were essential in this study. The only feasible control would be to attempt to obtain a score representing information on the resources available to the classes studied, and use partial correlation. This was not done, however.

4. *Instrument decay.* Inasmuch as each team of observers watched only three classes during one afternoon, it seems unlikely that fatigue or boredom affected their observations.

5. *Data collector characteristics.* This threat could have been controlled best by using only one pair of observers in all classrooms. An alternative would have been to use several teams, all with the same balance of gender, ethnicity, age, and so forth. This was deemed not feasible under the study conditions, however; hence, the existence of this threat remained a possibility.

6. *Data collector bias.* It would have been a good idea to have different teams of observers assess each variable for each class so that the scores for each class would come from different observers. Better yet, each team could have assessed only one of the variables. This approach is quite feasible in many studies and might have been arranged here, although it would have complicated the logistics. Using data collectors ignorant of the hypothesis would have been preferable. The fact that pairs of observers, observing independently, obtained good agreement with each other lends some confidence that their scores on the two variables were not contaminated. It does not rule out the possibility, however, since both may have been equally biased.

7. *Testing.* No testing threat was present because the subjects were not asked to respond to any instruments.

8. *Extraneous events.* This one is a bit tricky. Many extraneous events might affect class motivation during an observation period. This is one reason that it is a good idea to observe a class several times to get a reliable measure of what goes on in that class. But even if only one observation is made, it is unlikely that internal validity would be threatened, because such external events are unlikely to have any relationship to the second variable in the hypothesis—openness. You should give this point some thought. We will return to it later in the chapter.

9. *Maturation.* No maturation threat existed because no time interval was involved in the study.

10. *Attitude of subjects.* Attitude was not likely to have been a threat because the presence of observers, if it had any effect, should have been the same for all classes.

11. *Regression.* A regression threat does not apply because the group being studied was not selected on the basis of extreme scores. A regression threat does not apply to correlational studies. Can you see why?[1]

12. *Implementation.* In the usual sense, there are no implementers (of a particular treatment) in this study. However, this category is a useful reminder of a threat that may well exist: Differences in teacher characteristics may account for any re-

lationship found between openness and motivation.

Unlike a comparison-group study, a correlational study poses no possibility of manipulating implementers. Thus, the researcher should obtain information on any variables presumed, or known, to affect the variables being studied. In this case, information on general teaching skill, for example, should have been obtained. The method of controlling this threat for specific variables (such as teaching ability) is the same as for subject characteristics—partial correlation.

Note
1. Because only one group is involved in testing the hypothesis. In this case, it is a group of classrooms.

At this point, you may have learned more about internal validity than you ever wanted to know. We hope, however, that you agree with us that it is not only one of the most important aspects of planning a study, but also one of the most interesting. It is not unusual for students to feel somewhat overwhelmed at this stage. Perhaps it seems that so many possibilities for alternative explanations exist that the task of controlling them is endless.

In one sense, this is correct: A researcher can probably never be certain that all such possibilities have been eliminated in a single study. This is another reason that studies should be replicated. On the other hand, the situation is not as bad as it may seem. As you have seen, many potential threats to internal validity can be reasonably well controlled; and many others can be judged as unlikely to occur. In the next section, we propose some guidelines to help you evaluate the probable seriousness of a particular threat in a given study. In actuality, we have already been making use of these guidelines.

Guidelines for Handling Internal Validity: Comparison-Group Studies

The evaluation of specific threats to internal validity in comparison-group studies follows three steps.

Step 1. Ask: What specific factors either are known to affect the dependent variable or may logically be expected to affect this variable? Note that researchers need *not* be concerned with factors *un*related to what they are studying.

Step 2. Ask: What is the likelihood of the comparison groups differing on each of these factors? A difference between groups cannot be explained away by a factor that is the *same* for all groups. Note that all the efforts at controlling the threats previously discussed have this as their intent—to equate the comparison groups.

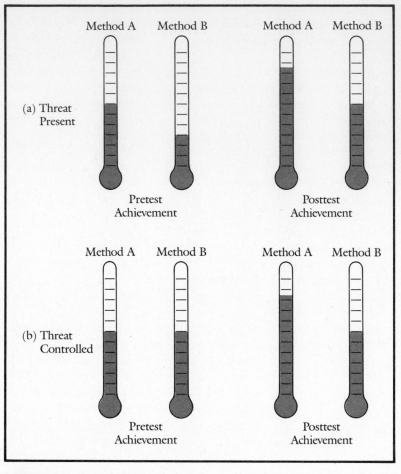

FIGURE 11.1
Illustration of Step 2: Guidelines For Handling Internal Validity in Comparison Group Studies

The importance of step 2 is illustrated in Figure 11.1. In each diagram the thermometers depict the performance of subjects receiving method A compared to those receiving method B. In diagram (a), subjects receiving method A performed higher on the posttest but *also* performed higher on the pretest; thus the difference in pretest achievement accounts for the difference on the posttest. In diagram (b), subjects receiving method A performed higher on the posttest but did *not* perform higher on the pretest; thus the posttest results *cannot* be explained by, or attributed to, different achievement levels prior to receiving the methods.

Step 3. Evaluate each identified threat on the basis of how likely it is to have an effect and plan to control it if possible. If a given threat cannot be controlled, acknowledge this fact and discuss it.

Let us consider an example to show how these three steps might be used. Suppose that a researcher wishes to investigate the effects of lecture vs. inquiry instruction on the critical thinking ability of students (as measured by scores on a critical thinking test). The instructor plans to compare two groups of eleventh graders, one group being taught by an instructor who uses the lecture method, the other group being taught by an instructor who uses the inquiry method. We list below the threats to internal validity discussed in Chapter Nine, followed by our evaluation of each.

Subject Characteristics

Although there are many possible subject characteristics which might affect critical thinking ability, we identify only two here—initial critical thinking ability and gender.

Initial Critical Thinking Ability. *Step 1*: Initial critical thinking ability of students in the two groups is almost certainly related to posttreatment critical thinking ability. *Step 2*: Groups may well differ unless they are randomly assigned or matched. *Step 3*: The likelihood of this threat having an effect unless it is controlled is high.

Gender. *Step 1*: Gender may be related to posttreatment ability. *Step 2*: If groups differ significantly in the proportions of each gender, a threat exists. Although possible, this probably is unlikely. *Step 3*: The likelihood of this threat having an effect unless it is controlled is low.

Loss of Subjects

Step 1: Subject loss is likely to affect posttreatment scores on any measure of critical thinking ability, since those subjects who drop out or are otherwise lost would likely have lower scores. *Step 2*: Groups probably would not differ in numbers lost, but this should be verified. *Step 3*: The likelihood of this threat having an effect unless it is controlled is moderate.

Location

Step 1: If the location of treatment and/or of data collection differs for the two groups, posttreatment scores on the critical thinking test could be affected. Posttreatment scores would be expected to be affected by class size, availability of reading materials or films, and other resources. *Step 2*: Groups may differ unless a control is instituted by standardizing locations for implementation and data collection. The classrooms using each method may differ systematically unless steps are taken to ensure that resources are comparable. *Step 3*: The likelihood of this threat having an effect unless it is controlled is moderate to high.

Instrument Decay

Step 1: Instrument decay may affect any outcome. *Step 2*: Groups could differ, but this should not be a major problem, providing all instruments used are carefully examined and any alterations found are corrected. *Step 3*: The likelihood of this threat having an effect unless it is controlled is low.

Data Collector Characteristics

Step 1: Data collector characteristics might affect scores on the critical thinking test. *Step 2*: Groups might differ unless a control is instituted by using the same data collector(s) for all groups. *Step 3*: The likelihood of this threat having an effect unless it is controlled is moderate.

Data Collector Bias

Step 1: Collector bias could certainly affect scores on the critical thinking test. *Step 2*: Groups might differ unless a control is instituted by training them in administration of the instrument and keeping them either ignorant of the hypothesis or of which treatment group they are testing. *Step 3*: The likelihood of this threat having an effect unless it is controlled is high.

Testing

Step 1: Pretesting might well affect posttest scores on the critical thinking test. *Step 2*: Presumably, the pretest would affect both groups equally, and would not seem likely to favor either method since instructors using both methods are teaching critical thinking skills. *Step 3*: The likelihood of this threat having an effect unless it is controlled is low.

Extraneous Events

Step 1: It is difficult to think of extraneous events that might affect critical thinking skills, but they might include such things as a special TV series on thinking, attendance at a district workshop on critical thinking by some students, or participation in certain extracurricular activities (e.g., debates) that occur during the course of the study. *Step 2*: In most cases, these events would likely affect both groups equally, and hence are not likely to constitute a threat. *Step 3*: The likelihood of this threat having an effect unless it is controlled is low.

Maturation

Step 1: Maturation could affect outcome scores, since critical thinking is presumably related to personal growth. *Step 2*: Assuming that the instructors teach each method over the same time period, maturation should not be a threat. *Step 3*: The likelihood of this threat having an effect unless it is controlled is low.

Attitude of Subjects

Step 1: Subject attitude could affect posttest scores. *Step 2*: Presumably, neither treatment group is being treated as more "special" than the other. *Step 3*: The likelihood of this threat having an effect unless it is controlled is low.

Regression

Step 1: Regression is unlikely to affect posttest scores unless subjects are selected on the basis of extreme scores. *Step 2*: It is unlikely, though possible, that groups will be affected differently. *Step 3*: The likelihood of this threat having an effect unless it is controlled is low.

Guidelines for Handling Internal Validity: Correlational Studies

The evaluation of specific threats to internal validity in correlational studies follows a procedure similar to that for comparison-group studies.

Step 1. Ask: What are the specific factors that are known to affect one of the variables being correlated or that logically could affect it? It does not matter which variable is selected, although it is usually helpful to select the variable thought to be dependent on the other.

Step 2. Ask: What is the likelihood of each of these factors also affecting the *other* variable being correlated with the first? Note that the researcher need *not* be concerned with factors that are unrelated to *both* variables.

Step 3. Evaluate each threat in terms of its likelihood and plan to control it. If a given threat cannot be controlled, this fact should be acknowledged and discussed.

You may recall our earlier discussion of one or more extraneous events affecting the open classroom study. We judged this threat to be of little concern because external events that might affect student motivation would be unlikely to affect classroom openness, which is largely a matter of overall classroom organization.

The rationale behind the principle that a factor must be related to *both* variables being studied in order to explain any correlation between them is illustrated in Figure 11.2. Diagram 1 in the figure illustrates a correlation between variables A and B. This is shown by the overlap in circles: The greater the correlation, the greater the overlap. Diagram 2 shows a third circle (C), which represents the additional variable that is being considered as a possible threat to internal validity. Since it is correlated with *both* A and B, it may be considered a possible explanation for at least part of the correlation between them. This is shown by the fact that C overlaps *both* A and B. By way of contrast, diagram 3 shows that whereas C is correlated with B, it is *not* correlated with A (there is no overlap). Since C overlaps only with B (i.e., it does not overlap with both variables), it *cannot* be considered a possible alternative explanation for the correlation between A and B.

As we did with comparison-group studies, let us consider an example to show how these steps might be applied. Suppose a researcher wishes to study the relationship between social skills (as observed) and job success (as

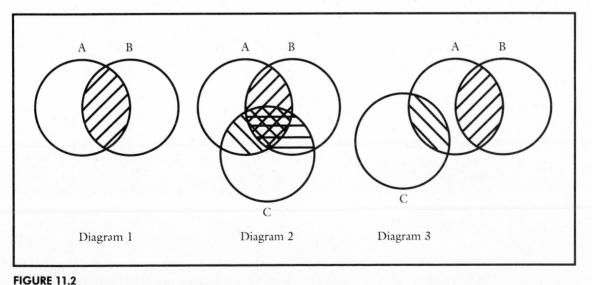

Diagram 1   Diagram 2   Diagram 3

FIGURE 11.2
Circle Diagrams Illustrating Relationships among Variables

rated by supervisors) of a group of young adults with developmental delays in a career education program. Listed below are several threats to internal validity and our evaluation of each.[3]

Subject Characteristics

Here we will consider only four of many possible subject characteristics.

Severity of Handicap. *Step 1*: Rated job success can be expected to be related to severity of handicap. *Step 2*: Severity of handicap can also be expected to be related to social skills. Therefore, severity should be assessed and controlled (using partial correlation). *Step 3*: The likelihood of this threat having an effect unless it is controlled is high.

Socioeconomic Level of Parents. *Step 1*: Socioeconomic level is likely to be related to social skills. *Step 2*: Parental socioeconomic status is not likely to be related to job success for this group. Although it is desirable to obtain socioeconomic data (to find out more about the sample), it is not of high priority. *Step 3*: The likelihood of this threat having an effect unless it is controlled is low.

Physical Strength and Coordination. *Step 1*: Physical factors may be related to job success. *Step 2*: Strength and coordination are not likely to be related to social skills. Although it is desirable to obtain such information, it is not of high priority. *Step 3*: The likelihood of this threat having an effect unless it is controlled is low.

Physical Appearance. *Step 1*: Appearance is likely to be related to social skills. *Step 2*: Appearance is also likely to be related to rated job success. Therefore, this variable *should* be assessed and controlled (again by using partial correlation). *Step 3*: The likelihood of this threat having an effect unless it is controlled is high.

Loss of Subjects

Step 1: Lost subjects are likely to have poorer job performance. *Step 2*: Lost subjects are also more likely to have poorer social skills. Thus, loss of subjects can be expected to reduce the magnitude of correlation.[4] *Step 3*: The likelihood of this threat having an effect unless it is controlled is moderate to high.

Location

Step 1: Since the subjects of the study would (inevitably) be working at different job sites and under different conditions, location may well be related to rated job success. *Step 2*: If observation of social skills is done on site, it may be related to the specific site conditions. Although this threat could be controlled by independently assessing the job site environments, a

---

[3] Remember that these are our judgments; other researchers or authorities might disagree with our assessments.

[4] This point may become clearer if you examine the correlation design in Figure 9.1. Note what happens if you use your fingers to cover the X's that are low on both variables.

better solution would be to assess social skills at a common site such as that used for group training. *Step 3*: The likelihood of this threat having an effect unless it is controlled is high.

Instrument Decay

Step 1: Instrument decay, if it occurs, is likely to be related to how accurately social skills are measured. Observations should be scheduled, therefore, so as to preclude this possibility. *Step 2*: Instrument decay would be unlikely to affect job ratings. Therefore, its occurrence would not be expected to account for any relationship found between the major variables. *Step 3*: The likelihood of this threat having an effect unless it is controlled is low.

Data Collector Characteristics

Step 1: Collector characteristics may well be related to job ratings, since interaction of data collectors and supervisors is a necessary part of this study and reactions to the data collector could affect ratings. *Step 2*: Characteristics of data collectors presumably would not be related to observation of social skills; nevertheless, to be on the safe side, this possibility should be controlled by having the same data collectors observe all subjects. *Step 3*: The likelihood of this threat having an effect unless it is controlled is moderate.

Data Collector Bias

Step 1: Observations of social skills may be related to preconceptions of observers about the subjects. *Step 2*: Ratings of job success should not be subject to data collector bias. However, observers should have no prior knowledge of job ratings, since such information might well affect their assessment of social skills. *Step 3*: The likelihood of this threat having an effect unless it is controlled is high.

Testing

Step 1: Performance on the first instrument administered (whichever it is) cannot, of course, be affected by performance on the second. *Step 2*: In this study, scores on the second instrument (whichever it is) cannot be affected by performance on the first, since the subjects are unaware of their performance on the first instrument. *Step 3*: The likelihood of this threat having an effect unless it is controlled is zero.

At this point, return to each of the specific threats to your proposed study that you identified in Chapter Nine. Use the guidelines just presented to evaluate the seriousness of each threat and state your conclusion in the space provided below. Then state how you would try to control for the threat in your own study.

1. *Subject characteristics*. Possible threat? Yes _____ No _____

If a possible threat, how serious? High _____ Moderate _____

Low _____

I would control it by _____

_____

_____

2. *Loss of subjects*. Possible threat? Yes _____ No _____

If a possible threat, how serious? High _____ Moderate _____

Low _____

I would control it by _____

_____

_____

3. *Location*. Possible threat? Yes _____ No _____

If a possible threat, how serious? High _____ Moderate _____

Low _____

I would control it by _____

_____

_____

4. *Instrument decay*. Possible threat? Yes _____ No _____

If a possible threat, how serious? High _____ Moderate _____

Low _____

I would control it by _____

_____

_____

5. *Data collector characteristics*. Possible threat? Yes _____ No _____

If a possible threat, how serious? High _____ Moderate _____

Low _____

I would control it by _____

_____

_____

6. *Data collector bias*. Possible threat? Yes _____ No _____

If a possible threat, how serious? High _____ Moderate _____

Low _____

I would control it by _____

_____

_____

7. *Testing*. Possible threat? Yes _____ No _____

If a possible threat, how serious? High _____ Moderate _____

Low _____

I would control it by _____

_____

_____

8. *Extraneous events*. Possible threat? Yes _____ No _____

If a possible threat, how serious? High _____ Moderate _____

Low _____

I would control it by _____

_____

_____

9. *Maturation*. Possible threat? Yes _____ No _____

If a possible threat, how serious? High _____ Moderate _____

Low _____

I would control it by _____

_____

_____

10. *Attitude of subjects*. Possible threat? Yes _____ No _____

If a possible threat, how serious? High _____ Moderate _____

Low _____

I would control it by _____

_____

_____

11. *Regression*. Possible threat? Yes _____ No _____

If a possible threat, how serious? High _____ Moderate _____

Low _____

I would control it by _____

_____

_____

12. *Implementation*. Possible threat? Yes _____ No _____

If a possible threat, how serious? High _____ Moderate _____

Low _____

I would control it by _____

_____

_____

Summary

In this chapter, we reconsidered the various threats to internal validity discussed in Chapter Nine, and considered a number of ways to prevent (or at least minimize) their occurrence.

Key Concepts Discussed in This Chapter

holding a variable constant	planned ignorance
standardizing conditions	matching

How Far Along Should I Be at This Point?

By now, you should be able to suggest at least one way that each of the threats to internal validity discussed in Chapter Nine can be controlled in both comparison-group and correlational studies. You should have evaluated the seriousness of each of these threats for your study, and stated how you would control any that are likely to occur.

Evaluate your progress, therefore, by checking the following. At this point, you should have:

- Accomplished each of the tasks listed at the end of the preceding chapters. (If not, review and accomplish them before going any further.)
- Thought about how to control each of the threats to internal validity discussed in Chapter Nine.
- Evaluated the seriousness of each of these threats for your own study.

■ *What's Next?*

In the next chapter, we identify and discuss some of the more common techniques that researchers use to analyze the data they collect in the course of their research.

■ *For Further Reading*

Howe, E., et al. 1989. Validity and teacher influence. *Educational Researcher*, 18(7):11–15, 26.

Millman, J., & Gowin, D. B. 1974. *Appraising educational research: A case study approach*. Englewood Cliffs, NJ: Prentice-Hall.

Shaver, J. P. 1983. The verification of independent variables in teaching methods research. *Educational Researcher*, 12(8):3–9.

Richey, H. W. 1976. Avoidable failures of experimental procedure. *Journal of Experimental Education*, 45:10–13.

Rosnow, R. L., & Davis, D. J. 1977. Demand characteristics and the psychological experiment. *Et Cetera*, 34:301–313.

Chapter Twelve

DATA ANALYSIS

Once a researcher has obtained information through the use of research instruments (tests, rating scales, interview schedules, and so forth), he or she must make sense of it. How is the information to be used to answer the research question or test the research hypothesis? Statistical procedures help researchers answer such questions. They enable them to organize and simplify the information they have collected. In this chapter, previously mentioned studies will be used to provide examples of the most commonly used statistical techniques.

By the time you have finished this chapter, you should be able to identify some of the more common techniques that researchers use in data analysis and to describe where their use would be appropriate. You should also have decided on techniques to use in your proposed study.

■ Scores

Earlier in the text, we pointed out the usefulness of scores as summaries of individual or group performance, characteristics, and the like. Whenever a researcher is working with a measured variable, scores on that variable provide the best means of describing the characteristics of a group or an individual, or of testing hypotheses.

There are many different types of scores, some of which you are probably familiar with. The initial score that is obtained when totaling items on a test or a rating scale, for example, or frequencies on an observational category sheet, is called a *raw score*. In the open classroom study, the scores obtained on the rating scale for openness and on the observation record for motivation were raw scores.

For purposes of describing the performance of a particular individual or group, raw scores have serious limitations. Suppose we know that a particular classroom has received a score of 3.5 on openness and a score of 64 on motivation. What does this tell us? Practically nothing! We do not know whether each of these scores represents high, low, or intermediate amounts of openness and motivation. A score of 64 may be the highest score received by any of the classes in the open classroom study—or the lowest. We have no way of telling if we do not know what the score *means* relative to other scores.

We give meaning to a score by comparing it with something else—most commonly with *other* scores obtained by other individuals, classes, and so forth. The comparison is made by converting a raw score into what is called a *derived score*. The most common derived scores are the percentile rank (typically, although incorrectly, referred to as a percentile), the grade-equivalent score, and the age-equivalent score. Although all these scores are useful in giving meaning to a particular raw score, they are not the best scores to use for research purposes.[1] Whenever possible, another type of derived score, the *standard score*, is to be preferred. Many published instruments include tables for converting raw scores to standard scores. Lacking these, a researcher can, without too much difficulty, make his or her own conversions.[2] Conversion generally is not necessary, however, since in most studies raw scores will give results very similar to those of standard scores; our main point here is that the other types of derived scores mentioned above should *not* be used.

◼ Statistics for Comparison-Group Studies

The most obvious way to compare the scores of two groups is to calculate the average score for each group. Although several different types of averages exist, the one most commonly used is the *arithmetic mean* (usually referred to simply as the *mean*). It is determined by adding up all the scores in a group and dividing the sum by the total number of scores in the group. The simple formula shown below summarizes the process.

$$\text{Mean} = \frac{\text{sum of scores}}{\text{number of scores}} \quad \text{or} \quad \overline{X} = \frac{\Sigma X}{N}$$

In this formula, X represents any particular raw score, N represents the total number of scores in the group, Σ tells us to sum whatever follows, and $\overline{X}$ indicates the mean.

Although the arithmetic mean is the most commonly used average, it suffers from two limitations. The first is that it sometimes is misleading. Whenever the average score of one group is compared with that of another (as in comparing the mean scores of two treatment groups or comparing the average test score of scientists with the average score of engineers), researchers want to know which group performed better "as a group." The mean does provide an index of a group's performance, but it is not always a very accurate indication. Let us show you why.

Consider the following group of scores:

$$10, 12, 15, 16, 20, 50$$

The arithmetic mean for this group of scores is 123/6 = 20.5, which is not a very accurate indication of the group's performance. Only one of the six scores falls above 20.5. These numbers illustrate the sort of situation in

---

[1] The reason requires a technical explanation that is beyond the scope of this text. If you are interested, consult any standard statistics text. See, for example, F. J. Gravetter & L. B. Wallnau. 1988. *Statistics for the behavioral sciences* (2nd Ed.). St. Paul, MN: West Publishing Co.

[2] Although they are not especially difficult, the calculations used to make these conversions are beyond the scope of this text. Again, consult a standard statistics text.

which the arithmetic mean should *not* be used—namely, whenever there are a few extreme scores that are much higher or much lower than the rest of the scores in the group. When this is the case, a different type of average, the median, should be used. The *median* is the point in a group of scores below and above which 50 percent of the scores fall. If there are an even number of scores, as in the example above, the median falls halfway between the division into the upper and lower halves. In this example, the median is 15.5, a much more appropriate index of the group's performance than the mean. In the absence of extreme scores, the mean should be calculated, however, as it is the more useful index.

The second limitation of the mean is that it omits quite a bit of useful information (as does any average). An average provides only a single numerical index to describe an entire group of scores. Consider the following two sets of scores:

Set A   44, 48, 50, 54, 59
Set B   5, 36, 50, 65, 99

The mean for both of these sets of scores is 51; the median for both sets is 50. Yet the two sets are clearly different in composition. In Set A, the scores cluster around the average; in Set B, they are much more spread out. Simply reporting either the mean or the median, therefore, would not provide a researcher with a very useful description of how the two sets of scores differ.

In order to handle this problem, statisticians have devised other kinds of numerical indices to indicate how much the scores in a group are spread out. The simplest of these is the *range*, or the difference between the highest and lowest scores in a group. In Set A, for example, it is 15; in Set B, it is 94. The most widely used index of "spread," however, is the *standard deviation* (SD). Although a detailed interpretation of this index is beyond the scope of this text, a simple explanation is that the larger the numerical value of the standard deviation, the more spread out the scores in a group of scores. (In Set A, the SD is 5.1; in Set B, it is 31.3.)

The standard deviation and other indices of spread are useful pieces of information for a researcher to have. For the most complete description of a group of scores, however, a frequency polygon should be used. A *frequency polygon* is a graphic illustration of all the scores in a group. A comparison of frequency polygons is the most meaningful way to evaluate groups of scores. Let us illustrate how to construct one.

Suppose that we have obtained the scores for two groups of students on the Test of Ability to Explain.[3] One group has been taught by the inquiry method and the other by the lecture method. On the 40-item test, the highest score received by a student in either group is 32, and the lowest score is 3. There are 60 students in each group. Let us construct a frequency polygon for the inquiry group first.[4]

Step 1. Determine the difference between the highest and lowest scores. In this case, $32 - 3 = 29$.

Step 2. Divide this difference by 15 and round to the nearest whole number. In this example, $29/15 = 1.93$, which rounds to 2. This number is the size of the intervals to be used in the polygon.

---

[3] See Chapter Six.

[4] Frequency polygons, and in fact all the statistics presented in this chapter, can be obtained with relatively little effort by using a computer. However, in order to avoid misinterpretation it is essential that you understand the steps involved in obtaining these statistics; these are not evident in the output that the computer produces.

TABLE 12.1 Distribution of Scores for Two Groups on a Test of Ability to Explain

Inquiry Group Score	Lecture Group Score
31–32	31–32
29–30	29–30
27–28	27–28
25–26	25–26
23–24	23–24
21–22	21–22
19–20	19–20
17–18	17–18
15–16	15–16
13–14	13–14
11–12	11–12
9–10	9–10
7–8	7–8
5–6	5–6
3–4	3–4

Step 3. Beginning with the lowest score, set up intervals as shown in Table 12.1. Make one interval schedule for each group.

Step 4. Determine the number of scores in each interval for each group and enter the tally in the table in a column entitled "Frequency." We have done this, using fictitious data, in Table 12.2. As you can see, there are seven scores of 25 or 26 in the inquiry group and four scores of 25 or 26 in the lecture group.

Step 5. Draw a pair of axes as shown in Figure 12.1. Mark off points on the *x* axis to represent the score intervals. The lowest interval is placed near

TABLE 12.2 Table 12.1 with Frequency of Scores in Each Interval Added

Inquiry Group		Lecture Group	
Score	Frequency	Score	Frequency
31–32	1	31–32	0
29–30	3	29–30	2
27–28	5	27–28	3
25–26	7	25–26	4
23–24	9	23–24	4
21–22	9	21–22	7
19–20	6	19–20	9
17–18	6	17–18	8
15–16	4	15–16	7
13–14	4	13–14	6
11–12	2	11–12	4
9–10	1	9–10	4
7–8	2	7–8	1
5–6	0	5–6	1
3–4	1	3–4	0

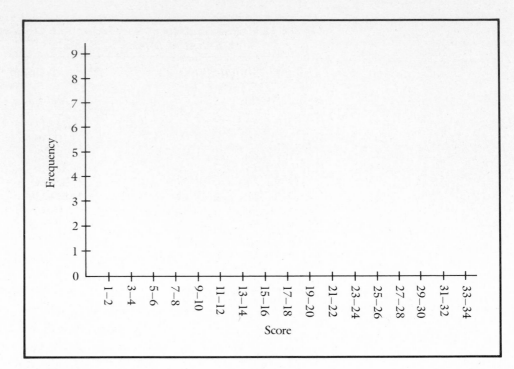

FIGURE 12.1
Frequency Polygon Axes

the y axis. The distance between points must remain constant. Then mark off points on the y axis to represent frequencies. These must begin with 0. The highest point is the largest frequency in either group. In this example, the largest frequency is 9.

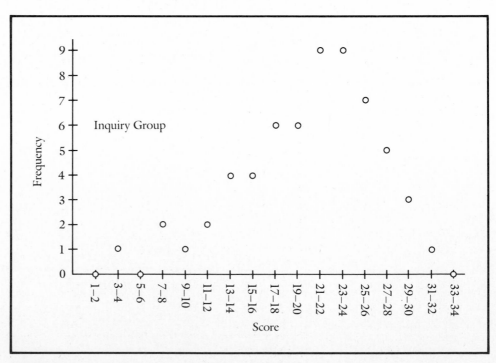

FIGURE 12.2
A Plotting of the Scores of the Inquiry Group on the Test of Ability to Explain

Step 6. Plot each frequency for each interval for one of the groups. We shall plot the frequencies for the inquiry group. Thus, we place an open dot directly opposite a frequency of 1 on the *y* axis and directly above the 3–4 interval on the *x* axis. We place another dot directly opposite a frequency of 0 on the *y* axis and directly above the 5–6 interval on the *x* axis, another dot directly opposite a frequency of 2 on the *y* axis and directly above the 7–8 interval, and so on (see Figure 12.2). We also plot the frequency (which is zero) for one interval below and one interval above the actual range of scores.

Step 7. Connect the points in sequence, being sure not to skip any interval (see Figure 12.3). Notice that the line must touch the *x* axis at both ends; that's why we plotted zero frequencies at interval 1–2 and interval 33–34.

We have now constructed the frequency polygon for the inquiry group. Notice that it provides a visual representation of all the scores in the group. How would you describe the inquiry group's performance on this test?

_____

_____

_____

_____

_____

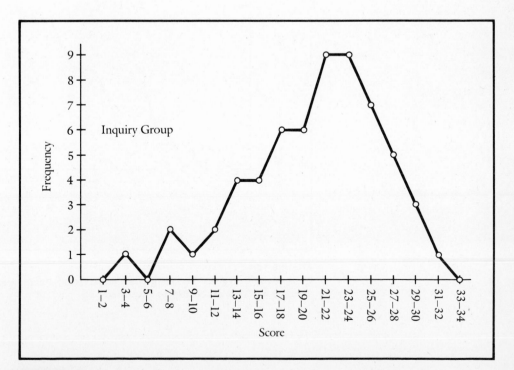

FIGURE 12.3
Completed Frequency Polygon of the Scores of the Inquiry Group on the Test of Ability to Explain

AUTHORS' COMMENTS

The inquiry group, in general, scored high on the test. As the frequency polygon reveals, there were many more high scores than low scores.

Now check your ability to construct a polygon by plotting the frequencies for the lecture group on this same pair of axes, as shown in Figure 12.4. We have started you off by using shaded dots to plot the frequencies for the three lowest intervals. After you have plotted all the frequencies for the lecture group, connect the points. Take care that you do not (1) forget that every interval must have a frequency entered—even if it is zero (as for the inquiry group at interval 5–6) and (2) use the y axis to represent individuals: the number 6 on the y axis means "6 people"—not person number 6.

How would you interpret the difference in performance, as shown in Figure 12.4, between the inquiry and lecture groups?

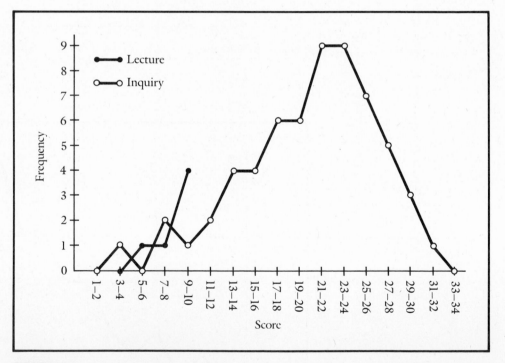

FIGURE 12.4
Frequency Polygons Showing the Comparative Performances of Inquiry and Lecture Groups on Test of Ability to Explain

AUTHORS' COMMENTS

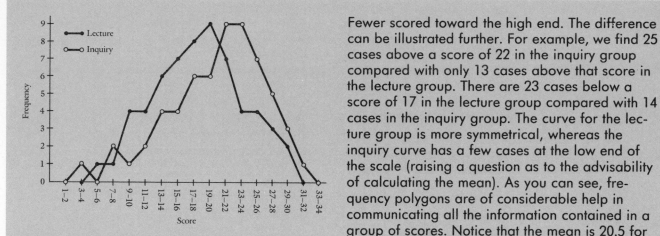

Your completed frequency polygon should look like the one shown above.

The lecture group performed, overall, at a lower level than the inquiry group. A greater number of students in the lecture group scored toward the low end of the distribution of scores.

Fewer scored toward the high end. The difference can be illustrated further. For example, we find 25 cases above a score of 22 in the inquiry group compared with only 13 cases above that score in the lecture group. There are 23 cases below a score of 17 in the lecture group compared with 14 cases in the inquiry group. The curve for the lecture group is more symmetrical, whereas the inquiry curve has a few cases at the low end of the scale (raising a question as to the advisability of calculating the mean). As you can see, frequency polygons are of considerable help in communicating all the information contained in a group of scores. Notice that the mean is 20.5 for the inquiry group and 18.5 for the lecture group. The median is 20.9 for the inquiry group and 18.4 for the lecture group. Notice again that the frequency polygon provides far more information than does simply the calculation and presentation of these averages.

■ *Statistics for Correlational Studies*

The visual analog to the frequency polygon for correlational studies is the scatterplot. You have already encountered it in Chapter Nine. A *scatterplot* is a pictorial representation of the relationship between two measured variables. Scatterplots are easy to construct, provided some common pitfalls are avoided. (First, in order for data to be plotted, there must be a score on each variable for *each* individual. Second, each individual must be represented by one, and only one, point of intersection.) The data in Table 12.3 were used to construct the scatterplot shown in Figure 12.5. Four steps are involved.

TABLE 12.3   Data Used to Construct Scatterplot in Figure 12.5

	Score	
Individual	*Variable 1*	*Variable 2*
Pedro	12	41
John	21	76
Alicia	9	29
Charles	7	21
Bonnie	13	43
Phil	11	37
Sue	7	14
Oscar	18	63
Jean	15	54
Dave	14	39

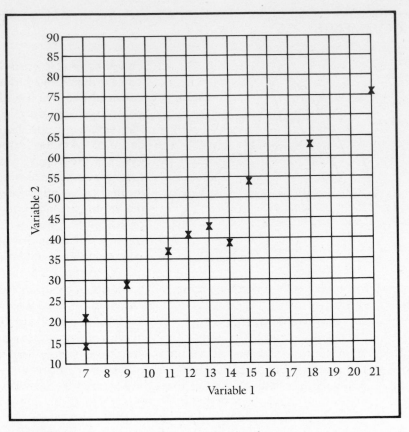

FIGURE 12.5
Scatterplot of Data Presented in Table 12.3

Step 1. Decide which variable will be represented on each axis. It makes no difference which variable is placed on which axis. We have used the horizontal (*x*) axis for variable 1 and the vertical (*y*) axis for variable 2.

Step 2. Divide each axis so that all scores on the variable represented on that axis can be included. It is helpful to use graph paper.

Step 3. Plot each person at the point where his or her scores on the variables intersect. For example, Pedro had a score of 12 on variable 1, so we locate 12 on the horizontal axis. He had a score of 41 on variable 2, so we locate 41 on the vertical axis. We then draw imaginary lines from each of these points until they intersect, and mark an **x** at that point.

Step 4. In the same way, plot the scores of all ten students on both variables. The completed result is a scatterplot.

INTERPRETING SCATTERPLOTS

How do researchers interpret scatterplots? What are they intended to reveal? A researcher wants to know not only *if* a relationship exists between variables, but also *to what degree*. The degree of relationship, if one exists, is what a scatterplot illustrates.

Consider Figure 12.5. What does it tell us about the relationship between variable 1 and variable 2? This question can be answered in several ways:

- We could say that high scores on variable 1 go with high scores on variable 2 (as in John's case), and that low scores also tend to go together (as in Sue's case).
- We could say that by knowing a student's score on one variable, we can estimate his or her score on the other variable fairly closely. Suppose, for example, that a new student attains a score of 13 on variable 1. What would you predict his or her score to be on variable 2? You probably would *not* predict a score of 65, or one of 25. (We would predict a score somewhere from 35 to 50.)
- We could say that there is a strong or high degree of relationship between the two variables. If all the plotted points were on a straight line, we would speak of it as a "perfect linear relationship." Such relationships are very rare, however, and are probably never attained in educational research.

CORRELATION COEFFICIENTS

Figure 12.6 presents several other examples of scatterplots. Studying them will help you understand degrees of relationship, and also give meaning to a widely used statistic—the correlation coefficient. The *correlation coefficient*, designated by the symbol *r*, is a numerical way of expressing the degree of relationship that exists between two variables. Just as with a scatterplot a *positive* correlation exists when high scores on one of the variables are accompanied by high scores on the other, when low scores on one are accompanied by low scores on the other, and so forth. A *negative* relationship exists when high scores on one variable are accompanied by low scores on the other, and vice versa.

Correlation coefficients are never more than + 1.00, indicating a perfect positive relationship, or − 1.00, indicating a perfect negative relationship. Perfect positive or negative correlations, however, are rarely if ever

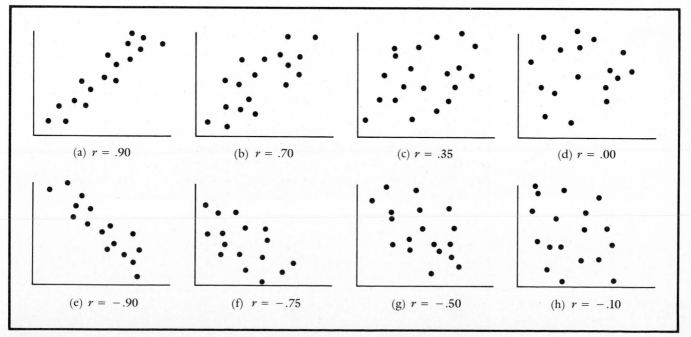

FIGURE 12.6
Scatterplots and Correlation Coefficients Showing Different Degrees of Relationship

achieved. If the two variables are highly related, a coefficient somewhat close to +1.00 or −1.00 will be obtained (e.g., .85, −.93). The closer the coefficient is to either of these extremes, the greater the degree of the relationship. If there is no or hardly any relationship, a coefficient of .00 or close to it will be obtained. The coefficient is calculated directly from the same scores used to construct the scatterplot. With practice, you can learn to estimate the correlation coefficient from inspection of the scatterplot.

The scatterplots of Figure 12.6 illustrate differing degrees of correlation along with the correlation coefficient obtained from the same scores. Both positive and negative correlations are shown. Scatterplots (a), (b), and (c) illustrate differing degrees of positive correlation; scatterplots (e), (f), (g), and (h) illustrate differing degrees of negative correlation. Scatterplot (d) indicates no relationship between the two variables involved.

Actually, there are many different correlation coefficients, each applying to a particular circumstance and each calculated by means of a different computational formula. The formula we have been illustrating is the one most frequently used—the Pearson product-moment correlation coefficient.

In order to better understand the meaning of different values of the correlation coefficient, we suggest that you try the following two exercises with Figure 12.6.

Exercise 1

Lay a pencil flat on the paper on scatterplot (a) so that the entire length of the pencil is touching the paper. Place it in such a way that it touches or covers as many dots as possible. Take note that there is clearly one "best" placement. You would not, for example, maximize the points covered if you placed the pencil horizontally on the scatterplot. Repeat this procedure for each of the scatterplots, noting in the space provided below what occurs as you move from one scatterplot to another.

Exercise 2

Draw a horizontal line on scatterplot (a) so that about half of the dots are above the line and half are below it. Next draw a vertical line so that about half the dots are to the left of the line and half are to the right. Repeat the procedure for each scatterplot and note in the space provided below what you observe as you move from one scatterplot to another.

AUTHORS' COMMENTS

Exercise 1. In scatterplot (a), the pencil covers the greatest number of dots if it is placed at an angle from lower left to upper right. Further, most of the dots are covered or touched. As you move to scatterplot (b) or (c), it is still quite clear that the best place to put the pencil is as before, at the same angle. However, fewer dots are covered in (b) than in (a), and fewer are covered in (c) than in (b). In (d), there is no placement of the pencil that covers more dots than any other. In scatterplot (e), it is once again clear where the pencil should be placed—this time at an angle from upper left to lower right. As you progress to scatterplots (f), (g), and (h), the placement remains the same but there are more and more dots that are missed by the pencil.

Exercise 2. In scatterplot (a) most of the dots are in the upper right and lower left quadrants. As you move to (b) and (c), this is still true, but to a lesser extent. In (d), there are equal numbers in all quadrants. In (e), most of the dots are in the upper left and lower right quadrants. As you move to scatterplots (f), (g), and (h), the numbers in each quadrant become more similar. If you spend some time associating these patterns with the corresponding numerical values for the correlation coefficients, we think the meaning of these coefficients will become clearer.

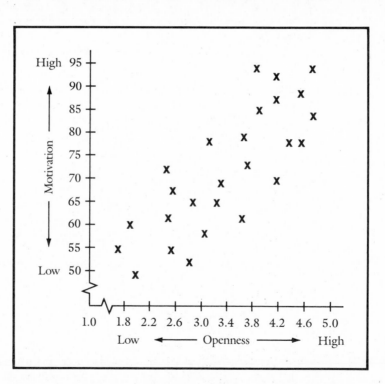

FIGURE 12.7
A Scatterplot Showing a Relationship Between Two Variables

To check your understanding, let us return again to the open classroom study. Suppose that we made a scatterplot and it turned out as shown in Figure 12.7. What would you say about the relationship between openness and motivation as displayed in this scatterplot? Do the variables appear to be related? If so, how would you describe the relationship?

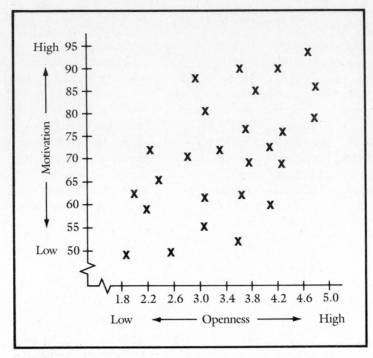

FIGURE 12.8
A Second Scatterplot Showing a Relationship Between Two Variables

Now suppose the scatterplot turned out like Figure 12.8 instead. What would you say now about the relationship between openness and motivation? Do the variables appear to be related? If so, how would you describe the relationship?

_____

_____

_____

Next, use the data on openness and motivation in Table 12.4 to construct a scatterplot from the actual data on the axes shown in Figure 12.9. We have entered the scores for classrooms 1 and 2; your task is to enter the scores for the remaining classrooms.

When you have finished, your scatterplot should be identical to the one shown in Figure 12.10.

How would you interpret the scatterplot that you constructed from the data in Table 12.4? What can you say about the relationship between openness and motivation as shown in the scatterplot? Do the variables appear to be related? If so, how would you describe the relationship?

_____

_____

_____

_____

_____

TABLE 12.4 Raw Data on Openness and Motivation for 26 Classrooms

Classroom	Openness Rating	Motivation (% of Attendees)
1	4.5	97
2	4.0	88
3	2.4	77
4	1.9	64
5	1.8	67
6	4.7	91
7	1.7	82
8	1.9	89
9	4.1	99
10	4.2	67
11	4.1	83
12	4.2	94
13	4.4	85
14	4.7	84
15	3.4	93
16	3.2	90
17	3.3	86
18	4.4	73
19	3.4	74
20	1.9	70
21	4.6	85
22	3.1	96
23	4.7	54
24	4.5	90
25	3.7	82
26	4.0	75

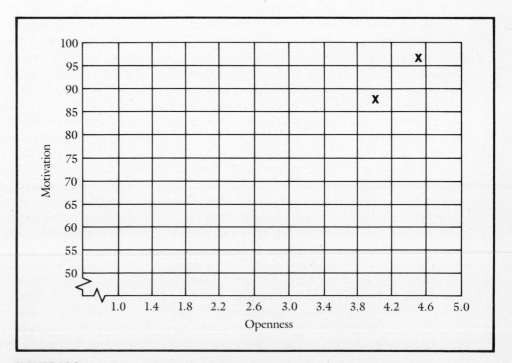

FIGURE 12.9
Scatterplot Showing Relationship Between Openness and Motivation for 26 Classrooms

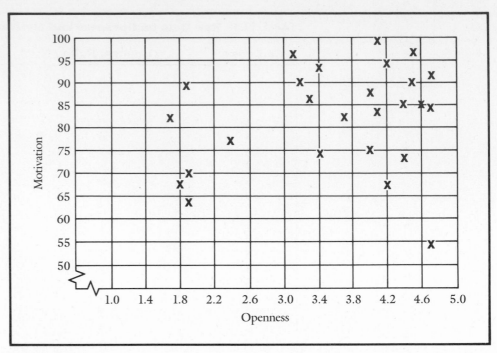

FIGURE 12.10
Completed Scatterplot Showing Relationship Between Openness and Motivation for 26 Classrooms

AUTHORS' COMMENTS

The scatterplot in Figure 12.7 indicates a strong relationship between openness and motivation. Classrooms rated high in openness also score high in motivation. Classrooms rated lower in openness score lower in motivation.

The scatterplot in Figure 12.8 indicates a much weaker relationship. The fact that there are no classrooms in the upper left and lower right portions indicates some degree of relationship, but it is not very strong.

Figure 12.10 (the actual data) indicates that there is (alas!) very little relationship between openness and motivation in these classrooms. The correlation coefficient is .26. There is a slight tendency for classrooms at the high end of the openness scale to also be at the high end on the motivation scale, but it is not very pronounced. Several classrooms that were rated high on openness scored low on motivation. Similarly, those classrooms that were rated low in openness received a wide range of motivation scores. (Keep in mind the many limitations of this study that we discussed earlier. Recall, in particular, the lack of representativeness of the sample and the poor reliability and validity of the measures due to the use of only one observation period. Consequently, these data do not provide an adequate test of the research hypothesis.)

Figure 12.10 also illustrates that there are two distinct groupings of classrooms with regard to openness. Six classrooms are clustered at the low end of the scale; the remainder are at the high end. As it happens, these groups correspond to the original reputation of the classrooms. Ordinarily, the correlation would provide evidence of the validity of the openness rating—*except* that most of the observers knew of the reputations of these classrooms before observing them. (This possible source of bias was discussed in Chapter Nine.)

A further interpretation is that there are greater differences in degree of motivation in the classrooms rated more open that in those rated less open. This interpretation is a very tentative one, however, and must be viewed with caution owing to the small size of the sample.

Studies Involving Only Categorical Variables

Up to this point we have discussed data analysis in studies using a comparison-group design in which one variable is measured, or the correlational design in which both variables are measured. Most educational research involves use of the statistical procedures we have just discussed. There are times, however, when a researcher wishes to study the relationship between two (or more) categorical variables. Such studies require different statistical procedures, the most common being the *crossbreak table* (also known as a contingency table).

The simplest crossbreak is a 2 × 2 table, as shown in Table 12.5. Each individual is tallied in one, and only one, cell, which corresponds to the combination of his or her gender and grade level. Notice that the numbers in each of the cells in Table 12.5 represent totals—the total number of individuals who fit the characteristics of the cell (e.g., junior high males). Although percentages and proportions are sometimes calculated for cells, we do not recommend it, as the calculations are often misleading.

TABLE 12.5 Hypothetical Relation Between Teacher Gender and Grade Level

	Male	*Female*	*Total*
Junior high school teachers	40	60	100
High school teachers	60	40	100
Total	100	100	200

It probably seems obvious that Table 12.5 reveals a relationship between teacher gender and grade level. A junior high school teacher is more likely to be female; a high school teacher is more likely to be male. Often, however, it is useful to calculate "expected" frequencies in order to see results more clearly. What do we mean by "expected"? If there is no relationship between variables, we would "expect" the proportion of cases within each cell of the table corresponding to a category of one variable to be identical to the proportion within that category for the entire group.

Look, for example, at Table 12.6. Exactly one-half (50 percent) of the entire group of teachers in this table are female. We would "expect," there-

TABLE 12.6 Repeat of Table 12.5 with Expected Frequencies Added (in Parentheses)

	Male	*Female*	*Total*
Junior high school teachers	40 (50)	60 (50)	100
High school teachers	60 (50)	40 (50)	100
Total	100	100	200

fore, that exactly one-half of the junior high school teachers would be female. Similarly, we would "expect" that one-half of the high school teachers would be female. The expected frequencies, in other words, would be 50 female junior high school teachers and 50 female high school teachers, rather than the 60 female junior high school and 40 female high school teachers that were actually obtained. These expected frequencies along with the actual (or observed) frequencies are shown in each cell in Table 12.6. The expected frequencies are given in parentheses.

There is a numerical index, called the *contingency coefficient*, that can be used with crossbreak tables. It is interpreted in much the same way as the Pearson correlation coefficient. With the contingency coefficient, however, the maximum possible value is not 1.00, but depends on the number of categories for each variable. Table 12.7 presents some of these values.

TABLE 12.7 Contingency Coefficient Values for Different-sized Crossbreak Tables

Size of Table	Upper Limit*
2 × 2	.71
3 × 3	.82
4 × 4	.87
5 × 5	.90
6 × 6	.91

* The upper limits for unequal-sized tables (such as 2 × 3 or 3 × 4 tables) are unknown, but can be estimated from the values given. Thus, the upper limit for a 3 × 4 table would approximate .85.

Look back at Table 12.5. This is a 2 × 2 table (there are two categories for each variable); hence, the highest possible value of the contingency coefficient would be .71.

It is time again to check your understanding. For each of the examples that follow, write in the statistical procedure that you would use to clarify the data, and also make a diagram to show how the results might look. Use the figures presented earlier in the chapter as models. In some cases, more than one statistical procedure may be appropriate.

Case 1
Comparing students in special classes with similar students not in special classes on scores on a self-concept test.

_____

_____

_____

Case 2
Relating the number of positive counselor comments contained in audiotapes of interviews to the gain in counselee scores over a 3-month period on a test of ego strength.

_____

_____

_____

Case 3
Comparing answers of a group of fifth graders to these two questions:

"How do you feel about your teacher?"
"Do most of the kids in the room like their classmates?"

Each student's response to each question is classified as "Generally Positive," "Neutral," "Generally Negative," or "Indeterminate."

_____

_____

_____

Case 4
Comparing first, second, and third graders' answers to interview questions about how much they like school. Each answer is categorized as "Very Much," "Some," "A Little," or "Not Much."

_____

_____

_____

Case 5
Relating scores on the odd-numbered items of the QE Intelligence Test[5] to scores on the even-numbered items for a group of college sophomores.

_____

_____

_____

Case 6
Relating teacher scores on the Picture Situation Inventory[6] to the number of controlling statements made over several observation periods as judged by observers.

_____

_____

_____

[5] See Chapter Six.
[6] See Chapter Six.

AUTHORS' COMMENTS

Case 1. Frequency polygon and/or mean or median (two groups compared on a measured variable).

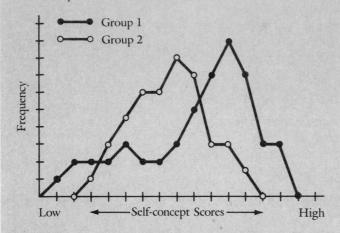

Case 2. Correlation coefficient and/or scatterplot (one group, both variables measured).

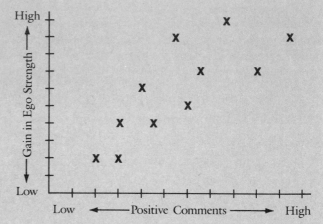

Case 3. Crossbreak table (one group, both variables best treated as categorical). If "Indeterminate" as is deleted, correlation could be used by assigning points (e.g., positive = 3; neutral = 2; negative = 1).

Feelings about Teacher

		Positive	*Neutral*	*Negative*	*Indeterminate*
	Positive	20	5	10	4
Liking of Classmates	Neutral	5	10	5	3
	Negative	5	5	15	2
	Indeterminate	3	2	2	1

Case 4. a. If numbers are assigned to categories of liking, frequency distribution and/or mean or median for each of the three groups. See case 1.

b. If categories are treated as given, crossbreak table.

Case 5. Correlation coefficient and/or scatterplot (one group, both variables measured). See case 2.

Case 6. Correlation coefficient and/or scatterplot (one group, both variables measured). See case 2.

Rating

		Very Much	Some	A Little	Not Much
	3				
Grade Level	2				
	1				

Describe below the statistical procedures you think would be appropriate to use in your proposed study and give an illustration of how the data might appear.

What procedures will you use? _____

_____

Why will you use these procedures? _____

_____

_____

Draw a sketch or diagram below to illustrate how the results might look.

_____

Assessing the Magnitude of a Relationship

Now that you are familiar with some of the ways of studying relationships in different kinds of studies, the next question that arises is: When is a relationship sizable enough to be important? By this time, you most likely do not expect there to be a simple answer to the question—and you are right!

The key question in most comparison-group studies is this: How large does a difference between the mean scores of two groups have to be in order to "make a difference"? Unfortunately, in most educational research, this is a very difficult question to answer. Sometimes, prior experience can be helpful. One of the characteristics of IQ scores is that, over the years, many educators have had enough experience with them to make differences between them meaningful. Most experienced counselors, administrators, and teachers realize, for example, that a difference of less than 5 points between the mean scores of two groups has little importance. They also know that a 10-point difference between mean scores is enough to have important implications.

At other times, a researcher may have available a frame of reference, or standard, to use in interpreting the magnitude of a difference between means. One such standard consists of the mean scores of known groups. In a study of critical thinking in which one of the authors participated, the end-of-year mean score for a group of eleventh graders who received a special curriculum was shown to be higher than is typical of the mean score of eleventh graders in general *and* close to the mean score of a group of college students. By contrast, a comparison group scored lower than both. Since the special curriculum group also demonstrated a fall-to-spring mean gain twice that of the comparison group, the total evidence obtained through performance comparisons with other groups indicated that the gains made by the special curriculum group were important.

Another technique for assessing the magnitude of a difference between the means of two groups is to calculate *effect size* (ES). Effect size takes into account the *size* of the difference in means that is obtained. One common index of effect size, known as delta (Δ), is obtained by dividing the difference between the means of the two groups being compared by the standard deviation[7] of the comparison group. Thus,

$$\text{Delta} = \frac{\text{mean experimental group} - \text{mean comparison group}}{\text{standard deviation of comparison group}}$$

When pretest to posttest gains in the mean scores of two groups are compared, the formula is modified as follows:

$$\text{Delta} = \frac{\text{mean experimental gain} - \text{mean comparison gain}}{\text{standard deviation of gain scores of comparison group}}$$

The standard deviation of gain scores is obtained by first getting the gain score (posttest minus pretest score) for each individual and then calculating the standard deviation as usual.

Although effect size is a useful tool for assessing the magnitude of a difference between the means of two groups, it does not, in and of itself, answer the question of how large an ES must be for researchers to consider it important. Once again, this is essentially an arbitrary decision. Most researchers consider that a delta of .50 (i.e., half a standard deviation of the comparison group's scores) or larger is an important finding. If the scores are typically distributed, such an ES indicates that the difference in means between the two groups is about one-twelfth the distance between the highest and lowest scores of the comparison group. When you are assessing the magnitude of a difference between the means of two groups, therefore, we recommend that you (1) always make use of data on the means of known groups if such data are available; (2) calculate delta; and (3) interpret a delta of .50 or larger as important.

In correlational studies, the key question is: How large must a correlation coefficient be to indicate an important relationship? What does an important relationship look like on a scatterplot? As you know by now, doing or evaluating research is not cut and dried; it is not a matter of following a set of rules. Rather, it requires informed judgment. In judging correlation coefficients, you must first assess their appropriateness.

Consider, for example, Figure 12.11. All five scatterplots shown represent a Pearson correlation of about .50. Only in (a), however, does the coefficient completely convey the nature of the relationship. In (b), the relationship is understated by the coefficient since it is a curvilinear one.

---

[7] Appendix C shows how to calculate the standard deviation.

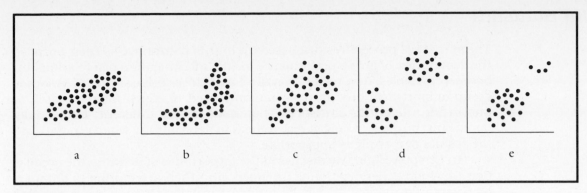

FIGURE 12.11
Scatterplots with a Pearson r of .50

In (c), the numerical index does not reflect the fan-shaped nature of the relationship. In (d), the coefficient does not reveal that there are two distinct subgroups. In (e), the coefficient is greatly inflated by a few unusual cases. Although these illustrations are a bit exaggerated, similar results can be found in real data.

If the Pearson correlation coefficient is an adequate summary,[8] we believe that most researchers would agree, when testing a hypothesis, to the interpretations shown in Table 12.8.

When both, or all, variables are categorical, assessment of the magnitude of a relationship is even more difficult. Sometimes it is helpful to inspect the crossbreak table, particularly for discrepancies between expected and obtained frequencies. The contingency coefficient referred to earlier is also useful; we recommend the same general guidelines as for the Pearson coefficient (see Table 12.8), with the recognition that the number of categories of each variable affects the maximum value that this index can have.

TABLE 12.8 Interpretation of Correlation Coefficients (r) When Testing Research Hypotheses

Magnitude of r	Interpretation
.00 to .40	Of little practical importance, except in unusual circumstances. Perhaps of theoretical value.*
.41 to .60	Large enough to be of practical as well as theoretical use.
.61 to .80	Very important, but rarely obtained in educational research.
.81 or above	Probably an error in calculation. If not, a very sizable relationship.

* When a very few people are selected from a large group, even correlations this small may be useful.

[8] We would say it is only for scatterplot (a) in Figure 12.11.

■ *Inferential Statistics*

The statistical procedures discussed up to this point have as their purpose the description of group performance, or the identification of a relationship between variables. As a result, they are called *descriptive statistics*. Another group of statistical procedures commonly used in educational research is known as *inferential statistics*. They have a very different, but equally important, purpose: to assist researchers in determining when generalizing the results of a study is appropriate.

In Chapter Eight, we discussed the importance of defining the population to which generalization is intended, and then attempting to obtain a representative sample, ideally by random selection. Even when a random sample is used, however, a researcher cannot expect to obtain exactly the same results in the sample as would have been obtained for the entire population.

In the open classroom study, for example, suppose that a correlation of .60 had been obtained between classroom openness and motivation, rather than the .26 that was actually obtained, and that the sample of classrooms had been randomly selected. The question of interest is: What is the correlation in the population? It would be naive to expect it to be precisely .60, but might it be .50? Might it be .20? Inferential statistics can help us answer these questions.

Both the theory behind this class of statistics and the calculations of specific indices are beyond the scope of this text. We will, however, explain the rationale underlying inferential statistics sufficiently so that you can interpret them should you come across them in reading a research study. Our discussion will also help you know which statistics are applicable to differing situations. You should remember, however, that the use of inferential statistics is based on the assumption of random selection of the sample. If the sample in a study has not been randomly selected, the application of such statistics is highly questionable.

The outcome of *all* inferential statistical procedures is expressed in one or both of two ways.

1. *The outcome can be expressed as the probability of getting a discrepancy from a hypothesized population value as large as or larger than the one obtained in the study.* We might, for example, determine the probability of obtaining a sample mean of 20.5 (or larger), as we did in our earlier example for the inquiry method, if the population mean is 15.0. Let us suppose that the calculation of inferential statistics results in a probability of .05. This means that we will get a sample mean of 20.5 or larger 5 times in 100 if the population mean is 15.0. Probability is always expressed as a decimal (.20 means 20 times in 100; .01 means 1 time in 100; .002 means 2 times in 1000, and so forth). What accounts for our sample value differing from the population value? Often, the explanation given is that the discrepancy is due to "chance."

A more satisfying explanation attributes the discrepancy to "sampling error," with the recognition that any particular sample mean is likely to differ from the population mean simply because it *is* a sample. Since a sample is only a portion (and often a very small portion) of the population, it would be very surprising if the sample mean were identical to the population mean. Another way of saying this is that if we were to take a very large number of random samples of the same size, we would expect to find a mean that differs from the population mean by as much as (or more than) ours does in 5 out of every 100 samples. We can also state that our result is "statistically significant" at the .05, or 5 percent, level.

The great value of inferential statistics is that they make possible an estimate of the size of the "sampling error" so that the probability of obtaining a particular result can be calculated. When evaluating relationships, researchers customarily use a number representing no relationship at all as the hypothetical population value. In comparison-group studies, this means determining the probability that an obtained difference between means would occur if the population difference was 0. In correlational studies, the obtained correlation is tested against a hypothetical population correlation of .00. This is usually referred to as "testing the null hypothesis." If the probability is small (it is customary to define small as less than .05), the researcher "rejects" the null hypothesis and concludes that the relationship in the population is greater than 0. Note that even though the relationship is greater than 0, it might be very slight. For this reason, some researchers (including ourselves) prefer the second interpretation of inferential statistics, described in item 2 below.

The logic of testing the null hypothesis is that of setting up a "straw man" in hopes of knocking it down. Figure 12.12 illustrates the decision-making process. First the "straw man" is set up by stating the null hypothesis (typically as $\overline{X}_1 - \overline{X}_2 = 0$, or $r = .00$). This states that, for the population in question, there is *no* relationship between the variables being studied. Next, the appropriate inference statistic is calculated, leading to a statement of probability which indicates how often the *sample result* (e.g., $\overline{X}_1 - \overline{X}_2 = 20$, or $r = .56$) would be obtained as a result of sampling error *if* the null hypothesis is true. Finally, one of two decisions is made. Either it is concluded that the sample result *is* one of these sampling error occurrences and the null hypothesis is retained *or* it is concluded that the sample result is *not* a sampling error occurrence and the null hypothesis is wrong, that is, the relationship in the population is not zero. The smaller the probability, the less likely it is that the sample value is due to sampling error. Because the researcher hopes that the sample result is not just due to chance, he or she is pleased by obtaining a small probability which justifies rejection of the null hypothesis.

2. *The outcome can be expressed by placing boundaries around the sample value.* This interpretation permits us to make statements such as the following about our previous example: "We can be confident that the population mean is between our sample mean and ± 5.5, with the probability of being wrong equal to .05. That is, we will be wrong 5 times in 100 if we state that the population mean is between 15.0 and 26.0." The interval of 15–26 is called the *confidence interval*. In this case, it is the 95 percent

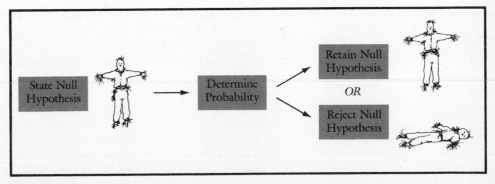

FIGURE 12.12
The Null Hypothesis Decision-Making Process

confidence interval because the probability is .95 that the population value lies inside this interval, and only .05 that it lies outside the interval. Other limits can be established, but the 95 percent and 99 percent confidence intervals are the ones most commonly used.

In our example comparing the inquiry and lecture methods, we obtained a difference between the means of the two groups of 2.0 (mean of inquiry group minus mean of lecture group, or 20.5 − 18.5 = 2.0). Inferential statistics enable us to place boundaries around this—such as, "The population difference is 2.0 ± 0.6 (i.e., between 1.4 and 2.6)"—knowing we will be correct 95 percent of the time.

In the open classroom study, we can place boundaries around the obtained correlation coefficient of .26. Thus, we can make statements such as this: "The correlation in the population is .26 ± .20 (i.e., between .06 and .46), with a confidence level of 95 percent."[9]

Check your understanding of the foregoing discussion with the following exercises.

Exercise 1
A researcher obtains a sample mean of 70 and wishes to determine the probability of such a mean occurring if the population mean is 60. The researcher obtains a probability of .10. What does this tell the researcher?

_____

_____

_____

Exercise 2
A researcher obtains a mean of 120 for a random sample of males and a mean of 129 for a random sample of females on an achievement test. What is the null hypothesis? If the resulting probability is .01, what is your interpretation?

_____

_____

_____

Exercise 3
In exercise 2, the 95 percent confidence interval is found to be 2 to 16 (9 ± 7). How do you interpret this finding?

_____

_____

_____

[9] Remember that we are only explaining how this process works. In order to actually calculate such intervals, you would need more knowledge of statistics than we present in this text. This statement would be accurate if the number of classrooms was 100.

Exercise 4
A random sample of college students reveals a correlation of .65 between high school GPA and college GPA. What is the null hypothesis? If the resulting probability is less than .001, what is your interpretation?

_____

_____

_____

Exercise 5
In exercise 4, the 95 percent confidence interval is .65 ± 25. What are the boundaries of the interval? How do you interpret this information?

_____

_____

_____

AUTHORS' COMMENTS

Exercise 1. A mean of 70 or larger will occur 10 percent of the time as a result of sampling error if the population mean is 60.

Exercise 2. The null hypothesis states that there is *no* (zero) difference between males and females in the population from which the samples were selected. A probability of .01 means that the obtained difference of 9 would occur 1 time in 100 in random samples of the same size.

Exercise 3. The researcher will be correct 95 percent of the time in concluding that the population difference is between 2 and 16.

Exercise 4. The null hypothesis is that the correlation in the population is .00. We would be correct 99.9 percent of the time in concluding that the population correlation is not .00. We would be wrong in this conclusion only 1 time in 1000.

Exercise 5. The boundaries are .40 to .90. If we conclude that the correlation in the population is between these values, we will be correct 95 percent of the time.

■ *ADDENDUM 1: Statistical Matching*

You will recall from Chapter Eleven our discussion of statistical matching as a means of controlling the threat to internal validity posed by subject characteristics. At that time, we promised an explanation of the rationale behind the procedure. We want to present this explanation now. Let us first describe its application to a correlational study.

To review, whenever two or more characteristics of individuals are correlated, there is a possibility that yet *other* characteristics of these individuals may explain any relationships that are found. The other characteristics of subjects can be controlled through a technique known as *partial correlation*.

Let us use an example in which a researcher sought to study a possible relationship between teachers' expectations of failure and the amount of disruptive behavior by students in their classes. This relationship is shown in scatterplot (A) in Figure 12.13.

The researcher desires to control, or "get rid of," the variable of class "ability level," since it is logical to assume that it might be a cause of variation in the other two variables. In order to control for this variable, the researcher needs to measure the ability level of each class. He or she can then construct scatterplots (B) and (C) as shown in Figure 12.13. Scatterplot (B) shows the correlation between amount of disruptive behavior and class ability level; scatterplot (C) shows the correlation between teacher expectation of failure and class ability level.

The researcher can now use scatterplot (B) to predict the disruptive behavior score for class 1, based on the class's ability score. In doing so, the researcher assumes that the line[10] shown in scatterplot (B) correctly represents the relationship between these variables (class ability level and amount of disruptive behavior) in the data. Next, the researcher subtracts the *predicted* disruptive behavior score from the *actual* disruptive behavior score. The result is the *adjusted* disruptive behavior score—that is, the score has been "adjusted" by taking out the influence of ability level. For class 1, the predicted disruptive behavior score is 7 (based on a class ability score of 5). In actuality, this class scored 11 (higher than expected), so the adjusted score for amount of disruptive behavior is 4 (11 − 7). The same procedure is then followed to adjust the teacher expectation score for class 1 for the effect of class ability level, as shown in scatterplot (C) (10 − 7 = 3). After repeating this process for the entire sample of classes, the researcher is now in a position to determine the correlation between the *adjusted* disruptive behavior scores and the *adjusted* teacher expectation scores. The result is the correlation between the two major variables—amount of disruptive behavior and teacher expectation of failure—with the effect of class ability eliminated, and thus controlled. This entire procedure can be repeated ("adjusting" the adjusted scores) to control additional variables. In practice, the calculations required are greatly simplified.

In the comparison-group design, the same rationale is used, the difference being that only one measured variable is "adjusted." The difference between each individual's original score and the predicted score is again used (the adjusted score). The mean (or median) of each group is then calculated. When a pretest is used as the matching variable, the resulting adjusted score is called a *regressed* gain score. This score is preferable to the more straightforward gain score (posttest minus pretest score) primarily because it is more reliable.

---

[10] This line is called the regression line or "best fit" line. It is the straight line which best represents the relationship. Its placement can be estimated visually, but is actually determined mathematically.

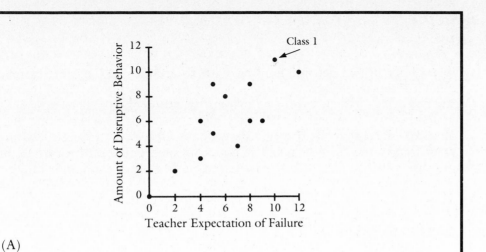

(A)
Amount of Disruptive Behavior in Class as Related to Teacher Expectation of Failure

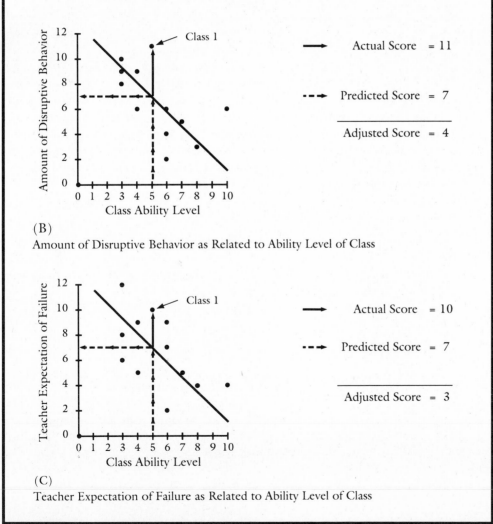

(B)
Amount of Disruptive Behavior as Related to Ability Level of Class

(C)
Teacher Expectation of Failure as Related to Ability Level of Class

FIGURE 12.13
Scatterplots for Combinations of Variables

■ ADDENDUM 2: Specific Inferential Statistics

It is important to become familiar with the names of the most commonly used inferential techniques so you will be able to recognize them in reading the research literature and also to identify which ones may be applicable to your study.[11] Remember that they all require random sampling. In the absence of random sampling, the probabilities that are produced are in error to an unknown degree. The potential usefulness of these statistics is another powerful argument for attempting to obtain random samples.

The following techniques are used to compare the means of groups for statistical significance.

critical ratio. Used only when each of two groups contains at least 30 scores.

⌐ t *test for independent means.* Used when two groups are made up of different individuals.

⌐ t *test for correlated means.* Used when two means are based on same individuals, or when groups have been matched.

⌐ *analysis of variance (ANOVA).* Used instead of the *t* test for independent means when comparing means of two or more independent groups.

analysis of covariance (ANCOVA). Used instead of the *t* test for correlated means when two or more groups are matched statistically.

Mann-Whitney U test. Used to compare two independent groups when scores are ranks.

Kruskal-Wallis one-way analysis of variance. Used to compare two or more independent groups when scores are ranks.

sign test. Used to compare two matched groups as an alternative to the *t* test for correlated means.

Friedman two-way analysis of variance. Used to compare two or more matched groups.

The following technique is used to evaluate the statistical significance of correlation coefficients.

t *test for* r. Used with the Pearson correlation coefficient.

The following technique is used to evaluate the statistical significance of relationships shown in a crossbreak table.

chi-square. Used when the data are in the form of frequency counts.

---

[11] Each of these requires certain conditions or assumptions that you should check whenever you have occasion to use them. Any basic statistics text will identify these assumptions.

▇ *Summary*

In this chapter, we identified some of the more common techniques that researchers use to analyze data. We explained the difference between descriptive and inferential statistics, and described when the use of each is appropriate. We discussed how to construct frequency polygons, scatterplots, and crossbreak tables.

▇ *Key Concepts Discussed in This Chapter*

raw score	correlation coefficient
derived score	crossbreak table
standard score	statistical matching
statistic	effect size
arithmetic mean	descriptive statistics
median	inferential statistics
range	null hypothesis
standard deviation	statistical significance
frequency polygon	confidence interval
scatterplot	

▇ *How Far Along Should I Be at This Point?*

By now, you should understand what is meant by the terms "descriptive statistics" and "inferential statistics" and when each should be used in research. You should also understand how frequency polygons, scatterplots, and crossbreak tables are used in educational research and be able to interpret them.

Evaluate your progress, therefore, by checking the following. At this point, you should have accomplished each of the tasks listed at the end of the preceding chapters. (If not, review and accomplish them before going any further). Furthermore, you should be able to:

• Explain what is meant by the terms "descriptive statistics" and "inferential statistics."
• Prepare a frequency polygon.
• Determine the mean and median of a set of scores.
• Construct a scatterplot and a crossbreak table.
• Estimate the correlation coefficient from a scatterplot.
• Explain the purpose and use of inferential statistics.
• Describe the statistical procedures you would use in your own study.

■ *What's Next?*

In the next chapter, we put everything you have learned so far together as we examine an actual research proposal prepared by a student in one of our classes. We analyze both the strengths and the weaknesses of this student's work. We then ask you to draw together all of the parts of your proposed study that you have prepared to date into a single document. Finally, we present both the initial and revised versions of another student's proposal to illustrate how a proposal can change in the process of development.

■ *For Further Reading*

Hollander, M., & Proschan, F. 1984. *The statistical exorcist.* New York: Marcel Dekker.

Jaeger, R. M. 1984. *Statistics: A spectator sport* (2nd Ed.). Beverly Hills, CA: Sage.

Moore, D. S. 1985. *Statistics: Concepts and controversies.* New York: W. H. Freeman and Company.

Rowntree, D. 1981. *Statistics without tears: A primer for nonmathematicians.* New York: Charles Scribner's Sons.

Schutte, J. G. 1977. *Everything you always wanted to know about elementary statistics (but were afraid to ask).* Englewood Cliffs, NJ: Prentice-Hall.

Chapter Thirteen

THE RESEARCH PROPOSAL

In this chapter, you will have the opportunity to examine a complete research proposal that was prepared by a student in one of our classes, and to read our comments on both its strengths and weaknesses. We will then present another example in which you will see both an initial and a revised version of a student's work. You will thus have an opportunity to compare your work with that of other students who used the materials in this book in the past and who prepared satisfactory proposals.

Finally, we suggest that you pull together all of the various parts of your proposed study that you have prepared up to now into a single document. When you have done this, you will, in essence, have completed a research proposal. We feel fairly confident that parts of this proposal have been changed as you have worked on it—that is to be expected.

When you have finished this chapter, you should have completed the final draft of your proposed study—your research proposal.

An Example of a Student Research Proposal

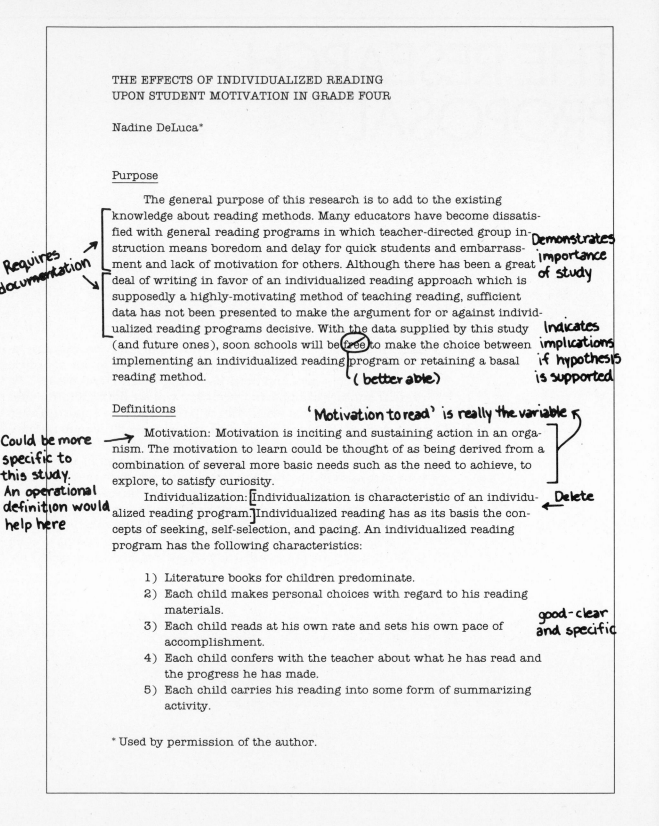

THE EFFECTS OF INDIVIDUALIZED READING
UPON STUDENT MOTIVATION IN GRADE FOUR

Nadine DeLuca*

Purpose

The general purpose of this research is to add to the existing knowledge about reading methods. Many educators have become dissatisfied with general reading programs in which teacher-directed group instruction means boredom and delay for quick students and embarrassment and lack of motivation for others. Although there has been a great deal of writing in favor of an individualized reading approach which is supposedly a highly-motivating method of teaching reading, sufficient data has not been presented to make the argument for or against individualized reading programs decisive. With the data supplied by this study (and future ones), soon schools will be free to make the choice between implementing an individualized reading program or retaining a basal reading method.

[margin note: Requires documentation]

[margin note: Demonstrates importance of study]

[margin note: Indicates implications if hypothesis is supported]

[margin note: (better able)]

Definitions

Motivation: Motivation is inciting and sustaining action in an organism. The motivation to learn could be thought of as being derived from a combination of several more basic needs such as the need to achieve, to explore, to satisfy curiosity.

Individualization: [Individualization is characteristic of an individualized reading program.] Individualized reading has as its basis the concepts of seeking, self-selection, and pacing. An individualized reading program has the following characteristics:

[margin note: Could be more specific to this study. An operational definition would help here]

[margin note: 'Motivation to read' is really the variable]

[margin note: Delete]

1) Literature books for children predominate.
2) Each child makes personal choices with regard to his reading materials.
3) Each child reads at his own rate and sets his own pace of accomplishment.
4) Each child confers with the teacher about what he has read and the progress he has made.
5) Each child carries his reading into some form of summarizing activity.

[margin note: good-clear and specific]

* Used by permission of the author.

6) Some kind of record is kept by the teacher and/or the student.
7) Children work in groups for an immediate learning purpose and leave group when the purpose is accomplished.
8) Word recognition and related skills are taught and vocabulary is accumulated in a natural way at the point of each child's need.

Prior Research

Abbott, J. L., "Fifteen Reasons Why Personalized Reading Instruction Doesn't Work." Elementary English (January, 1972), 44:33-36.

This article refutes many of the usual arguments against individualized reading instruction. It lists those customary arguments then proceeds to explain why the objections are not valid ones. **ok**
It explains how such a program can be implemented by an ordinary classroom teacher in order to show the fallacy in the complaint that individualizing is impractical. Another fallacy involves the argument that unless a traditional basal reading program is used, children do not gain all the necessary reading skills.

Barbe, Walter B., Educator's Guide to Personalized Reading Instruction. Englewood Cliffs, New Jersey: Prentice-Hall, Inc., 1961.

Mr. Barbe outlines a complete individualized reading program. He explains the necessity of keeping records of children's reading. **ok** The book includes samples of book-summarizing activities as well as many checklists to ensure proper and complete skill development for reading.

Hunt, Lyman C., Jr., "Effect of Self-selection, Interest, and Motivation upon Independent, Instructional and Frustrational Levels." Reading Teacher (November, 1970), 24:146-151.

Dr. Hunt explains how self-selection, interest, and motivation *A good beginning* (some of the basic principles behind individualized reading), when *Additional material* used in a reading program, result in greater reading achievement. *should be added*

Miel, Alice, Ed., Individualizing Reading Practices. New York: Bureau of Publications, Teachers College, Columbia University, 1959.
Veatch, Jeanette, Reading in the Elementary School. New York: The Roland Press Co., 1966.
West, Roland, Individualized Reading Instruction. Port Washington, New York: Kennikat Press, 1964.

Good - shows relevance to present study

The three books listed above all provide examples of various individualized reading programs actually being used by different teachers. (The definitions and items on the rating scale were derived from these three books.)

Hypothesis

Variables are clear. Hypothesis is directional

The greater the degree of individualization in a reading program, the higher will be the students' motivation.

Population

Right

An ideal population would be all fourth grades in the United States. Because of different teacher-qualification requirements, different laws, and different teaching programs, though, such a generalization may not be justifiable. One that might be justifiable would be a population of all fourth-grade classrooms in the San Francisco-Bay Area.

Sampling

good sampling plan

random !! →

The study will be conducted in fourth-grade classrooms in the San Francisco-Bay Area, including inner-city, rural, and suburban schools. The sample will include at least one hundred classrooms. Ideally, the sampling will be done randomly by identifying all fourth-grade classrooms for the population described and using random numbers to select the sample classrooms. As this would require excessive amounts of time, this sampling might need to be modified by taking a (sample) of schools in the area, identifying all fourth-grade classrooms in these schools only, then taking a random sample from these classrooms.

Instrumentation

appears to have good logical validity. Items are consistent with definition

Instrumentation will include a rating scale to be used to rate the degree of individualization in the reading program in each classroom. A sample rating scale is shown below. Those items on the left indicate characteristics of classrooms with little individualization.

Should state how data on different days will be used. It can be used to check stability

Reliability: The ratings of the two observers who are observing separately but at the same time in the same room will be compared to see how closely the ratings agree. The rating scale will be repeated for each classroom on at least three different days.

Three days may not be sufficient to get reliable scores

Validity: Certain items on the student questionnaire (to be discussed in the next section) will be compared with the ratings on the rating scale to determine if there is a correlation between the degree of individualization apparently observed and the degree indicated by stu- *good*

Can't use the same item for both variables!

dents' responses. In the same manner, responses to questions asked of teachers and parents can be used to indicate whether the rating scale is a true measure of the degree of individualization.

Would parents be qualified to judge this?

Another means of instrumentation to be used is a student questionnaire. A sample questionnaire is included. The following questions have as their purpose to determine the degree of motivation by asking how many books read and how the child indicates that he feels about reading: questions numbered 1 ④ 5, 6, 7, 9, 10, 11, 12, and 13. Questions 2, 3, ④ and 8 have as their purpose to help determine the validity of the items on the rating scale. Questions 14 and 15 are included to determine the students' attitudes toward the questionnaire to help determine if their attitudes are possible sources of bias for the study. Questions 8 and 9 have an additional purpose which is to add knowledge about the <u>novelty</u> of the reading situation in which the child now finds himself. This may be used to determine if there is a relationship between the novelty of the situation and the degree of motivation. ⟶ *But why?*

good

Most items appear to have logical validity but the lack of definition of motivation to read makes it difficult to judge

Good idea but may not be enough items to give a reliable index

Good idea but maybe too few items to give a reliable index

To control novelty as an extraneous variable?

RATING SCALE

	Scale	
1. Basal readers or programmed readers predominate in room.	1 2 3 4 5	There is an obvious center in the room containing at least five library books per child.
2. Teacher teaches class as a group.	1 2 3 4 5	Teacher works with individuals or small groups.
3. Children are all reading from the same book series.	1 2 3 4 5	Children are reading various materials at different levels.
4. Teacher initiates activities.	1 2 3 4 5	Student initiates activities.
5. No reading records are in evidence.	1 2 3 4 5	Children or teacher are observed to be making notes or keeping records of books read.
6. There is no evidence of book summarizing activities in the room.	1 2 3 4 5	There is evidence of book summarizing activities around room (e.g., student-made book jackets, paintings, drawings, models of scenes or characters from books, class list of books read, bulletin board displays about books read . . .).

RATING SCALE

7. Classroom is arranged with desks in rows and no provision for a special reading area.

1 2 3 4 5

Classroom is arranged with a reading area so that children have opportunities to find quiet places to read silently.

8. There is no conference area in the room for the teacher to work with children individually.

1 2 3 4 5

There is a conference area set apart from the rest of the class where the teacher works with children individually.

9. Children are doing the same activities at the same time.

1 2 3 4 5

Children are doing different activities from their classmates.

10. Teacher tells children what they are to read during class.

1 2 3 4 5

Children choose their own reading materials.

11. Children read aloud in turn to teacher as part of a group using the same reading textbook.

1 2 3 4 5

Children read silently at their desks or in a reading area or orally to the teacher on an individual basis.

Student Questionnaire

Is your intent here to get at socioeconomic level?

Age _____ Grade _____ Father's work _____

Mother's work _____

Appears valid 1. How many books have you read in the last month? _____

Appears valid 2. Do you choose the books you read by yourself? _____

If not, who does choose them for you? _____

Appears valid 3. Do you keep a record of what books you have read? _____

Does your teacher? _____

Appears valid 4. What different kinds of reading materials have you read this year?___

Questionable validity 5. Do you feel you are learning very much in reading this year? _____

Why or why not? _____

Some indication of the scoring system should be given. Open-ended questions must rely on content analysis of responses. You could use examples from your pilot study.

6. Complete these sentences:

    Books _____ *How scored?*

    Reading _____

7. Do you enjoy reading time? _____ *Appears valid*

8. Have you ever been taught reading a different way? _____ *Appear valid as indicators of novelty*

    When? _____ How was it different? _____

    _____ *Generally not a good idea to have one item (9) dependent on another item (8)*

9. Which way of learning to read do you like better? _____

    _____ Why? _____

10. If you couldn't come to reading class for some reason, would you be *Appears valid*

    disappointed? _____ Why? _____

11. Is this classroom a happy place for you during reading time? _____ *Appears valid*

12. Do most of the children in your classroom enjoy reading? *Questionable validity*

    _____

13. How much of your spare time at home do you spend reading just for *Appears valid*

    fun? _____

14. Did you like answering these questions or would you have preferred

    not to? _____ *} Good idea*

15. Were any of the questions confusing? _____

    If so, which ones? _____

    How were they confusing? _____

Student Questionnaire:

Reliability: An attempt will be made to control item reliability by asking the same question in different ways and comparing the answers. *Which items will be compared?*

Validity: Validity may be questionable to some degree since school children may be reluctant to report anything bad about their teachers or the school. *Good point* Observers will be reminded to establish rapport with children as much as possible before administering questionnaires and to assure *Good idea* them that the purpose of the questions does not affect them or their school in any way.

Why do you want this information?

A teacher questionnaire will also be administered. A sample questionnaire is included. Some of the questions are intended to indicate if the approach being used by the teacher is new to her and what her attitude is toward the method. These questions are numbered 1, 2, 3, and 4. Question 5 is supposed to indicate how (available) reading materials are so that this can be compared to the degree of student motivation. Questions 6 and 8 will provide validity checks for the rating scale. Question 7 will help in determining a relationship between socioeconomic levels and student motivation.

Why? how is this related to your hypothesis

May be too few items to give reliable index

Good

Reliability: Reliability should not be too great a problem with this instrument since most questions are of a factual nature.

Incorrect. It is the reliability of information that counts. Persons may or may not be consistent in giving factual information. It does seem likely that these questions would provide reliable data.

Validity: There may be a question as to validity depending upon how the questions are asked (if they are used in a structured interview). The way they are asked may affect the answers. An attempt has been made to state the questions so that the teacher does not realize what the purposes of this study are and so prejudice her answers.

Good

Teacher Questionnaire

Why include? As a means of controlling 'experience'?

1. How long have you been teaching? _____

Why? to assess novelty?

2. How long have you taught using the reading approach you are now using? _____

Why?

3. What other approaches have you used? _____
   _____

Why?

4. If you could use any reading approach you liked, which would you use?
   _____

   Why? _____

Why?

5. In what manner do you obtain reading materials? _____
   _____

   Where did you get most of those you now use? _____
   _____

Appears valid for individualization

6. How often are the children grouped for reading? _____
   _____

Under procedures, you explain that items 1-5 and 7 are intended as attempts to control extraneous variables. This is a very good idea but the purpose should be made clear earlier (in this section).

7. From what neighborhood or area do most of the children in this class come? _____

_____

To assess socio-economic status

8. How do you decide when and how word recognition skills and vocabulary are taught to each child? _____

_____

Appears valid for individualization

If it were feasible, an excellent instrument would be a parent questionnaire. The purpose of it would be to determine how much the child reads at home, his general attitude toward reading, and any changes in his attitude the parent has noticed.

Good idea. Parents should be able to judge 'motivation to read'

Procedures

Since the sample of one hundred classrooms is large and each classroom will need to be visited at least three times for thirty minutes to one hour during each visit on different weeks, quite a large team of observers—probably around twenty—will be needed. They will work in pairs observing independently. They will spend about one-half hour each visit on the rating scale. The visits should take place between Monday and Thursday, since activities and attitudes are often different on Fridays. The investigation will not begin until after school has been in session for at least six weeks so that all programs have had sufficient time to function smoothly.

Good idea

Control of extraneous variables: Sources of extraneous variables might include that teachers using individualized reading might be the more skillful and innovative teachers. Also, in cases where the individualized reading program is a new one, teacher enthusiasm for the new program might carry over to students. In this case it might be the novelty of the approach and teacher enthusiasm rather than the program itself that is motivating. An attempt will be made to determine if there is a relationship between novelty and teacher enthusiasm and student motivation by correlating the results of the teacher questionnaire (showing newness of program and teacher preference of program), indications from questions on student questionnaire, and statistics on motivation in a scatterplot. The influence of student socioeconomic levels on motivation will be determined by comparing the answers to the question on the teacher questionnaire concerning what area or neighborhood children live in, the question on parental occupations on the student

Good

Good

Good

o.k. but could be clearer

Good

This section does a good job of identifying and attempting to control variables likely to be detrimental to internal validity

Good but how will information be scored?

questionnaire, and student motivation. The amount and availability of materials may influence motivation also. This influence will be determined by the answers of teachers concerning where and how they get materials.

Isn't it likely that all classrooms would be affected the same? Further, it seems unlikely that your second variable (individualization) would be affected. If so, it's no problem so far as internal validity is concerned

The presence of observers in the classroom may cause distraction and influence the degree of motivation. By having observers repeat procedures three or more times, later observations may prove to be nearly without this procedure bias. By keeping observers in the dark about the purpose of the study, it is hopeful that will control as much bias in their observations and question-asking as possible. *Good idea. However, since they both observe (individualization) and administer your questionnaire (motivation) they may well figure out the hypothesis. If there is concern that this 'awareness' could influence their ratings and/or administration of the questionnaire, it would be preferable to have each instrument administered by different persons.*

Will you use all of them?

Data Analysis

Observations on the rating scale and answers on the questionnaires will be given number ratings according to the degree of individualization and amount of motivation respectively. The average of the total ratings will then be averaged for the two observers on the rating scale, and the average of the total ratings will be averaged for the questionnaires in each classroom to be used on a scatterplot to show the relationship between motivation and individualization (in each classroom.) Results of the teacher questionnaire will be compared similarly with motivation on the scatterplot. The correlation will be used to further indicate relationships.

Right

Delete. This is incorrect. Do you see why?

Unclear, delete

But teacher questions lack logical validity as indicators of 'motivation.' Items 6 and 8 can check 'individualization' however.

PILOT STUDY

Procedure

The pilot study was conducted in three primary grade schools in San Francisco. The principals of each school were contacted and were asked if one or two reading classes could be observed by the investigator for an hour or less. The principals chose the classrooms observed. About forty-five minutes was spent in each of four third-grade classrooms. No fourth grades were available in these schools. The instruments administered were the student questionnaire and the rating scale.

Both the questionnaire and rating scale were coded by school and by classroom so that the variables for each classroom might be compared. The ratings on the rating scale for each classroom were added together then averaged. Answers on items for the questionnaire were rated "1" for answers indicating low motivation and "2" for answers indicating high motivation. (Note: Some items had as their purpose to test validity of rating scale or to provide data concerning possible biases, so these items were not rated.) Determining whether answers indicated high or low motivation created no problem except on Item #1. It was decided that fewer than eight books (two books per week) read in the past month indicated low motivation, while more indicated high motivation. The ratings for these questions were then added and averaged. Then these averaged numbers for all the questionnaires in each classroom were averaged. The results were as follows:

Room	Individualization	Motivation
#1	1.4	1.3
#2	2.1	1.6
#3	3.0	1.8
#4	3.2	1.7

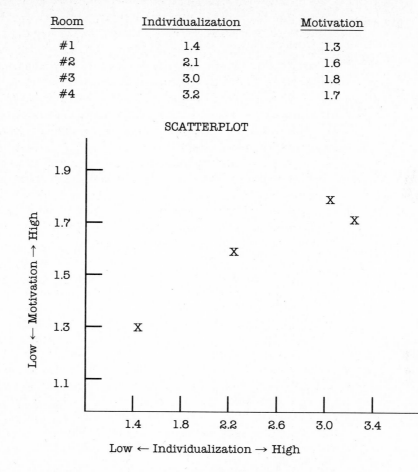

SCATTERPLOT

Although this pilot study could not possibly be said to uphold or disprove the hypothesis, we might venture to say that if the actual study were to yield results similar to those shown on the graph, there would be a strong correlation (estimate: $r = .90$) between individualization and motivation. This correlation is much too high to be attributed to chance with a sample of 100 classrooms. If these were the results of the study

random

described in the research proposal, the hypothesis would seem to be upheld.

Indications

     Unfortunately, I was unable to conduct the pilot study in any fourth-grade classrooms which immediately throws doubt upon the validity of the results. In administering the student questionnaire, I discovered that many of the third-graders had difficulty understanding the questions. Therefore, the questioning took the form of individual structured interviews. Whether or not this difficulty would hold for fourth-graders, too, would need to be determined by conducting a more extensive pilot study in fourth-grade classrooms.

     It was also discovered that Item #7 in the rating scale was difficult to rate. Perhaps it should be divided into two separate items—one concerning desk arrangement and one on the presence of a reading area—and worded more clearly.

     Item #8 on the student questionnaire seemed to provide some problems for children. Third-graders, at least, didn't seem to understand the intent of the question. There is also some uncertainty as to whether the answers on Item #15 reflected the students' true feelings. Since it was administered orally, students were probably reluctant to answer negatively about the test to the administrator of the test. Again, a more extensive pilot study would be helpful in determining if these indications are typical.

     Although the results of the pilot study are not very valid due to its size and the circumstances, its value lies in the knowledge gained concerning specific items in the instruments and problems that can be anticipated for observers or participants in similar studies.

Good observation

Right

Right

Right

A Second Example of a Student Research Proposal

In teaching our classes in educational research, we have found it to be a useful learning experience to have students provide constructive criticism of one another's research proposals as they develop. We think that you too will find it instructive to critique a proposal in its first draft. Accordingly, we now present a first, rough draft of a student's proposal. It contains some serious problems and errors. In the space provided, evaluate each section of the proposal and try to recommend ways to improve it. Later, you will see the final version of this proposal. (You may wish to read the complete proposal before commenting on each section.)

THE EFFECTS OF A PEER-COUNSELING CLASS
ON SELF-ESTEEM (FIRST DRAFT)

Purpose/Justification

The justification for my study is to understand the effectiveness of a major educational delivery system that teaches facilitative interpersonal communication skills and techniques to laypersons and to understand and measure the overall impact on the student's view of self.

If the hypothesis is supported, implications are that students enrolled in a peer-counseling class will see gains in self-concept, self-esteem, academic achievement, and attendance.

My suggestions for improvement (if any) are the following:

_____

_____

_____

Hypothesis

Students enrolled in a peer-counseling class show more improvement in self-esteem than students not so enrolled.

My suggestions for improvement (if any) are the following:

_____

_____

_____

Definitions

Self-esteem is an individual's conscious awareness of self. It is operationally defined as the score on the Piers-Harris Children's Self-Concept Scale.

The second variable is categorical: peer-counseling class vs. no peer counseling. A peer-counseling class is defined as a one-semester class in which high school students are taught a variety of interpersonal helping behaviors that can be used by nonprofessionals when they assume a helping role with others. This variable is operationally defined as enrollment (or nonenrollment) in a peer-counseling class as verified by school records.

My suggestions for improvement (if any) are the following:

_____

_____

_____

Prior Research

(Omitted from this exercise.)

Instrumentation*

The instrument to be used to measure self-esteem is the Piers-Harris Children's Self-Concept Scale. It is appropriate for students in grades 3–12. It consists of 80 statements about oneself to which the respondent answers either yes or no. A factor analysis indicated the items covered six general areas: behavior, intellectual and school status, physical appearance and attributes, anxiety, popularity, and happiness/satisfaction.

The scale was standardized on 1183 children in grades 4–12 in one Pennsylvania school district. There appear to be no consistent gender or grade differences in means. The internal consistency of the scale ranges from .78 to .93, and retest reliability ranges from .71 to .77. Correlations with similar instruments are in the mid-.60s, and the scale has teacher and peer validity coefficients on the order of .40. Care was taken that the scale not correlate unduly with social desirability, and substantial success was achieved; however, quite high correlations ($-.54$ to $-.69$) exist with a measure of anxiety. The authors believe this represents a true trait correlation rather than reflecting response style. It appears that this scale has adequate reliability and validity for use in the proposed study.

As part of my study, I will check content reliability by giving the odd-numbered items to a subgroup of my sample and the even-numbered items to another such group. I will check retest reliability by giving the scale a second time. I will get content-related evidence of validity by checking to see whether counselors and teachers have noted any behavioral changes in students. I will obtain criterion-related evidence of validity by using the Coopersmith Self-Esteem Inventory, which resembles the Piers-Harris in format and age levels.

* Information is summarized from the Piers-Harris test manual and reviews in the Mental Measurements Yearbook.

My suggestions for improvement (if any) are the following:

_____

_____

_____

Population/Sample

The ideal (target) population is all students enrolled in any secondary school with a peer-counseling program in the San Francisco Unified School District. I intend to obtain my sample as follows:

1. Obtain a list of schools that offer peer-counseling classes.
2. Obtain a list of names of students enrolled in these schools.
3. Assign the name of each student a number.
4. Decide on the number of subjects I need.
5. Use a table of random numbers to select my subjects.

I am entitled to generalize to all students in San Francisco public schools that offer peer-counseling classes because my sample is random.

My suggestions for improvement (if any) are the following:

_____

_____

_____

Procedures/Internal Validity

I recognize that I would need to get cooperation from the school district to identify students and that I might be required to obtain consent forms to administer the self-esteem scales to all students shortly before and shortly after the peer-counseling class is given, although such scales are often used as a part of such classes and in other classes.

With respect to internal validity, I foresee problems in subject selection because some students will enroll only to acquire credit whereas others will be enrolled because they want to learn the skills. My groups should be similar because they are randomly selected. Location may be a problem because classes in some schools may have a better atmosphere than in others. Extraneous events could certainly interfere with the effectiveness of the training. Attitude of subjects may be a problem because adolescents may resist taking the scales. I don't see any problems in loss of subjects because it should be the same in both groups. Maturation and testing also should be the same for both groups. Data collection should not be a problem because the answer sheets will be computer-scored.

My suggestions for improvement (if any) are the following:

_____

_____

_____

Data Analysis

I will obtain a gain score from pretesting to posttesting for each student. To test my hypothesis, I will use frequency polygons and means (or medians), since I have a comparison-group design. To check content reliability, I will use a scatterplot with even-numbered item scores on one axis and odd-numbered item scores on the other. To check reliability over time, I will use a scatterplot with scores on the first test on one axis and scores on the second test on the other axis. To assess criterion-related evidence of validity, I will use a scatterplot with Piers-Harris scores on one axis and Coopersmith scores on the other. The appropriate inference technique for my study is a *t* test for means. The resulting probability is precise because I have a random sample.

My suggestions for improvement (if any) are the following:

_____

_____

_____

AUTHORS' COMMENTS

Purpose/Justification. The introductory paragraph is satisfactory as an overview of the intent of the study. It does not, however, indicate why the study should be done. Why is the question an important one to investigate? Why is it important to study self-esteem? Why does the researcher expect self-esteem to be improved by a class that teaches helping skills?

The stated implications are not implications; the first two outcomes are what is being studied (although elsewhere only self-esteem is referred to); the latter two (academic achievement and attendance) are leaps of faith not justified by this study. Implications should state, specifically, what support for this hypothesis would mean for general knowledge and/or for practice.

Hypothesis. The statement indicates clearly the variables to be studied and predicts the outcome—directionally.

Definitions. Self-esteem is, admittedly, difficult to define. However, review of the pertinent literature, including that pertaining to the tests to be used, should certainly lead to a much clearer statement. The operational definition is helpful in that the scale can be reviewed to judge just what it measures. The definition of peer counseling is adequate, although a little more specificity of content would be helpful. The operational definition is clear enough, but weak in that a reader has no idea as to what extent the classes fit the definition—any class so designated in the records would be accepted. Verification of content by observation, questionnaire, or the like would be preferable.

Instrumentation. The review of the Piers-Harris is good, although some discussion of the low validity coefficients and specification of the time intervals on retest reliability would improve it. The means of checking content reliability is incorrect. Reliability (and validity) can be checked only by having two scores on each person—comparing groups is virtually meaningless. The time interval for checking retest reliability should be given. Content-related evidence of validity cannot be assessed in the manner described. Knowledgeable people must review the instrument for consistency with the definitions of the variable—and this is virtually impossible until self-esteem is more clearly defined. Use of another, similar scale in getting criterion-related evidence of validity is common, but weak since, in effect, the second instrument (Coopersmith) is more like an equivalent form of the primary instrument (Piers-Harris). A better criterion would be ratings by teachers or counselors as alluded to (incorrectly) under content-related evidence of validity.

Population/Sample. The stated population is a sensible accessible population. In most such studies, however, the researcher's target, or ideal, population is much broader. The procedure for selecting a random sample is a good one (assuming the peer-counseling class is open to all students), but it does not provide the necessary comparison groups. Either the sample so selected must be subsequently divided into "peer-counseling" vs. "no peer-counseling" groups—which is very inefficient, since there would presumably be far fewer in the peer-counseling group—or the populations must be divided initially (an easy thing to do using class enrollments) and then a random sample selected from each subpopulation. The intended size of each sample should be stated. Generalization to all schools that offer the career-counseling class *at the time of the study* is justified.

Procedures/Internal Validity.   In some instances, the principle that a threat exists only if the comparison groups differ on extraneous variables seems to be understood (with regard to loss of subjects and maturation, for example). In other instances, there appears to be some confusion. The issue regarding subject selection is whether the two groups (peer counseling vs. no peer counseling) will differ in ways related to self-esteem. This, of course, depends on how the two groups are obtained, and the selection procedure has not been made clear. Since the course is an elective, it is probable that the groups will differ on such characteristics as social skills, academic skills, and altruism, all of which are likely to be related to self-esteem. Even more important, the groups are likely to differ initially in self-esteem. Random selection does *not* solve this problem. Random assignment would, but it is not possible in this study. The fact that some students may be taking the class for the "wrong reasons" may weaken the impact of the class, but it is not a threat to internal validity—it is an unavoidable, built-in part of the method.

Similarly, the fact that some peer-counseling classes may be more effective than others is an inevitable part of the method—not a threat to internal validity. Extraneous events could constitute a threat, but only if they affect the peer-counseling group differently from the comparison group, which seems unlikely, since both "treatment" groups are found in each school. Attitude of subjects is a threat only if one comparison group is more negative than the other; this may well be the case, since the peer-counseling group is more likely to see the scales as making sense. Data collection may be a problem, since self-esteem scales are presumably susceptible to influence by the tester's demeanor, directions, and (possibly) personal characteristics (gender, age, and so forth).

We view the categories of subject characteristics, attitude of subjects, and data collector bias as the most serious threats. The proposal should indicate what will be done to eliminate or reduce them.

Data Analysis.   The procedures to be used are correct. Gain scores are not the best way to control pretest self-esteem (statistical matching would be better), but the idea is correct. The statement that the probability that results from calculation of the *t* test for means is precise is correct *unless* a sizable number (we would say more than 10 percent) of the subjects are lost. In a study such as this that includes several schools, it is advisable to compare the peer-counseling and no peer-counseling groups at each school in addition to making overall comparisons.

After several discussions with the instructor and fellow students, the student revised the initial draft of her work. The revised draft is presented below.

THE EFFECTS OF A PEER-COUNSELING CLASS
ON SELF-ESTEEM (REVISED DRAFT)

Purpose/Justification

Many adolescents are believed to engage in self-defeating behaviors because they were never taught how to understand and accept themselves. Participating in a peer-counseling class should promote a higher level of self-awareness and subsequently a lower level of gang-related activity, drug use, and other self-defeating behaviors that presumably result, in part, from low self-esteem.

If the hypothesis is supported, efforts should be made to expand the offering of such classes. These results would also support the idea that learning ways to help others helps one to accept and like oneself.

Hypothesis

High school students enrolled in a one-semester peer-counseling class will demonstrate more gain in self-esteem than students not so enrolled.

Definitions

Self-esteem is a relatively stable set of self-attitudes reflecting both a description and an evaluation of one's own behavior and attributes. It is operationally defined as the score on the Piers-Harris Children's Self-Concept Scale. It is a measured variable.

The second variable is categorical: peer counseling vs. no peer counseling. A peer-counseling class is defined as a one-semester class in which high school students are taught a variety of interpersonal helping behaviors that can be used by nonprofessionals when they assume a helping role with others. These include skills in tutoring, advising, leading discussions, listening, and clarifying. The operational definition of participation in such a class is official enrollment throughout the semester in a class that is identified as addressing the skills previously described by both the school administration and the instructor of the class.

Prior Research

(Omitted from this exercise.)

Instrumentation*

The instrument to be used to measure self-esteem is the Piers-Harris Children's Self-Concept Scale. It is appropriate for students in grades 3–12. It consists of 80 statements about oneself to which the respondent answers either yes or no. A factor analysis indicated the items covered six general areas: behavior, intellectual and school status, physical appearance and attributes, anxiety, popularity, and happiness/satisfaction.

The scale was standardized on 1183 children in grades 4–12 in one Pennsylvania school district. There appear to be no consistent gender or grade differences in means. The internal consistency of the scale ranges from .78 to .93, and retest reliability ranges from .71 to .77. Correlations with similar instruments are in the mid-.60s, and the scale has teacher and peer validity coefficients on the order of .40. Care was taken that the scale not correlate unduly with social desirability, and substantial success was achieved; however, quite high correlations ($-.54$ to $-.69$) exist with a measure of anxiety. The authors believe this represents a true trait correlation rather than reflecting response style. It appears that this scale has adequate reliability and validity for use in the proposed study.

As part of my study, I will check content reliability by comparing the score from the odd-numbered items with the score from the even-numbered

---

* Information is summarized from the Piers-Harris test manual and reviews in the Mental Measurements Yearbook.

items for each subject on the pretest. I will check retest reliability by giving the scale to a subgroup of at least 50 subjects 4 weeks following the posttest and comparing the two posttest scores for each of these subjects. I will get content-related evidence of validity by having several counselors compare the items on the scale with my definition of self-esteem. I will obtain criterion-related evidence of validity by comparing pretest scores with ratings of the same students made by teachers and/or counselors.

Population/Sample

The ideal (target) population is all students in large, urban high schools in the United States. Realistically, my accessible population is all students in the public high schools in San Francisco. I intend to obtain my sample as follows:

1. Obtain a list of all schools in the San Francisco Unified School District that offer a class in peer counseling (estimated to be six schools).
2. Obtain the class lists of all students who have enrolled for the next semester.
3. Use a table of random numbers to select at least 20 students from each school. (I recognize that in some schools this may be all students taking the class.)
4. Obtain the list of all students in each school.
5. After eliminating those enrolled (present or past) in the peer-counseling class, randomly select at least 20 students at each school to be the comparison group.

I am entitled to generalize to all students in San Francisco public high schools that offer a peer-counseling class.

Procedures/Internal Validity

I recognize that I would need to get cooperation from the school district to identify students and give my scales. I might also be required to obtain consent forms to administer the Piers-Harris scale. The scale would be administered immediately before and after the peer-counseling class is given at each school, and again 4 weeks after the class to a subgroup to check validity.

With respect to internal validity, I do not see serious threats due to location, loss of subjects, extraneous events, or maturation, since these should be the same for both treatment groups. Subject characteristics that may create a threat include initial level of self-esteem, academic ability, gender, ethnicity, and socioeconomic status. I will control gender and ethnicity by mechanical matching at each school and initial self-esteem, academic ability, and socioeconomic status by statistical matching or equating of my groups. Attitude of subjects may be a threat, since students in the peer-counseling classes may take the Piers-Harris scale more seriously and respond more honestly. I will have the person who administers the scale explain that we are trying to better understand our students and hope that this can overcome the problem. I will also ask this person to fill out a form describing students' behavior during the scale administration. The data collector will be the same throughout, a person selected for skill and experience in collecting such information. He or she will not know the purpose or hypothesis of the study.

Data Analysis

I will obtain a gain score from pretesting to posttesting for each student. To test my hypothesis, I will use frequency polygons and means (or medians), since I have a comparison-group design. To check content reliability, I will use a scatterplot with even-numbered item scores on one axis and odd-numbered item scores on the other. To check reliability over time, I will use a scatterplot with scores on the first test on one axis and scores on the second test on the other axis. To assess criterion-related evidence of validity, I will use a scatterplot with Piers-Harris scores on one axis and teacher/counselor ratings on the other. The appropriate inference technique for my study is a t test for means. My resulting probability will be imprecise to the extent that subjects are lost as a result of dropping out and of matching my groups.

AUTHORS' COMMENTS

The revised draft takes into account many of the comments made by the instructor on the first draft. As you can see, a number of changes were made. If the author of this proposal decided to actually carry out the study, some additional changes would probably have to be made (particularly with regard to sampling and the control of extraneous variables). Nevertheless, we consider the revised draft to be an acceptable piece of work by a student who has completed a first course in educational research.

We have now reached the end of your proposal. You have learned a lot about educational research, and about how to put together a research proposal. It is time to draw together the various parts of the study that you have been preparing into a single document—the final draft of your proposal.

Summary

In this chapter, we examined a research proposal prepared by a student in one of our classes, and analyzed both the strengths and the weaknesses of this student's work. Next, we presented both the initial and later revised drafts of another student's proposal in order to illustrate how proposals can change in the process of development. Finally, we asked you to draw together all the parts of your proposed study into a single document—your own completed research proposal.

How Far Along Should I Be at This Point?

By now, you should be familiar with many of the basic ideas involved in educational research, including research problems and hypotheses, variables and definitions, sampling and generalizability, the use of instruments, reliability and validity, research designs, internal validity, and descriptive and inferential statistics. You should have applied these concepts to a research proposal of your own choosing.

Evaluate your progress, therefore, by checking the following. At this point, you should have:

- Accomplished each of the tasks listed at the end of the preceding chapters. (If not, review and accomplish them before going any further.)
- Completed the research proposal for your proposed study.
- Discussed all the topics listed below in your report:
  purpose
  justification
  ethics
  hypothesis
  variables
  definitions
  prior research
  instrumentation, including reliability and validity
  sampling
  generalizability
  procedures, including internal validity
  data analysis

What's Next?

In the next chapter, we will examine several additional methodologies used by researchers in education. We will then present examples of how these methodologies might actually be used by teachers and other professionals in schools to investigate questions of interest.

For Further Reading

Behling, J. H. 1984. *Guidelines for preparing the research proposal* (Rev. Ed.). Lanham, MD: University Press of America.

Davitz, J. R., & Davitz, L. L. 1977. *Evaluating research proposals in the behavioral sciences.* New York: Teachers College Press.

Fraenkel, J. R., & Wallen, N. E. 1990. Writing research proposals and reports. In *How to design and evaluate research in education.* New York: McGraw-Hill, pp. 440–462.

Krathwohl, D. R. 1977. *How to prepare a research proposal* (2nd Ed.). Syracuse, NY: Syracuse University Bookstore.

Chapter Fourteen

DOING RESEARCH IN SCHOOLS

In this chapter, we want to acquaint you with a few additional research methodologies that you should be aware of, and that you may want to learn more about. We then shall provide you with some examples of how these methodologies, along with the others we have talked about in this book, can be used by teachers and other professionals in the field of education to investigate problems and questions of interest in their work.

When you have finished this chapter, you should be familiar with a variety of methodologies that are used by researchers in education. You should also be able to see how these methodologies might be used to investigate problems and questions of interest in your own work.

◼ A Brief Review

In this book, we have been concerned primarily with four types of research: true experiments, quasi-experiments, causal-comparative studies, and correlational studies. Let us review the essential characteristics of each of these briefly.

True Experiments

When a researcher is able to conduct a true experiment, he or she arranges for one or more groups of subjects to receive different treatments. The subjects are (usually) randomly assigned to treatment and control (or comparison) groups, and administration of the treatment(s) is controlled by the researcher. The performance or achievement of the subjects after differing treatments is compared by means of their scores on a test or other instrument. The intent is to assess the effect of an independent variable on one or more dependent variables. The results of the study may be generalized to the population from which the sample was selected, provided the sample was chosen randomly at the outset.

Quasi-Experiments

When random assignment is not possible, a researcher may conduct a quasi-experiment. Although two or more groups of subjects are still compared (usually), the subjects are *not* randomly assigned to the treatment and control groups. Intact groups (e.g., existing classes) are used, or a specific individual or group is assessed repeatedly over a time period. Administration of the treatment variable is controlled by the researcher. The intent, again, is to assess the effect of an independent variable on one or more dependent variables. The researcher is entitled to generalize the results of the study beyond the sample involved—*provided* each group is a random sample from a specified population *and* is not substantially altered by matching procedures.

Causal-Comparative Studies

When a researcher conducts a causal-comparative study, two or more groups that already differ in certain ways are compared on one or more variables. There is no manipulation or intervention on the part of the researcher other than that required to administer the instrument(s) necessary to collect the data. The intent is to explore possible causation between group membership and the other variable(s). The researcher may be entitled to generalize the results of the study if he or she knows that the subjects involved were randomly selected from specified populations.

Correlational Studies

When a researcher conducts a correlational study, only a single group of subjects is involved. As in causal-comparative research, the variables are not manipulated. The scores of the subjects on two or more different measures are correlated. The intent is to determine the degree of relationship that exists between the variables involved. Generalization to a defined population is defensible if the sample was randomly selected and loss of subjects is minimal.

Which of the four types of research methodologies summarized above did you plan to use in your proposed study?

_____ An experimental methodology

_____ A quasi-experimental methodology

_____ A causal-comparative methodology

_____ A correlational methodology

Could you have investigated the research question in your proposed study by another one of the methodologies listed above (besides the one you chose)?

Yes _____ If so, which one? _____

No _____ If not, why not? _____

_____

_____

Some Additional Methodologies

Educational researchers also conduct other kinds of research besides the four mentioned above. The most common are surveys, case studies, content analyses, and ethnographies. Let us describe each one briefly.

SURVEYS

When a researcher conducts a survey, a written questionnaire, test, or interview is administered, either by mail or in person, to one or more groups of subjects. No treatment is involved, nor is a relationship (usually) studied. The responses of the subjects to the questions are summarized, analyzed, and reported. The intent is to obtain a sizable amount of information about the characteristics of a particular group. The researcher is entitled to generalize the findings to a larger group if the sample surveyed was randomly selected from that group and not too many are "lost."

When a researcher conducts an interview, an interview schedule (a carefully designed set of questions) is prepared and administered orally to one or more groups of subjects. The essential difference between a questionnaire and an interview is that data are usually collected from fewer individuals in an interview, but the information is far more detailed. Interviews also permit a researcher to probe and follow up on questions of particular interest. Since interviews usually involve a fairly small sample that was not selected randomly, generalization is rarely appropriate.

Here are three examples of research questions that would lend themselves to being investigated by means of a survey:

"What do students like about their high school courses?"

"What improvements would teachers suggest to make teaching as a career more attractive to young people?"

"To what extent do 'regular' teachers favor mainstreaming students with special problems?"

Could you have investigated the research question in your proposed study by means of a survey?

Yes _____ No _____ If not, why not? _____

_____

_____

CASE STUDIES

When a researcher conducts a case study, he or she collects data on a single individual or group in depth, often using a variety of instruments, over a longer period of time than is the case in a survey. The intent is to find out as much as possible about the characteristics, actions, ideas, and other attributes of a single individual or group. Generalization is not considered to be appropriate.

Here are three examples of research questions that would lend themselves to a case study:

"Why is Joanna having such trouble learning to read?"
"Why is Mrs. Rogers so well liked by students?"
"What makes Ms. Chin such an effective therapist?"

Could you have investigated the research question in your proposed study by means of a case study?

Yes _____ No _____ If not, why not? _____

_____

_____

CONTENT ANALYSES

A content analysis is just what its name implies—an analysis of the written or visual contents of a document. The conscious and unconscious beliefs, attitudes, values, and ideas of people or groups are often revealed in the things they write (or draw, paint, and so on). By examining the contents of one or more documents—magazines, newspapers, advertisements, novels, plays, books—the researcher can determine the occurrence of various words, statements, concepts, pictures, images, and ideas. To analyze the contents of a document, however, a researcher first needs to plan how to select and order the contents that are available for analysis. Pertinent categories must be developed that will allow the researcher to identify and then count and compare elements which he or she thinks are important. Sometimes these categories can be developed in advance; more commonly, they must emerge after the researcher has become familiar with the content.

The nub of content analysis is defining as precisely as possible those aspects of content that the researcher wants to investigate and then formulating relevant categories to identify and analyze them. These categories should be so explicit that another researcher who used them to examine the same material would find essentially the same proportion of topics emphasized or ignored. Frequencies of occurrence in each of the categories of interest are evaluated and then reported. The intent is to come to some conclusions about how often certain characteristics, ideas, positions, and images are presented in the documents analyzed. The researcher is entitled to generalize the findings to the extent that the documents examined are representative of some larger group of documents. Here are two examples of research questions that would lend themselves to being investigated by means of content analysis:

"What images do U.S. history textbooks present of people of color?"
"To what extent did the authors of studies reported in educational journals over the last 10 years use random samples?"

Could you have investigated the research question in your proposed study by means of a content analysis?

Yes _____ No _____ If not, why not? _____

_____

_____

ETHNOGRAPHIES

When a researcher conducts an ethnography, one or more individuals are extensively observed going about their daily activities in naturalistic settings. These activities, and how they are performed, are described in considerable detail and, typically, clarified through interviews with "key informants." No manipulation or intervention on the part of the researcher takes place. The intent is to "paint a portrait" of what the individuals do (and why) as clearly and in as much detail as possible. Generalization is usually highly questionable, because the subjects chosen by the researcher and the observations made are highly selective.

For example, an ethnographic researcher might be interested in the following question: "What is life like in an inner-city high school?" The researcher's goal is to document or portray the daily, ongoing experiences of the teachers, students, administrators, and staff in an inner-city school. The school would be regularly visited over a considerable length of time (a year is not uncommon). Classrooms would be observed on a regular basis, and an attempt made to describe, as fully and as richly as possible, what exists and what happens in those classrooms. Several of the teachers, students, administrators, and support staff would be interviewed in depth.

The researcher's descriptions (a better word might be "portrayals") might include the social atmosphere of the school; the intellectual and emotional experiences of students; the manner in which administrators and teachers (and staff and students) act toward and react to others of different ethnicities, genders, or abilities; how the "rules" of the school (and the classroom) are learned, modified, and enforced; the kinds of concerns teachers (and students) have; and the views students have of the school, and how these compare with the views of the administration and the faculty.

Here are two examples of research questions that would lend themselves to being investigated through an ethnography:

"What goes on in an elementary class for gifted students during an average week?"
"What leadership style do newly appointed principals use during their first year of administration?"

Could you have investigated the research question in your proposed study through an ethnography?

Yes _____ No _____ If not, why not? _____

_____

_____

▪ *Examples of How Research Could Be Done in Schools*

At this point, you may be wondering how these various methodologies can be applied by education professionals in conjunction with their other duties. Is it possible, for example, for elementary and secondary school teachers, administrators, or counselors to use some of these methods to do research in the schools? Might other professionals use them in their work to investigate questions of interest? The answer is a definite yes! Research does not have to be left to "outside" investigators.

There are many kinds of questions that lend themselves very well to being investigated in schools. For example, what kinds of methods work best with what kinds of students? How can teachers encourage students to think about important issues? How can content, teaching strategies, and activities be varied to help students of differing ages, genders, ethnicities, and abilities? How can subject matter be presented so as to maximize understanding? What can teachers and administrators do to capture and maintain the interest of students in schooling? What can counselors do? What can other education professionals do?

Classroom teachers, counselors, supervisors, and administrators can help provide some answers to these (and other) important questions. If several teachers in different schools within a district, for example, were to investigate the same question in their classrooms (thereby "replicating" the research of their peers), they could begin what might become a steadily accumulating base of knowledge about important aspects of teaching and learning, a knowledge base that, although badly needed, does not at present exist.

Let us present some examples, therefore, of what could be done.[1]

INVESTIGATING THE TEACHING OF SCIENCE CONCEPTS BY MEANS OF AN EXPERIMENT

Mrs. Gonzales, a first-grade teacher, is interested in the following question:

> "Does the use of drama improve understanding of basic science concepts in first graders?"

How might Mrs. Gonzales proceed?

Although it could be investigated in a number of ways, this question lends itself particularly well to experimental research. Mrs. Gonzales could randomly assign students to classes in which some teachers use dramatics and some do not. She could compare the effects of these contrasting methods by testing the conceptual knowledge of the students in these classes at specified intervals with a test designed to measure conceptual understanding. The average score of the different classes on the test (the dependent variable) would give Mrs. Gonzales some idea of the effectiveness of the methods being compared.

---

[1] Although we use school-based settings for the examples we present, it takes only a little imagination to conceptualize conducting similar studies in agencies and institutions other than schools (e.g., mental health institutions, volunteer organizations, community service agencies).

Of course, Mrs. Gonzales wants to have as much control as possible over the assignment of individuals to the various treatment groups. In most schools, the random assignment of students to treatment groups (classes) would be very difficult to accomplish. Should this be the case, comparisons still would be possible using a quasi-experimental design. Mrs. Gonzales might, for example, compare student achievement in two or more *intact* classes in which some teachers agree to use the drama approach. Since the students in these classes would not have been assigned randomly, this design could not be considered a true experiment; but if the differences between the classes in terms of what is being measured are quite large, and if students have been matched on pertinent variables (including a pretest of conceptual understanding), the results could still be suggestive with regard to how the two methods compare.

1. What difficulties, if any, do you foresee for Mrs. Gonzales?

_____

_____

_____

2. What might Mrs. Gonzales do to eliminate or minimize these difficulties? What else might she do to improve the quality of her study?

_____

_____

_____

3. What other method(s), if any, might Mrs. Gonzales use to investigate her

question? _____

_____

_____

AUTHORS' COMMENTS

1. The classes might differ with regard to important variables that could affect the outcome of the study. If Mrs. Gonzales is the data collector, she could unintentionally favor one group when she administers the instrument(s).

2. Mrs. Gonzales should make an attempt to control for all extraneous variables (student ability level, age, instructional time, teacher characteristics, and so on) that might affect the outcome under investigation. Several control procedures were described in Chapter Eleven—teaching during the same or closely connected periods of time, using equally experienced teachers for both methods, matching students on ability and gender, having someone else administer the instrument(s), and so forth.

3. Mrs. Gonzales might decide to use the causal-comparative method if some classes are already being taught by teachers using the drama approach.

DETERMINING WHAT STUDENTS LIKE ABOUT SCHOOL BY MEANS OF A SURVEY

Mr. Abramson, a high school guidance counselor, is not interested in comparing instructional methods. He is interested in how students feel about school in general. Accordingly, he asks the following questions:

"What do students like about their classes? What do they dislike? Why?"

"What types of subjects are liked the best or least?"

"How do the feelings of students of different ages, sexes, and ethnicity in our school compare?"

What might Mr. Abramson do to get some answers?

These sorts of questions can best be answered by a survey that attempts to measure student attitudes toward their classes. Mr. Abramson will need to prepare a questionnaire, taking time to ensure that the questions he intends to ask are directed toward the information he wants to obtain. Next, he should have some other members of the faculty look over the questions and identify any they feel will be misleading or ambiguous.

There are two difficulties involved in such a survey. First, Mr. Abramson must ensure that the questions to be answered are clear and not misleading. He can accomplish this, to a fair extent, by using objective or "closed-ended" questions, ensuring that they all pertain to the topic under investigation, and then further eliminating ambiguity by pilot testing a draft of the questionnaire with a small group of students. Second, Mr. Abramson must be sure that a sufficient number of questionnaires are completed and returned so that meaningful analyses can be made. He can improve this rate of return by giving the questionnaire to students to complete when they are all in one place. Once he has the completed questionnaires collected, he should tally the responses and see what he's got.

The big advantage of questionnaire research is that it has the potential to provide a lot of information from quite a large sample of individuals. If more details about particular questions are desired, Mr. Abramson can also conduct personal interviews with students. As we have mentioned before, the advantage there is that Mr. Abramson can ask open-ended questions (those giving the respondent maximum freedom of response) with more confidence, and pursue particular questions of special interest or value in depth. He would also be able to ask follow-up questions, and explain any items that students find unclear.

1. What difficulties, if any, do you foresee for Mr. Abramson?

_____

_____

_____

2. What might Mr. Abramson do to eliminate or minimize these difficulties? What else might he do to improve the quality of his study?

_____

3. What other method(s), if any, might Mr. Abramson use to investigate his

questions? _____

_____

_____

AUTHORS' COMMENTS

1. Some students may not understand the questions, or they may not return their questionnaire.

2. Mr. Abramson has an advantage over many survey researchers in that he can probably ensure a high rate of return by administering his questionnaire directly to students in their classrooms. He must be careful to give directions that facilitate an honest and serious set of answers, and to ensure the anonymity of the respondents. Although difficult, he also should try to get data on both reliability (perhaps by giving the questionnaire to a subsample a second time after an appropriate time interval—say, 2 weeks) and validity (perhaps by selecting a subsample who are interviewed immediately after they individually fill out the questionnaire). Checking reliability and validity requires sacrificing anonymity for *those* students since he must be able to identify individual questionnaires.

3. None. A survey is the most appropriate methodology to use to investigate the research question.

CHECKING FOR BIAS IN ENGLISH ANTHOLOGIES BY MEANS OF A CONTENT ANALYSIS

Ms. Hallowitz, an eighth-grade English teacher, is concerned about the accuracy of the images or concepts that are presented to her students in their literature anthologies. She asks the following questions:

"Is the content presented in the literature anthologies in our district biased in any way? If so, how?"

What might Ms. Hallowitz do to get answers?

To investigate these questions, a *content analysis* is called for. Ms. Hallowitz decides to look particularly at the images of heroes that are presented in the literature anthologies used in the district. First, she needs to select the sample of anthologies to be analyzed—that is, to determine which texts she will peruse. (She restricts herself to only the current texts available for use in the district.) She then needs to think about the specific categories she wants to look at. Let us assume she decides to analyze the physical, emotional, social, and mental characteristics of heroes that are presented. She could then break these categories down into smaller coding units such as the following:

Physical	Emotional	Social	Mental
weight	friendly	ethnicity	wise
height	aloof	dress	funny
age	hostile	occupation	intelligent
body type	uninvolved	status	superhuman
.	.	.	.
.	.	.	.
.	.	.	.

Ms. Hallowitz can prepare a coding sheet to tally the data in each of the categories that she identifies in each anthology she studies. Comparisons among categories can then readily be made to see, for example, whether white males are portrayed as "white collar" workers and "males of color" are portrayed as "blue collar" workers.

A major advantage of content analysis is that it is unobtrusive. Ms. Hallowitz can "observe" without being observed, since the contents being analyzed are not influenced by her presence. Information that she might find difficult or even impossible to obtain through direct observation or other means can be gained through a content analysis of the sort sketched above.

A second advantage is that content analysis is fairly easy for others to replicate. Finally, the information that is obtained through content analysis can be very helpful in planning for further instruction. Data of the type sought by Ms. Hallowitz can suggest additional information which students may need to gain a more accurate and complete picture of the world they live in, the factors and forces which exist within it, and how these factors and forces impinge on people's lives.

1. What difficulties, if any, do you foresee for Ms. Hallowitz?

_____

_____

_____

2. What might Ms. Hallowitz do to eliminate or minimize these difficulties? What else might she do to improve the quality of her study?

_____

_____

_____

3. What other method(s), if any, might Ms. Hallowitz use to investigate her

questions? _____

_____

_____

AUTHORS' COMMENTS

1. Ms. Hallowitz's major problem lies in being able to define clearly the categories that will suit her questions. If, for example, nonwhite males are less often portrayed as "professionals," does this indicate bias in the materials or does it reflect reality?

2. She should try to identify all the anthologies being used in her district and then either analyze each one or select a random sample.

3. Ms. Hallowitz could survey teacher and/or student opinions about bias, but that would answer a different question.

PREDICTING WHICH KINDS OF STUDENTS ARE LIKELY TO HAVE TROUBLE LEARNING ALGEBRA BY MEANS OF A CORRELATIONAL STUDY

Let's turn to mathematics for our next example. Mr. Thompson, an algebra teacher, is bothered by the fact that some of his students have difficulty learning algebra while other students learn it with ease. As a result, he asks:

"How can I predict which sorts of individuals are likely to have trouble learning math?"

What might Mr. Thompson do to investigate this question?

If Mr. Thompson could make fairly accurate predictions in this regard, he might be able to suggest some corrective measures that he or other teachers could use to help students so that large numbers of "math haters" are not produced. In this instance, *correlational research* is an appropriate methodology. Mr. Thompson could utilize a variety of measures to collect different sorts of data on his students: their performance on a number of "readiness" tasks related to algebra learning (e.g., calculating, story problems); other variables that might be related to success in algebra (anxiety about math, critical thinking ability); familiarity with specific concepts ("constant," "variable," "distributed"); and any other variables that might conceivably point up how those students who do better in algebra differ from those who do more poorly.

The information obtained from such research can help Mr. Thompson predict more accurately which students will have learning difficulties in algebra and should suggest some techniques for him to try in order to help students learn.

1. What difficulties, if any, do you foresee for Mr. Thompson?

2. What might Mr. Thompson do to eliminate or minimize these difficulties? What else might he do to improve the quality of his study?

_____

_____

_____

3. What other method(s), if any, might Mr. Thompson use to investigate his

question? _____

_____

_____

AUTHORS' COMMENTS

1. The main problem for Mr. Thompson is likely to be getting adequate measurements on the different variables he wishes to study. Some information should be available from school records; other variables will probably require special instrumentation. (He must remember that this information must apply to students *before* they take the algebra class.)

2. Mr. Thompson must, of course, have an adequately reliable and valid way to measure proficiency in algebra. He must also try to avoid incomplete data (i.e., missing scores for some students on some measures).

3. Other methodologies are less appropriate, although an ethnographic study might clarify the variables that should be examined as predictors.

COMPARING TWO DIFFERENT WAYS OF TEACHING CHEMISTRY BY MEANS OF A CAUSAL-COMPARATIVE STUDY

Mrs. Algonquin, a first-year chemistry teacher, is interested in discovering whether students in past classes achieved more in, and felt better about, chemistry when they were taught by a teacher who used "inquiry science" materials. Accordingly, she asks the following question:

"How has the achievement of those students who have been taught with inquiry science materials compared with that of students who have been taught with traditional materials?"

What might Mrs. Algonquin do to get some answers to her question?

If this question were to be investigated experimentally, two groups of students would have to be formed, and then each group taught differently by the teachers involved (one teacher using a standard text, let's say, and the other using the inquiry-oriented materials). The achievement and attitude of the two groups could then be compared by means of one or more assessment devices.

To test this question using a *causal-comparative design*, however, Mrs. Algonquin must find a group of students who *already* have been exposed to the inquiry science materials and then compare their achievement with that of another group taught with the case study materials. Do the two groups differ in their achievement and feelings about chemistry? Suppose they do. Can Mrs. Algonquin then conclude with confidence that the difference in materials produced the difference in achievement and/or feelings? Alas, no, for other variables may be the "cause." To the extent that she can rule out such alternative explanations, she can have some confidence that the materials are at least one factor in causing the difference between groups.

1. What difficulties, if any, do you foresee for Mrs. Algonquin?

_____

_____

_____

2. What might Mrs. Algonquin do to eliminate or minimize these difficulties? What else might she do to improve the quality of her study?

_____

_____

_____

3. What other method(s), if any, might Mrs. Algonquin use to investigate

her question? _____

_____

_____

AUTHORS' COMMENTS

1. Mrs. Algonquin's main problems are in getting a good measure of achievement and in controlling extraneous variables. The latter is likely to be difficult, since she needs to have access to prior classes in order to get the relevant information (such as student ability and teacher experience).

2. She might locate classes that were as similar as possible with regard to extraneous variables that might affect results.

3. Unless she has a special reason for wanting to study previous classes, Mrs. Algonquin might be advised to compare methods that are being used currently. She might be able to use the quasi-experimental approach (by assigning teachers to methods and controlling the way in which the methods are carried out). If not, her causal-comparative approach would permit easier control of extraneous variables if current classes were used.

FINDING OUT HOW MUSIC TEACHERS TEACH THEIR SUBJECT BY MEANS OF AN ETHNOGRAPHIC STUDY

Mr. Adams, the director of curriculum in an elementary school district, is interested in knowing more about how the district's music teachers teach their subject. Accordingly, he asks:

"What do music teachers do as they go about their daily routine—in what kinds of activities do they engage?"

"What are the explicit and implicit rules of the game in music classes that seem to help or hinder the process of learning?"

What can Mr. Adams do to get some answers?

To gain some insight into these questions, Mr. Adams could choose to carry out an *ethnography*. He could try to document or portray the activities that go on in a music teacher's classes as the teacher goes about his or her daily routine. Ideally, Mr. Adams should focus on only one classroom (or a small number of them at most) and plan to observe the teacher and students in that classroom on as regular a basis as possible (perhaps during a preparation period). He should attempt to describe, as fully and as richly as possible, what he sees going on.

The data to be collected might include interviews with the teacher and students, detailed prose descriptions of classroom routines, audiotapes of teacher–student conferences, videotapes of classroom discussions, examples of teacher lesson plans and student work, and flowcharts that illustrate the direction and frequency of certain types of comments (e.g., the kinds of questions that teacher and students ask of one another, and the responses that different kinds of questions produce).

Ethnographic research can lend itself well to a detailed study of individuals as well as classrooms. Sometimes much can be learned from studying just one individual. For example, some students learn how to play a musical instrument very easily. In hopes of gaining insight into why this is the case, Mr. Adams might observe and interview one such student on a regular basis to see if there are any noticeable patterns or regularities in the student's behavior. Teachers and counselors, as well as the student, might be interviewed in depth. Mr. Adams might also conduct a similar series of observations and interviews with a student who finds learning how to play an instrument very difficult, to see what differences can be identified. As in the study of a whole classroom, as much information as possible (study style, attitudes toward music, approach to the subject, behavior in class) would be collected. The hope here is that through the study of an individual, insights can be gained that will help the teacher with similar students in the future.

In short, then, Mr. Adams's goal should be to "paint a portrait" of a music classroom (or an individual teacher or student in such a classroom) in as thorough and accurate a manner as possible so that others can also "see" that classroom and its participants, and what they do.[2]

---

[2] Although it may appear that ethnographic research is relatively easy to do, it is, in fact, extremely difficult to do well. If you wish to learn more about this method, consult one or more of the following references: H. B. Bernard. 1988. *Research methods in cultural anthropology.* Newbury Park, CA: Sage Publications. J. P. Goetz & M. D. LeCompte. 1984. *Ethnography and qualitative design in educational research.* San Diego, CA: Academic Press. Y. S. Lincoln & E. G. Guba. 1985. *Naturalistic inquiry.* Newbury Park, CA: Sage Publications. C. Marshall & G. B. Rossman. 1989. *Designing qualitative research.* Newbury Park, CA: Sage Publications.

1. What difficulties, if any, do you foresee for Mr. Adams?

_____

_____

_____

2. What might Mr. Adams do to eliminate or minimize these difficulties? What else might he do to improve the quality of his study?

_____

_____

_____

3. What other method(s), if any, might Mr. Adams use to investigate his

questions? _____

_____

_____

_____

AUTHORS' COMMENTS

1. One of the difficulties in conducting ethnographic research is that relatively little advice can be given beforehand. The primary pitfall is allowing personal views to influence the information obtained and its interpretation.

2. We believe that an ethnographic study should be done only under the guidance of someone with prior training and experience in using this methodology.

3. Mr. Adams could elect to use a more structured observation system and a structured interview. This would reduce the subjectivity of his data, but it might also detract from the richness of what he reports.

■ *All Have Value*

It is to be stressed at this point that all of the research methodologies we have described in this book have value. Each constitutes a different way of inquiring into the realities that exist within classrooms and schools, and into the minds and emotions of students, teachers, and other professionals. Each represents a different sort of tool to use in order to understand, analyze, and draw conclusions about schooling and education. But it is inappropriate to consider any one or two of these approaches as being "superior to," or "better than," any of the others, for the effectiveness of a particular methodology depends in large part on the nature of the research question asked and the specific context within which the investigation is to take place.

In our view, it is unwise to compare the effectiveness of one methodology using the criteria of another, or attempt to impose a single model's standards on all educational research. Investigators need to gain insights into what goes on in education from as many perspectives as possible, and hence need to construe research in broad rather than narrow terms. So far as we are concerned, research in education should ask a variety of questions, move in a variety of directions, encompass a variety of methodologies, use a variety of tools, and be undertaken by a variety of people. Different research orientations, perspectives, and goals should not only be allowed for, but encouraged.

An Example of In-School Research

It seems appropriate to conclude this chapter with a real-life example of how even one of the most difficult types of research to do in schools (a quasi-experiment) can be carried out in the context of ongoing school activities and responsibilities. The following study[3] was carried out by one of our students, Darlene DeMaria, in her special class for learning-disabled students in a public elementary school near San Francisco, California. Ms. DeMaria hypothesized that male learning-disabled students in elementary schools who receive a systematic program of relaxation exercises would show a greater reduction in off-task behaviors than students who do not receive such a program of exercise.

Using an adaptation of an existing instrument, Ms. DeMaria selected 25 items (behaviors) from a 60-item scale previously designed to assess attention deficit. The 25 items selected were those most directly related to off-task behavior. Each item was rated from 0–4 on the basis of prior observation of the student, with a rating of 0 indicating that the behavior had never been observed and a rating of 4 indicating that the behavior had been observed so frequently as to seriously interfere with learning.

Three weeks after school began, Ms. DeMaria and her aide filled out the rating scale for each of the 18 students independently. The score provided the basis for assessing improvement and for matching two groups prior to intervention.

Since the students were assigned to the Resource Room (where Ms. DeMaria taught) approximately 1 hour a day in groups of 2 to 4, and their schedules had been set previously, random assignment was not possible. It was, however, possible to match students across groups on grade level and (roughly) on initial ratings of off-task behavior. The class included students in grades 1 through 6. Students selected to be in the experimental group received the relaxation program on a daily basis for 4 weeks (Phase I), after which both Ms. DeMaria and her aide again independently rated all 18 students. Comparison of the groups at this time provided the first test of the hypothesis. Next, the relaxation program was continued for the original experimental group and *begun* for the comparison group for another 4 weeks (Phase II), permitting additional comparison of groups and resolving the ethical question of excluding one group from a potentially beneficial experience. At the end of this time, all students were again rated independently by Ms. DeMaria and her aide.

---

[3] D. DeMaria. 1990. A study of the effect of relaxation exercises on a class of learning-disabled students. San Francisco, CA: San Francisco State University. Unpublished master's degree thesis.

The results showed that after Phase I the experimental group showed deterioration (*more* off-task behavior—contrary to the hypothesis), whereas the comparison group showed little change. At the end of Phase II, the scores for both groups remained about the same as at the end of Phase I. Further analysis of the various subgroups (each instructed during a different time period) showed that little change occurred in the group that received only 4 weeks of training. Of the three subgroups that received 8 weeks of training, two showed a substantial *decrease* in off-task behavior and one showed a marked *increase.* The explanation for the latter appears clear. One student who was placed in the Resource Room program just prior to the onset of training had an increasingly disruptive effect on the other members of his subgroup, an influence that the training was not powerful enough to counteract.

What do you think the strengths of this study are? the limitations?

_____

_____

_____

_____

_____

AUTHORS' COMMENTS

This study demonstrates how research on important questions can be conducted in real-life situations in schools and can lead to useful, although tentative, implications for practice.

Like any study, this one has several limitations. The first is that agreement between Ms. DeMaria and her aide on the pretest was insufficient and required further discussion and reconciliation of differences, thus making the pretest scores somewhat suspect. Agreement, however, was satisfactory (an r above .80) for both posttests.

A second limitation is that the comparison groups could not be precisely matched on the pretest, since the control group had more students at both extremes. Although neither group initially showed more off-task behavior overall, this difference as well as other uncontrolled differences in subject characteristics could conceivably explain the different outcomes for the two groups. Further, the fact that the implementer (Ms. DeMaria) was one of the raters could certainly have

influenced the ratings. That this did not happen is suggested by the fact that Ms. DeMaria's Phase II scores for the original experimental group were in fact higher (contrary to her hypothesis) than in Phase I. Evidence of retest reliability of scores could not be obtained during the time available for the study. Evidence for validity rests on the agreement between independent judges. Generalization beyond this one group of students and one teacher (Ms. DeMaria) clearly is not justified. The analysis of subgroups, although enlightening, is after the fact, and hence the results are highly tentative.

Despite these limitations, the study does suggest that the relaxation program may have value for at least some students if it is carried out long enough. One or more other teachers should be encouraged to replicate the study. An additional benefit was that the study clarified, for the teacher, the dynamics of each of the subgroups in her class.

Classroom teachers and other professionals can (and should, we would argue) conduct studies like the one you have just read. As mentioned earlier, there is much in education about which we know little. Many questions remain unanswered; much information is needed. Classroom teachers, counselors, and administrators can help to provide this information. We hope you will be one of those who do.

Summary

In this chapter, we reviewed the four main methodologies presented in this book, and then briefly described a few additional methodologies that are often used in research studies. We then presented some examples of how teachers and other professionals in the field of education can use these methodologies to investigate problems and questions of interest in their work.

Key Concepts Discussed in This Chapter

research methodology	causal-comparative study
experiment	survey
quasi-experiment	interview
correlational study	case study
content analysis	ethnography

How Far Along Should I Be at This Point?

By now you should be familiar with a variety of methods used in educational research: their application and their strengths and limitations. You should be able to see how they can be used in schools, classrooms, and other settings as well as in large-scale research efforts.

Evaluate your progress, therefore, by checking the following. At this point, you should have accomplished each of the tasks listed at the end of the preceding chapters. (If not, review and accomplish them before going any further.) Furthermore, you should be able to:

• Explain briefly what each of the following research methodologies involves:
  experiment
  quasi-experiment
  causal-comparative study
  correlational study
  survey
  case study
  content analysis
  ethnography
• Offer some ideas about how to use research in your own work.

■ *What's Next?*

In the next (and last) chapter of the book, we provide you with a set of criteria for evaluating research reports. We use these criteria to critique a published report of research conducted in the past by one of the authors.

■ *For Further Reading*

Barnes, R. P. 1964. *Research for the practitioner in education.* Washington, DC: Department of Elementary School Principals, National Education Association.

Borg, W. R. 1987. Action research. In *Applying educational research: A practical guide for teachers* (2nd Ed.). New York: Longman.

Bransford, J., et al. 1986. Teaching thinking: Evaluating evaluations and broadening the data base. *Educational Leadership,* 44(2):68–70.

Budd, W. C., & Kelly, S. P. 1970. *Educational research by practitioners: An elementary casebook.* New York: Harper & Row.

Merriam, S. B. 1988. *Case study research in education: A qualitative approach.* San Francisco: Jossey-Bass.

Chapter Fifteen

CRITIQUING RESEARCH REPORTS

Wfae have almost completed our journey. You should, at this point, have a pretty good idea of many of the basic ideas involved in educational research. You have learned about research problems and hypotheses, about variables and definitions, about sampling and generalizability, about the use of instruments and research design, about reliability and validity, and about methods of data analysis. You have also applied many, if not all, of these concepts to a research proposal of your own choosing. Finally, you have learned how the research methodologies we have discussed can be used in schools to investigate questions of interest.

Before we end our journey, let us examine one final matter—how to assess the value of the many research reports that are published in the professional literature. Writing proposals and investigating questions of interest are only part of what research is about. Knowledgeable professionals, as well as researchers, should be able to read and evaluate published reports. Many beginning students of research have difficulty determining the adequacy of a particular study. Accordingly, in this chapter, we shall give you a set of criteria you can use to evaluate research reports that relate to your particular interests.

When you have completed this chapter, you should be able to read and critique most educational research reports.

Criteria for Evaluating Research Reports

Reviewing a research study involves the same concepts that are important in designing a study. As they plan an investigation, researchers must think about the various aspects of a study that we have discussed in this book: the

TABLE 15.1   Criteria for Evaluating Research Reports

Purpose. Is the intent of the author(s) clear?

Justification. Is the importance of the study made clear? Are implications specified? Are ethical issues discussed?

Definitions. Are the variables clear? Are the major terms defined? If so, how? constitutively? operationally?

Prior Research. Is it extensive? Is it relevant? Are the results summarized?

Hypotheses. Are hypotheses clearly stated? implied? directional?

Sampling. Is the intended population described clearly? Is it implied? Is the sample described clearly? Is it representative? random? Is sample size adequate?

Instruments. Is instrumentation adequately described? Were reliability and validity checks performed? Is evidence of reliability sufficient? Is evidence of validity sufficient for the purpose of the study?

Procedures/Internal Validity. Are the procedures clearly described? Have threats to internal validity been discussed? How adequately have they been controlled?

Data Analysis. Are the statistics that were used appropriate? Are limitations discussed?

Results. Are results presented clearly? Is the written description consistent with the data? Are there a minimum of inferences?

Discussion. Are the authors' interpretations consistent with the obtained results? Are they relevant to the purpose of the study? Do they place the study in a broader perspective? Are limitations on population generalizability discussed? Are limitations on ecological generalizability discussed?

---

question to be investigated, the formulation of a hypothesis, the appropriate research methodology, the clarity of terminology, the selection of a sample, the choice of instruments, the analysis of data, and so forth. All these must be put together into a feasible and justifiable research plan.

In critiquing a study, you need to look at what researchers have actually done, and how well. To assist you in this regard, Table 15.1 presents a list of criteria that are useful for reviewing and evaluating studies. Notice that almost all of these topics are ones we have reviewed earlier in the text. The two that have not been previously considered are "results" and "discussion"; these are examined in the following section.

RESULTS AND DISCUSSION

The *results* section of a study presents in writing the findings that have emerged, usually with accompanying tables and/or charts. In examining a study, you should always note whether the written description of the findings is appropriate and consistent with the data presented. In most cases, you will find this to be the case. Occasionally, however, there may be a discrepancy between the findings as reported in tables and the way in which they are described in writing.

The *discussion* section of a report, in contrast, is the place where researchers consider their findings in a broader context. It is also the place for investigators to recapitulate any difficulties that were encountered in the study and to make suggestions for possible improvement in future studies.

It is of particular importance that the results and discussion sections of a study be kept distinct from each other. A good discussion section will typically go considerably beyond the data in attempting to place the findings in a broader perspective. It is important that the reader not be misled into thinking that the investigator has obtained evidence for something that is only speculation. To put it differently, there should be no room for disagreement regarding the statements in the results section of the report. The statements should follow very clearly and directly from the data that were obtained. There may be much argumentation and disagreement about the broader interpretation of these results, however.

Let us consider the results of the study on teacher personality and classroom behavior described in Chapter Six (see page 118). As hypothesized in that study, significant correlations of .40 to .50 were found between a test of control need on the part of the teacher and (1) the extent of controlling behavior in the classroom as observed and (2) ratings by interviewers as "less comfortable with self" and "having more rigid attitudes of right and wrong." These were the results of the study and should clearly be identified as such in a report. In the discussion section, however, these findings might be placed in a variety of controversial perspectives. Thus, one investigator might propose that the study provides support for selection of prospective teachers, arguing that anyone scoring high in control need should be excluded from a training program on the grounds that this characteristic and the classroom behavior it appears to predict are undesirable in teachers. In contrast, another investigator might interpret the results to support the desirability of attracting people with higher control need into teaching. The investigator might cite such data as those reported in another example in Chapter Six (see page 118) to support the position that, at least in inner-city schools, teachers scoring higher in control need are likely to have more businesslike classrooms.

Clearly, both of these interpretations go far beyond the results of the particular study. There is no reason the investigator should not make such an interpretation, provided that it is clearly identified as such and does not give the impression that the results of the study provide direct evidence in support of the interpretation. Many times a researcher will sharply differentiate between results and interpretation by placing them in different sections of a report and labeling them accordingly. At other times a researcher may intermix the two, making it difficult for the reader to distinguish the results of the study from the researcher's interpretations.

A Critique of a Research Report

Your task in this section is to read and critique the following research article, published by one of the authors and two of his colleagues.[1] Although the research was conducted a number of years ago, the focus of the study is current. Critical thinking has recently reemerged as a topic of considerable interest to the educational community. In addition, the teaching method used in the study remains a major approach supported by advocates of critical thinking.

Use the outline presented in Table 15.1 to critique the study.

[1] N. E. Wallen, V. E. Haubrich, & I. Reid. 1963. The outcomes of curriculum modifications designed to foster critical thinking. *The Journal of Educational Research*, 56:529–534. Used by permission.

THE OUTCOMES OF CURRICULUM MODIFICATIONS
DESIGNED TO FOSTER CRITICAL THINKING

Critical thinking appears to be a universally accepted objective of
education, though we are frequently unclear as to what we mean by it and to
what extent we wish to live with its consequences. As has been pointed out
elsewhere (5), various definitions of critical thinking seem to encompass some
or all of the following features:

1. Use of scientific methods, including emphasis on evidence and the
   nature of hypotheses.
2. The tendency to be inquisitive, critical, and analytical with respect to
   issues, personal behavior, etc. A derivative of this attribute is lack of
   susceptibility to propaganda.
3. Use of correct principles of logic.

The emphasis is on the development of that elusive philosophical idea,
the rational man.

With respect to methods of fostering critical thinking, two major
approaches have been advocated. The first is "progressive education." Critical
thinking is presumed to be but one of the objectives which are fostered by a
greater degree of self-determination, flexibility of curriculum, and freedom of
behavior. The results of the Eight-Year Study provided some support for this
position. Further support of an indirect type is provided by studies which
indicate that questioning and critical behaviors are less likely to occur in rigid,
highly formalized situations where deviation is punished (2).

The second approach emphasizes the tools rather than the attitude of
critical thinking, while recognizing the importance of a milieu conducive to the
use of the tools. Thus, emphasis is placed on acquainting students with the
principles of logic and experimentation and with their use. It is this approach
toward which this study was directed.

Method

The basic design of the study was as follows:

It involved seven teachers of U.S. history (eleventh grade) in three Salt
Lake City high schools who introduced the curriculum modifications and
an additional two who served as controls. During the first year, one class
(selected at random) taught by each of the nine teachers was tested in the fall
and again in the spring to establish the amount of gain to be expected over a
year's time under the present curriculum. The tests were the Cooperative U.S.
History Test, the Watson-Glaser Test of Critical Thinking, and the IDS Critical
Thinking Test. During the summer of 1960, the experimental teachers attended

a 1-week workshop at the University of Utah campus under the direction of Dr. Vernon Haubrich, during which time they received training in the curriculum procedures and materials presently available as well as experience in the development of new materials. During the following academic year, two of their classes were again tested in the fall and the spring, as were those of the control teachers. During this year the staff members worked with the teachers in the utilization and development of materials. The resulting data permitted comparisons of gains made from year to year under the same teacher and from teacher to teacher within a given year.

The statistical analysis used was analysis of covariance, which permits comparison of end-of-year scores—adjusted for beginning-of-year scores under the different treatments. Thus (in effect) the mean gain achieved by the experimental teachers during the first year—regular curriculum—is compared with the mean gain achieved under the modified curriculum. Further, the mean gain achieved by the experimental teachers using the modified curriculum is compared with the mean gain achieved by the control teachers during the same year.

Curriculum Modifications

The overall plan of curriculum modification called for the teaching of a unit in "critical thinking" followed throughout the year by application to the content of the course as rather broadly defined. As an example, the students were encouraged to examine their textbook, their newspapers, and their teachers for examples of fallacious logic. This approach has been extensively developed in the Illinois Curriculum Program under the direction of B. Othanel Smith and his associates. In a comprehensive application of the plan in Illinois, a total of 36 teachers and approximately 1,500 high school students in English, geometry, science, and social studies participated. As of this writing, only a preliminary report has been published (5). It appears that the study was carefully conducted and that the students experiencing the experimental method showed greater gain on measures of critical thinking than the control group without showing impairment in mastery of course content.

Thus, the present study is, to a large extent, a replication of the Illinois study to determine whether similar results are obtained—a procedure woefully lacking in educational research. In addition, the present study contains some methodological improvements, notably the use of a "baseline" for gauging change which is based on the same teachers who institute the curriculum changes.

For convenience, the curricular practices may be divided into (1) materials presented during the unit on critical thinking, and (2) application materials throughout the remainder of the year.

1. <u>Unit on Critical Thinking</u>. This unit required approximately 3 weeks for all teachers and was conducted—at the teachers' convenience—sometime during the second or third month of school.

The sequence of presentation varied from teacher to teacher but included the following topics and in this general order:

a. Definitions—abstract and concrete
b. Logical fallacies—<u>post hoc</u> fallacy, etc.
c. Deductive principles
    syllogisms
    if-then statements
    validity and truth
d. Inductive principles
    the nature of evidence
    analysis of arguments, including recognition of implicit assumptions
    reliability of sources

In addition to their notes and experiences during the workshop, the teachers were provided with <u>Applied Logic</u> by Little, Wilson, and Moore, and copies of <u>Guide to Clear Thinking</u> developed by the Illinois Curriculum Program. Also, it was intended that each student be provided with or have access to <u>A Guide to Logical Thinking</u> by Shanner. In one school, however, a misunderstanding resulted in these booklets not being available to all students.

As can be seen from the topics listed above, the intent was to present to these students many of the more salient developments in the areas of logic, semantics, and philosophy of science, but in a fashion which they would comprehend.

2. <u>Application</u>. Throughout the remainder of the year, the teachers attempted to utilize the ideas and skills taught during the unit wherever feasible. To this end, many of the exercises developed by the Illinois group were used. Also, the teachers showed considerable ingenuity and expenditure of effort in materials which they developed. Some of the flavor of the materials may be conveyed by the following illustrative exercises.

a. A statement on page 77 of the text states: "The Articles of Confederation granted considerable power to a Congress of the United States." Is this definition, explanation, or opinion? What criteria are provided?
b. Analyze the argument for unfair advantages in big business on page 368 of the text. Are there any irrelevancies? Fallacies? Do the reasons justify the conclusion?
c. Is there a fallacy in the following argument? Life under a strong government in Great Britain was tyrannical. We must not allow a strong government to develop in this country.

Tests Used to Evaluate Outcomes

The measuring devices used to assess the outcomes of the program included the Watson-Glaser Critical Thinking Appraisal and the IDS Critical Thinking Test—both constructed to assess skills in critical thinking—and the Cooperative U.S. History Test, which was used to assess change in the more typical content of the course.

1. Watson-Glaser Test. This test was originally published in 1942 and was revised in 1956. It contains five subtests: inference, assumptions, deductions, interpretation, and arguments. It has been used in numerous studies and is quite adequate in terms of technical considerations such as reliability and norms. Ennis (3) has, however, questioned its validity on the grounds that some items are questionable and that it gives too high a score to the "chronic doubter."

2. IDS Test. This test was developed in 1957 by Ennis, in part as an attempt to overcome his objections to the Watson-Glaser. As such, the items are, on logical grounds, superior. Preliminary data suggest that it is adequate from a technical standpoint.

3. Cooperative U.S. History Test. This test is considered to be one of the best standardized tests of the typical content of American history courses. It contains items designed to test knowledge of historical facts; understanding of cause-and-effect relationships, trends, and developments; and ability to recognize chronological relationships, interpret historical maps, and locate historical information, with emphasis on political and diplomatic history. It is somewhat weak in the area of contemporary affairs.

Results

Table 1 shows the means of the various groups as well as some additional data pertaining to the IDS test. Tables 2 and 3 show mean values for the Watson-Glaser and Cooperative History tests, respectively. These data support the following interpretation.

TABLE 1 Means of Experimental and Control Groups in the Present Study and of Other Comparison Groups on the IDS Test

	N	Mean, Fall	Mean, Spring	Gain
Experimental teachers Regular curriculum—year 1	140	8.8	10.2	1.4
Experimental teachers Modified curriculum—year 2	280	9.1	11.8	2.7
Control teachers Regular curriculum—year 1	36	6.8	8.4	1.6
Control teachers Regular curriculum—year 2	53	7.5	9.0	1.5
Normative data—high school juniors*			9.0	
Normative data—high school seniors*			9.6	
College educational psychology students*			12.3	
High school students in courses emphasizing critical thinking*			12.1	

* R. H. Ennis. 1963. Interim report: The development of the IDS critical thinking test. Personal communication.

1. The IDS Test

a. Considered as a group, students of the experimental teachers showed significantly greater gain ($p < .01$)[2] the second year—that is, under the modified curriculum—as compared with the previous year. The amount of the difference, when compared with available norms, indicates the improvement to be of practical importance. The students under the revised curriculum began the year with a mean score very near that typical of eleventh graders and, by the end of the year, scored at a level almost up to that of a sample of unselected college students and almost as high as previously reported groups in high school classes emphasizing critical thinking. Students of these teachers but without the revised curriculum showed the amount of gain to be expected during the course of a year. Both groups began the year with nearly identical mean scores.

b. The significant ($p < .05$) teacher-by-method interaction suggests that the curricular modifications are more effective with some teachers than with others.

c. When students experiencing the revised curriculum were compared with students in the regular curriculum (during the same year—different teachers), they showed significantly greater gain ($p < .01$). The gain for the students in the regular curriculum (two teachers) was almost identical for the 2 years.

It seems legitimate to conclude that the revised curriculum had a rather marked effect on critical thinking as measured by the IDS Test.

[2] Authors' Note: Tables showing the details of all statistical analyses involving inferential statistics have been omitted, since they require technical knowledge beyond the scope of this text.

TABLE 2 Means of Experimental and Control Groups on the Watson-Glaser Test

	N	Mean, Fall	Mean, Spring	Gain
Experimental teachers Regular curriculum—year 1	120	62.3	64.9	2.6
Experimental teachers Modified curriculum—year 2	240	61.6	64.0	2.4
Control teachers Regular curriculum—year 1	30	56.8	60.0	3.2
Control teachers Regular curriculum—year 2	53	59.6	62.0	2.4

2. The Watson-Glaser Test

a. The results for this test do not support the IDS Test results. There is essentially no difference between the two groups of students taught by the experimental teachers in amount of gain. In both years the gain is 2.8. The group experiencing the modified curriculum was slightly lower on the fall testing. For the first-year group, the gain is from a percentile rank of 77 to 83, while for the second-year group (modified curriculum), the gain is from the 74th to the 81st percentile rank based on high school norms. Grade equivalent scores are not available for this test.

b. The comparison of experimental and control groups during the second year is consistent with the foregoing analysis only in showing no significant difference between the groups.

The results for this test provide no evidence for the modified curriculum. This finding is particularly disappointing in light of the fact that the Illinois study did find a significant superiority in amount of gain shown on this test by students in the experimental group.

TABLE 3 Means of Experimental and Control Groups on the Cooperative U.S. History Test (Standard Scores: $\underline{X} = 50$, $\underline{S} = 10$)

	N	Mean, Fall	Mean, Spring	Gain
Experimental teachers Regular curriculum—year 1	140	44.1	49.3	5.2
Experimental teachers Modified curriculum—year 2	280	41.3	49.7	8.4
Control teachers Regular curriculum—year 1	36	44.1	47.6	3.5
Control teachers Regular curriculum—year 2	51	39.5	46.9	7.4

3. The Cooperative U.S. History Test

a. Students under the modified curriculum made significantly more gain during the year than did students with the same teachers during the preceding year ($p < .001$). In both instances, the students at the end of the year scored slightly below national norms. The experimental group, however, scored considerably lower at the beginning of the year.

b. The experimental group (modified curriculum) showed more gain than the control group during the same year, but not significantly so.

c. The control teachers achieved significantly ($p < .05$) more gain the second year.

d. The gain of the experimental teachers was not significantly greater than the gain achieved by the control teachers during the second year. Because of the gain achieved by the experimental teachers, we are tempted to suggest that the curricular modifications may have fostered greater interest and/or skill in dealing with course content, hence, greater mastery. But since the gain was not significantly greater than that achieved by the control teachers during the second year, it is possible that other factors were operative, possibly that the second-year students began the year with somewhat poorer background. It is clear that the modifications did not result in a decrease in the mastery of course content.

Reactions of Teachers, Students, and Parents

An additional measure of the outcomes of a plan such as this is to be found in the reactions of the persons involved in it. Although no systematic attempt was made to collect such data in the present study, some information, almost inevitably, is present. It is recognized that impressions such as those which follow are subject to many criticisms on the grounds of selective sampling and bias of several kinds; they are nevertheless presented as valuable, though for the most part subjective, data.

1. The several experimental teachers have all expressed considerable enthusiasm for the program as an interesting and worthwhile attempt in an important area, although some are quite skeptical as to the results achieved, particularly among the less able students. Even accounting for the expected desire to comfort the researchers and to justify their own efforts, it is our opinion that this represents an honest reaction on the part of the teachers. One bit of supportive data is that they have all indicated an intention to use at least part of the materials next year and have expressed the hope that further work of this kind will be undertaken.

The consensus seems to be that the material on fallacies and definitions was easiest to put across, with the material on syllogisms the most difficult, as would be expected. As to organization of presentation, some of the teachers indicated that they would prefer to spread the topics out during the year and introduce them as smaller units. One teacher would, in the future, not teach the material as a distinct unit but rather would attempt to incorporate it throughout the course.

2. As reported by the teachers, the reactions of students was varied. Some expressed the view that it was difficult. Others wondered what it was for (i.e., "Why don't we just have history?"). Our expectation was that some students would be psychologically threatened by the material; this seems to have been the case but to a lesser extent than we expected. On the other hand, some became intrigued and enjoyed it. Several teachers reported students making use of material in arguments and particularly in debate, though some of the same material frequently is presented in debate (and in psychology) courses. Several incidents of carryover to other activities were reported:

a. Letters were written to several advertisers and to a weatherman requesting definition of terms. The former were not satisfactorily answered; the latter was—and in some detail.
b. As a result of a difference of opinion in class regarding a syllogism, several students wrote to a professor of philosophy at the University of Utah for clarification.

3. There appears to have been little reaction from parents. As expected, some parents feared that knowledge of history was being sacrificed for some new silliness, but the teachers were able to provide an explanation which was at least in some cases considered adequate.

We had expected some objection from parents along the lines that their children were beginning to question some of the eternal verities. That this did not happen may be attributable to the parents' confidence in the schools, to parental indifference, or to lack of impact of our program.

Summary

This report describes a 2-year project which introduced into three high schools a curriculum plan designed to foster critical thinking and which attempted to assess its effectiveness. The curriculum plan was patterned after a similar program developed at the University of Illinois and consisted of the presentation of a 3-week unit on the tools of logical analysis, semantics, and scientific method at a level appropriate to eleventh graders, followed by an application of these tools to the content of the course in U.S. history throughout the year. The seven participating teachers were provided a workshop prior to the introduction of the unit and were provided the services of the project staff, as well as the benefits of several group discussions throughout the year. Their interest and effort expended in the project was such as to leave no question but that the approach received an adequate trial.

The results of the evaluation demonstrate quite clearly that mastery of the typical content of the U.S. history course was not impaired by the curriculum modification. The effectiveness of the program in fostering critical thinking is not unequivocally demonstrated, since one of the tests to assess this change did not show any difference between experimental and control groups. The other test, however, which on logical grounds may be argued to be a better test, did show rather impressive differences in favor of students who received the revised curriculum. Further, the reactions of teachers and students, though not intensively studied, strongly support the value of the program.

References

1. Aschener, M. J. 1956. Teaching the anatomy of criticism. The School Review, 64:317-322.

2. Carpenter, F. 1956. Educational significance of studies on the relationship between rigidity and problem solving. Science Education, 40:296-311.

3. Ennis, R. H. 1958. An appraisal of the Watson-Glaser critical thinking test (1957-1958). Journal of Educational Research, 52:155-158.

4. Ennis, R. H. 1963. Interim report: The development of the IDS critical thinking test. Personal communication.

5. Henderson, K. B. 1958. The teaching of critical thinking. Phi Delta Kappan, 39:280-282.

Write your critique of this study in the spaces provided below.

Purpose/justification: _____

_____

_____

_____

_____

Clarity/definitions: _____

_____

_____

_____

_____

Prior research: _____

_____

_____

_____

_____

_____

Hypotheses: _____

_____

_____

_____

_____

Sampling: _____

_____

_____

_____

_____

Instrumentation: _____

_____

_____

_____

_____

Procedures/internal validity: _____

_____

_____

_____

_____

Data analysis: _____

_____

_____

_____

_____

Results: _____

_____

_____

_____

_____

Discussion: _____

_____

_____

_____

_____

Summary of critique: _____

_____

_____

_____

_____

AUTHORS' COMMENTS

We view this article as an example of good research. It is to be expected that we are somewhat less critical than others, perhaps you.

PURPOSE/JUSTIFICATION

The authors relied on the "current acceptance" of its importance to justify studying critical thinking. Although this is often done, we believe a reader deserves a more thorough treatment, perhaps something like the following:

Many respected thinkers, including Dewey, Adler, Toffler, and Taba, have defended the necessity of students' learning to be critical thinkers rather than passive channels for the transmission of information. The rate of information generation is such that no one can expect to master even a limited content area for more than a very short time. In academic areas, therefore, one must learn to evaluate new information and to see its relationship to previous knowledge. In the more general arena of daily life, the necessity for citizens of a democracy to sift and evaluate competing claims for their allegiance and endeavors has been recognized since the framing of the U.S. Constitution.

A reader might also expect some rationale for the teaching method involved. Although implied in the report, a more explicit statement might be the following:

If our definition of critical thinking is accepted, one teaching approach that is immediately suggested is direct instruction in the component skills (e.g., the recognition of logical fallacies). Each skill is presented to students in a manner commensurate with their level of knowledge; opportunities to practice the skills and receive feedback are provided.

Further, the reader might expect to find an exposition of the implications of study outcomes for theory and practice:

If it is shown that the method is effective, additional support is provided for those wishing to disseminate it more widely. Teachers and others will have reason to expect that the desired outcomes will, in fact, occur. Further, such results would also support the general theory espoused by Bruner and others, that high school students are capable of learning content customarily taught in college. Finally, additional evidence would exist to support the proposition that critical thinking can be taught in a straightforward manner to all high school students in much the same ways as other more typical content, rather than depending on greater maturity or special talent on the part of students or teachers.

Finally, the authors should have indicated, at the outset, that the study was a replication of other work and provided more details regarding the prior study.

We see no reason for concern about the ethical implications of the study, although the authors did state, near the end of their report, that they had anticipated some objections from parents because students were being encouraged to question commonly held assumptions. Discussion of the philosophical/political ramifications of this issue is beyond the scope of a research report, but the authors might have explained why they had such expectations.

CLARIFY/DEFINITIONS

The focus of the study seems clear—to obtain evidence of the extent to which the curriculum modifications improve critical thinking in high school students and affect acquisition of customary knowledge of history. The primary outcome variable, "ability to think critically," is clear at the outset. Other outcome variables, however, were not mentioned until near the end of the study. These variables—reactions of teachers, students, and parents—should have been mentioned in the introduction.

No specific section on definitions was provided. The authors did provide somewhat of a constitutive definition of *critical thinking*. However, the statement that various definitions encompass "some or all" of these features is imprecise. Did the authors intend to include all the features? If not, which ones were to be included? Further explication would have been helpful, especially of the "correct principles of logic." Additional clarity could easily have been achieved by defining critical thinking operationally as the scores on the Watson-Glaser and IDS tests. The essentials of the curriculum modifications are probably clear in context later in the report, but might have been called to the reader's attention earlier. The four items listed in the "Unit on Critical Thinking" section might well have been given as the definition of critical thinking, since they are more specific both as to the intent of the curriculum and its content.

PRIOR RESEARCH

The reference to prior research is not very extensive. The two research studies cited, however, do appear to be directly related to the study and the results of the study are indicated. The authors could not have been expected to review all the studies pertaining to critical thinking prior to that time, but some additional references would have been helpful.

HYPOTHESES

Hypotheses were not stated explicitly. We would argue that they should have been, since the study was clearly intended to test the efficacy of a particular method. The following four hypotheses were clearly implied, however.

During the new curriculum year, as compared with the preceding year, the classes of the experimental teachers would demonstrate:

1. Greater gain in critical thinking.
2. Approximately the same amount of gain in knowledge of history.

During the same year, classes taught the new curriculum (by the experimental group teachers), as compared with classes taught the usual curriculum (by the control group teachers), would demonstrate:

3. Greater gain in critical thinking.
4. Approximately the same amount of gain in knowledge of history.

SAMPLING

The sample was clearly not obtained in a random manner, including as it did a total of nine teachers in three high schools and a total of 27 intact classes of students, all in one particular city. The authors did not argue for representativeness, since they would have had to offer evidence that the teachers and students were similar to a population of interest in some important ways (e.g., ability level, socioeconomic level of the students, years of experience of the teachers). In fact, the mean scores of the Cooperative U.S. History Test (see Table 3 in the study) suggest that the student sample was very similar to, but slightly below, the normative group for that test. The sample, then, was a convenience sample, with all of its inevitable limitations.

Whether or not the authors wanted to argue for the generalizability of the results, they should have provided some demographic data. For example, the ethnic makeup of both the teacher and student samples can be presumed (from the location of the study) to be predominantly Anglo (as, in fact, was the case). Further, some readers would likely infer (again because of location) that the attitudes of the teachers would be highly conservative (although this was *not* the case). Since these variables would be expected to influence outcomes, some information on them should have been provided. The sample of students is large in all comparisons of interest, but the sample of teachers is not (only seven experimental and two control). Although actually larger than in many studies of this type, this sample size—particularly that of the control group—presents further limitations.

INSTRUMENTATION

The authors did a poor job of addressing reliability. They are guilty of the typical "quick shuffle" in stating that usage and "other evidence" were sufficient. They should, at the very least, have reviewed previous evidence as to type of reliability and the magnitude of reliability coefficients and then assessed their applicability to this study. Since the student sample appeared to be quite similar in performance on these tests to available norm groups, prior data might have been applicable. However, there is still no excuse for not reporting internal consistency coefficients, since they could easily have been obtained from the data available. While pre-post correlations are somewhat misleading as indicators of reliability in a treatment study (since inconsistency is to be expected pre to post), they are nevertheless of interest, particularly for comparisons between the groups. If the new curriculum turned out to be effective, less pre-post consistency might be expected for students exposed to this curriculum, since new treatments are, by their nature, trying to disturb the predictable pattern of development.

The authors provided a brief logical analysis of the two critical thinking tests. They did not, however, discuss these tests in relation to the curriculum modifications introduced in the study. Readers can make their own comparisons between the five subtests of the Watson-Glaser test and the outline of curriculum topics, but they should not have to do so. It appears that all five subtests have logical relevance to the curriculum topics, but that two topics (definitions and reliability of sources) may not have been tested. The authors had a responsibility to defend their use of this test as it relates to the content taught.

Even less information was provided on the validity of the IDS test. Although use of independent judges to assess the validity of these tests for the purposes of this study may be less crucial than in many studies, it would have greatly strengthened the authors' report. Reliability and validity data on the Cooperative U.S. History Test should have been discussed.

Finally, the authors neglected to report a very useful piece of information. They had a built-in empirical check on validity—the correlation between the two tests—which could easily have been obtained from the data at hand. It would be very helpful to have this correlation (both pre and post) separately for each major treatment group. The results of the group comparisons do suggest that these correlations were not high, but the details are important.

PROCEDURES/INTERNAL VALIDITY

The description of the situational manipulation that was the crucial aspect of the study (i.e., the curriculum modification) is described extensively, although it must be acknowledged that in such a study precisely what occurred is difficult to describe completely. The study would have been strengthened by some observational data on the teachers at various times to support the contention in the summary that curriculum modifications were carried out as intended. The design of the study appears to be a good one. It permits comparison of curriculum and control classes during the same year; it also permits comparison of curriculum and control classes during two successive years while holding the teacher variable constant.

Subject Characteristics. The characteristics of subjects are always of concern when random assignment of sizable numbers of subjects is not used. Analysis of covariance and similar techniques (e.g., analysis of regressed gain scores) do make it possible to match groups with respect to measured variables (in this case, pretest scores), but cannot ensure comparability on other variables, such as student attitude toward social studies or interest in analytic processes.

Loss of Subjects. Mortality would not have been expected to favor the new curriculum groups, since it occurred either by absence from class or by random deletion.

Location. It seems unlikely that the experimental classes would have had any additional resources not available to the control classes, since year 1 vs. year 2 classes were those of the same teachers and during year 2 the control classes were in the same schools.

Instrument Decay. Decay seems unlikely with the test data provided the test booklets were reviewed for any markings.

Data Collector Characteristics. More detail should have been provided. In actuality, all testing was done by one white male graduate student. The characteristics of the data collector were thus held constant.

Data Collector Bias. It seems unlikely that bias would have been introduced by test scoring, since all tests were machine-scored. Information on test administration should have been included, however. The administration of tests by teachers is notorious for violations of standard testing procedures. Had this been the case, the experimental teachers might have been suspected of giving assistance or additional time in taking the tests. This, of course, would have favored their students. In actuality, this threat was minimal, since a project-trained assistant administered all tests.

Attitude of Subjects. A Hawthorne effect was a major concern in this study. Since both teachers and students knew that they were part of a special project and since the experimental teachers received special summer training, it could be argued that this special attention accounted for the obtained results. The only way to control for this threat would be to provide similar special attention to the students in the control groups.

Testing. Pretesting should not have given an advantage to the new curriculum group, since it was done in all groups. It might be argued that the pretest interacted with the method to result in an advantage to the experimental group, but this seems unlikely in that the pretest items were only a sample of the tasks emphasized all year long. Omission of the pretest would have eliminated this possibility at the sacrifice of statistical matching of groups.

It is conceivable that the new curriculum students would have done more poorly on the posttest because of increased critical ability, but this is contrary to the hypotheses and the outcomes obtained.

Extraneous Events. It is always conceivable that one or more other factors, instead of the independent variable, may be responsible for the outcome(s) of a study. In this study, such factors might have included a schoolwide disruption (i.e.,

a teachers' strike during year 1 of the study), or the introduction of critical thinking materials into the physical science curriculum during year 2. In any study, the integrity and acumen of the researchers must be relied on to identify and discuss such factors. Since none were mentioned here, we can only infer that none were known to the researchers. The study design—comparing groups both across years and within the same year—is probably the best way to rule out such possibilities, since "other factors" would not have been expected to favor the new curriculum group under both circumstances.

Maturation of students would have affected all comparison groups in the same way, since the pre-post testing interval was the same for all. Maturation of teachers might have accounted for the superiority of year 2 over year 1 results if the teachers were relatively inexperienced (this was not the case, however), but would have been unlikely to have accounted for differences in year 2 alone.

Regression. A regression effect is unlikely, since extreme groups were not used. If anything, such an effect would favor the control group during year 2, since it had lower pretest scores.

Implementation. In a methods study such as this, researchers must be concerned about possible differences between teachers of the two groups—perhaps the experimental teachers were just better teachers than the control teachers. Use of the same teachers for both methods—as in part of this design—is the best way to control for this threat.

DATA ANALYSIS

Descriptive Statistics. The statistics presented are appropriate, although the omission of standard deviations is unfortunate. Standard deviations are important, in that they permit the assessment of the magnitude of the differences in mean gain. This is particularly important when inferential statistics are suspect. Effect size also should have been reported.

Another method of judging the magnitude of change is by comparison with other known groups. As the authors pointed out, the year 1 and year 2 experimental teacher groups began at very near the expected mean. Although the year 1 group gained somewhat more than might be expected from normative data, the additional gain of the year 2 groups (to that attained by "special groups") does seem sufficient to warrant the conclusions drawn.

Inferential Statistics.   Analysis of covariance is an appropriate procedure for this study. Since the assumption of random sampling was violated, however, the authors were obligated to indicate that the resulting probabilities were not exact and should be interpreted only as general indications. This they did not do. It is legitimate to use the probabilities as indicators of greater gain on the IDS test than on the Watson-Glaser, although the comparison of means (see Tables 1 and 2 in the study) makes the same point. What is not defensible (although common) was the reporting and interpreting of probabilities as though they could be taken at face value.

RESULTS

The description of results is consistent with the tables presented and is clearly written. The description is largely free of interpretive comments with the exception of a comment under the Cooperative U.S. History Test, which states that it is possible that certain factors were operating in one situation. However, the wording seems to make it clear that this is an inference.

DISCUSSION

Relatively little interpretation is provided. At several points the authors compare the findings of their study with those of the original, replicated study. The inclusion of the material on reactions of teachers under the results section may be questionable, since some of the statements are not clearly supported by the data presented within the study itself. Overall, the data did, in our opinion, justify the interpretations made.

Population Generalizability.   To their credit, the authors did not overgeneralize their results to "teachers" and "students," but rather phrased both their discussion of results and their summary in terms of the outcomes obtained for just the teachers and students involved in the study. They failed to discuss the serious limitations imposed by their convenience sample, however. Also, their use of inferential statistics without qualification implies, we believe, that they thought their results were generalizable. They did mention that the study was a partial replication and that the replicated data did not support previous findings, but we would argue that they should have included a statement somewhat like the following at the end of their summary:

> In total, our evidence indicates that further use and study of this method are warranted. We found no evidence of negative effects and some evidence of positive impact. Since, however, our results were equivocal and, in specifics, inconsistent with a prior study, and since our sample does not permit generalization to a defined population, these results must be treated as tentative.

Ecological Generalizability.   The authors made no comments about the ecological generalizability of the study. They did not commit the (not uncommon) error of recommending this method in all social studies courses or at a variety of grade levels, or in the absence of a university support system, but neither did they warn against such overgeneralization.

SUMMARY OF CRITIQUE

The principal criticisms of the study appear to be of two kinds: (1) the authors could have included additional detail on several points—particularly regarding the description of the sample and the testing procedures—and provided a word of caution with regard to statistical probabilities; and (2) the nature of the sampling raises questions about generalizing. The fact that some of the results were similar to those of the previous study lends confidence to generalizing, but the fact that some results were not the same is a negative feature.

Your last assignment is to critique a research report following the format of the preceding critique. You may wish to use one of the studies that you located in Chapter Four. However, this exercise will be more valuable if your critique is of a fairly sophisticated study, so you may wish to locate a new one. Summarize and critique this study in the space provided below, using the categories presented in Table 15.1.

Title of study: _____

_____

Author(s): _____

_____

Year of publication: _____

Journal in which published (title, volume, date of article, pages): _____

_____

Brief Summary of Study

Procedures (What did the researchers do?) _____

_____

_____

_____

_____

_____

_____

_____

Results (What did the researchers find?) _____

_____

_____

_____

Your Critique of Study

Purpose/justification: _____

_____

_____

_____

Clarity/definitions: _____

_____

_____

_____

Prior research: _____

_____

_____

_____

_____

_____

_____

_____

_____

Hypotheses: _____

_____

_____

_____

Sampling: _____

_____

_____

_____

Instrumentation: _____

_____

_____

_____

_____

_____

_____

Procedures/internal validity: _____

_____

_____

_____

_____

_____

_____

Data analysis: _____

_____

_____

_____

_____

_____

_____

Results: _____

_____

_____

_____

_____

_____

_____

Discussion: _____

_____

_____

_____

_____

_____

_____

Summary of critique: _____

_____

_____

_____

_____

_____

_____

■ *Summary*

In this chapter, we presented several criteria you can use to evaluate published reports of research that you read in the professional literature. We provided a study conducted by one of the authors in the past, and asked you to critique it and compare your evaluation of the study with ours.

■ *Key Concepts Discussed in This Chapter*

purpose	instruments
justification	data analysis
prior research	procedures
hypotheses	internal validity
variables	results
definitions	interpretations
sampling	

■ *How Far Along Should I Be at This Point?*

By now, you should have completed your research proposal. You should have a basic idea of many of the concepts of educational research, and some ideas about how research can be done in schools. You should also use criteria to evaluate published reports of educational research, and have critiqued at least one such published report.

Evaluate your progress, therefore, by checking the following. At this point, you should have:

• Accomplished each of the tasks listed at the end of the preceding chapters. (If not, review and accomplish them now.)
• Completed your research proposal.
• Learned many of the basic concepts of educational research.
• Gained some idea of how research can be done in schools.
• Gained knowledge of criteria you can use to evaluate published reports of educational research.
• Critiqued at least one published report of educational research.

■ *What's Next?*

Take a break (we suggest dinner at a nice restaurant with a good friend).
We hope you enjoyed the book.
Good luck!

■ *For Further Reading*

Fraenkel, J. R., & Wallen, N. E. 1990. Analysis of the study. In *How to design and evaluate research in education.* New York: McGraw-Hill, pp. 266–269, 297–300, 323–325, 359–360, 403–405.

Katzer, J., Cook, K. H., & Crouch, W. W. 1982. *Evaluating information: A guide for users of social science research* (2nd Ed.). Reading, MA: Addison-Wesley.

Richardson-Koehler, V. 1987. What happens to research on the way to practice? *Theory into Practice,* 26(1):38–43.

APPENDIXES

Appendix A

GENERAL GLOSSARY OF RESEARCH TERMINOLOGY

ABAB design A single-subject experimental design in which measurements are repeatedly made until stability is presumably established (baseline), after which treatment is introduced and an appropriate number of measurements are made; the treatment phase is followed by a second baseline phase, which is followed by a second treatment phase.

accessible population The population from which the researcher can realistically select subjects for a sample, and to which the researcher is entitled to generalize findings.

achievement test An instrument used to measure the proficiency level of individuals in given areas of knowledge or skill.

age-equivalent score A score that indicates the age level for which a particular performance (score) is typical.

baseline the graphic record of measurements taken prior to introduction of an intervention in a time-series design.

case study An in-depth investigation of an individual, group, or institution to determine the variables, and relationship among the variables, influencing the current behavior or status of the subject of the study.

categorical data variables Data (variables) that differ only in kind, not in amount or degree.

causal-comparative research Research that attempts to determine the cause for, or consequences of, existing differences in groups of individuals; also referred to as ex post facto research.

cluster sampling / cluster random sampling The selection of groups of individuals, called clusters, rather than single individuals; all individuals in a cluster are included in the sample; the clusters are preferably selected randomly from the larger population of clusters.

comparison group The group in a research study that receives a different treatment from that of the experimental group.

concurrent validity (evidence of) The degree to which the scores on an instrument are related to the scores on another instrument administered at the same time, or to some other criterion available at the same time.

confidence interval An interval used to estimate a population value. It is constructed in such a way that the interval has a predetermined probability of including the value.

constant A characteristic that has the same value for all individuals.

constitutive definition Explanation of the meaning of a term by using other words to describe concisely what is meant.

construct-related validity (evidence of) The degree to which an instrument measures an intended hypothetical psychological construct, or nonobservable trait.

content analysis The process of inductively establishing a categorical system for organizing open-ended information.

content-related validity (evidence of) The degree to which an instrument logically appears to measure an intended variable, as determined by expert judgment.

control group The group in a research study that is treated "as usual."

convenience sample A sample that is easily accessible.

correlational research Research that involves collecting data in order to determine the degree to which a relationship exists between two or more variables.

criterion-related validity (evidence of) The degree to which performance on an instrument is related to performance on other instruments intended to measure the same variable, or to other variables logically related to the variable being measured.

data Any information obtained about a sample.

data collector bias Unintentional behaviors or expectations on the part of data collectors that may create a threat to the internal validity of a study.

dependent variable A variable affected or expected to be affected by the independent variable; also called criterion or outcome variable.

derived score A score obtained from a raw score in order to aid in interpretation. Derived scores provide a quantitative measure of each subject's performance relative to a comparison group.

descriptive research / study Research that attempts to describe existing conditions without analyzing relationships among variables.

descriptive statistics Data analysis techniques enabling the researcher to meaningfully describe data with numerical indices or in graphic form.

directional hypothesis A relational hypothesis stated in such a manner that a direction, often indicated by "greater than" or "less than," is hypothesized for the results.

ecological generalizability The degree to which results can be generalized to environments and conditions outside the research setting.

effect size An index used to indicate the magnitude of an obtained result or relationship.

empirical Based on observable evidence.

equivalent forms Two tests identical in every way except for the actual items included.

equivalent-forms method A way of checking consistency by correlating scores on equivalent forms of an instrument in order to obtain a reliability coefficient; also referred to as alternate-forms reliability.

errors of measurement Inconsistency of individual scores on the same instrument.

ethnography / ethnographic research The collection of data on many variables over an extended period of time in a naturalistic setting, usually using observation and interviews.

experiment A research study in which one or more independent variables are systematically varied by the researcher to determine the effects of this variation.

experimental group The group in a research study that receives the treatment (or method) of special interest in the study.

experimental research Research in which at least one independent variable is manipulated, other relevant variables are controlled, and the effect on one or more dependent variables is observed.

experimental variable The variable that is manipulated (systematically altered) in an intervention study by the researcher.

external validity The degree to which results are generalizable, or applicable, to groups and environments outside the research setting.

extraneous event An event that is not part of an intervention but that may affect performance on the dependent variable, thereby influencing results and affecting internal validity; also referred to as a history threat to internal validity.

extraneous variable A variable that makes possible an alternative explanation of results; an uncontrolled independent variable.

frequency polygon A graphic method of showing all the scores obtained by a group of individuals.

generalizing See **ecological generalizability; population generalizability.**

grade-equivalent score A score that indicates the grade level for which a particular performance (score) is typical.

Hawthorne effect A positive effect of an intervention resulting from the subjects' knowledge that they are involved in a study, or their feeling that they are in some way receiving special attention.

hypothesis A tentative, reasonable, testable assertion regarding the occurrence of certain behaviors, phenomena, or events; a prediction of study outcomes.

implementer threat The possibility that results are due to variations in the implementation of the treatment in an intervention study, thereby affecting internal validity.

independent variable A variable that affects (or is presumed to affect) the dependent variable under study and is included in the research design so that its effect can be determined; sometimes called the experimental or treatment variable.

inferential statistics Data analysis techniques for determining how likely it is that results based on a sample or samples are similar to results that would have been obtained for an entire population.

instrument Any procedure or device for systematically collecting data.

instrumentation The entire process of collecting data in a study.

interjudge reliability The consistency of two (or more) independent scorers, raters, or observers.

internal validity The degree to which observed differences on the dependent variable are directly related to the independent variable, not some other (uncontrolled) variable.

intervention A specified treatment or method that is intended to modify one or more dependent variables.

interview A form of research in which individuals are questioned orally.

Kuder-Richardson approaches Procedures for estimating the internal consistency reliability of a test or other instrument from a single administration of the test without splitting the test into halves.

level of confidence The probability associated with a confidence interval; the probability that the interval will contain the population value. Commonly used confidence levels in educational research are 95 and 99 percent.

level of significance The probability that a discrepancy between a sample statistic and a specified population parameter is due to sampling error, or chance. Commonly used significance levels in educational research are .05 and .01.

literature review The systematic identification, location, and analysis of documents containing information related to a research problem.

location threat The possibility that results are due to characteristics of the setting or location in which a study is conducted, thereby producing a threat to internal validity.

loss-of-subjects threat The possibility that subjects who are "lost" to a study (for whatever reason) may differ from those who remain so that their absence has a significant effect on the results of the study. Also referred to as mortality.

matching design A technique for equating groups on one or more variables so that each member of one group has a direct counterpart in another group.

maturation threat The possibility that changes which occur in subjects as a direct result of the passage of time affect their performance on the dependent variable and thereby affect internal validity.

measured variable Data that differ in amount or degree, along a continuum from less to more.

multiple-baseline design A single-subject experimental design in which baseline data are collected on several behaviors for one subject, after which the treatment is applied over a period of time to each behavior in sequence until all behaviors are under treatment.

nondirectional hypothesis A prediction that a relationship exists without specifying its exact nature.

null hypothesis A statement that any difference between an obtained sample statistic and a specified population value is due to sampling error, or chance.

observer bias The possibility that an observer does not observe objectively and accurately, thus producing invalid observations and a threat to the internal validity of a study.

one-group pretest-posttest design A weak experimental design involving one group that is pretested, exposed to a treatment, and posttested.

operational definition Explanation of the meaning of a term by stating the actions, processes, or operations used to measure or identify examples of it.

outcome variable See **dependent variable.**

percentile rank An index of relative position indicating the percentage of scores that fall at or below a given score.

pilot study A small-scale study conducted before an actual study in order to reveal defects in the research plan.

population The group to which the researcher would like the results of a study to be generalizable; it includes *all* individuals with certain specified characteristics.

population generalizability The extent to which the results obtained on a sample are generalizable to a larger group.

prediction The estimation of scores on one variable from information about one or more other variables.

prediction study An attempt to determine variables that are related to (predict) a criterion variable.

probability The relative frequency with which a particular event occurs among all events of interest.

problem statement A statement that indicates the variables of interest to the researcher and any specific relationship between those variables which is to be (or was) investigated; it includes a description of background and rationale (justification) for the study.

projective device An instrument that includes vague stimuli that subjects are asked to interpret. There are no correct answers or replies.

purposive sample A nonrandom sample selected because prior knowledge suggests it is representative.

random assignment The process of assigning individuals or groups randomly to different treatment conditions.

random numbers (table of) A list of numbers that provides the best means of random selection or random assignment.

random sample A sample obtained in such a way that every member of the population has an equal chance of being selected.

random sampling The process of selecting a random sample.

raw score The total score attained by an individual based on all the items on a test or other instrument.

regression threat The possibility that results are due to a tendency for groups, selected on the basis of extreme scores, to regress toward a more average score on subsequent measurements, regardless of the experimental treatment.

reliability The degree to which scores obtained with an instrument are consistent.

reliability coefficient An index of the consistency of scores on the same instrument. There are several methods of computing a reliability coefficient, depending on the type of consistency and characteristics of the instrument.

replication Conducting a study again, either as a direct repetition of the original study, using different subjects, or as a modified version with specified aspects of the study changed.

research The formal, systematic application of scholarship, disciplined inquiry, and most often the scientific method to the study of problems.

research hypothesis A statement of the expected relationship between two or more variables, or other expected outcomes.

research proposal A detailed description of a proposed study designed to investigate a given problem.

research report A description of how a study was conducted, including results and conclusions.

researcher bias The possibility that the researcher's expectations concerning the outcomes of a study may contribute to producing those outcomes, thereby creating a threat to internal validity.

sample The group of subjects on which information is obtained; sample subjects should be selected in such a way that they represent the larger group (population) from which they were obtained.

sampling The process of selecting a sample.

sampling error Expected chance variation in sample statistics that occurs when successive samples are selected from a population.

scatterplot The plot of points determined by the cross tabulation of scores on coordinate axes; used to represent and illustrate the relationship between two measured variables.

scientific method A way of knowing that is characterized by the public nature of its procedures and conclusions and by rigorous testing of its conclusions.

Solomon four-group design An experimental design that involves random assignment of subjects to each of four groups. Two groups are pretested, two are not; one of the pretested groups and one of the unpretested groups receive the experimental treatment, and all four groups are posttested.

split-half procedure A method of estimating the internal consistency reliability of an instrument by giving the instrument once but scoring it twice—for each of two equivalent "half tests." These scores are then correlated.

stability (of scores) The extent to which scores are reliable (consistent) over time.

standard score A derived score that expresses how far a given raw score is from the mean, in terms of standard deviation units.

statistic(s) A numerical index describing a characteristic of a sample.

statistically significant The conclusion that results are unlikely to have occurred through sampling error, or chance; an observed correlation or difference probably exists in the population.

stratified sampling The process of selecting a sample in such a way that identified subgroups in the population are represented in the sample in the same proportion as they exist in the population.

subject characteristics threat The possibility that characteristics of the subjects in a study may account for observed relationships, thereby producing a threat to internal validity.

survey study / research An attempt to obtain data from members of a population (or a sample) to determine the current status of that population with respect to one or more variables.

target population The population to which the researcher, ideally, would like to generalize results.

test of significance A statistical test used to determine whether the obtained results for a sample are likely to represent the population.

test-retest method A procedure for determining the extent to which scores from an instrument are reliable over time by correlating the scores from two administrations of the same instrument to the same individuals.

testing threat A threat to internal validity posed by the fact that improved scores on a posttest may be a result of subjects having taken a pretest.

threat to internal validity An alternative explanation for research results—namely, that an observed relationship is an artifact of another variable.

time-series design An experimental design involving one group that is repeatedly pretested, exposed to an experimental treatment, and repeatedly posttested.

treatment group A group receiving a specified intervention.

treatment variable See **experimental variable.**

unit of analysis The unit (usually a score for an individual or a group) that is used in data analysis.

validity The degree to which correct inferences can be made on the basis of results obtained from an instrument; it depends not only on the instrument itself but also on the instrumentation process and the characteristics of the group studied.

validity coefficient An index of the validity of scores on an instrument; a special application of the correlation coefficient.

variability The extent to which scores differ from one another.

variable A characteristic that can assume any one of several values (e.g., cognitive ability, height, aptitude, teaching method).

z-score The most basic standard score. It expresses how far a score is from a mean in standard deviation units.

Appendix B

SPECIALIZED GLOSSARY OF STATISTICAL TERMINOLOGY

W e recognize that a variety of statistical terms are presented in research reports. Although we cannot provide detailed explanations for these terms—their usage, rationale, or calculation—we are including a brief explanation of the most common ones so that they will have some meaning for you when you encounter them. Many of the terms have not been discussed in this text.

analysis of covariance (ANCOVA) A statistical technique for equating groups on one or more variables when testing for statistical significance; it adjusts scores on a dependent variable for initial differences on other variables, such as pretest performance or IQ.

analysis of variance (ANOVA) A statistical technique for determining the significance of differences among means; it can be used with two or more groups.

average A number representing the typical score attained by a group of subjects. See **measures of central tendency.**

biserial correlation An approximation of the Pearson r that is used when one variable is arbitrarily divided into two categorical variables.

chi square (χ^2) A nonparametric test of significance appropriate when data are in the form of frequency counts; it compares frequencies actually observed in a study with expected frequencies to see if they are significantly different.

coefficient of determination (r^2) The square of the correlation coefficient. It indicates the degree of relationship between two variables.

contingency coefficient An index of relationship derived from a crossbreak table.

contingency table See **crossbreak table.**

correlation coefficient (r) A decimal number between .00 and ± 1.00 that indicates the degree to which two measured variables are related.

Cronbach alpha (α) An internal consistency or reliability coefficient for an instrument requiring only one test administration.

crossbreak table A table of all combinations of two or more categorical variables which portrays the relationship (if any) between the variables.

degrees of freedom A number indicating how many instances out of a given number of instances are "free to vary"—that is, not predetermined.

discriminant function analysis A statistical procedure for predicting group membership (a categorical variable) from two or more measured variables.

Duncan's New Multiple-Range Test A technique used following analysis of variance with three or more groups to determine which differences among groups are statistically significant.

eta An index that indicates the degree of a curvilinear relationship.

expected frequency The frequency in each cell of a crossbreak table that is expected based on marginal totals or theoretical prediction. It is used in the calculation of chi square.

factor analysis A statistical method for reducing a set of variables to a smaller number of factors.

factorial design An experimental design that involves two or more independent variables (at least one of which is manipulated) in order to study the effects upon a dependent variable of the variables acting individually and in interaction with each other.

F-ratio (F-test) The final calculation in analysis of variance. It is the ratio of two estimates of population variance.

Kruskal-Wallis one-way analysis of variance A nonparametric inferential statistic used to compare two or more independent groups for statistical significance of differences.

log-linear models. Statistical procedures for simplifying the analysis of complex crossbreak tables.

Mann-Whitney U Test A nonparametric inferential statistic used to determine whether two uncorrelated groups differ significantly.

mean / arithmetic mean ($\overline{X}$) The sum of the scores in a distribution divided by the number of scores in the distribution; the most commonly used measure of central tendency.

measures of central tendency Indices representing the average or typical score attained by a group of subjects. The most commonly used in educational research are the mean and the median.

measures of variability Indices indicating how spread out the scores are in a distribution. Those most commonly used in educational research are the range, standard deviation, and variance.

median That point in a distribution having 50 percent of the scores above it and 50 percent of the scores below it.

mode The score that occurs most frequently in a distribution of scores.

multiple correlation (R) A numerical index describing the relationship between predicted and actual scores using multiple regression; the correlation between a criterion and the "best combination" of predictors.

multiple regression A technique using a prediction equation with two or more variables in combination ($y = a + b_1X_1 + b_2X_2 + b_3X_3 \cdots$) to predict a criterion.

nonparametric technique A test of significance appropriate when the data represent an ordinal or nominal scale, or when assumptions required for parametric tests cannot be met.

obtained frequency The actual frequency obtained for each cell in a crossbreak table. It is used in the calculation of chi square.

parameter A numerical index describing a characteristic of a population.

parametric technique A test of significance appropriate when the data represent an interval scale and meet other specified assumptions.

path analysis A sophisticated type of analysis investigating causal connections among correlated variables.

Pearson r An index of correlation appropriate when the data represent either interval or ratio scales; it takes into account each and every score and produces a coefficient between .00 and ± 1.00.

range The difference between the highest and lowest scores in a distribution; a measure of variability.

Scheffe Test A technique used following analysis of variance with three or more groups to determine which differences among groups are statistically significant.

standard deviation (SD) The most stable measure of variability; it takes into account each and every score in a distribution.

standard error of a statistic The standard deviation of the sampling distribution of a statistic.

standard error of estimate An estimate of the size of the error to be expected in predicting a criterion score.

standard error of measurement An estimate of the size of the error to be expected in an individual's test score.

standard error of the difference (SED) The standard deviation of a distribution of differences between sample means.

standard error of the mean (SEM) The standard deviation of sample means which indicates by how much the sample means can be expected to differ if other samples from the same population are used.

statistic(s) A numerical index describing a characteristic of a sample.

statistically significant The conclusion that results are unlikely to have occurred as a result of sampling error, or chance; an observed correlation or difference probably exists in the population.

t test for correlated means A parametric test of significance used to determine whether there is a significant difference between the means of two matched, or nonindependent, samples. It is also used for pre-post comparisons.

t **test for independent means** A parametric test of significance used to determine whether there is a significant difference between the means of two independent samples.

Type I error The rejection by the researcher of a null hypothesis that is actually true. Also called alpha error.

Type II error The failure of a researcher to reject a null hypothesis that is really false. Also called beta error.

variance (SD²) The square of the standard deviation; a measure of variability.

Appendix C

CALCULATION OF SOME COMMONLY USED STATISTICS

◼ The Standard Deviation

The *standard deviation* is the most useful index of spread or variability. As with the mean, every score in the distribution is used to calculate it. The steps involved in calculating the standard deviation are straightforward:

1. Calculate the mean of the distribution.
2. Subtract the mean from each score. The results are called deviation scores and are symbolized by small x's.
3. Square each of the deviation scores.
4. Add up all the squared deviation scores.
5. Divide the total by the number of scores. The result is called the *variance.*
6. Take the square root of the variance. This is the standard deviation.

The above steps can be summarized as follows:

$$\text{Standard deviation} = \sqrt{\frac{\text{sum of squared deviation scores}}{\text{number of scores in the distribution}}}$$

Expressed as a formula, this is:

$$\text{SD} = \sqrt{\frac{\Sigma x^2}{n}}$$

where SD is the symbol for standard deviation, Σ is the symbol for sum of, x is the symbol for a deviation score, and n represents the number of scores in the distribution.

This procedure sounds more complicated than it is. It really is not difficult to calculate. Let us calculate the standard deviation for this distribution of ten scores: 80, 85, 60, 55, 25, 70, 40, 45, 50, 30.

1. Calculate the mean. (It turns out to be 54.)
2. Subtract the mean from each raw score to get a deviation score.
3. Square each of the deviation scores.
4. Add up the squared deviation scores.
5. Divide by the total number of such scores. (The total is 3640, which, divided by 10, equals 364.) This is the variance.
6. Take the square root of the variance. (It is 19.08.) This is the standard deviation.

The full computation is shown in the table below.

Raw Score	Mean	Deviation Score	Square of the Deviation Score	
85	−54	31	961	
80	−54	26	676	
70	−54	16	256	
60	−54	6	36	
55	−54	1	1	Variance
50	−54	− 4	16	$(SD^2) = 3640/10 = 364$*
45	−54	−10	81	
40	−54	−14	196	Standard deviation
30	−54	−24	576	$(SD) = \sqrt{364} = 19.08$†
25	−54	−29	841	
		Total	3640	

* The symbol for the variance of a sample is sometimes shown as s^2; the symbol for the variance of a population is σ^2.

† The symbol for the standard deviation of a sample is sometimes shown as s; the symbol for the standard deviation of a population is σ.

You will notice that the more spread out scores are, the greater the deviation scores will be, and hence the larger the standard deviation. The closer the scores are to the mean, the less spread out they are, and hence the smaller the standard deviation. Thus, if we were describing two sets of scores on the same test, and we stated that the standard deviation of the scores in Set A was 2.7, whereas the standard deviation in Set B was 8.3, we would know that there was much less variability in Set A—that is, the scores were closer together.

Once we know the mean and the standard deviation of a distribution, we can make useful interpretations and comparisons.

■ Chi Square

Chi square is the inference technique used to determine statistical significance of a relationship expressed in a crossbreak table. We shall use the data in the table below for our explanation.

	White	Nonwhite	Total
Males	200 (185)	100 (115)	300
Female	170 (185)	130 (115)	300
Total	370	230	600

The first number in each cell represents the obtained frequency; the number in parentheses represents the expected frequency. Let us use the letter O to represent obtained frequencies, and the letter E to represent expected frequencies. The calculation of chi square then proceeds as follows:

1. For cell 1:
   a. Subtract E from O: $(O - E) = 200 - 185 = 15$
   b. Square the result: $(O - E)^2 = 15^2 = 225$
   c. Divide the result in (b) by E: $\dfrac{(O - E)^2}{E} = \dfrac{225}{185} = 1.22$

2. Repeat this process for *each* cell (you can do this in any order, just be sure that all cells are calculated).

   cell 2: a. $170 - 185 = -15$
   b. $(-15)^2 = 225$
   c. $\dfrac{225}{185} = 1.22$

   cell 3: a. $100 - 115 = -15$
   b. $(-15)^2 = 225$
   c. $\dfrac{225}{115} = 1.96$

   cell 4: a. $130 - 115 = 15$
   b. $(15)^2 = 225$
   c. $\dfrac{225}{115} = 1.96$

3. Add results across all cells:

$$\sum \frac{(O - E)^2}{E} = 1.22 + 1.22 + 1.96 + 1.96 = 6.36 = \text{chi square } (\chi^2)$$

After the value for χ^2 has been calculated, we want to determine how likely it is that such a result could occur if there were no relationship in the population (i.e., if the obtained frequencies do not exist in the population, but occurred because of the particular sample that was selected). As with all inferential tests, we determine this by consulting a probability table (similar to the one shown in Appendix E). You will notice that this table has a column headed "Degrees of Freedom."* Degrees of freedom are calculated in crossbreak tables as follows:

1. Subtract 1 from the number of rows (e.g., $2 - 1 = 1$).
2. Subtract 1 from the number of columns (e.g., $2 - 1 = 1$).
3. Multiply step 1 by step 2 ($1 \times 1 = 1$).

---

* This concept is important with regard to many inferential statistics. In essence, it refers to the number of scores in a frequency distribution that are "free to vary"—that is, not fixed. For example, suppose you had a distribution of only three scores, *a*, *b*, and *c*, which must add up to 10. It is apparent that *a*, *b*, and *c* can have a number of different values (e.g., 3, 5, and 2; 1, 6, and 3; 2, 2, and 6) and still add up to 10. But once any two of these values are fixed, then the third is also set—it cannot vary. Thus, should $a = 3$ and $b = 2$, *c must* equal 5. Hence, we say that there are two degrees of freedom in this distribution—any two of the values are "free to vary," so to speak, but once they are set, the third is also fixed.

Thus, in our example above, there is only one degree of freedom. If we look opposite one degree of freedom in the chi-square table, we find under .05 (the .05 significance level) a value of 3.84. Since our obtained chi-square (χ^2) value of 6.36 exceeds 3.84, we conclude that our obtained results are unlikely to have occurred (only a 5 percent probability) if there is no such relationship in the population.

The final step in the process is to calculate the contingency coefficient (symbolized by the letter C), to which we referred in Chapter Twelve. This is done as follows:

1. Add the obtained chi-square value to n, the number of cases (e.g., 6.36 + 600 = 606.36).
2. Divide the chi-square value by step 1 (6.36/606.36 = .01).
3. Take the square root of step 2 ($\sqrt{.01}$ = .10). This is the contingency coefficient (C).

The Correlation Coefficient (Pearson r)

When the data for both of the variables in a study are expressed in terms of measured scores, the Pearson r is the appropriate correlation coefficient to calculate. The Pearson r requires that each individual in the group have a score on each of the variables being correlated. The formula for calculating the Pearson r coefficient is:

$$ r = \frac{\Sigma XY - \dfrac{(\Sigma X)(\Sigma Y)}{n}}{\sqrt{\left(\Sigma X^2 - \dfrac{(\Sigma X)^2}{n}\right)\left(\Sigma Y^2 - \dfrac{(\Sigma Y)^2}{n}\right)}} $$

where X and Y are variables and n is the number of pairs of scores. Don't be alarmed! The Pearson formula looks a lot more complicated than it really is. It does have a lot of steps to follow before we finally get to the end, but each step is easy to calculate. We need two sets of scores to calculate a correlation coefficient.

Let's imagine that we have the following sets of scores for two variables, X and Y, for five students:

Student	Variable X	Variable Y
A	20	20
B	18	16
C	18	20
D	15	12
E	10	10

What we would like to know is whether these two variables are related, and if so, how—positively? negatively? Or are they not related? To answer these questions, we apply the Pearson formula and calculate the correlation coefficient for the two sets of scores.

Student	X	Y	X²	Y²	XY
A	20	20	400	400	400
B	18	16	324	256	288
C	18	20	324	400	360
D	15	12	225	144	180
E	10	10	100	100	100
	81	78	1373	1300	1328
	ΣX	ΣY	ΣX^2	ΣY^2	ΣXY

As you can see, ΣX equals the sum of the scores on the X variable. ΣY equals the sum of the scores on the Y variable. ΣX^2 equals the sum of the squares of each of the X scores. ΣY^2 equals the sum of the squares of each of the Y scores. ΣXY equals the sum of the products of the X and Y scores (i.e., the sum of each X score multiplied by its corresponding Y score). Now we simply substitute each of these sums into the formula. In our example, n (the number of pairs of scores) is 5.

$$r = \frac{1328 - \frac{(81)(78)}{5}}{\sqrt{\left(1373 - \frac{(81)^2}{5}\right)\left(1300 - \frac{(78)^2}{5}\right)}} = \frac{64.4}{\sqrt{(60.8)(83.2)}} = \frac{64.4}{71.1} = .91$$

Let's proceed now step by step.

1. Multiply ΣX by ΣY and divide by n. This equals 1263.6.
2. Subtract step 1 from ΣXY. This equals 64.4.
3. Divide $(\Sigma X)^2$ by n. This equals 1312.2.
4. Subtract step 3 from ΣX^2. This equals 60.8.
5. Divide $(\Sigma Y)^2$ by n. This equals 1216.8.
6. Subtract step 5 from ΣY^2. This equals 83.2.
7. Multiply step 4 by step 6. This equals 5058.56.
8. Take the square root of step 7. (Use a calculator!) This equals 71.1.
9. Divide step 2 by step 8. This equals .91, the correlation coefficient (the Pearson r). In short, $r = + .91$.

Appendix D

TABLE OF RANDOM NUMBERS

(a)	(b)	(c)	(d)	(e)	(f)	(g)	(h)	(i)
83579	83978	49300	01577	62244	99947	76797	00365	01172
51262	49969	56628	09946	78523	11984	54415	00641	07889
05033	90862	53849	93440	24273	51621	04425	23084	54671
02490	84667	67313	68029	00816	38027	91829	99524	68403
51921	09986	09539	58867	09215	97495	04766	21763	86341
31822	39187	57384	31877	91945	05078	76579	12364	59326
40052	40394	79717	51593	29666	35193	85349	22757	04243
35787	57263	95876	90361	89136	44024	92018	33831	82072
10454	46051	22159	54648	40380	72727	06963	55497	11506
09985	39854	74536	79240	80442	59447	83938	38467	40413
57228	04256	76666	95735	40823	82351	95202	87848	85275
04688	70407	89116	52789	47972	89447	15473	04439	18255
30583	58010	55623	94680	16836	63488	36535	67533	12972
73148	81884	16675	01089	81893	24114	30561	02549	64618
72280	99756	57467	20870	16403	43892	10905	57466	39194
78687	43717	38608	31741	07852	69138	58506	73982	30791
86888	98939	58315	39570	73566	24282	48561	60536	35885
29997	40384	81495	70526	28454	43466	81123	06094	30429
21117	13086	01433	86098	13543	33601	09775	13204	70934
50925	78963	28625	89395	81208	90784	73141	67076	58986
63196	86512	67980	97084	36517	99414	39246	68880	79787
54769	30950	75436	59398	77292	17629	21087	08223	97794
69625	49952	65892	02302	50086	48199	21762	84309	53808
94464	86584	34365	83368	87733	93495	50205	94569	29484
52308	20863	05546	81939	96643	07580	28322	22357	59502
32519	79304	87539	28173	62834	15517	72971	15491	79606
29867	27299	98117	69489	88658	31893	93350	01852	86381
13552	60056	53109	58862	88922	41304	44097	58305	10642
73221	81473	75249	88070	22216	27694	54446	68163	34946
41963	16813	31572	04216	49989	78229	26458	89582	82020
81594	04548	95299	26418	15482	16441	60274	00237	03741
27663	33479	22470	57066	31844	73184	48399	05209	17794
07436	23844	45310	46621	78866	30002	91855	14029	84701
53884	59886	40262	38528	28753	14814	71508	91444	94335
45080	08221	30911	87535	66101	95153	36999	60707	10947
42238	98478	80953	25277	28869	69513	93372	98587	64229
49834	43447	29857	75567	85500	24229	23099	96924	23432
38220	82174	85412	66247	80642	45181	28732	76690	06005
61079	97636	62444	07315	78216	75279	75403	49513	16863
73503	47241	61985	91537	25843	89751	63485	34927	11334
18326	96584	45568	32027	97405	06282	75452	26667	46959
89596	26372	01227	23787	33607	69714	28725	43442	19512
45851	81369	08307	58640	14287	10100	43278	55266	46802
87906	42482	50010	31486	23801	08599	32842	47918	40894
24053	02256	03743	26642	03224	93886	57367	78910	38915
20525	69314	34939	70653	40414	94127	99934	35025	50342
30315	62283	53097	99244	08033	97879	92921	68432	68168
69240	41181	08462	99916	88851	43382	28262	10582	25126
59159	99994	25434	73285	54482	91218	49955	01232	55104
33137	42409	49785	02790	98720	89495	00135	27861	39832

Table of Random Numbers (*Continued*)

(a)	(b)	(c)	(d)	(e)	(f)	(g)	(h)	(i)
03772	83596	01998	19683	03807	22324	16596	54549	15292
38223	26962	41821	84290	65223	83106	93175	24427	40531
38910	45316	82279	98066	67103	33755	85437	09309	75265
15780	60337	25069	47937	23687	40781	94043	74876	58012
59645	03262	42485	73462	41946	75704	61738	72335	96817
63333	68207	01070	92462	14781	82511	15065	46306	02456
85151	46866	48722	48086	20474	36574	69470	58413	37706
11531	34955	57169	04940	35640	98230	65837	36680	41477
96319	74374	15695	79458	31647	53067	13571	12179	99589
30134	59746	31665	13134	17529	39398	33946	73628	40643
04416	96960	85645	04216	28945	25137	60714	75168	83151
42928	79955	97819	45369	55359	17937	83239	11295	58130
52948	73337	82355	44257	52712	87726	91823	94251	98289
83365	12321	79618	53832	12536	21188	89557	96752	54411
17668	39848	04395	20304	74086	19150	86215	23346	84632
16488	84810	05643	70033	90915	95334	64949	45891	43946
87762	53973	04659	74735	31564	70225	76596	56131	90245
09545	67121	31566	88183	82886	45188	66813	56750	13472
50075	92832	23965	05293	84834	53872	13978	00210	77150
50014	56960	70470	84533	37605	35882	26829	09730	78137
27461	22430	70494	09014	81705	80986	72819	72797	20603
85455	36779	76804	65884	42010	20583	87053	01910	96843
46186	36401	36356	68021	41599	42851	79517	59232	37616
52865	88615	68405	17169	66648	89528	77078	45204	54016
19677	10382	66142	29876	62918	45150	73732	69810	82674
28445	84222	59854	57384	92011	14740	51517	21596	97755
80247	85449	88336	88043	86893	76735	08150	38847	06776
19069	16727	51768	37181	67709	08832	61876	83914	85457
07850	52649	32868	07651	77211	29598	13084	68633	88783
49746	61632	51796	53973	37340	46210	19822	28946	77191
32966	34486	41597	04154	32647	84479	92920	73104	97780
72920	05779	55936	34629	58795	95807	47141	57443	11846
96183	28273	32998	87991	37407	76595	49199	80466	75910
26410	63387	73201	37246	28831	18261	32480	95368	87073
25940	24468	45166	82520	94541	81832	56388	20212	81172
06149	87534	80183	38237	70561	15886	86544	56381	10014
07765	24744	91075	54307	72266	37821	89684	25908	17081
79930	48815	95288	00162	72993	37305	00922	57012	38192
86624	43304	96428	37148	61842	66107	26714	35042	33438
06874	26347	61749	34324	70973	00303	62882	70944	75589
22058	65172	55633	98434	63643	02538	79073	16385	44285
12825	40453	81056	09429	53089	47280	93450	25837	01359
09520	05545	62075	11026	92864	21694	94113	59588	07072
14123	63054	13983	27314	21748	26306	05480	58202	23461
07260	84731	51977	34707	40477	66515	42171	09292	43919
12494	23659	44181	58492	08178	20422	41828	73576	86239
82127	96579	74270	27091	21850	49286	75057	54749	66583
23184	99161	16549	28711	67847	90570	61705	02104	77154
55739	74047	33846	00562	85265	68479	28594	52163	79804
97799	90967	92906	67741	79498	76903	27121	32486	43435

TABLE OF CHI SQUARE VALUES

The table entries are critical values of χ^2.					
Degrees of Freedom (df)	Proportion in Critical Region				
	0.10	0.05	0.025	0.01	0.005
1	2.71	3.84	5.02	6.63	7.88
2	4.61	5.99	7.38	9.21	10.60
3	6.25	7.81	9.35	11.34	12.84
4	7.78	9.49	11.14	13.28	14.86
5	9.24	11.07	12.83	15.09	16.75
6	10.64	12.59	14.45	16.81	18.55
7	12.02	14.07	16.01	18.48	20.28
8	13.36	15.51	17.53	20.09	21.96
9	14.68	16.92	19.02	21.67	23.59
10	15.99	18.31	20.48	23.21	25.19
11	17.28	19.68	21.92	24.72	26.76
12	18.55	21.03	23.34	26.22	28.30
13	19.81	22.36	23.74	27.69	29.82
14	21.06	23.68	26.12	29.14	31.32
15	22.31	25.00	27.49	30.58	32.80
16	23.54	26.30	28.85	32.00	34.27
17	24.77	27.59	30.19	33.41	35.72
18	25.99	28.87	31.53	34.81	37.16
19	27.20	30.14	32.85	36.19	38.58
20	28.41	31.41	34.17	37.57	40.00
21	29.62	32.67	35.48	38.93	41.40
22	30.81	33.92	36.78	40.29	42.80
23	32.01	35.17	38.08	41.64	44.18
24	33.20	36.42	39.36	42.98	45.56
25	34.38	37.65	40.65	44.31	46.93
26	35.56	38.89	41.92	45.64	48.29
27	36.74	40.11	43.19	46.96	49.64
28	37.92	41.34	44.46	48.28	50.99
29	39.09	42.56	45.72	49.59	52.34
30	40.26	43.77	46.98	50.89	53.67
40	51.81	55.76	59.34	63.69	66.77
50	63.17	67.50	71.42	76.15	79.49
60	74.40	79.08	83.30	88.38	91.95
70	85.53	90.53	95.02	100.42	104.22
80	96.58	101.88	106.63	112.33	116.32
90	107.56	113.14	118.14	124.12	128.30
100	118.50	124.34	129.56	135.81	140.17

Source: From Table VII (abridged) of Fisher & Yates. *Statistical Tables for Biological, Agricultural, and Medical Research,* Published by Longman Group Ltd. London (previously published by Oliver & Boyd Ltd. Edinburgh) and reprinted by permission of the authors and publishers.

INDEX

INDEX

A

AB design, 205–206
  (*See also* Experimental designs)
ABA design, 203–208
  (*See also* Experimental designs)
ABAB design, 206
  (*See also* Experimental designs)
Ability tests, 108–115
Age-equivalent scores, 237
  (*See also* Scores)
Analysis of covariance (ANCOVA), 264
Analysis of variance (ANOVA), 264
Application of Generalizations test, 111
  example, 112
  responses to, 114
Applied research, 5
Arithmetic mean (*See* Mean)
Attitude of subjects threat (to internal validity),
    175–176
  controlling, 216
  in innovative curriculum study, 183, 220
  in open classroom study, 186, 224
Attitude scale (*See* Rating scale)
Averages, 236–238
  mean, 237–238
  median, 237

B

Baseline period, 205–208
Basic research, 5
Bibliographic card, 63
Boolean operators, 71

C

Card catalog, 56, 57
Case studies, 290–291
Categorical variables (*See* Variables)
Causal-comparative research, 194–198, 289
  and experimental research, 197–198
  types of, 195
Causal-comparative studies, 191
  (*See also* Causal-comparative research)
Chi-square test, 264
  calculation of, 347–349
Clarity, in research questions, 14–19
  (*See also* Research questions)
Cluster sampling (*See* Sampling)
Comparison group (in experimental research), 191–192
Comparison group design, 160–162
  (*See also* Research designs)
Computer search:
  Boolean operators, 71
  sample printout, 73
  steps in, 69–74
Confidence intervals, 259–260
  95 percent, 259–260
  99 percent, 260
Confidentiality of research data, 40
  (*See also* Ethical principles)
Content analysis, 291–292; 296–298
Contingency coefficient, 252
  values for different-sized crossbreak tables, 252
Contingency table (*See* Crossbreak tables)
Control group (in experimental research), 191–192
Control group design (*See* Pretest-posttest control
    group design)
Construct-related evidence of validity, 94–95
Content-related evidence of validity, 89–92
Convenience sampling (*See* Sampling)
Coopersmith Self-Esteem Inventories (review of),
    120–122